A POLITICAL BIOGRAPHY OF ALEXANDER POPE

EIGHTEENTH-CENTURY
POLITICAL BIOGRAPHIES

Series Editor: J. A. Downie

TITLES IN THIS SERIES

1 Daniel Defoe
P. N. Furbank & W. R. Owens

2 Jonathan Swift
David Oakleaf

3 Delarivier Manley
Rachel Carnell

4 Henry Fielding
J. A. Downie

5 Richard Steele
Charles Knight

FORTHCOMING TITLES

John Arbuthnot
Angus Ross

John Toland
Michael Brown

William King
Christopher Fauske

Eliza Haywood
Kathryn King

Joseph Addison
Charles Knight

A POLITICAL BIOGRAPHY OF ALEXANDER POPE

BY

Pat Rogers

LONDON AND NEW YORK

First published 2010 by Pickering & Chatto (Publishers) Limited

Published 2016 by Routledge
2 Park Square, Milton Park, Abingdon, Oxfordshire OX14 4RN
711 Third Avenue, New York, NY 10017, USA

First issued in paperback 2015

Routledge is an imprint of the Taylor & Francis Group, an informa business

© Taylor & Francis 2010
© Pat Rogers 2010

All rights reserved, including those of translation into foreign languages. No part of this book may be reprinted or reproduced or utilised in any form or by any electronic, mechanical, or other means, now known or hereafter invented, including photocopying and recording, or in any information storage or retrieval system, without permission in writing from the publishers.

Notice:
Product or corporate names may be trademarks or registered trademarks, and are used only for identification and explanation without intent to infringe.

BRITISH LIBRARY CATALOGUING IN PUBLICATION DATA

Rogers, Pat, 1938–
A political biography of Alexander Pope. – (Eighteenth-century political biographies)
1. Pope, Alexander, 1688–1744. 2. Poets, English – 18th century – Biography. 3. Politics and literature – Great Britain – History – 18th century.
I. Title II. Series
821.5-dc22

ISBN-13: 978-1-138-66518-7 (pbk)
ISBN-13: 978-1-8519-6846-6 (hbk)

Typeset by Pickering & Chatto (Publishers) Limited

CONTENTS

Acknowledgements	vii
Abbreviations	viii
Dates and Quotations	ix
Sources	x
Introduction	1
Part I: William and Anne, 1688–1714	
1 Nature and Nurture	7
2 The Flowers of the Forest	29
3 The Piping Time of Peace	51
Part II: George I, 1714–27	
4 Civil and Religious Rage	77
5 Toil, Trouble, South Sea Bubble	103
6 A Dull Duty and a Public Cause	123
Part III: George II, 1727–44	
7 Dunce the Second Reigns	151
8 Libels and Satires	175
9 Friendship and Opposition	201
Epilogue: After Walpole	225
Notes	233
Works Cited	243
Index	249

For Robert DeMaria

ACKNOWLEDGEMENTS

The present book draws in places on material used in previous studies, although this has naturally been adapted, compressed and reordered to suit the biographic context. In particular I have made use of a number of entries in *The Alexander Pope Encyclopedia*, published by Greenwood Press in 2004, and acknowledge permission to recast the information contained there.

My greatest debt on a personal level is to Adrienne Condon, for her support and encouragement. In addition I wish to thank Alan Downie, the general editor of this series, and Mark Pollard of Pickering & Chatto Publishers, for their patience and consideration as the writing of the book stretched out beyond the time that was originally planned and expected by us all.

It is a pleasure to record the enlightenment and inspiration given by Pope scholars, including the work of earlier giants such as Maynard Mack, George Sherburn, David Foxon and John Butt. The writings of numerous contemporary scholars have enhanced my appreciation of the poet, most pervasively Paul Baines, Howard Erskine-Hill, David Fairer, Christine Gerrard, Dustin Griffin, Isobel Grundy, Brean Hammond, James McLaverty, George Rousseau, Valerie Rumbold and Howard Weinbrot. Among those who have contributed to my understanding of Pope's world are historians past and present, including G. V. Bennett, John Bossy, John Carswell, H. T. Dickinson, Ragnhild Hatton, David Hayton, J. H. Plumb, W. A. Speck and E. P. Thompson.

ABBREVIATIONS

Anecdotes J. Spence, *Observations, Anecdotes, and Characters of Books and Men*, ed. J. M. Osborn, 2 vols (Oxford: Clarendon Press, 1966).

Corr. *The Correspondence of Alexander Pope*, ed. G. Sherburn, 5 vols (Oxford: Clarendon Press, 1956).

TE *The Twickenham Edition of the Works of Alexander Pope*, ed. J. Butt et al., 11 vols (London: Methuen, 1938–68).

INTRODUCTION

A political biography must first of all be a biography. In other words, it needs to tell the story of a life with special reference to politics – which we could roughly define as the subject's interactions with public controversy of his or her time. There are particular grounds for caution in the case of an individual like Pope, for whom the vocation of writing mattered far more than the day-to-day struggles in parliament, and who (for good reasons, to be spelled out shortly) seldom intervened directly in the political process. This book does not seek to conduct a full structural analysis of the party system in the early Hanoverian age, or to offer a minute description of the course of events in Westminster, the streets of London or the shires. Nor shall I give a comprehensive account of the leading players in the ideological battles Pope witnessed. What the book attempts is to locate Pope's position in the major controversies of the day, and to say enough of the issues to make sense of the stance he took – or in some cases did not take. Many key figures in the contests and dissentions, such as the Duke of Marlborough, the Earl of Oxford, Lord Bolingbroke, Robert Walpole, Francis Atterbury and William Pulteney, were well known to him: some became intimate friends. The pages that follow will explore these relationships, but in the context of Pope's own development as a man and a writer. It is the trajectory of his career that determines the shape of this narrative, rather than the external course of politics.

His personal inclinations, as well as issues of health and religion, debarred Pope from activity in the public sphere – something that marks him off from many of his contemporaries in the literary world. Unlike Swift and Manley, he did not conduct journals or write pamphlets in the cause of party. Unlike Addison and Steele, he did not enter parliament or accept posts awarded by government patronage. Unlike Prior, he did not represent Britain in a diplomatic role. Unlike Gay, he was never sent abroad in the retinue of an official embassy. Unlike Congreve, he held no comfortable sinecure. Unlike Rowe, he was not awarded a position at court as laureate. Unlike Arbuthnot, he gained no foothold in the royal establishment.

Again, Pope left us few clues with regard to his opinions on some of the most contentious issues of the day. He wrote no abstract statement of his views on the 'Revolution principles' that had helped to inspire the overthrow of James II and the installation of William and Mary in 1688/9. Almost all we can say for certain is that he held James in little esteem, hated William, felt more kindly towards Anne, disliked George I and steadily lost any respect he may once have felt for George II. No clear-cut evidence exists that he ever lifted a finger to take up the cause of the Pretender, yet the elective affinities expressed in his friendships, with Protestants and Catholics alike, seem to argue a quiet loyalty to the Stuarts against the house of Nassau or Brunswick. So do actions such as his character reference at the 'trial' (strictly a parliamentary bill of pains and penalties) of Atterbury. As we shall see in this book, his allegiance to the old faith underpinned most of the big decisions he took in the course of his life.

Yet, despite this reticence in making open political commitments, it cannot be denied that Pope was deeply influenced by his times. Almost from the beginning his work dealt with the most urgently debated topics of the moment, whether war and peace, the Jacobite risings, the South Sea Bubble, the Atterbury plot, the Excise crisis or the development of the patriot opposition to Walpole. When he wrote a poem on the highly contentious Treaty of Utrecht in 1713, along with dozens of willing poetasters, his work *Windsor-Forest* stood almost alone in mentioning the notorious slave contract that formed part of the diplomatic deal. Equally, he was alive to religious, philosophic, musical and scientific quarrels passing before him, as they caught up important historical figures who included Isaac Newton, George Friderick Handel, George Berkeley and Lady Mary Wortley Montagu. Theatrical disputes often had a political dimension, and here he came into contact with the greatest members of the acting profession, among them Thomas Betterton, Colley Cibber and Anne Oldfield. Both his friendships and his enmities helped to define the nature of his social, economic and constitutional issues – allies such as Jonathan Swift and John Gay, opponents such as Joseph Addison and Lord Hervey. The bitter collapse of his once good relations with Lady Mary had links with party strife as well as implications for gender politics.

It is on account of factors like these that the book has been divided into three parts. The first section covers the years from Pope's birth in 1688 to the end of the Stuart era in 1714, that is the reign of William and Mary followed by that of Anne. The second is devoted to the years 1714 to 1727, when George I occupied the throne. The third embraces the first thirteen years of George II, from 1727 until 1740, with an epilogue taking the story down to Pope's death in 1744. These days it looks a shade old-fashioned to pay to so much attention to regnal divisions. But early eighteenth-century politics allows such a proceeding, and may even require it. Almost everything changed in public life the moment that the new monarch took the helm, something that events in 1688/9, 1702 and 1714 abundantly showed. People confidently expected a similar palace revolution in 1727, and though this did not exactly occur the nature of politics at court and at Westminster did shift in myriad ways. We could say that *The Dunciad* invents a succession crisis waiting to happen.

On the last two occasions that the monarchy changed hands during his lifetime, many things were in flux for Pope himself (he had been too young in 1688 and 1702). Each of the years when the first two Georges successively took the throne represents a natural break in the story of Pope's career. This is because 1714 marks the end of his early phase as a writer of pastoral and witty *vers de société*, typified by *An Essay on Criticism*, *Windsor-Forest* and *The Rape of the Lock*. For more than a decade after this, he would be preoccupied by the translation of Homer and the 'dull duty of an editor',[1] in other words his edition of Shakespeare. Only after the accession of George II was Pope ready to emerge with a new harsher vein of satire, exemplified by highly personalized attacks such as *Peri Bathous* and *The Dunciad*. These works set the stage for his more openly political works of the 1730s, including the *Imitations of Horace* and the *Moral Essays*. During this period he also brought out his most wide-ranging excursion into philosophic (and political, some would say) terrain, *An Essay on Man*. Following this trajectory through, we find the last stage opening around 1738, almost coinciding as it happens with the death of Queen Caroline one year earlier. The poetic output declines, and only one substantial item, the new version of *The Dunciad*, appeared before Pope's death. By that time his mighty enemy Walpole had left the political arena, and a new politics had begun to emerge which called for a different mode of literary scrutiny.

In each phase, this book will devote the closest attention to works with a major political component. These include *Windsor-Forest*, *The Dunciad* and (seen here as prolonged commentary on the Whigs' treatment of Tory leaders after they came to power in 1715) the *Epistle to Bathurst*. Other works, however important from a literary standpoint, will receive much more cursory treatment. Certain threads will reappear throughout the narrative, among them the lasting impact left by the Jacobite rising, especially the execution of one of the rebel lords, the Earl of Derwentwater – who, it emerges, had close ties to some members of Pope's most intimate circle.

No biography like this can pretend to offer a fully nuanced account of the structure of politics in the early eighteenth century. Modern research has found ever more complex strands in the history of the parties in this era, as it played out in the struggles between (and within) the Whig and Tory factions. I hope that specialists will excuse a measure of simplification, necessary in the interests of clarity, as we follow the main lines of Pope's career. Most work on his political stance has tended to fall into one of two categories: discussion of his attitude towards the Jacobite cause, and assessment of his relations with the opposition to Walpole in the 1730s. In this book I have tried to give adequate coverage on both issues, and in the former case especially I have adduced new information and fresh perspectives on the material. However, I also seek to deal thoroughly with other aspects of his involvement in public affairs.

In one particular way we have tended to overlook a key component of the poet's political identity. As all students of his works know, his father was a City businessman and Catholic convert. Many scholars, headed by Maynard Mack, have explored the implications of the poet's religious background as it affected his life and his oeuvre.[2] But since Pope moved as a young boy to the rural shelter of Berkshire (a move that was itself prompted by anti-Catholic legislation), and later settled in his suburban retreat at Twickenham, we usually forget just how strong his roots in the capital were. He maintained close friendships with individuals who lived and worked in the financial and commercial heart of the City. As his poems reveal, he kept a close eye on London politics, which exhibited intense municipal rivalries as well as playing a crucial part in the national contest for power.

Many of Pope's loyalties, as already indicated, had a hereditary or even atavistic base. This applies especially to the religious outlook he imbibed from his education, his ancestry (more strongly from his mother's side of the family) and his early contact with the Catholic gentry of the English home counties. Some of the contacts that he established in this process would last for most of his lifetime: people like the Dancastles of Binfield, the Blounts and the Carylls remained at the emotional centre of his being. Other allegiances owe more to his bookish nature, and his addiction to reading from early childhood. As an aspirant writer he had a group of literary mentors, who mostly came from a Protestant background but did not take not an aggressively Whiggish line. The major influence was exerted by Sir William Trumbull, a rural neighbour who had retired from an active role at court and in diplomacy. As we have just seen, a number of core values to which Pope clung had their origin in his father's involvement in the mercantile life of London. Only when he became an adult, and started to make his own way as a writer, did Pope get to know the grandees of Church and state: people like Oxford, Bolingbroke, Atterbury, Bathurst, Burlington, Lady Mary Wortley Montagu and many more. Such aristocratic individuals often served as patrons and allies in the culture wars – Lady Mary more briefly than the others named – but generally they receive more attention than they sometimes deserve. For one thing, Pope never joined the ruling elite: his health and his religion alone would keep him on the margins. In the second place, we need to remember that most of his major sponsors had aligned themselves against Walpole during the prime minister's long period at the helm of national affairs. At various junctures, several of them grew disenchanted with the course of events, and retreated into an ostentatiously 'private' life. So they, too, often stood outside the mainstream of national politics.

All the factors just mentioned had the effect of turning Pope into an oppositional figure: but that is not quite the same thing as a figure of significant opposition in the day-to-day sequence of events. We should never delude ourselves into thinking that the big decisions in public affairs were made in coffee-houses, newspaper printing offices or in the streets of English cities. (Scotland and Ireland each represents a special case, though the independence of both Edinburgh and Dublin was in large measure a token phenomenon.) Most of the time the course of national business was determined at Westminster, a fact that Walpole never forgot. With a relatively weak executive branch, the prime minister needed the support of rank-and-file MPs and peers to get measures through, as well as the suffrage of the King and the royal entourage at court. He also wanted, but did not always have, a compliant system of law courts. Finally, he required an efficient power base up and down the country, capable of managing elections and administering justice at a local level. If a 'public sphere' did exist, then it was one with circumscribed authority. Opinion could be mobilized at rare intervals to deflect the minister from his intended actions, as at the time of the Excise crisis in 1733. But although, as a result of that episode, Walpole lost much of his popularity in the City of London and suffered an unaccustomed parliamentary reverse, he did not lose his office. He simply backed down on the issue and got on with governing.

Like most men and women of his day, then, Pope stood at two or three removes from genuine political influence. The story we shall trace shows him as a close student of politics and an enlightening commentator on events of the time. But the groups with whom the poet naturally allied himself seldom had a strong impact on the course of government. This applies in particular to the Catholic gentry of the Thames Valley, where he found his deepest allegiances. As Joseph Stalin might have asked, 'Pope's friends? How many divisions have *they* got?'

PART I: WILLIAM AND ANNE, 1688–1714

1 NATURE AND NURTURE

Like most of us, Alexander Pope was formed both by his family and by a broader environment. His genetic inheritance, as the child of quite elderly parents, merged with the effects of his upbringing, which took place first in the heart of London, then briefly in the outlying village (as it then was) of Hammersmith, and finally in the rural seclusion of Windsor Forest. Over the years the young man joined a set of wider communities, each of which had its own particular religious, social and geographic base. These separate influences combined to make him by the age of twenty-five essentially the man he would remain. Equally they contributed a great deal to the character of his poetry, and to the nature of the writer that he ultimately became.

1

> Unspotted Names! and memorable long,
> If there be Force in Virtue, or in Song.
> Of gentle Blood (part shed in Honour's Cause,
> While yet in Britain Honour had Applause)
> Each Parent sprung.
>
> *Epistle to Arbuthnot* (*TE*, vol. 4, p. 126)

Once upon a time – it now seems very distant – people generally cared more about the obligations of children than the responsibilities of parents. As a dutiful son, Alexander Pope felt a strong sense of filial respect. His lifelong behaviour shows that he loved his father and mother, and strove to be a proud and worthy offspring. On the face of things they were ordinary enough, and they certainly could not have anticipated that their child would make such a mark in the world. From his father, the younger Pope took not just his name but a deep commitment to the values of the principled recusant community, who were forced to give up so much because of their loyalty to their Catholic faith. We know less of his mother, and since she lived her days entirely in the domestic sphere it is likely that she embodied for Alexander qualities of Christian charity, homely virtue and simple piety. In her later years he saw her as a beacon in his life, or more precisely a lighted taper, as in a letter to Lady Mary Wortley Montagu around 1718:

> I have yet a Mother of great age and infirmitys, whose last precarious days of life I am now attending, with such a solemn pious kind of officiousness, as a melancholy Recluse watches the last risings and fallings of a dying Taper.
>
> (*Corr.*, vol. 1, p. 469)

This phrase, as Maynard Mack pointed out,[1] must go back to a line in the Apocrypha. It reads in the Douai Bible version Ecclesiasticus 26:22: 'As the lamp shining upon the holy candlestick, so is the beauty of the face in a ripe age'. Pope remained devoted to his mother for as long as she lived, citing her objections as a prime reason why he could never convert to Anglicanism. She even pretended to find his ministrations to her in old age unduly burdensome, as Magdalen Rackett reported: 'Mrs *Pope* complain'd that most Children plagu'd their Parents with Neglect; that he did so much with perpetually teasing [irritating] her with his Over-fondness and Care'.[2] When Edith died peacefully just short of her ninetieth birthday, her son described the bedside scene with a pardonable hint of exaggeration: 'It wou'd afford the finest Image of a Saint expir'd, that ever Painting drew' (*Corr.*, vol. 3, p. 374).

Edith, or Editha, Pope (1643–1733) came from a family long settled in York, as one of probably sixteen children who were born to William Turner (1597–1665) and his wife Thomasine, née Newton (1604–81).[3] She was christened at Worsborough, Yorkshire, on 18 June 1643. This was a village near Barnsley, in a part of this largely unindustrialized county that was already known for coal mining and metalwork. Daniel Defoe gave the place a miss, with just a reference in passing to

> a Town call'd *Black Barnsley*, eminent still for the working in Iron and Steel; and indeed the very Town looks as black and smoaky as if they were all Smiths that liv'd in it; tho' it is not, I suppose, call'd *Black Barnsley* on that Account, but for the black Hue or Colour of the Moors, which being covered with Heath, (or Heather, as 'tis called in that Country) look all black, like Bagshot Heath, near Windsor.[4]

Pope made a single trip to York, doubtless in part as a sentimental journey to his mother's old home, but he does not appear to have relished an encounter with Black Barnsley. It would have been a reasonably familiar landscape, since his sister lived on the edge of Bagshot Heath, and he had to cross this notoriously dangerous stretch of the highway when travelling between London and Berkshire.

A little information has come to light on Edith's eldest sister Christiana as a result of her marriage to Samuel Cooper (1609–72), the greatest English miniature painter of the seventeenth century. Edith had three brothers, but none of them survived into her son's lifetime. She may have left York before her mother's death. At some date following June 1684 she married the widower Alexander Pope senior. Her only child was the poet, born in 1688. Like many members of the Turner family, she adhered to the Catholic faith. After the death of her husband in 1717, she continued to live with her son and moved to Twickenham in 1719. By this time, with her health infirm, she received the loving care of her son. She suffered from intermittent fevers and from jaundice. Sometimes in his absence she was attended by Martha Blount. From the later 1720s she spent her life as an almost permanent invalid. In October 1730, after a fall into the fire at home, her clothes were set in flames, but luckily she escaped burns and made a slow recovery (see Chapter 8). At this stage Pope feared that she was on the point of death, but again her resilient constitution saw her through. She was, however, lapsing into some form of senile dementia.

We can trace back Pope's ancestry for several generations on both sides. His maternal ancestors, the Turners, have been located as early as the fifteenth century. The family was settled around York until shortly before the poet's day. Its members had hovered between Catholic and Protestant faiths for several generations: some of Edith's siblings clung to the Roman Catholic faith, while others were Protestants. In the *Epistle to Arbuthnot* Pope paid a warm tribute to his parents, quoted as the epigraph above. The gentle blood that he claimed his family had shed refers to the death of two of Edith's brothers, who took up the royalist cause in the Civil War. It appears that Edith inherited most of the family's money, including some possibly left by another brother who is said to have become a general in the Spanish army. However, there are signs that this fortune had been steadily depleted in the first half of Mrs Pope's life.

The most famous individual on either side of the family tree was the painter Samuel Cooper, who as we have seen married Pope's maternal aunt. The young man did not know any of his uncles, but Christiana Cooper, his godmother, survived until he was almost five and bequeathed him a painted china dish, and (subject to a life interest on the part of her sister Elizabeth) her books, pictures and medals, 'set in gold or otherwise'.[5] In turn, Elizabeth Turner lived until he reached manhood: a spinster, she seems to have lived with the Popes, and she must have been the 'old aunt' who taught the boy to read (*Anecdotes*, vol. 1, p. 8). Another sister, Jane, survived until after Christiana's death in 1693. From his aunt Alice descended a family, the Mawhoods, with whom Pope later had some contact. In the poet's own lifetime, he would forge his most significant contacts with the family of his half-sister Magdalen Rackett.

Alexander Pope, senior (1646–1717), father of the poet, worked as an import-export merchant dealing in 'Hollands', that is, Flemish lace. On the paternal side, the Popes derived from Hampshire and most if not all adhered to the reformed religion. Alexander's great-grandfather kept an inn at Andover, in the north of the county, and the publican's son became an Anglican clergyman who served in the parish of Thruxton in Hampshire, close to Andover. The merchant was the posthumous child of the clergyman Alexander I (d. 1646), who had married Dorothy Pine (d. 1670). Meanwhile a sister, Mary (1636–94), became the second wife of another man of the church, Rev. Ambrose Staveley, rector of Pangbourne, Berkshire. Ambrose died a matter of weeks after young Alexander was born, so there cannot have been any first-hand contact between the two. But as Mary Staveley lived on for another six years, she may have been known to the poet – the family seat of his close friends the Blounts lay at Mapledurham, barely two miles away on the other side of the Thames from Pangbourne. Family relations had apparently been good: in 1676 Anne Staveley, a daughter of the vicar by his first wife, left considerable bequests to her step-mother and step-uncle. She also remembered William Pope, a brother who came between Mary and Alexander. After the death of Alexander I, his widow Dorothy had moved a fairly short distance to Micheldever, on the other side of Andover, where her father also served as a parson in the Church of England. These facts show how solidly rooted the Popes were in the adjoining counties of Hampshire and Berkshire, and how many ties they had to the clergy.

However, the career of Alexander II took a completely different turn. He went into business in London with William, and is said to have completed his apprenticeship by 1669, when his mother divided between her sons the considerable sum of £1,000 to give them a good start.[6] If so, he must still have adhered to the Protestant faith at this date. He may have spent time pursuing his trading career in either Lisbon or more likely Flanders. By 1671 he had come back to London and lodged for the next two years at least in the parish of St Bennet Fink, a huddle of just eight streets and alleys which clustered around the newly restored church in Threadneedle Street. A document in 1675 places him in Broad Street, which ran into the same road a little way up from the Royal Exchange: part of this thoroughfare lay in the parish of St Bennet. Within three years he had become a householder, with a wife, boy (a short-lived son) and a certain Mary – who is most likely Mary Beach, the child's wet-nurse. She performed the same function when little Alexander was born, ten years later, and stayed with the family right up to her death in 1725. After his first wife Magdalen died, he went into lodgings again with a neighbour, having presumably left his daughter and Mary with the Staveleys in Pangbourne. Thus far the archives, scanty as they are, are sufficient to indicate an orthodox progress in commercial life, with a gradually increasing position in the community until he met with a reverse in the loss of Magdalen.[7] He conducted much of his trade with the American colonies.

We know very little about the elder Pope's first wife, except that she passed away in August 1679 and was buried at St Bennet Fink's church on 1 September.

Possibly she died in giving birth to her daughter, the poet's half-sister Magdalen, later Rackett (d. 1749). The couple had two children: as well as the girl, there was a boy named after his father, who died at an early age in August 1682. This time the burial took place at Pangbourne, conducted by Ambrose Staveley, brother-in-law of the child's father. It may be, as Mack has speculated, that the bereaved husband left the two infants in the care of the Staveley family while he carried on his business and looked for a new wife.[8] In any case, at some date after June 1684 the widower entered into matrimony once more. His bride, Edith Turner, was over forty by the time of the marriage.

A hiatus then appears in the records. We pick up traces of Alexander senior in the summer of his son's birth, when the ratebooks show him again as a 'landlord' in the Lombard Street precinct. After the ascent of William and Mary to the throne, he was listed in a roll of declared papists, now a suspect group, as a 'merchant' in the parish of St Edmund, the church that stood physically nearest to his son's birthplace in Plough Court. In 1690 the rating assessment describes him as a papist and as 'unfree', that is not a member of a City guild who had been 'freed' after completing his apprenticeship. He has a wife, two children and three servants. The assessment of just over one guinea (£1.05) indicates that he was levied at the double rate imposed on Catholics.

After he had established a cosy fortune of something like £10,000, Pope senior was able to retire in 1688. One motive for this action seems to have been a quarrel with his brother William, although a more likely reason for his abrupt exit may lie in the political realities of the day, caused by 'the immediate crackdown of William and Mary's government on London papists'.[9] By this time he had taken up residence in Plough Court in the City, where his famous son was born in the year of his retirement.

The elder Pope seems to have become pretty thoroughly urbanized, with his concerns focused chiefly on the trading world. Indeed, he might well have stayed in London for the remainder of his retirement, which lasted almost thirty years, had not government legislation forced his hand. After the Revolution of 1688, papists endured a series of restrictive measures imposed by parliament. Eventually the Popes made a token compliance with the Ten Mile Act and moved out from the City to Hammersmith, west of London. This was their home from the summer of 1692 until the end of the decade. As we shall shortly see, Mr Pope later acquired a house at Binfield in Berkshire from his son-in-law, Magdalen's husband Charles Rackett. The family moved out to the country around 1700 and remained there until around April 1716, when further anti-Catholic measures led the family to settle at Chiswick. By the standards of the time, this was an itinerant way of life. In following the writer's career, we shall be able to observe how this pattern of disruption helped to form his view of recent history, as well as opening up different vistas on which his poetic imagination could feed. In this sense the personal was always political for Alexander junior.

2

Like (probably) Daniel Defoe and (barely) John Keats, but unlike other authors of the Cockney school, Pope was born within the sound of Bow Bells. He came into the world near the heart of the 'square mile', during the same year that his father retired from his business as a linen merchant, 1688.[10] No evidence has come to light showing that the elder Pope served an apprenticeship or gained his freedom. Even if he did, as a converted Catholic, Alexander senior would have found great difficulty in swearing the oath of loyalty to the monarch, as freemen were required to do: within six months of the birth of the new son, William of Orange had landed at Torbay and within three more he had accepted the throne along with his wife Mary. By that time Mr Pope had given up trade, having made a competent fortune.

He had run his business from a narrow four-storey house at the foot of Plough Court, looking towards the eastern end of Lombard Street, long known as a hub of banking, close to where it meets Gracechurch Street. The area had been devastated in the Great Fire, and the Popes' plain but sturdy brick home must have dated from the period of reconstruction. Despite heavy damage sustained in the Blitz, Plough Court itself remains as a covered alleyway, about sixty yards long, running south to Lombard Court. Tradition has it that the Popes rented no. 2, a house which survived into the middle of the nineteenth century. Soon after it was occupied by Salem Osgood, a Quaker who also worked in the drapery trade. This property passed in 1715 to the Bevan family, who became one of the leading pharmaceutical firms in the capital. They too were Quakers, and also mainstays of the anti-slavery movement. The character of the area at this period in this era is well conveyed in John Strype's edition (1720) of *The Survey of London*:

> But now for the South side of Lombard Street. Betwixt Grasschurch Street and St. Clements Lane, are these Courts and Alleys, viz. White Hart Court, which hath a Passage through an Entry, into another Court so called, which leadeth into Grasschurch Street, a Place well inhabited by Wholesale Dealers, and most by Quakers, where they have their Meeting-house ... Plough Yard hath a good Free Stone Pavement, and the Houses well built and inhabited. Three Kings Court, well inhabited by Wholesale Dealers and others.[11]

If not exactly an upscale area, it was a busy, prosperous part of town, where the ambitious could pursue their goals in life. Sadly for Alexander and his family, after 1688 these opportunities existed only in an attenuated form, if at all, for people like them.

The Popes' residence lay just a short walk from the newly rebuilt Royal Exchange, as well as from East India House, and not much further from the historic centre of municipal affairs, the Guildhall. In 1694–5 the newly founded Bank of England would open its doors first at Mercers' Hall and then at Grocers' Hall, off Poultry, both close to the Exchange and a comfortable step from Plough Court. (Only in 1734 would the Bank acquire its more famous location in Threadneedle Street.) Further along Lombard Street to the west came the General Post Office, overseeing a significant sector of mercantile communications, and next door from 1691 Lloyd's coffee-shop, the home of the growing insurance industry. Across the road lay the entrance to Exchange Alley, which was to achieve a dubious fame as the epicentre of speculative activity at the time of the South Sea Bubble. Pope senior would not live to see that event or the erection of the new South Sea House in Threadneedle Street, though he would have known the old structure on this site. His son, an investor in the company, undoubtedly grew familiar with both buildings. Taken together, these institutions constituted the main locus of the Financial Revolution, a series of developments which dominated City life during the lifetime of Alexander Pope junior. They would feature prominently in his poetry of the 1730s, as we shall see in Chapter 8. The symbolism of this topographic connection seems all too neat.

In this house young Alexander spent the first four or five years of his life. The property stood across the road from Plough Court, in the small parish of St Edmund the King, which Christopher Wren and Robert Hooke had rebuilt after the Fire. In 1679 Pope senior buried his first wife Magdalen in another restored church, St Bennet Fink, about a hundred yards north of his home.[12] The Popes' home belonged to Langbourn Ward, a narrow straggling area that extended from the eastern end of Fenchurch Street to the junction of Poultry and Cornhill – in very approximate modern terms, the stretch between the Bank and the Lloyd's building.[13] Like much of the inner city, the ward experienced several convulsions in this era, reflecting the nature of the divided society within its boundaries. The leading merchants and goldsmith-bankers mostly took a consistently pro-Whig position, while proportionately the smaller tradesmen and retailers harboured a stronger admixture of Tory sentiment. Matters came to a head at the aldermanic poll in 1712, when a fierce party clash led to uproar in the City's common council amid allegations of fraud and manipulation on behalf of the Whig Lord Mayor. For much of Pope's lifetime the bigger battalions were able to have their way and the ward generally seems to have supported ministerial and court candidates against those allied with Tory and country interests. The alderman so controversially elected in 1712 was Peter Delmé (d. 1728), a Levant merchant of Huguenots origins, and a director of the Bank, who would be knighted by George I as soon as he acceded to the throne – in short, a classic City plutocrat. Delmé became Lord Mayor in 1723, but not before a highly contentious election following a blocking manoeuvre by Tory councilmen in the previous year.[14] The newspapers made much of this episode and it could hardly have escaped Pope.

This then was the world which opened up before the eyes of Pope in his earliest years. London had moved into full reconstruction mode after the ravages of the Great Fire, which had taken place little more than twenty years prior to his birth. Above the low rooflines of the city, as they would seem today, loomed the massive dome of St Paul's, which did not achieve its final shape until Pope was a young adult. All around stood the monuments of England's rise to political and mercantile power. As the poet grew up, he would witness many impressive construction works: not just the new Exchange, the General Post Office, East India House in nearby Leadenhall Street, and closer to the river the Custom House, but a variety of public and private buildings erected either to replace structures lost in the Fire or to satisfy the emerging needs of the mercantile community. Before he died Pope would see the completion of the Bank of England, South Sea House and the Admiralty offices in Whitehall, and the new Mansion House had begun to rise at the western end of Lombard Street. St Thomas's hospital had recently been restored and it was joined in the 1720s by Guy's. Several of the City churches had already been rebuilt, but there were more to come in the shape of the so-called Queen Anne churches. Pope took a particular interest in one of these, St Mary le Strand, designed by his friend James Gibbs – as was St Martin's in the Fields, a project separate from the Queen Anne programme. Meanwhile, some of the magnificent town houses of the aristocracy had disappeared over the previous century, but in their place arose mansions such as Burlington House and Marlborough House. Unlikely as it would have seemed in the 1690s, the boy growing up in Plough Court ultimately gained entrée to these palatial homes.

It is hard for us to imagine the visual excitement which this riot of construction stirred in men and women of the time. Daniel Defoe could hardly contain his enthusiasm when he came to write about the changing face of his hometown. While the sprawling unplanned growth of the city generally gave him concern, he revelled in the scale and magnificence of individual buildings, as they expressed the reborn confidence of his fellow citizens. He peppered a section on the capital in his *Tour thro' the Whole Island of Great Britain* (1724–6) with phrases such as 'The *Royal Exchange*, the greatest and finest of the Kind in the World'.[15] On top of this, he printed a long description of the scheme for a new palace of Whitehall, to replace the ramshackle old complex that succumbed to fires during Pope's early years. Such colossal architectural development had a psychological rather than an aesthetic impact: above all, it reminded people that Britain was expanding materially and politically. Pope can never have forgotten the sights which met his infant's gaze.

But there were some catches. In the first place, where Defoe lauded 'that beautiful Column, called the *Monument*',[16] Pope saw only a memorial to bigotry. The Doric column of Portland stone had been put up in the 1670s ostensibly to commemorate the survival of the city after the Great Fire. It rose 200 feet from ground level in Fish Street Hill, with an emblematic statue on its base by Caius Gabriel Cibber, whose son Colley would become the king of Pope's dunces. Tendentious Latin inscriptions were carved into the stone, blaming the Catholic population for starting the fire. After the Exclusion Crisis in 1681, to add further insult to this injurious claim, a new clause suggested that 'Popish frenzy' was still about its work in London. Luckily we can no longer decipher these words, as they were chiselled away in the nineteenth century. Close by, the authorities erected a plaque with an equally incendiary message on the site of the outbreak of the fire in Pudding Lane. It was taken down when James II sat on the throne, and reinstalled as soon as William III supplanted him. The Monument itself stood no more than a hundred yards from Plough Court: a couple of minutes' stroll down Gracechurch Street from the Popes' home. Small wonder that the poet never got over this lasting rebuke to the community in which he grew up:

> Where London's column, pointing to the skies,
> Like a tall bully, lifts the head, and lyes.
>
> (*TE*, vol. 3.ii, p. 340)

Secondly, the city was run not by hard-working small businessmen like Alexander Pope, senior. The great magnates and mercantile princes who dominated the economic activity of London also had a stranglehold on the corporation, guilds and ancillary bodies which controlled almost every aspect of commerce. It was to them that London chiefly owed the glut of new buildings dotting its skyline. These individuals exercised a key role in parliament. Whiggish, Protestant and Williamite to a man – they were all male – they stood for the new order in finance and society. The humble merchant in Plough Court, even though he was an overseas trader, did not belong to their number. His son came to harbour deep suspicions about the process that took place with bewildering speed in the first two decades of his own life. Pope's conservative humanist outlook clashed with the values of the moneyed men, and like most Tories he had serious doubts over expansionist overseas policies. This too marked him off from Defoe, who in a stream of pamphlets and private letters urged the government to make ever greater investment in trading settlements round the world.

In other ways, too, the pair stood on opposite sides of a major divide in political ideology. They had a similar origin under some aspects: Daniel Foe, to give him the name by which he still went, started out in the hosiery trade just before Pope was born, fitting out his warehouse in Freeman's Yard off Cornhill – a stone's throw from Plough Court. But the differences were stark. James Foe, father of the future novelist, held a position of some importance in civic affairs as a freeman of the City, a prominent member and warden of the Butchers' Company and a churchwarden. He took an active part in the resistance of the City oligarchy to attempts by the Stuart monarchs to limit its traditional power. In practice none of these avenues was open to Pope senior, though ways did exist sometimes to evade the requirements for oaths of loyalty and certificates of attendance at Anglican churches. Meanwhile Daniel took time off to take part in the rebellion of the Duke of Monmouth in 1685: he saw the Protestant cause defeated at the battle of Sedgmoor, but in the long run it turned out that he had joined the winning team. By contrast Pope's family background was peopled mainly by those who supported the Stuarts, and as time went on this dwindled into an increasingly desperate and marginal faction. History came down on the side of other groups, and the former elite could only watch in impotent fury while their opponents inherited the new world of wealth and power. Nowhere did the lines of this contest stand out in sharper definition than in London, which became more than ever the hub of the nation.

3

Being a child was a largely passive experience in early modern England. Despite the more liberal attitudes promoted by John Locke, the job of young boys, and even more girls, was to soak in the world as their elders mediated it to them. Soon Alexander would find his agency further diminished by his invalid status, constraining him to an almost feminine range of activity. But before that he would have gone about his life mainly as an observer, absorbing impressions and storing up memories for future use. Since he had a poet's heightened receptivity, he obviously took in more than most children of his age.

Plough Court operated as a workplace as well as a home. If we can trust the well-founded story that the Pope's residence occupied no. 2, then the ground floor and cellar served as the business premises, with some part of the second and third floors together with the garret containing domestic offices. We must picture the bustling activity at street level, with traders from far afield mingling with the locals. As international commerce grew, London served as a major entrepot, but it also had a large manufacturing section on the edge of the historic City, and as Alexander grew up it was becoming a major financial centre for the first time in its history. Just down the road at the coffee-house which bore his name, Edward Lloyd started his club of marine underwriters when the boy was three. Almost next door, a dog-legged passageway ran from the Royal Exchange to the Post Office: it was called Exchange, or more familiarly Change, Alley. Here from his office at Jonathan's coffee-house, John Castaing began in January 1698 to publish the prices of stocks and commodities with his *Course of the Exchange*.

This network formed the basis of the Stock Exchange, and around this spot in Change Alley some of the most vivid drama of the South Sea Bubble would play out in 1720, as investors jostled one another first to put their money into the company and then to seek to withdraw it. The Bubble echoed through Pope's later verse as insistently as it resonated within the entire psyche of the nation. All this shows that the key developments forging a new political and cultural identity for Britain had their visible expression within yards of his birthplace.

Besides this, the metropolis echoed to the sounds of street theatre and civic pageantry. The derisive Pope-burnings which had stoked up anti-Catholic feeling in the reign of Charles II had naturally died away during the reign of his papist brother, but these ceremonies of the 1670s and 1680s, before and after the Exclusion crisis, were etched into Catholic memory for generations to come. Besides, Protestants could still find plenty of occasions when they could display their zeal for the cause. The best opportunity, of course, came on 5 November, and after William's arrival at Torbay on this date in 1688 it tuned into a dual festival. In principle the annual Lord Mayor's show marked a less divisive occasion, but even this could be – and was – used to make a political point on one side or another. 'Public anniversaries were essentially designed to sanctify the political order', the historian Nicholas Rogers has written, 'to observe the memorable events in its creation, and by extension to provide opportunities for ruling-class liberality and spectacle'. He adds a telling comment: 'The populace was invited to occupy public space on these occasions, to share in the jubilation of a polity's creation and regeneration, to reverence its legitimacy'.[17] At its outset the regime of William and Mary stood in desperate need of legitimizing. The Whig dynasts and the bench of bishops had endorsed their takeover, but many of the common people remained obstinately unconvinced. Even those who had detested the headlong descent into prejudice and discrimination under James II feared the constitutional precedent set by removing an anointed monarch on what were fundamentally political grounds: this debate ran and ran, up into the time of Edmund Burke and beyond.

A second issue raised by the observations of Nicholas Rogers gives rise to a fascinating speculation. Was Alexander senior, with his newborn son on his shoulder, among the 'populace' who witnessed the proclamation of William and Mary in front of the Royal Exchange in February 1689? Probably not: he had too clear a sense of what was in store for him. But more plausibly: did the boy ever find himself among the throngs of Londoners who lined the streets each October to watch the Lord Mayor's Day procession, with its mixture of propaganda, carnivalesque rites and simple junketing? The question is a real one, because of the extensive use Pope makes of the occasion in *The Dunciad* (see Chapter 7 below). Maynard Mack has argued with great cogency that lines in the poem go back to impressions formed in the poet's earliest years by the elaborate special effects seen in the procession. He suggests that the verses hark back to residues of a more primitive response, reaching far back into a child's mixed sensation of delight and terror as he stares from some lowly perch at what seem to be towering figures gliding by:

> 'Twas on the day when thro' the broad Cheapside
> Gigantic Forms in Cars triumphal ride ...

It would hardly be surprising if their vague menace as sensed at the time by a child were to surface later on, giving physical body to what the rational (now grown-up) mind of the poet interpreted as solely an intellectual and cultural threat.[18]

The gigantic forms on view would include the fifteen-feet tall figures of Gogmag and Corineus, who were now restored to duty after their enforced inactivity during the Commonwealth, when Cromwell had them destroyed. Unfortunately rats ate out the entrails of the new statues. According to a contemporary pamphlet, 'the dissolution of the two old, weak and feeble giants gave birth to the two present substantial and majestic giants ... [which were] immediately advanced to [their] lofty stations in the Guildhall.'[19] Thus in 1708 the famous pair of wooden statues representing Gog and Magog were set up to replace effigies destroyed in the Fire. They were too heavy to haul out from their ceremonial plinth, but replicas were constructed each year as props in the Lord Mayor's procession until they perished in the Blitz – and in their modern incarnation, after a new set was supplied in 1953, they still fulfil this role.

Crude pageantry of this sort lies behind much of *The Dunciad*, with the gods and demons early on (*TE*, vol. 1, p. 76), and the monsters later: 'All sudden, Gorgons hiss, and Dragons glare, / And ten-horn'd fiends and Giants rush to war' (*TE*, vol. 1, p. 177). These nouns recall the stock allegories of civic ceremonial in Pope's youth and beyond. We may remember that Gog and Magog figure in the text of Geoffrey of Monmouth, author of a work in which Pope displayed some interest, and that the poet intended in his unfinished epic to 'moralize the old fables concerning *Brutus, Gogmagog, &c*'.[20] 'Gog from the land of Magog' was mentioned in the Book of Ezekiel as an invader of Israel, while the two names figure among the hosts of the Antichrist in Revelations. Such emblems of discord could serve a cathartic purpose in the pageants, like Herod in a mummers' play or a pantomime villain. In *The Dunciad* the giants provide another means to link dulness with Satan.

The single episode which may have impacted most deeply on the Pope family (although not, of course, on little Alexander, who was only sixteen months old) occurred at the Lord Mayor's show of 1689. William's supporters determined to make this a set-piece of unforgettable impact, and it was described at the time as having outdone 'all that had been seen before on the like occasion' – a large claim, in view of the opulence of these affairs under the early Stuarts. The show commemorated the installation of Sir Thomas Pilkington, 'perhaps the most acerbic of the Whig magistrates', and spared little by way of expense or effort:

> [It] was celebrated by the Whigs as 'London's Great Jubilee', a tribute to the Revolution and to the rescue of the City from oppression. The affair was rich with symbolism, studded with Whig talent, and most importantly, open to the people ... Participation was extended vicariously to the guildsmen, drawn up by company along the way, and to the people, who lined the streets and crowded the balconies. On his return from Westminster, the Lord Mayor officially reviewed four pageants presented in Cheapside and left standing until dark for the people's edification. An added attraction in 1689 was the stunning entrance of William and Mary in a cavalcade headed by the Earl of Monmouth.[21]

This passage needs something by way of gloss. First, the title 'Earl of Monmouth' had only been recently bestowed: it covers the identity of a figure better known as Charles Mordaunt, Earl of Peterborough (1658–1735), who had become one of Pope's closest friends by the time of *The Dunciad*, and about whom the poet told Joseph Spence a number of picturesque anecdotes. Second, it is striking that in his draft version of the work Pope imagined the menacing giants as looming over Cheapside, where the pageants were staged in 1689 – especially as he does not describe this section of the route in the published poem. Third, we should note the presence of the 'guildsmen' in organized blocks within the crowd lining the route, a testimony to the residual strength of the livery companies in all City business.

Soon William and Mary gained a seemingly unbreakable hold on power, a process confirmed by the defeat of James's Catholic forces in Ireland. As time went on, however, cracks began to appear. The death of Queen Mary from smallpox at the end of 1694 struck a personal and political blow at the King, and some of his most trusted lieutenants also departed from the scene. The public grew resentful of the Dutch mafia who seemed to be in control of royal decision-making. Simultaneously the attritional Nine Years War against Louis XIV dragged on, with the allies led by William bogged down in an apparently endless stalemate. In 1697 the Peace of Ryswick brought an end to this conflict, only for an even more costly European struggle to break out in 1701 with the War of the Spanish Succession. By the turn of the century British feelings about the great deliverer of 1688 took an emphatically mixed form. This allowed a loyal opposition to grow up, mostly non-Jacobite in complexion. The rump of Tories and royalists who had been alienated by James's policies, and then left on their knees after the Revolution swept them aside, gradually found a new role. They were able to capitalize on the growth of a Country party to oppose the Court faction: this embraced some radical commonwealth men, disenchanted Whig gentry and nostalgic Tory squires. The Pope family stood outside each of these categories, but they had some affinities with both of the latter two groups.

Needless to say, neither Alexander nor Edith, for overlapping reasons to do with religion and gender, had the vote. As it happened, the City had an unusually large electorate, since the franchise was open to some 8,000 members of the livery companies. Men with a less substantial business than the one Mr Pope abandoned in 1688 would have been able to exercise the right to vote – something he had renounced when he underwent conversion to the proscribed faith. Mostly the constituency was represented by the great magnates of London commerce. Financiers like Sir Robert Clayton rose to the top of the hierarchy, while bankers such as Sir Charles Duncombe, who sat for constituencies outside the capital, gained huge power. But there were overseas traders too, perhaps most notably Sir Gilbert Heathcote, who first stood for election in 1698 and gained a seat in 1701. He operated on a vast scale, and had fingers in every financial pie including the Bank and the New East India Company. As we shall see, Pope would make derisive references to Heathcote in his poetry. Many of the smaller merchants favoured the Tory party, but the oligarchs were mostly Whigs.

We cannot say with absolute certainly where the loyalties of Pope's father would lie; but his later behaviour and his few known proclivities suggest that he would have supported candidates from the Country party against those of the Court. What his son came to believe is apparent from many references in his writing. To take just one example, in one of the imitations of Horace there is a bitter recollection of the harsh laws imposed on people like the elder Pope and his family:

> But knottier Points we knew not half so well,
> Deprived us soon of our Paternal Cell;
> And certain Laws, by Suff'rers thought unjust,
> Deny'd all Posts of Profit or of Trust:
> Hopes after Hopes of pious Papists fail'd,
> While mighty WILLIAM's thundring Arm prevail'd.
> For Right Hereditary tax'd and fin'd,
> He stuck to Poverty with Peace of Mind;
> And me, the Muses help to undergo it;
> Convict a Papist he, and I a Poet.

(*TE*, vol. 4, p. 169)

The lines speak with heart-rending directness of the climate in which Pope grew up.

4

His co-religionists constituted a small percentage of the national population. They formed a conspicuous block of society in only a few parts of the country, notably Lancashire and Cheshire, although there was an important group of recusant gentry in the Thames Valley, with whom Pope made lasting connections during his youth. Some humbler folk in the provinces retained an allegiance to the old faith, but as yet there had been no large-scale immigration from Catholic countries to major centres, so that the urban poor were Protestant for the most part – often virulently so. Within months of Pope's birth, James II was ousted from the throne, having lost popularity in considerable measure because of his attempts to impose freedom of worship, that is official tolerance of Catholicism.

The backlash which followed under William and Mary saw the introduction of severe penal laws against the papist community.[22] Excluded from succession to the throne, Catholics had to take oaths of loyalty, on pain of losing most civic rights. Out of fear that insurrection would break out they were forbidden to keep arms, ammunition or, bizarrely, a horse worth more than £10 (1 Will. & Mar., c. 15). A few years later, a new measure, 7 & 8 Will. III, c. 24, closed the professions of counsellor-at-law, barrister, attorney and solicitor to all Catholics. Yet another (7 & 8 Will. III, c. 27) laid down that anyone refusing to take the oaths of allegiance and supremacy, when lawfully tendered, should be liable to suffer as a popish recusant convict (the phrase that Pope recalls in the last line of the passage just quoted); and that no one refusing this should be admitted to vote at the elections for a member of parliament. The most striking and astonishing of all these laws had still to come. This took the form of a particularly invidious statute (11 & 12 Will. III, c. 4) passed in 1700, which the great constitutional scholar Erskine May, writing in the more tender-minded Victorian period, called 'an act no less factious than bigoted, – which cannot be read without astonishment'.[23] It incapacitated all Roman Catholics from inheriting or purchasing land, unless they formally abjured their religion. If they refused, their property was legally transferred for life to their next of kin in the Protestant faith. They were even prohibited from sending their children abroad, to be educated in their own faith. Finally, the measure laid down that any Catholic priests caught exercising their vocation should be imprisoned for life, and it set a reward of £100 for informing against priests who said mass.

In terms of year-by-year living, there was one further disability which few could escape. While no regular system of income tax had yet come into being, property taxes were imposed annually, and special levies raised from time to time to meet special needs such as supplies for a war. One convenient way of harvesting more money was to assess rates for Catholics at double the standard rate, for both national and local taxes. This had happened in the Caroline period, and parliament renewed this policy with extra vigour in 1692 – an imposition that remained in place until 1794. The need to finance the wars with France led to much greater government borrowing, precisely the increase in credit that the new institutions such as the Bank of England had been set up to facilitate. Tories claimed that the benefits went to the City moneyed men who funded large loans, and the costs were loaded on to taxpayers generally, including landowners who had to pay during wartime at the rate of four shillings in the pound, that is 20 per cent, on rental values. More and more the poet's natural affinities drew him to those hardest hit by such measures, especially the papist community.

Each draconian addition to the statutes had a direct and personal impact on the Popes. Partly, at least, because of these laws, the poet's family left London shortly after the Revolution of 1688: even their ultimate refuge involved a legal fiction, since they were not permitted to buy their house in the country. As time went on, the operation of the laws underwent some relaxation under Queen Anne, and several of Pope's friends and neighbours continued to send their children, both boys and girls, to Continental Europe for a Catholic education. But the Hanoverian accession in 1714 led to a renewal of the old laws and the introduction of even more stringent measures, with consequences we shall explore in Chapter 4.

Another issue is relevant. While it did not impact directly upon most people in their everyday lives, the passage of the Act of Settlement in 1701 (12 & 13 Will. III, c. 5, s. 2) made an important statement. This act had as its principal aim the establishment of the Hanoverian succession to the British throne. It stipulated what should happen if the reigning monarch William or his sister-in-law Anne (who would actually succeed a year later) died without an heir. Urgency had grown with the death of Anne's only surviving child, the Duke of Gloucester, in 1699. In its opening paragraph the measure named Sophia, Electress of Hanover and granddaughter of James I, as the designated successor. After her, the throne would pass to her heirs, 'being protestant'. This foreshadowed the actual course of events in 1714: Sophia died that summer, but after the death of Anne – who survived only until 1 August – the throne passed without too much fuss to the new Elector, Sophia's son, who duly became King George I. Other provisions of the Act required that the sovereign should always be a member of the Church of England, and that the monarch should not leave England without the consent of parliament.

Despite all that, the real sting in the wording came in certain clauses that explicitly proscribed a Catholic monarchy. These required the new monarch to take a coronation oath enacted in 1689 which contained a promise to uphold the Protestant reformed religion. In the clearest language of all, the new law repudiated the claims of anyone who 'is, are or shall be reconciled to, or shall hold communion with, the See or Church of Rome, or shall profess the popish religion, or shall marry a papist'. This ban has lasted into the twenty-first century, though many people today think its time has long past. Contemporaries did not fail to observe that something like fifty persons with a stronger claim were debarred from the succession simply by virtue of their faith. But everyone knew that the whole object of the exercise was to exclude both the deposed King, James II, and his son, the so-called Old Pretender, James Edward Stuart. As it turned out, the former monarch died within three months of the passage of the Act. There was also a daughter, Louisa Maria, born after the King's exile, who was still a child of eight: she would die from smallpox in 1712 without ever being seen as a major contender to succeed. James Edward of course remained a focus of anxiety for decades to come, most obviously when he led the abortive rising in 1715–16. Most likely Pope did not care greatly about some of these issues; and he always held a low opinion of James II. Still, the naked contempt with which parliament had spurned the claims of his fellow Catholics must have fuelled a lurking sense that he was no more than a second-class citizen. In spite of all his later achievements, he never completely overcame this feeling.

We can hardly feel surprise that the Revolution of 1688, a bold pre-emptive strike on behalf of the aristocracy, provoked considerable insecurity. This in turn bred some of the fiercest anti-Catholic measures, which seem extraordinarily petty, as well as repressive, to modern eyes. As we have just seen, the year after Pope was born, parliament brought in a measure to expel papists from London. By this Act (1 Will. & Mar., c. 9) the justices of London and the home counties were empowered to arrest all such persons 'as are or are reputed to be Papists'. If the suspect then refused to take an oath of allegiance, he or she would be 'esteemed and adjudged a Popish Recusant Convict'. It was then forbidden for the individual to 'remaine continue or be within the sayd City or Cityes [London and Westminster] or Ten miles distance from the same'.[24] Unquestionably, it was this Act that prompted Pope's father to retreat from the capital around 1692. He moved first to Hammersmith, which, as George Sherburn says, 'if not ten miles from Hyde Park Corner, was remote enough from the City to show his good intentions'.[25] Not until about 1700 did the family move to Binfield in Windsor Forest. We may be inclined to congratulate the poet on his good luck in escaping from urban squalor, so that he could enjoy his upbringing amid the rural delights of this sylvan refuge. But the young Pope must have felt in his inner self a strong contrary influence. A sense, that is, that he was being shifted gradually further and further from the centre of things: a consciousness of exclusion and exile. Pope's later drive for success may be seen as an attempt to recapture an inheritance denied him. All the wry jokes in his poems and letters count for little beside the brutally stark phrasing of the statute. Whig historians have described some 'precarious' toleration for the Catholics through non-enforcement of such laws; but a 'Popish Recusant Convict' needed no persecution complex to feel that he was being driven out from society.[26] With the passage of time came further inroads into the poet's freedom of civic action. We shall look at these over the course of this narrative.

By late 1691 Mr Pope had begun to contemplate a move from the City. He paid a fine in lieu of serving as a parish constable, as most people who could afford it chose to do. The vestry minutes record the suggestion that he may have been planning to quit the ward by the following midsummer, in which case he would be entitled to a rebate on the fine. Next year he was assessed at the double rate for the poll tax covering the Lombard Street precinct; but in the second quarter a new occupant appears in the list. This man, a certain George Oldner, continued to pay the tax in the fourth quarter, but in addition the house's residents still included 'Mr. Popes servant and John Taverner'. The former was probably Mary Beach, the nursemaid; and the second can certainly be identified as the family's domestic priest, otherwise known by the name of Banister. Why these two remained after the married couple and their children had moved out, we have no idea.[27]

Some equally mysterious circumstances surround the family's new home. It remains unclear exactly when, where and why they took up residence in Hammersmith. The poet never mentions this phase in this life, even though the Popes were there until about 1700. The few facts that have emerged make the removal no less enigmatic. By 1695 Alexander's half-sister Magdalen, still aged only about sixteen, had married Charles Rackett, a member of a family well established in the area. The couple had a daughter who died at the age of seven months in April 1696. Official documents list Charles as a 'gentleman', and while not an exact term this indicates that he was a man of some substance. However, his later life did not always go well and the Rackett children were to cause the poet considerable trouble over the years. Soon afterwards, Rackett bought a house in Berkshire, in the village of Binfield, where he briefly took up residence. This would be the house where young Alexander spent the most influential period of his childhood and adolescence. In July 1698 it was sold by Rackett to Mr Pope, described in the deeds as 'of Hammersmith ... Merchant'. However it was another year or two before the family moved in. Meanwhile the Racketts settled in a more impressive property on the eastern edge of Windsor Forest, near Bagshot, and Pope would visit here regularly afterwards. Hall Grove lay no more than seven miles from Binfield as the crow flies, but no prudent crow – or poacher – would have crossed the carefully policed woodlands without informing traffic control. That was something the Racketts would learn to their cost in the course of time.

In defiance of the strict legalities, the Thames-side village of Hammersmith where the family took up residence lay no more than four miles west of Hyde Park Corner. Travellers on their way from central London along the road to the west would pass some imposing structures at Knightsbridge, Campden House and Holland House. But once they had left the park itself behind, they would encounter open fields on either side for most of their journey. The village had started to become fashionable in the later seventeenth century, and by 1725 Defoe could report that it was no longer 'a long scattering Place', but 'a Wood of great Houses and Palaces', with 'a noble Square built as it were in the middle of several handsome Streets, as if the Village seem'd enclin'd to grow up into a City'.[28]

This evocative description nonetheless conceals the real reason why Mr Pope must have decided to bring his family to this particular spot. Yet again we have to seek the reason in religious politics. A local historian of the nineteenth century explains the issues at stake: 'If there is one spot in the neighbourhood of London to which the English Roman Catholics look with greater veneration than another ... that spot is Hammersmith, which contains an unusual number of establishments belonging to the members of that faith'.[29] Entering the village from the east, the traveller would soon have come on a Benedictine convent. Allegedly this had been founded before the Reformation, but 'escaped the general destruction of religious houses from its want of endowment'.[30] Here a girls' school had been set up in the reign of Charles II (who himself had passed a great deal of time in the village), and under the instigation of his Queen, Catherine of Braganza. She induced Frances Bedingfield (1616–1704) to establish the house, and to act as superior until moving to another school in York in 1686. Suggestively, the institution in the north had been founded by Bedingfield as early as 1676: could Edith Turner have met her there? Contemporary accounts suggest that 'professed religious ladies, who were nuns in disguise' staffed the establishment.[31] The school stood close to the country home of the Portuguese ambassador, a site which always became the focus for recusant activity. After the death of Charles in 1685, his widow, the Queen dowager, spent the next few summers at the convent school which owed its foundation to her initiative.

Some crucial facts bear a little emphasis here. The largest of the English Benedictine convents in France, at Dunkirk, was headed from 1663 to 1712 by Mary Caryll, aunt of one of Pope's very closest friends, John Caryll – whose mother was another Frances Bedingfield.[32] As for the religious named Frances Bedingfield, she belonged to a prominent recusant family with whom Pope also had many ties. Among the girls educated at Hammersmith around the turn of the century was Mary Bedingfield, daughter of a barrister who was also a member of the Pope circle. Subsequently Mary married Sir John Swinburne, son of a friend and correspondent of the poet, Mary Swinburne, a member of the Berkshire Englefields. We shall hear more of this family in Chapter 4. Mary Bedingfield's schoolfellows included three daughters of Sir John Webb, one of whom would marry the ill-fated Earl of Derwentwater, beheaded on Tower Hill in 1716.

Once more these individuals had personal connections with Pope's family (see Chapter 4).[33] By chance the nearby district of Brook Green, then an outlying subdivision of Hammersmith, came to be known as 'Pope's Corner', as a result of the unusual number of Catholic institutions.

The close association of the village with Catholic activity had been reinforced during the hysteria provoked by the alleged Popish Plot in 1680. At this time the notorious Titus Oates launched an inquisitorial raid on the house in the company of an armed posse. As a contemporary news sheet reported:

> A house at Hammersmith having been much frequented by persons whose mien and garb rendered them suspected, Dr. Oates was informed that several jesuits and priests lay there concealed, but on strict search found no man there but an outlandish [foreign] gentleman, who appeared to be secretary to the ambassador of the Spanish King, upon the list of his servants in the secretary's office. It seems the mistress of the house, who is much admired for her extraordinary learning, beyond her sex and age, understanding excellently well the Latin, Hebrew, Greek, and several modern languages, being also very well read in most parts of philosophy and the mathematics, has been often visited by ingenious men, foreigners, and others, her admirers, which gave occasion to the information against her, but being examined before his Majesty's council, and making oath that she harboured no such obnoxious persons as had been suggested by Dr. Oates, she was immediately acquitted, and the gentleman was delivered to the ambassador, his master.[34]

The Popes may have been already acquainted with the Carylls and the Bedingfields. In any case, there is no serious ground for doubting that they made Hammersmith their choice because of its recent history. Many existential decisions in the past came down to such religious considerations – something far less true in the modern western world.

Pope's own formal schooling began at the time that his family was living in Hammersmith. After his aunt had taught him to read, he received the basic rudiments from the domestic priest in Plough Lane, a man named Edward Taverner, alias John Banister. It is a pity that we know virtually nothing of Taverner, since he seems to have played a major role in the development of his charge.[35] At the age of about eight the boy was sent for a year to one of the many Catholic schools which managed like the convent at Hammersmith to survive in flagrant contradiction of the laws. Taverner may have accompanied him to this establishment, operated at Twyford near Winchester by a certain Wait with the help of an equally obscure figure named John Grove. All we know of this spell comes from what Pope's sister Magdalen Rackett told Joseph Spence, to the effect that he was whipped after writing a satire on the masters, and promptly withdrawn by his parents (*Anecdotes*, vol. 1, pp. 8–9).

Better things lay in store. The youngster went to study under Thomas Deane (1651–1735), who kept a school in Marylebone. The master had held an Oxford fellowship, which he forfeited when converting to the Catholic faith after the accession of James II. He had suffered various penalties, including a spell in the pillory, for his subsequent activities, which may have included serving as a priest. Soon after Alexander got there, the school had to be moved to a new location on the north side of Piccadilly near Hyde Park Corner, as a result of the unduly close surveillance it had received from a local magistrate in its old setting – the justices of the peace actually 'broke up' the school on instructions from the Duke of Bedford in 1696, a short while before the young man arrived. He spent something like two or three years here just before the turn of the century. Though Pope did not think that he learnt very much under Deane, the school provided a more liberal atmosphere than Twyford had done. Three decades later, when Deane was again in trouble for seditious writing, Pope and John Caryll joined other supporters to come to his relief with a pension.

If we can interpret accurately the remarks Pope made much later to Spence, he made little progress at either school, having lost the little he had learnt under his first instructor, Taverner. Nor did he join in the playtime activities of his schoolmates at Deane's academy, preferring to 'amuse himself with Drawing, and such like improving and rational Accomplishments'.[36] It does not sound like a recipe for popularity. But deep within the boy there lay an unquenchable urge to acquire knowledge and to improve his understanding of the world. The chance to satisfy these needs came only after the family once more upped sticks and left Hammersmith for their new home at Binfield. There he found the perfect environment for the studies which would lay the foundation for his literary career, and more widely instil in him the particular outlook that characterized his views on life – including politics.

2 THE FLOWERS OF THE FOREST

> Both in the flower of youth, Arcadians both,
> Equal in song and eager to respond.
>
> Virgil, *Eclogues* 7, trans. P. Alpers

Most of the formative experiences of Pope's lifetime took place while he resided in Windsor Forest. From the age of twelve Whitehill House at Binfield was his family home, and it remained the main locus of his spiritual life until fresh acts of oppression by the Hanoverian government led to its disposal when he was twenty-eight. Although not literally his native heath, it became the place to which his fondest memories constantly returned.

From this point in his development, we know more about Alexander's boyhood and adolescence than usually happens with individuals born in earlier centuries. Several reasons lie behind such a comparative glut of information. For one thing, in his poems and letters the adult writer often harked back to this phase. The scattered woodlands around Windsor became symbolic 'Groves of *Eden*' (*TE*, vol. 1, p. 148) in his work. The poet himself, as well as several others who knew him at the time (including his sister), gave Joseph Spence their recollections of the manner in which he spent his life in the forest. Then again, his daily companions in Binfield were his parents and his nurse Mary Beach – each of these lived to a good old age, and constituted a living aide-memoire. Pope kept many of the friends he had acquired in his youth, and continued to visit his old haunts even after the property had passed from his family. His sister, as we have seen, lived on the edge of the forest. Finally, the area was replete with historical, courtly and even mythical associations. The Thames washed its northern edge, and the main road to Salisbury and Exeter skirted its southern boundary. In some ways the retreat that the poet would construct for himself at Twickenham served as a replacement for the scenes of his boyhood. Halfway between Binfield and Lombard Street, the riverside house enabled him to recapture some of the values enshrined in his youthful home.

In retrospect, the time Alexander passed growing up in the forest stood out as a sort of Arcadian interlude. What he lacked in good health, he made up for with the nervous energy and capacity for fun that characterize most young people. His letters show more delight in flippancy and self-mockery than in later years. He made friendships that would last for decades. All the while he was steadily mastering the craft which meant most to him, writing. Most of all, he had an acute sense of belonging, as he got to know more of his co-religionists and more people who shared his love of literature. After he became an adult, he saw many of these certainties fractured by the course of events that he could no longer passively observe from a comfortable distance.

1

On the face of things, Pope's main concerns had little to do directly with politics. Literature provided the driving force in his life, and his sojourn in the forest allowed him to pursue this passion with few distractions. As he told his friend Martha Blount, he 'read whole days there under the trees'. His father encouraged his bent for composing poetry, but could prove a hard taskmaster. Much later Edith told Joseph Spence, 'He was pretty difficult in being pleased and used often to send [his son] back to new turn them. "These are not good rhymes," he would say, for that was my husband's word for verses' (*Anecdotes*, vol. 1, pp. 7, 20).

The boy had already acquired an enduring fascination with the work of Homer, which he had first encountered through the medium of a translation of the *Iliad* by John Ogilby in the sumptuous folio edition of 1660. Later on Pope would become aware of the cultural politics bound up in the great classical epics, but at this stage he responded most directly to the heroic canvas, the human drama and the vivid scene-painting he found in Homer. The idea of embarking on his own translation crystallized in his years at Binfield. At the same time he was expanding the scope of his reading. Lifelong favourites such as Erasmus, Montaigne and Ovid surfaced in his consciousness. Like most autodidacts, he began by following his own instincts: 'In a few years I had dipped into a great number of the English, French, Italian, Latin, and Greek poets. This I did without any design but of pleasing myself, and got the languages by hunting after the stories.' The most notable inclusion here concerns Italian, at a time when few British readers knew very much about the language or literature. He retained this interest, and as late as 1740 he brought out an edition in two volumes of Latin poetry written by modern Italian authors. Perhaps the most striking thing Pope said about this phase occurs in the same conversation with Spence: 'I followed everywhere as my fancy led me, and was like a boy gathering flowers in the woods and fields just as they fall in his way. I still look upon these five or six years as the happiest part of my life' (*Anecdotes*, vol. 1, p. 24).

Much of his time obviously went on studying the most significant works of earlier English literature. In 1701 a neighbour called Gabriel Young, the former owner of Whitehill House, presented him with a black letter Chaucer from 1598 in folio, and this also would ultimately lead Pope to produce his own version of some Chaucerian tales. Spenser, Sidney's *Arcadia*, the poems of Ben Jonson and *Paradise Lost* were on his self-imposed curriculum, along with Shakespeare. Among recent writers, by far the biggest influence was exerted by John Dryden, who died in the year that the Popes moved out to Berkshire. Pope may once have seen the older poet regaling the patrons at Will's coffee-house in Covent Garden, but if so their personal dealings went no further. Pope conducted a lasting virtual relationship with Dryden, seeing his predecessor as a model both in literary skills and in the construction of a career. Another critical example given by Dryden was his continuing loyalty to the Catholic faith he had embraced under James II, even though this meant he was stripped of his post as poet laureate under William and lived out his days as a marginalized figure.

Just before or just after the move to the country – we cannot be sure which – Pope fell victim to the spinal tuberculosis which would limit his activity for the rest of his days. He had contracted Pott's disease, named after the man who would first diagnose it a generation later, the London surgeon Percival Pott (1714–88). The main symptom is curvature of the spine, resulting from a tubercular condition of the bone and usually caused by infected milk. It produces an uneven contraction, so that one side of the body is affected more noticeably. Physicians refer to it as kyphoscoliosis, or curvature in two different planes. Pope was able to walk and ride in his youth, but gradually became dependent on help for the ordinary functions of everyday living. He needed to wear a corset in order to stand up. His height is generally stated at about four feet six inches. 'In effect', it has been said, 'he was as swaddled and dependent in his later years as a contemporary baby'.[1] The tubercular illness would help to explain the dangerous bouts of fever Pope underwent as a young man, for example in 1710. In order to combat the pain he needed to adopt a number of regimes: from the early 1730s he had recourse to a diet of asses' milk. Another lasting ailment, probably unconnected, came in the form of serious headaches, which may well have been what today we call migraine. When Sir Joshua Reynolds caught a glimpse of Pope at an auction, near the end of the poet's life, he noted an 'extraordinary countenance ... a pallid, studious look', and picked out with an artist's eye the signs both of deformity and pain in his face.[2]

As commonly happens, the disease progressed quite slowly. Typically the patient appears tired and languid, and in time has difficulty in using his or her limbs. By early adolescence the illness had taken this precise course, and Pope was condemned from now on to an invalid state as well as a grievously disfiguring hump and a tiny stature. Medical experts agree that the original cause almost certainly lay in the unsterilized milk of the time, perhaps even breast milk from his wet-nurse Mary Beach. We can discount the tale told by Magdalen Rackett that he had been gored and trampled by a cow as a young boy, with effects on his health thereafter – even though plenty of cows would have grazed in the fields around Hammersmith, as well as Binfield (*Anecdotes*, vol. 1, p. 3).

By the time he was well into his teens, then, Alexander had to reconcile himself to the limitations imposed by his 'little, tender, crazy Carcase', as the dramatist William Wycherley described it in 1709 (*Corr.*, vol. 1, p. 14). At one time he came to believe that he would not live very long, until he was advised to study less and ride very day, with a consequent improvement in his health. The famous physician John Radcliffe apparently gave this advice by means of a kind of distance diagnosis, without any contact with the patient: such things happened commonly enough at the time. But even with this more favourable prognosis, Pope's condition gave rise to potential embarrassments, as well as constraints. This is what a maid-servant employed by his friend, the second Earl of Oxford, reported after his death:

> He was unable to dress or undress himself, or get into bed without help; nor could he stand upright till a kind of stays, made of stiff linen, were laced on him, one of his first [*sic*] sides being contracted almost to the back-bone. He wanted much waiting on, but was very liberal to the maid-servants about him, so that he had never reason to complain of being neglected. These females attended him at night, and, in the morning, brought him his writing-desk to bed, lighted his fire, drew on his stockings, etc, which offices he often summoned them to perform at very early hours, so that, when any part of their business was left undone, their common excuse was, that they had been employed with Mr. Pope, and then no further reprehension was to be dreaded.[3]

Having to lead his life this way left its obvious mark. Pope grew accustomed to a marginal role, not quite a full participant in civic affairs. It drew him closer to his elderly and perhaps overprotective patents, it made it less likely he could attend Catholic schools (which would have meant living at a distance from his home, if not overseas), and it encouraged him to become even more absorbed in the private drama of his imagination. Later on, his deformity would expose him to cruel jibes which enemies launched in the public prints, for this was an age that knew nothing of political correctness. But at this stage, so far as we can tell, he met with little but sympathy and kindness.

Bookish and frail as he might be, Alexander did not spend all his days closeted in a library. He enjoyed life out of doors, got to know the flora and fauna of the surrounding countryside, and lent an ear to the forest murmurs as he sought out boyish haunts to combine play with reflection and dreams. Maynard Mack has written of the child's 'private kingdoms of forest and field', that induced 'a rapturous sense of seclusions, enclaves, inaccessible retreats'.[4] That captures very well the nature of Pope's imaginative world, with its abnormally acute sense of private fulfilment. Yet as time went on he learnt to focus more on the busy scene around him. Little of his poetry is about himself, in any simple way. To this extent he differs markedly from a poet like Wordsworth or Byron, even though they admired Pope and learnt from him. A good deal of politics comes up in *The Prelude*, but the events of the French Revolution, for example, are there because of their impact on the writer's own sensibility. By contrast, Pope often starts his imitations of Horace from local, personal and first-hand experience, and then modulates to the objective world of action in the public sphere which provides the real occasion for the work.

While at Binfield he came into contact with the rural sports that delighted the gentry and some of the humble citizens in the neighbourhood. He always had mixed feelings about activities which set as their goal inflicting pain or death on often harmless creatures. It is not too much of an exaggeration to say that he operated as a one-man Royal Society for the Prevention of Cruelty to Animals, long before such an organization existed in Britain or anywhere else. Still, he left a few signs that he envied the physical prowess of keen huntsmen such as John Caryll, the son of his friend in Sussex. A letter to John from Binfield in 1712 shows this:

> While you are pursuing the Sprightly Delights of the Field, springing up with activity at the Dawning Day, rouzing a whole Country with Shouts and Horns, and inspiring Animalls and Rationalls with like Fury and Ardor; while your Blood boils high in ev'ry Vein, your Heart bounds in your breast, and as vigorous a Confluence of Spirits rushes to it at the sight of a Fox as cou'd be stirrd up by that of an Army of Invaders; while the Zeal of the Chace devours the whole man, and moves him no less than the Love of our Country or the Defence of our Altars could do. While ... you are thus imployed, I am just in the reverse of all this Spirit and Life, confin'd to a narrow Closet, lolling on an Arm Chair, nodding away my Days over a Fire.
>
> (*Corr.*, vol. 1, p. 163)

Two years earlier the young man had written to a friend in town:

> I assure you I am look'd upon in the Neighborhood for a very Sober and well-disposd Person, no great Hunter indeed, but a great Esteemer of the noble Sport, and only unhappy in my Want of Constitution for that, and Drinking. They all say 'tis pitty I am so sickly, and I think 'tis pitty Thay are so healthy: But I say nothing that may destroy their good opinion of me.
>
> (*Corr.*, vol. 1, p. 81)

Some compensatory mechanism seems to have come into play. As Valerie Rumbold has observed, 'for many years he made strenuous efforts to live up to expectations of male robustness'; but a certain air of play-acting accompanied most of these efforts.[5]

While Pope would not have wished to live the life of some hard-drinking, boorish rustic – even if that had been possible – he might have liked to have had the choice. We can tell what he thought of such oafs in a delicious poem that he wrote a few years later, 'Epistle to Miss Blount, on her leaving the Town, after the Coronation'. *Rack* here means 'torment' or 'get the better of'; while *buss* means 'kiss'.

> Some Squire, perhaps, you take delight to rack,
> Whose game is Whisk, whose treat a toast in sack;
> Who visits with a gun, presents you birds,
> Then gives a smacking buss, and cries – No words!
> Or with his hound comes hollowing from the stable,
> Makes love with nods and knees beneath a table;
> Whose laughs are hearty, though his jests are coarse,
> And loves you best of all things – but his horse.
>
> (*TE*, vol. 6, p. 125)

The teenage Alexander obviously wanted to fit in with the people of the forest, even while he mocked the cruder aspects of rural living. Despite the obstacles provided by his health, his religion, his anomalous position in the class system and his bookish ways, he appears to have succeeded more than we might expect.

2

In June 1698 Mr Pope completed the purchase of the house in Binfield from his son-in-law at a price of £445, exactly the sum that Charles Rackett had paid for it three years earlier. (The precise match suggests some kind of collusion to avoid legal problems.) However, the family does not seem to have moved in immediately, and a tenant must have occupied the property. Pope senior then conveyed it in a deed dated April 1700, by which it was granted to Samuel and Charles Mawhood (pronounced 'Maud') in trust for his son Alexander. This was presumably to evade the law regarding the acquisition of estates by Catholics. Apparently Samuel Mawhood (1655–1736), a woollen draper in the Smithfield district of London, and a son of Edith Pope's sister Alice and her husband Richard, had abjured the hereditary faith. Samuel became a member of the Fishmongers' Company and a freeman of London by 1690; he also served on the City corporation as a Tory councilman for Farringdon Ward Without in the early Hanoverian years, both of which positions would have required taking the oaths. He had left the Mawhoods' home near Doncaster to serve an apprenticeship in the City, and as Valerie Rumbold has conjectured may have provided the link between the draper Alexander Pope and the Turner family into which he would marry.[6] Evidently Samuel prospered in business, as a result of getting a large army contract – precisely the sort of thing that Tories liked to complain about – and managed to give his daughter a huge dowry of £10,000.

Whitehill House was a small structure, probably timber-framed with some brickwork, suitable to the better sort of yeoman farmer rather than a member of the gentry. It has been enlarged and remodelled several times since, and the present-day building on this site better fits the name, Pope's Manor, which was bestowed on it in recent years. About fourteen acres of land surrounded the house, with two small parcels separately held. Today a suburb of the new town Bracknell called Popeswood contains a country park, 'Pope's Meadow', occupying part of the grounds of the manor, corresponding to wooded areas and farmland that ringed Whitehill House when the family resided there. Pope may have been thinking of the building when he wrote a jokey version of Horace, in the manner of his friend Swift, and mentioned 'my Paternal Cell, / A little House, with Trees a-row, / And like its Master, very low' (*TE*, vol. 4, p. 373), but if so there is a note of consciously scaling things down that commonly occurs in his poetry.

The house stood at the southern edge of the parish. Its site can be found near the southern end of what is now Murrell Hill Lane, north of the road from Wokingham to Bracknell (which ran approximately on the line of the present-day B3408 route). This road carried on to Staines and London, and Pope would have known the route intimately. Nearby, to the north-east, was a small grove of beech trees to which the teenager liked to retreat. In between this grove and the house stretched the parish common fields, still unenclosed, which had been stripped of their timber and were used chiefly for grazing. Large tracts of the forest had a bare and infertile look, some of it sprouting not much more than ferns or furze. The garden that Mr Pope seems to have constructed next to the house would have stood out more sharply from its surroundings than its suburban equivalent does today.

As for the village itself, it lay in the hundred of Cookham, north-west of Bracknell, which was itself a small settlement with just one street in Pope's day, and about three miles from the market town of Wokingham. At the beginning of the eighteenth century the population stood at around 500 people. The parish occupied 3,500 acres, containing a mixture of woodland and arable land, as well as the heath. It was situated in the heart of the forest – indeed picturesque legend claimed that the precise centre was marked by an ancient elm. This formerly stood in front of the village inn, once a hunting lodge used by royal gamekeepers. Binfield lies on a ridge with an elevation mostly between 200 and 300 feet above sea level. On the other side of the parish from Pope's home ran the Forest Road, leading from Reading to Windsor. Since 1597 the lords of the manor had been members of the Dancastle family, a Catholic line represented in the poet's day by his friend John Dancastle: their home lay on the eastern side of the village. It was also a good step to the church of All Saints, at the far north end of Binfield, with its fifteenth-century tower of puddingstone rubble. Only one topographic feature stands out, a stream or 'cut' that runs from south to north through the parish. Even with his limited mobility, young Alexander probably got to know every square inch of the place.

All in all, it was a pleasant spot to grow up, though in most respects a fairly unremarkable specimen of middle England. It boasted no visible features of great historic importance; it had no splendiferous mansion and no vastly rich grandee until, ten years after Pope died, William Pitt the elder built a stately pile on the site of the Dancastles' manor house. This was a working agricultural community, connected locally with Wokingham, and then at increasing distances with Windsor, Reading and ultimately London. Some forty miles away, the capital could be reached by a ride of a few hours. People who did not keep their own carriage, as the Popes seem not to have done, used the coach which ran to and from the White Swan in the Strand every day, along with the carrier's service to Wokingham on Tuesdays and Saturdays.

Windsor Forest itself shrouded the boy's early life. The medieval hunting area occupied a large portion of Berkshire, which had historically been set aside for royal use. Its borders extended fifteen miles from the River Thames to Bagshot in a north–south direction, and from the town of Windsor almost as far as Reading in an east–west direction. In the early eighteenth century it had a circumference of almost forty miles and comprised something like 100,000 acres. Most of the area enclosed was subject to forest law, as that had evolved over the course of several centuries since the Norman Conquest, and administered by a sizable legal bureaucracy. Such places were defined by their use and their legal status, not by their geographical character: originally, 'a Forest was a place of deer, not necessarily a place of trees'.[7] However, by a later date, forest law restricted unauthorized tree-felling as much as it precluded the poaching of deer. We shall return to these issues in a moment.

The Crown had its most obviously representation at Windsor Castle, with the Home or Little Park (just 300 acres with about the same number of fallow deer) adjoining it, and the Great Park with an acreage more than ten times larger that stretched towards the heart of the forest. The castle possessed a national as well as regional importance, as the site of monarchical power. It had also played a large part in England's chivalric past, as the home of the Order of the Garter, and the burial place of several kings and queens. Finally, the castle had a distinguished literary heritage, as it figured in major works by some celebrated writers. These elements would turn up in Pope's own poetry. For the rest, the landscape was made up of mixed regions of woodland, arable land, pasture and scrub. Especially on its edges, the forest included areas of marginal heath unfit for regular agricultural use, and these had been occupied by squatters and itinerant workers.

On the south-east corner was found an area of barren soil leading to the desolate stretches of Bagshot Heath.

Scattered across the region lay the homes of the gentry. Some of the larger estates straddled the boundaries of the forest, and their pleasure grounds were not subject to the same restrictions on hunting. Among the largest settlements were Maidenhead, Cookham and Bray at the northern edge. In the middle of the forest Wokingham was the only market town, while the most important centres of population had grown up on the fringes: Windsor, the seat of royal authority, and Reading, the county town. In addition assizes were held in Reading, which had its own as well hosting the nominations for election to the Berkshire constituency. At least 1,300 individuals were entitled to vote for the borough candidates in 1698, out of a population of around 6,000, which was half as much as the number of people living in the forest as a whole. Little Windsor had not much more than 1,000 inhabitants, but it elected two members as a 'scot and lot' borough, that is one where the franchise belonged to all male householders paying local taxes. Pope of course would never be allowed to cast his vote for members of parliament, and he did not take an active part in campaigning for the elections in 1710 and 1715. However, as we shall see, he was very well aware of what was happening on the political scene, locally as well as nationally. It could not have escaped his attention that his relative Richard Pottenger (1687–1739) – a first cousin once removed, descending from his aunt Mary Staveley – held the office of recorder, or chief legal officer, of Reading at the time when the Racketts found themselves embroiled in the Waltham Blacks affair in 1723, and indeed he gave bail for Charles Rackett (see Chapter 6). Later Pottenger became a Whig MP for the borough.

The poet had contacts throughout most of the forest. His immediate ties outside Binfield were with Easthampstead, the seat of his patron Sir William Trumbull. As we have seen, on the border in the direction of London lay the home of the Racketts. At Whiteknights, just short of Reading on the western perimeter, lived his close friends the Englefield family. Pope visited here often, sometimes en route to the Blount residence at Mapledurham, a little way beyond Reading. Scattered round the county lived a number of others who played a part in his life. From his youth, moreover, the forest became an important element in Pope's private world of the imagination. He often uses it as an emblem of retirement, peace and inspiration. But he knew about the social and political tensions that affected the area. These centred on the shifting application of 'forest law', the body of statutes and customary regulations by which the authorities administered the royal demesnes.

For centuries a prime cause of disaffection in the forest had been the grants made to royal favourites, limiting the rights of residents. As Simon Schama observes:

> Much of the angriest hostility against the royal forest regime, especially under the Angevin monarchs, came not from the common people, who somehow improvised ways and means of living with it, but from the propertied elite ... At its heart, then, the argument about the liberty of the greenwood was as much political as social.[8]

Nonetheless, the 'royalist romance of the greenwood'[9] was preserved under the Tudors and Stuarts, above all by John Evelyn, in his great work *Sylva* (1664).

An elaborate and overlapping system of judicial and administrative bodies, several of them oddly named, had grown up over this time to execute forest law. E. P. Thompson has carefully laid out its structure in Pope's time as part of his classic book *Whigs and Hunters*, and his diagrammatic presentation shows the bewildering array of functions and functionaries to be encountered in the forest.[10] They ranged from officials of the Swanimote court to the Chief Woodward, from the Verderers and Regarders to the Deputy Lieutenant of the Castle to the Master of the Royal Buckhounds. Pope must have known individuals in almost every category. These, however, are merely the roles that were allotted in terms of the specific management of Windsor Forest: behind them lay a mass of law-enforcement agencies which included the Church courts, manorial courts, justices of the peace and ordinary civil authorities. Common law and the statutes could be invoked as well as the special provisions of forest law. People often suppose that common law was overridden by these latter regulations, but this assumption has been shown to be untrue.

On the ground, battles generally raged between keepers, at the bottom of the administrative hierarchy, and humble residents – poachers, squatters or merely young tearaways. Sometimes yeoman and substantial farmers could find themselves on the wrong end of the law, as happened in the Waltham Blacks episode of 1722–3. Exceptionally, a member of the gentry became involved and the likelihood for this to happen grew larger if the individual chanced to belong to the recusant community. In addition, conflicts of interest sometimes arose, because the Verderers were elected by freeholders and not appointed by any Crown official, and even the appointed Regarders tended to come from a walk of life that put them on both sides of the fence. Such a conflict might surface at the meetings of the Swanimote court as well as at the more frequent sittings of the Court of Attachment, where two groups were represented: the keepers anxious to maintain tight control, along with the residents and users of the forest, who may have had an alternative agenda.

Charles I had rigorously applied forest law, but with his defeat came a total overthrow of the system. The Great Park was let out to tenant farmers, huge numbers of deer were killed until the stock had vanished and residents of the forest were able to assert with impunity what they regarded as their historic rights. In the royal forests generally a form of 'sylvan anarchy' emerged. As Schama puts it: 'After so many years of being fences off by contractors, whether parliamentarian or royalist, the woods were simply invaded by great armies of the common people who whacked and hacked at anything they could find'.[11] In turn this process came to an abrupt end with the return of Charles II, when the stocks of deer were replenished and the provisions of the forest law reactivated. Following this lead, James II kept up an equally fierce campaign against offenders. If the humble residents hoped that the balance would swing again with the accession of William Mary, they were to be disappointed. The courts were as active as ever in maintaining the existing law, and the government introduced a new measure (1 Will. & Mar., c. 10) to clamp down even more heavily on deer-stealing.

A brief respite came with the next monarch, Anne, when 'a genial laxity' prevailed in forest government: Thompson speculates that 'perhaps her frequent presence in the forest was more effectual in curbing offences than frequent court-keeping'. The same writer brings out statistics to show that prosecutions in the Swanimote courts fell a little in the reign of William, dropped almost to nothing under Anne, and then climbed precipitously when George I arrived, notably after 1717.[12] It can be said for certain that Pope would have been familiar with the broad history of the laws, for a hundred years back at least. The social tensions under Charles I had reached the very doorstep of Binfield parish: the residents of Sunninghill, just to the east, had complained they were taxed too highly in the 1630s. They were 'mean men, their grounds barren and the deer seldom out of them', whereas Binfield and adjoining hundred of Cookham were occupied by 'men of great estate'.[13] Besides, Sir William Trumbull had seen his own family's deer stock destroyed in the Cromwellian period, and had witnessed most of the ups and downs that have just been charted. He had to obey the law like any other subject of the Crown, and once in 1691 he had been refused permission to cut down a wood which he held on lease. In 1706 one of his servants was fined for an offence against forest law. According to Thompson, he 'observed forest law meticulously and took no venison except by warrant of the chief huntsman, Will Lorwen'.[14] Pope would soon have picked up from his principal mentor a sense of what was going on in the administration of the forest.

It may look as if all these squabbles hold only a parochial interest. In fact, the local tensions served as a microcosm of the clashes between competing forces at a national level – Thompson's book reads the entire episode of the Blacks as exposing to the light an allegedly repressive regime headed by Robert Walpole. Moreover, the forest supplied the cauldron where Pope first saw political antagonisms simmering among his fellow citizens. His sense of the issues at stake would inform one of his first major poems, entitled *Windsor-Forest*, mostly written a decade after his arrival at Binfield. The poem shows a double awareness: while it celebrates the literary and historical associations of the castle and the river, it portrays the landscape as fragile and vulnerable – open to 'ravishment' by unsympathetic rulers like William III. The scenery described by Pope is on the surface poetic or symbolic, and yet it contains a curiously realistic element. Thus, the wastelands peopled by squatters are present, and so in the allegorical set piece the mythical 'Lodona' stands for the real Loddon river, running into a loop of the Thames between Wokingham and Reading.

3

Although Pope senior had spent his life in the City as a member of the commercial class, he and his wife evidently gained rapid acceptance among the Catholic gentry of the home counties. Perhaps, as already suggested, this came about partly as a result of a friendship which Edith Turner may have forged with Frances Bedingfield, whose family had many connections with this group. We might also suspect that the boy Alexander, talented but physically handicapped, proved an object of sympathetic interest. The Popes would have immediately have come to the notice of John Dancastle (d. *c.* 1740), who was still lord of the manor at Binfield when the new arrivals settled in the village. He and his younger brother Thomas (d. 1728) lived at the manor with a resident priest. Pope maintained close relations with them for as long as they lived, and stayed at the house in 1717 after he had been uprooted with his parents in the previous year to move to Chiswick. The Dancastles had no pretensions either to grandeur or to intellectual weight, but they epitomized the worthy recusants among the lesser gentry who embodied many of the poet's most cherished values.

This friendship set off a chain reaction. In the seventeenth century a Dancastle had married into the Englefields, one of the most ancient Catholic families in Berkshire. Their seat lay at Whiteknights, just outside Reading: the house has been demolished, but the extensive parkland now forms a campus of the local university. It had been sequestrated 'for popish recusancy' following the Civil War, but the fines were removed after the Restoration. Young Pope made regular visits to the estate, staying there for example in 1711 and 1713. The patriarch was Anthony Englefield (1637–1712), one of the group of elders to whom the teenager looked up for advice and support. Pope called Anthony 'an extremely witty man, the delight of my youth'.[15] A good-natured old buffer with a taste for word games, he was admired by William Wycherley for his 'waggish ways'.[16] Anthony had a son named Henry (d. 1720), whose widow subsequently married Pope's schoolfellow Edward Webb. Among the trustees for the settlement when Catherine Englefield remarried were Michael Blount and John Caryll, both well known to the poet. One of Anthony's daughters married a local man named Lister Blount, and she became the mother of the sisters Martha and Teresa, who would play a large part in Pope's later life. Another daughter married a Northumberland baronet, Sir John Swinburne, who would be caught up together with his brothers in the 1715 rising, an event that caused the Blount girls and their admirer Pope some grief and possibly some embarrassment. Among Englefield's other relatives was a country gentleman from Sussex, John Caryll, and Alexander very likely met his close friend while on a visit to Whiteknights.

Pope knew John Caryll by the early years of the new century. He was the nephew of another John, Secretary of State to the Pretender, who granted his follower one of the fantasy peerages bestowed on Jacobites. As for Pope's friend, he endured imprisonment twice in 1696, on well-founded suspicions that he had known something of a plot to assassinate the King. Parliament sequestrated his estate near Petersfield for a time and gave it to a loyal servant of William III named Lord Cutts, whom Swift later mocked in a poem called 'A Description of a Salamander'. Right up to his death in 1736 Caryll remained a central figure in Pope's life. He was godfather to Martha Blount and he helped to arrange the marriage of her brother. However, his name survives in literary history chiefly because Pope made him the dedicatee of *The Rape of the Lock*, whose hero is modelled on Lord Petre, a ward of John Caryll.

We can now start to trace the tangled web of interrelationships among the recusant community. The gentry had only a limited pool of possible mates within their own class. Double taxation took its toll, and with dwindling funds to provide a dowry it was the young women in particular who felt the impact – hence in part the large number of girls who took up conventual life in France. Yet another of Anthony's daughters joined the Benedictine nunnery in Paris where the Blount sisters had studied. The inevitable result was that, ever since the Reformation, leading families had interbred across several generations. Their genealogies start to resemble a complex flow-chart, cut across by loops as one branch of the family spirals back into the main trunk in a regular process of feedback.

Very few of these involutions would seem important to anyone today. But they counted for a great deal more in the past, when power and identity inhered in hereditary groups bestowing patronage. We need only think of the table of kindred and affinity attached to the Book of Common Prayer in 1662, setting out the forbidden degrees of marriage, a document which many a bored congregation must have perused in the course of droning sermons. For Catholics, information on this topic held even greater urgency: not only were they a minority population, but the canons of the Church narrowed the range of possible partners more strictly than was the case with Anglicans. In fact, it took the Council of Trent to reduce the scope of prohibited affinity from the third to the second degree, meaning that marriage was possible with the second cousin of a deceased spouse. But in the case of direct consanguity, the bar extended as far as second cousins. Such considerations held more than an academic interest for the recusant community. In this circle, blood lines were as jealously hoarded as those in the thoroughbred stud-book. They helped, of course, to establish social standing and cultural hegemony, and we cannot remotely understand Pope's place within the politics of his time without allotting them their full weight.

Property formed the basis of power in early modern society. Sir William Blackstone, in his hugely influential *Commentaries on the Laws of England* (1765–9), set out in a series of charts the way that descent governed inheritance, and observed, 'The doctrine of descents, or law of inheritance in fee-simple, is a point of the highest importance; and is indeed the principal objects of the laws of real property in England'.[17] Successive acts of legislation had been designed to limit the ability of papists to make full use of the system, and thus inhibit their social agency.

The significance of these matters to a young man growing up as a Catholic in Berkshire at the start of the eighteenth century has been well conveyed by the historian John Bossy:

> A fairly sizeable group of families and houses in the Thames valley – Talbots, Webbs, Fermors, Stonors north of the river in Oxfordshire, Englefields, Blounts and others south of it in Berkshire – made for a congenial passage between the west Midlands and the far South. For this reason the Catholics of the region had an important role in the Elizabethan mission ... and in the quite different circumstances of 1700, when the woods had ceased to be a protective screen and become a pastoral environment, the milieu in which Pope found himself when his father moved to Binfield played a very similar role, integrating the Catholic gentry among themselves, and mediating between them and the metropolitan civilisation of London – functions memorably enacted in 'The Rape of the Lock'.[18]

Just as the missionaries used the Thames as a conduit for their activities, so the river supplied an imaginative corridor for the young poet, linking it in the process with many friends and co-religionists, together with numerous historic sites of the old faith. And – crucially – Pope knew members of every family named by Bossy, some on the most intimate terms. 'Blest *Thames*'s Shores the brightest Beauties yield, / Feed here my Lambs, I'll seek no distant Field' (*TE*, vol. 1, p. 67).

The overwhelming probability is that Pope first met the Blount sisters at Whiteknights, along with Martha's godfather John Caryll. In the years that followed, he would often stop off at the Englefields' home on his way to see the young ladies. Their home lay on the riverbank as the Thames meandered down to Reading, about five miles away. The Mapledurham estate had come into the possession of the Blounts – pronounced, and often spelt, 'Blunt' – in the late fifteenth century, and it has remained in the hands of their descendants right up to the present. One ancestor, Sir Walter Blount, died fighting for the King at the battle of Shrewsbury: Shakespeare gives him a decent walk-on part in *1 Henry IV* before he is slaughtered onstage. The beautiful Elizabethan-Jacobean mansion in the shape of an H, made of brick with tall gables, was begun by Sir

Michael Blount and completed by his son. Parliamentary forces sacked the house in 1643, and the estate was sequestrated for a time. However, it had largely recovered after the family took possession once more, well before the time that Lister Blount inherited it from a cousin. The period when Pope came to know Mapledurham, around 1707 in all probability, marked the end of a golden age. Lister's son Michael took over in 1710, and his extravagance coupled with the oppressive penalties imposed on the Catholic population led to a prolonged slide in family fortunes that took decades to arrest. As we shall see, Teresa and Martha were in effect ejected – driven 'out of house and home', Pope said (*Corr.*, vol. 1, p. 336) – and spent the rest of their lives in London. This was no great sacrifice for the elder girl Teresa, but an enduring cause of regret for Martha.

Over the course of time, Pope's relationship with the two women took two sharply diverging paths. He came to see Teresa as cold, self-seeking, worldly, uncaring and unreliable. Martha, familiarly known as Patty, represented the opposite qualities of modesty, loyalty, warmth and piety. He enshrined the younger sister as a pattern of womanhood in his *Epistle to a Lady*, and made her his most trusted confidante. She became his principal legatee at his death. At the heart of their friendship lay two things: their shared respect and affection for Edith Pope, and their joint allegiance to the Catholic Church. They had other friends in common, including Henrietta Howard and Lord Bathurst. But these things lay in the future. When Pope first met them, both were lively girls of about eighteen or nineteen, pretty and even coquettish. They engaged in literary games with other scions of recusant families in the Thames Valley, such as the Moores and the Jerninghams – the exchanges involved both sexes, and were not altogether as innocent as we might expect. Under fantastic pseudonyms they composed romantic missives: Teresa became Zephalinda, and Martha took the name of Parthenissa. On the fringe of this circle stood 'Cosen Bell', none other than Arabella Fermor, the young lady from Oxfordshire who would shortly achieve immortality as the model for the heroine Belinda in *The Rape of the Lock*.[19] By this stage it can occasion little surprise to find that Arabella was herself the granddaughter of Elizabeth Englefield, a member of the Whiteknights family Pope came to know so well. We should note that Teresa figured at least once in this correspondence as 'Bellinda'. We may well wonder if some foibles of the heroine of the *Rape* contain some light mockery of the spoilt, pretty, self-absorbed girl from Mapledurham with her arch glances and her beguiling dark locks.[20]

Such connections gave Pope access to a stable core of human values embodied in men and women who respected him in spite of his position outside the landed classes. Of course, things did not always run smoothly. There was friction with the Englefields over the marital problems of a woman named Elizabeth Weston. Nor did *The Rape of the Lock* go down well in all quarters, understandably in view of its tactless revelation of the games people played when they were forging dynastic marriages. But overall these years in the forest initiated Pope into an order of society where he felt comfortable. Soon he would add to his group of allies still more individuals who could be found on the Spaghetti Junction of interlinked family trees – Bedingfield, Stonor, Petre, Browne and several more. Some of his most lasting and reliable friends came from this source, notably Martha Blount and John Caryll. In case we are tempted to suppose that all these links came down to nothing more than money and self-advancement, it is worth recalling that Martha's godparents were John Caryll and his wife Elizabeth, who could never be accused of shirking their religious duties.

4

Both in his solitary vice of reading and in his growing social awareness, Pope enjoyed the support of influential friends and neighbours. Unquestionably the most regular and significant contact he forged outside his home, from the age of about seventeen (if not earlier), was Sir William Trumbull, the retired courtier and diplomat who owned Easthampstead Park, a large estate outside a village lying only two miles south of Whitehill House. The young Alexander made repeated visits to the mansion, and took to riding out in the forest with his new friend 'three or four days in the week, and at last almost every day' (*Anecdotes*, vol. 1, p. 31). This marked the start of a momentous stage in Pope's career, embodying his first sustained relationship with a non-Catholic, his first dealings with a cultivated and learned man of the world, and perhaps his first encounter with someone, apart from a doting parent, who believed in his potential as an author.

At first, the teenager probably felt some astonishment that a figure of Trumbull's standing would take notice of him. The new mentor, almost fifty years his senior, had enjoyed a varied and distinguished life in public service. He was a civil lawyer, educated at Oxford, where he became a fellow of All Souls in 1657. Knighted in 1684, he took part in a number of missions, including a spell in the weighty role of ambassador to Turkey. He also served as an MP for his old university, and then under William as Secretary of State. Forced out of office in 1697, he retired to his seat at Easthampstead. There, as we have already seen, Trumbull served as a Verderer, one of the officers supervising forest law. After the death of his first wife, he married in 1706 a local woman, Lady Judith Alexander, a daughter of the fourth Earl of Stirling. Sir William had been a patron of John Dryden and knew other writers such as William Wycherley, who then moved into Alexander's orbit. Having discovered the talented young poet in his neighbourhood, he devoted much of his remaining years to promoting the fortunes of his protégé. Pope would dedicate 'Spring', the first of his *Pastorals*, to Trumbull, who read the complete sequence before publication, and it was he who urged Pope to translate Homer. The pair continued in regular contact until the old man died in December 1716.

Formerly an ardent Whig, Trumbull seems to have acquired different political opinions as he aged, ending up as something close to a committed Tory, like his clergyman nephew Ralph Bridges. It is likely that Pope had Trumbull in mind in his portrait of the hermit-philosopher in a contrast of active and contemplative living built into the text of *Windsor-Forest*. He certainly wrote here that this noble retirement was the one embraced by Scipio, Atticus and 'Trumbal'; and elsewhere he claimed that he had celebrated Sir William's retirement to the groves of Windsor in that poem (*Corr.*, vol. 1, p. 328). According to Sir William, he had 'long since put' his young disciple on the subject of the forest and even given him 'severall hints' for it – possibly an exaggeration. In the last year of Trumbull's life, Pope addressed him in the guise of 'some Superior Being, that has been once among Men, and now sits above, at distance, not only to observe their actions, and weigh them with Truth and justice, but some times charitably to influence and direct them'. He wrote an eloquent epitaph on his old friend in 1717 (*TE*, vol. 6, pp. 169–70). About twenty letters survive between the two men, providing many shafts of insight into the early years at Binfield.

As he made his short way up a gentle declivity through the park, Pope must have experienced a sense of wonder at the mansion and its grounds. They very likely gave him his first notion of the great country house, an idea of civilized living and enlightened benevolence towards the community, which would often surface in poems such as the *Epistles* he later addressed to friends like Burlington and Bathurst. Here he drew on his friend's well-stocked library and met some of the wide circle of friends that the diplomat had acquired. The house lay on the site of a medieval hunting lodge and had been in the Trumbull family since the early seventeenth century. However, Sir William bought the manor of Easthampstead from John Dancastle only in 1696, on his retirement from politics. Over the course of years the property belonged in turn to William Trumbull I (d. 1635), to his son William II (d. 1668), and then to his grandson, Pope's friend. The house was surrounded by a park of some 250 acres. As Verderer for Easthampstead Walk, Trumbull had responsibility for a considerable area of the forest extending beyond the parish, all of which except the park was subject to royal jurisdiction.

In Pope's day the population of Easthampstead parish stood at only 200, though it covered over 5,000 acres. The Jacobean house was demolished in 1860 and replaced by a Victorian mansion, situated a little to the north of the old building. Today a conference centre and school occupy the site. The rural sports once practised here have been replaced by the less martial activities of a golf course. In fact, Pope would be unable to recognize his old haunts, for most of Easthampstead Park has been swallowed up in the designated new town of Bracknell. A little way off, in the direction of the modern town centre, stands the twelfth-century church of St Michael and St Mary Magdalene, heavily restored in the Victorian period with fine stained-glass windows by Burne-Jones. The Lady Chapel contains monuments of the Trumbull family, including Sir William's own. Noticeably, this tomb does not bear the epitaph that Pope composed for him: the only plausible explanation is anxiety in the fraught climate of 1717–18 about the political resentment simmering beneath its surface. However, we can still see in the north aisle of the church Pope's less contentious epitaph for Elijah Fenton, his collaborator on the *Odyssey* translation, and tutor to Sir William's son. 'Fat and indolent', as Pope called him, Fenton died in 1729 'of a great chair and two bottles of port a day'.[21]

Thanks to Trumbull, the young man had now joined a wider network. They included William Wycherley, Thomas Betterton, Samuel Garth and William Walsh. Wycherley had made his name early with two sparkling comedies in the 1670s, *The Country Wife* and *The Plain Dealer*. Since then he done nothing in particular, and done it very well. At Will's coffee-house he pontificated agreeably in the company of Dryden. When Pope was about sixteen he sought Wycherley out and in the course of their correspondence over the next few years he offered to revise some clumsy verses that the other had written. Naturally this produced cooling in their relations, but the youth's charm won over the older man, and he continued to support the budding poet. At least once he went to stay at Binfield. The letters that passed between them operate on a rather high-flown level, but on Pope's side they do reveal the beginnings of critical competence. The young man also displays some tact in dealing with an elderly man who was showing signs that he had slipped into a mild form of dementia. Pope never forgot the kindness he received as an unknown aspirant to fame from an established literary figure. His personal collection of obituaries has this entry: 'A writer famous for his knowledge of human nature, the first to gain my affection'.[22]

The phrasing of that entry suggests that Alexander was looking not so much for technical tips as for the kind of insights into the human condition that a dramatist might provide. Another of his new acquaintances, Betterton, was the last major figure of the Restoration theatre, and the most considerable tragic actor of his day. For Pope he remained simply 'the best actor I ever saw' (*Anecdotes*, vol. 1, p. 23). A shrewd businessman, he acquired a country property near Reading towards the end of his days, and the two seem to have met regularly in the last few years of Betterton's life. The actor delighted Pope with giddy stories of good King Charles's golden days, as they no doubt seemed in retrospect to a septuagenarian and an impressionable adolescent whose family had endured much under the monarchs who came after Charles II. It looks as if the youth got some encouragement for a strong but injudicious ambition that he had to write for the stage. When Betterton died in 1710, Pope inscribed in his commemorative list, 'The Roscius of his age, made his exit to the applause of all good men'.[23]

A more directly literary influence came from Samuel Garth. The doctor and poet had written the first important mock-heroic poem in English, *The Dispensary* (1699), which concerns squabbles in the medical profession between physicians and apothecaries over a dispensary for the poor. The work showed Pope how to use realistic detail within an overarching quasi-allegorical framework, how to build up effective character-sketches in paragraphs of witty couplets, and how to turn angry controversies into comic action. Garth presented Pope with a copy of his work in an edition of 1703, so they may have come together fairly soon after that date. But it was a friendship of opposites in many ways. Garth had the reputation of a blunt speaker, whereas Pope was oblique and sly. Again, Garth prospered at court, where he gained a post as royal physician and a knighthood in the early Hanoverian years: on the other hand Pope ostentatiously stood apart from the court and all its trappings. Garth kept to his strong Whig convictions and the unashamed posture of a freethinker in religion, a stance Pope could never have adopted. Three possible explanations might be given for their close relations. First, Pope admired the doctor for his literary talent. Second, he was making a conscious effort to widen his acquaintance and to embrace a more diverse body of friends. Third and most important, he regarded Garth as 'one of the best-natured men in the world', and 'the best good Christian ... / Altho' he knows it not' (*Anecdotes*, vol. 1, p. 44; *TE*, vol. 6, p. 129). The memorial summary makes it clear: 'An upright man and an elegant poet'.[24]

A further link in the chain was provided by William Walsh, another Whig poet of considerably less talent than Garth. Walsh served as an MP and held a small post at court. Samuel Johnson did not feel able to leave him out of the *Lives of the Poets*, such was his lingering presence in literary history, but the life left readers in no doubt that this was minor biography of a minor figure, whether as politician, poet or critic. Like the three men just described, Walsh had known Dryden well, and this provided one of the main attractions he held for Pope. At all events, his kindness to the fledgling writer earned him some favourable references. A portrait of Walsh hung in Pope's house, and he was awarded a commendatory entry in the book of remembrance: 'A wise critic, friend and good man'.[25]

These individuals drew Pope more into the orbit of fashionable London life and the world of celebrity. An Irish adventurer named Charles Wogan claimed long afterwards that he had introduced the young man to the set at Will's coffeehouse, bringing him 'up to London, from our retreat in the forest of Windsor, to dress à la mode'.[26] As Pope admitted himself, he arrived with a certain rustic awkwardness of manner. The hostile Charles Gildon, a victim in waiting for *The Dunciad*, called him a 'little *Aesopic* sort of animal in his own cropt Hair, and

Dress agreeable to the Forest he came from'.[27] The jibe combines a number of thrusts: according to legend, Aesop, a slave from the remote island of Samos, was deformed and ugly, and he came to the sort of violent end Gildon wished on Pope – Herodotus says he was pushed off a cliff. It was unfashionable for a man to go into society without a wig, while provincial dress probably meant the absence of rich clothes suitable for attendance at court.

Whatever his lack of polish, Pope further augmented his circle of friends in the capital. He formed his most intimate alliance from this period with an obscure man about town who has left little mark on history. Most likely he met Henry Cromwell (1659–1728) at Will's through the offices of Wycherley. This was a middle-aged bachelor, poetaster and would-be rake, who did not occasion much alarm to the parents of vulnerable girls. For a spell of about five years, starting in 1708, his boyish pose and manners of a dandy made a big impression on Pope, who was looking for some way to overcome his physical handicaps and become a ladies' man. They exchanged many letters, of which more than forty survive. In later years Cromwell occasioned a lot of embarrassment when in a heedless moment he gave his supposed mistress Elizabeth Thomas some of the poet's early letters. She promptly sold them to the unscrupulous publisher Edmund Curll, with predictable results (see Chapter 6).

At first glance the most arresting feature of this gallery of supporters relates to the sheer age of the people involved. Walsh, the youngest of them, had already reached his mid-twenties when Pope was born, and the older ones like Wycherley and Betterton counted as senile by the standards of the day. We could interpret this circumstance in various ways. Some might be tempted to see it as a quest for an alternative father: but in that regard Pope had been singularly blessed in having Alexander senior in that role. Others might wonder if, as a result of his upbringing with elderly parents, he felt at ease only with people of an earlier generation. Be that as it may, he certainly benefitted in a practical way from these contacts, which gave him an entrée to the literary world. Soon the disadvantaged boy would gather the fruits.

5

Three weeks before his twenty-first birthday, on 2 May 1709, Pope saw his first major work in print. It was a true coming of age. His four *Pastorals*, devoted in turn to each season of the year, appeared in the *Miscellanies* of Jacob Tonson, a long established series brought out by the most influential publisher of the day. The collection also contains two poems by Jonathan Swift, later to become his great ally in literary battles, but still comparatively unknown as a poet. Immediately Pope's name came to the attention of a broad reading public.

He made no attempt to disguise the debt he owed to his impressive corps of advisors. On the contrary, he flaunted their names in a note added to the first line of the opening item, 'Spring'. In a private communication much later, he reported that writing the poems had brought him to the attention of

> Dr. Garth, Mr. Walsh, Mr. Granville, with whom he both Convers'd and Corresponded and Sir Wm Trumbal, with whom on his having then resign'd the Office of Secretary of State, he lived familiarly being his near Neighbour. By some or other of these he was soon Introduc'd into the Acquaintance of the Duke of Shrewsbury Lord Somers Mr St. John and Ld Halifax.[28]

We can leave aside the last four names for the present, except to remark that all were very considerable persons in national life, with a high reputation as patrons of literature. Only Henry St John, later Lord Bolingbroke, would figure significantly in Pope's later life, and he happens to be the only individual on the list who was still in his twenties. The most noteworthy addition is that of George Granville, a politician and writer whom Pope would later choose as dedicatee of *Windsor-Forest*. Elsewhere he augmented his roster of advisors with more figures of considerable importance, including the dramatist Congreve, the politician Lord Wharton, the grandee Duke of Buckingham and the Marquess of Dorchester, a courtier now best remembered less for his own moderate achievements than for fathering Lady Mary Wortley Montagu. These demographics ensured that almost all the men who supervised Pope's earliest literary work had passed from the scene by the time he reached maturity as a writer. Only Bolingbroke would outlive him.[29]

Some of these men simply bestowed their name as a gesture of munificence, as patrons commonly did, though there is no evidence that they actually handed out largesse to the young poet – he actually got the respectable sum of ten guineas (£10.50), by no means niggardly for a complete beginner. However, he did chew over the work for many years with his informal advisory board. The most helpful of these mentors may have been William Walsh, who got Pope to visit him at his home in Worcestershire for six weeks in the late summer of 1707. Four pages containing passages of the *Pastorals* survive in manuscript with self-styled 'objections' and queries from the author together with detailed 'solutions' by Walsh. Some were straightforward verbal points – 'Wanton apply'd to a woman is equivocal and therefore not proper' – but others rested on broader issues of poetic decorum.[30] Once more Pope was happy to recall the nature of the help he had received from Walsh, who 'used to tell me that there was one way left of excelling, for though we had several great poets, we never had any one great poet that was correct – and he desired me to make that my study and aim' (*Anecdotes*, vol. 1, p. 32). Already the young man had formed the ambition to climb to the top of the literary pantheon by venturing on something unattempted yet in English poetry.

The pastorals mark the consummation of Pope's virtuoso skills, learned in an apprenticeship which began about the age of sixteen. Each of the four poems carries a dedication incorporated into its opening lines; the first three pay tribute to his mentors (Trumbull, Garth and Wycherley), while the last, 'Winter', is inscribed to the memory of a lady whom Walsh particularly admired. With their precocious fluency and assured technique, the *Pastorals* have seemed vacuous to many modern readers, but they show off what Pope could do in an established form, and that was the way writers needed to start in those days. One thing cannot be claimed for them – they are almost entirely innocent of political content, at a surface or latent level.

Nevertheless, as he reached his majority and made his debut before the literary audience, Pope had dipped a toe in the public sphere. He had assembled an extraordinarily diverse and accomplished team of supporters: often Grub Street hacks spent their lives trying to win the suffrage of one such name. The roster included high Tories such as Buckingham and solid Whigs like Garth, with many intermediary positions represented across the party spectrum. Up to 1710 he managed to remain largely aloof from day-to-day politics. Quite a lot of his correspondence survives from the early years, and yet it barely mentions the *va et vient* of affairs at Westminster, nor even the convulsions of a major war on the Continent. The British nation watched a dramatic spectacle of battles across Europe, many featuring the spectacular success attained at times by the Duke of Marlborough. The Duke, who effectively acted as Minister for War as well as Commander in Chief, bestrode the age with his imperious Duchess, while his coadjutor Godolphin served as Prime Minister and Minister for Finance. For years they attempted to keep a centrist policy to balance the demands of aggressive Whigs in the so-called Junto with the clamour of extreme Tories in parliament. Their efforts to bolster the administration with the help of the moderate Tory Robert Harley ultimately foundered. In 1709 and 1710 matters came to a head in a bitterly divisive sequence of events which led to a change in government. This affected even men or women who had no political influence and seemingly little interest in the subject – Pope among them. From now on, events would increasingly force such people to take sides.

3 THE PIPING TIME OF PEACE

> Why, I in this weak piping time of peace
> Have no delight to pass away the time ...
>
> Shakespeare, *Richard III*

From 1710 to 1715 Britain went through perhaps the most tumultuous phase of domestic politics witnessed during the entire eighteenth century. While Pope was not directly caught up in this sequence of events, many of his closest friends certainly were, and since he now spent longer periods in London he could not avert his eyes from the surrounding drama. For a good time he had maintained links with the capital, but after he reached his majority he began to stretch his wings. From this time on, visits to see friends such as Wycherley and Cromwell became more frequent. However, Pope did not embark on a prolonged stay in London over a period of months until 1713, a year that also saw his earliest poems with an unmistakable political flavour.

Flitting regularly between the city and the country, Pope had to endure persistent headaches which forced him to rest at intervals. In 1710 he lost his aunt Elizabeth and also his counsellor Thomas Betterton, both at an advanced age. At this time he naturally wished to capitalize on the reputation that the *Pastorals* had brought him. He worked on updated adaptations of Chaucer, and a miscellany issued in 1712 by Bernard Lintot, the bookseller who served as his main outlet for the next decade, offered him the chance to publish translations of classical poets along with the first brief version of *The Rape of the Lock*. This poem in two cantos gave the first signs of his powers in comedy, but today it is generally remembered only as the precursor to its brilliant reincarnation in five cantos, which appeared two years later. In the meantime he had streaked to the forefront of young poets with *An Essay on Criticism*, published in May 1711. The work scored an instant success, and remained the basic art of poetry for English readers up to the end of the century. Witty, erudite, beautifully constructed and laced with enough malice to provoke native responses in some quarters, it fulfilled all its creator's goals.

The *Essay* soon caught the attention of cantankerous John Dennis, a polemical man of letters always on the lookout for imaginary slights, and never able to resist a good bout of fisticuffs in print. The *Reflections upon a late Rhapsody, call'd, An Essay on Criticism* manages a few hits on detailed points amid a flurry of wild complaints. Dennis obviously resented the notice which the public chose to bestow on this callow youth – he himself had already reached his mid-fifties – and allowed full rein to his envious spite. His pamphlet marked the beginning of a long series of personal attacks which Pope had to endure ever after. Not content with calling his victim 'a hunch-back'd Toad', Dennis gave his readers helpful directions which might enable them to hunt out the offending creature in his home territory:

> And now if you have a mind to enquire between *Sunning-Hill* and *Ockingham*, for a young, squab, short Gentleman ... an eternal Writer of Amorous Pastoral Madrigals, and the very bow of the God of Love, you will be soon directed to him. And pray as soon as you have taken a Survey of him, tell me whether he is a proper Author to make personal Reflections on others; This little Author may extol the Ancients as much and as long as he pleases, but he has reason to thank the good Gods that he was born a Modern. For had he been born of *Graecian* Parents, and his Father by consequence had by Law had the absolute Disposal of him, his Life had been no longer than that of one of his Poems, the Life of half a day. Instead of setting his Picture to show, I have taken a keener Revenge, and expos'd his Intellectuals, as duly considering that let the Person of a Gentleman of his Parts be never so contemptible, his inward Man is ten times more ridiculous; it being impossible that his outward Form, tho' it should be that of downright Monkey, should differ so much from human Shape, as his immaterial unthinking part does from human Understandings.[1]

Such abuse focused on Pope's body, repeated with small variants year after year, must have accustomed him to the role of a stigmatized pariah, cast out by the cultural guardians on account of the mark of Cain he bore.

However, Dennis has an even more remarkable objection to make. He picks up on some lines in the *Essay* where Pope contrasts the reigns of Charles II and William III with regard to the moral tone of society. Evidently displeased by a reference to William's 'foreign reign', the vehemently Whiggish critic leaps to a hasty conclusion:

> Now I humbly conceive that he who Libels our Confederates, must be by Politicks a *Jacobite*; and he who libels all the Protestant Kings that we have had in this Island these threescore Years ... must ... derive his Religion from St. *Omer's*, as he seems to have done his Humanity and his Criticism, and is, I suppose, politickly setting up for Poet-laureate against the coming over of the Pretender.[2]

(The phrase about St Omer's contains a sneer about the English College set up near Lille by Robert Parsons in Elizabethan times, which remained the best known such seminary on the Continent.) Dennis was the first, but by no means the last, of Pope's adversaries to bring up this particular charge. Whatever its justification elsewhere, *An Essay on Criticism* provides no evidence. In any case Pope had drafted the poem mostly around 1709, before a new turn of events helped to politicize him, maybe against his will. As it stands, the *Essay* shows no awareness of an episode that had rocked the nation.

1

The crisis in 1710 came about as a result of a rash move by leaders of the government. They opted to bring to book the High Church clergyman Henry Sacheverell after he delivered an incendiary sermon at St Paul's cathedral, which in effect encouraged the people to resist the Revolution settlement. During the months of February and March 1710, the ministry staged a full-dress show trial before the House of Lords. Serious riots broke out in the streets while proceedings went ahead in Westminster Hall. When the verdict was announced, Sacheverell faced conviction on the two counts he faced, but only by a narrow margin. Most people considered the main sentence imposed, a three-year suspension from preaching, as good as an acquittal. Soon afterwards the condemned man set off on a triumphant tour, attracting fervent support from Tories up and down the country. A larger consequence followed, with the break-up of the ministry of Lord Godolphin and the Duke of Marlborough, who had led an increasingly fragile coalition of Whigs that no longer held the confidence either of the Queen or of the nation at large. Godolphin was dismissed as Lord Treasurer in August, and within four weeks the Tories had swept to a landslide victory in the general election. At the end of 1711 the Queen dispensed with the services of Marlborough too. Inside eighteen months, the whole political world had been turned upside down.

Pope left few clues as to what he thought about the man at the heart of this upheaval. Like most Tories, he probably agreed with Swift that the doctor was 'not very deep'.[3] After serving out his lenient sentence, Sacheverell received a plum rectory in London, at St Andrew's Holborn, but gradually his brief portion of fame began to fall away. Mobs on either side of the divide shouted his name in street affrays for some time to come, but he had dwindled into irrelevance long before he died in 1724. Nevertheless, he had helped to launch a series of events greater than himself. Almost all the peers with whom Pope enjoyed close relations over time had voted to acquit Sacheverell. The speech that the accused man made in his own defence came probably from the hand of Francis Atterbury, who later stood in need of Pope's testimony at another conspicuous trial before the House of Lords.

If the triumphant Tories believed in 1710 that they had inherited a secure tenure of power, events would soon teach them differently. From the start the ministry had to deal with fissions within its own party, as well as the harassment of disgruntled Whigs. The new leader Robert Harley, a moderate Tory, tried to introduce a centrist policy which would calm the nation after the upheavals caused by the Sacheverell affair. But a segment of the party detached itself under the banner of the October Club, and supported more aggressive measures backed by Harley's principal lieutenant, Henry St John, a politician of some ability but dubious loyalty. By 1711 Harley had become Lord Treasurer and Earl of Oxford, and a year later St John was made Viscount Bolingbroke – we shall refer to them by these names from now on. Pope, who got to know both leaders shortly afterwards, had a ringside seat as the coalition came to blows over the next two years. Almost all the high hopes with which the Tories took power had turned to ashes by 1714.

This precipitous slide had many causes. Queen Anne did not fully trust Bolingbroke at any stage, and as Oxford grew more vague and evasive with the passage of time she lost patience. The restive backbenchers could never aim a decisive blow against their more moderate colleagues in power, but they provided a nuisance factor which impaired the government's freedom of action. Only a minority of MPs within the party had openly declared for the Pretender, Anne's half-brother, but others were fellow-travellers who kept up links with the dispersed Jacobite movement in England, Scotland, Ireland and France. As often happened in the past, many members of the victorious party were more intent on feathering their own nests, or on heaping infamy on the defeated faction, than on taking an active share in governance of the nation. Family and personal interests coloured the decisions they took, inside and outside parliament. Some of them had as the first item on their agenda the opportunity to use to personal advantage their running feud with opponents inside the Godolphin or Marlborough clans, or to gain revenge for slights they had suffered at the hands of the Junto. Army officers were cashiered, postmasters sent packing, bishops ostracized, masters of colleges stripped of their powers. This process of fermentation went on every time a ministry changed, and the Whigs could institute an even larger upheaval when their turn came – they had a new monarch, a new dynasty, a new court and a fatally weakened opposition. A few of Pope's allies benefitted briefly when the Tories took power, but a greater number found themselves on the sidelines after the arrival of George I. Others, as we shall see, found themselves thrown into custody.

Along with such divisive issues as the succession, and the cries of the 'Church in danger' that had echoed throughout the Sacheverell affair, one big argument split parliament and the nation. This concerned the terms on which the nation should bring the War of the Spanish Succession to an end. The war had been lengthy and costly both in terms of human casualties and of depletion of national funds. In general the Tories wished to draw a line under the struggle as quickly as possible: to that end they initiated a military strategy which hamstrung commanders in the field and left the way clear for an agreed settlement. Whigs deplored their opponents' readiness to deal separately with the old enemy France while leaving other members of the alliance, especially the Dutch, out in the cold. They also opposed any weakening on one of the original aims of the war, that is placing the Habsburg claimant, Charles III, on the throne of Spain. But their slogan, 'No peace without Spain', rang with an increasingly hollow sound as hostilities dragged on without obvious benefit to the allied cause. More and more of the British people came to believe that the war had been prolonged mainly to fill the coffers of Marlborough, Godolphin, their acolytes such as the acquisitive paymaster of the forces James Brydges (later known to Pope as the Duke of Chandos) and their friends in the City of London. The burden seemed to fall unduly on those paying the land tax, including a good proportion of the country gentry whom Pope had encountered during his sojourn at Binfield.

The Tories whipped up a skilful publicity campaign under the control of their resourceful spin doctor, Jonathan Swift, and soon the ministry felt strong enough to deal directly with Louis XIV behind the back of the allies. What ultimately emerged, after complex negotiations, was the Treaty of Utrecht, signed in April 1713. The Austrians rejected the settlement, but another year of fruitless skirmishing persuaded them to come to the conference table and make their own peace with France. As a pendant to the main deal that had been sealed at Utrecht there followed a commercial treaty with Spain, which proved to be even more controversial and hard to ratify in parliament.

Among the key provisions of the peace treaty was the recognition by the French King of the Protestant succession, together with an undertaking on his part to expel the Pretender from the borders of his country – James Edward Stuart had maintained his shadow court at St Germain, just outside Paris, and after the failure of the rebellion in 1716 he retired to the papal territory of Avignon. Considerable portions of North America, some belonging to the Hudson's Bay Company, were returned to Britain, while Spain ceded Gibraltar – a concession with momentous after-effects. In addition Spain also transferred to British control the 'Asiento de Negras', a grant that allowed the exclusive right to export slaves from Africa to the New World. In theory this right was due to be exercised by the recently formed South Sea Company but in practice the arrangement would never come to fruition.

The Tories now had enough muscle in parliament to get the preliminary negotiations rubber-stamped by the Commons. However, the House of Lords presented more obstacles. Its members still contained a solid core of Williamite creations, and the opposition could generally count on the support of most of the bishops, who formed a latitudinarian cohort frequently at odds with the lower clergy, who took a higher line in the politics of Church and state. The preliminaries encountered fierce opposition in the upper chamber, and at the end of 1711 it looked as if the ministry faced certain defeat. Oxford persuaded the Queen reluctantly to dismiss Marlborough: she had always liked the Duke, but he became dispensable in the aftermath of her acrimonious break with her former favourite, the Duchess. Now desperate times called for desperate constitutional remedies, and without consulting his cabinet the Lord Treasurer submitted a bold démarche to Anne. On 1 January 1712, to the astonishment of political insiders and outsiders alike, the Queen created twelve new peers. They formed a diverse bunch. Among the inoffensive time-servers and promising sprigs of the loyal aristocracy, Oxford had chosen to elevate the husband of Anne's new favourite, Abigail Masham, and his own Jacobite son-in-law, Lord Dupplin. With the help of these overnight recruits to its number, the government was able to get its proposals past the House of Lords.

Some of the new peers were already known to Pope, although fewer than those acquainted with Jonathan Swift. Two names in particular stand out: George Granville, who became Baron Lansdowne, and Allen Bathurst, a young MP suspected of Jacobite leanings. We have come across Granville as one of Pope's sponsors for his *Pastorals*. He had been Secretary at War since 1710, and nourished a sizeable parliamentary interest through his ownership of strategic property in pliable Cornish boroughs. A month before he entered the purple, he had acquired a still greater claim to advancement when he acquired through marriage the hefty fortune of the Earl of Jersey's young daughter. As for Lord Bathurst, he proved to be one of Pope's most enduring friends, as well as the recipient of one of his very finest poems, the *Epistle* on the use of riches published in 1733. Bathurst had a character at once worldly and idealistic, with a passion for landscape gardening and country life, but at the same time a fondness for urban pleasures and a deep attachment to traditional Tory values. In the words of James Lees-Milne, 'Bathurst ... appealed to Pope as the very complement of himself. His openness, his disregard of all obstacles, and his gay vitality were balm to the other's jangling nerves.'[4] The durable peer lived long enough to enjoy the society of Laurence Sterne and he outlasted Pope, four years his junior, by three decades.

2

> It is history, the river of history, along which most of the significant events of the last two thousand years have taken place; but it is also the river as history.[5]

As the peace treaty moved towards a final settlement, a handful of commendatory poems began to trickle out. When news reached England on 2 April 1713 that negotiators had sealed the deal, this stream turned into a spate. The volunteer laureates included writers great and small, and some among them surpassed the usual level of such effusions. Only one of these works, however, has outlasted the occasion, and that of course was the one produced by Pope.

Windsor-Forest came out on 7 March, ahead of most of its rivals. This was the eve of Anne's accession to the Crown, which had marked what many considered a restoration of the Stuart line after a kind of interregnum under William. On the same date fell the second anniversary of an attempt by a French agent to murder Robert Harley, and as Swift told Stella this 'great day' had now acquired a dual significance at court since it marked the first minister's providential escape from death.[6]

The timing of publication was no coincidence. No one has ever doubted that *Windsor-Forest* is a Tory poem, celebrating a Tory peace. Two more controversial issues, apparently separate but ultimately linked, divide critics. The first centres on the question as to whether the work is actually a Jacobite manifesto in disguise. The second concerns the structure of the poem, split as it is between a section of pastoral and georgic describing the forest, and a section of prophecy and panegyric moving down the river from Windsor to London and the wider world. Neither debate has ever been conclusively resolved.

It will be best to consider the structural question first. A note Pope later supplied tells us that 'the poem was written at two different times: the first part of which relates to the country, in the year 1704, at the same time with the Pastorals; the latter part was not added till the year 1713, in which it was publish'd' (*TE*, vol. 1, p. 148). We usually need to take such statements by the author with caution, and few believe that the earlier portion was written so early, or the later portion so late. The opening segment is longer, reaching to line 290. It sets the scene, outlines the history of the area, describes rural activities, interjects an Ovidian episode on the myth of Lodona and pays tribute to a hermit-philosopher who has retreated to the 'shades' of the forest. The section comes to a conclusion with a passage on the literary giants who had celebrated Windsor, ending up (bathetically, we might feel today) with the poems' dedicatee, George Granville. This segues naturally into the opening lines of the second segment, which focus on Windsor Castle and its royal owners. By means of a fiat on behalf of the Queen, the tone changes with a panegyric on peace as her rule restores a golden age of cooperation among nations under Britain's beneficent guidance. By a simple but brilliantly effective stroke of imagination, Pope traces the course of English history as the poem follows the course of the timber from the oaks downstream, via Windsor past London to the wider ocean.

Many good critics have taken the line that this arrangement makes for a broken-backed composition, uneasily straddling the fence between pastoral and political elements. But the more closely we look at the text, the less this argument holds up. There is a myriad of connective filaments that run through the entire poem. We need consider only a few striking cases in point. The first section explores the fate of the forest under the Norman kings, while the second passes under review later monarchs who inhabited the castle. In the opening part we have the mock-battles of blood sports, in the second the real contests that had been fought in the war now reaching its end. Early on, the microcosmic harmony of the forest; later, the macrocosmic concord of nations. Part one has a mythological set piece charting the history of the rivulet Lodona, part two has an allegorical tableau of Father Thames and his tributary streams. First we get Anne as the huntress deity Diana, scouring the plains and protecting the 'Sylvan Reign' in a period of peace and plenty; then we are given Anne as the arbiter of international stability as her rule controls the oceans of the world. Part one brings with it the 'golden Years' of liberty; part two initiates 'Albion's Golden Days', marked by the freeing of slaves and the rescue of South American peoples from their bondage to Spain.

Examples could be multiplied many times over. Ultimately *Windsor-Forest*, for all the rich variety of its means, has a single end in view. From start to finish it is designed to link the conclusion of the war with the benefits of Anne's rule and the diplomatic, military and civil policy of Oxford's government. Before the poem has gone very far at all, we find the ecosystem of the forest linked to a particular dispensation: 'Rich Industry sits smiling on the Plains, / And Peace and Plenty tell, a STUART reigns' (*TE*, vol. 1, p. 152). This Edenic landscape had been threatened before, when the tyrannical Norman overlord despoiled the environment. It needs little extrapolation to see that the deeds of William I and his son Rufus have been replicated by the actions of a later foreign invader, William of Orange, and may now be reinforced by the German prince waiting in the wings to succeed Anne. At a personal level, Pope may have intuited that his family would itself be driven out of the forest by government measures, as indeed happened very soon after the Hanoverians took power – just three years after the poem appeared. But he probably felt too that William had already carried out a putsch worthy of the Norman kings when he banished people like Pope's family from the City in the early 1690s, and denied them the right to a home of their own.

For many years the figure of Nimrod in this section has been identified as a cover for William III. More recently, it has been suggested that the target was instead a foreign despot in the shape of Louis XIV, but this seems implausible on several grounds.[7] First, Pope explicitly states in a note that the passage concerning 'levelled towns' refers to 'the destruction made in the New Forest, and the tyrannies made there by William I' (*TE*, vol. 1, p. 155). It is an easy sideslip from one royal forest to another, and a short step from William I and William II to William III. On the other hand Louis had no relevance to the locale of the poem, no connection with the history of the chase and no Norman blood.

Second, Pope describes the death of Rufus in the forest, a passage with obvious links to the death of William III after a riding accident. Louis XIV did not die until a year after the poem came out, which precludes any such import. Third, the culmination of this excerpt sees 'Fair *Liberty*, Britannia's *Goddess*' reassume control of the sacred wood and introduce the 'golden years to come' (*TE*, vol. 1, p. 159). This hardly fits the real politics at work in Pope's day, since the French monarch held no sovereignty over British territory that would be reclaimed by the peace treaty. Nimrod clearly represents an incomer to the native haunts, like the Conqueror in former times and Dutch William in the present. Fourth, the claim that all will be well now that 'a STUART reigns once more' (*TE*, vol. 1, p. 152) makes no sense if the damage to the environment had been the work of a Bourbon prince. We must conclude that Pope has in mind the operation of forest law under William III, especially as a loosening of the reins took place under Anne.[8] Beyond that, the savage treatment meted out to the historic residents of Windsor stands as a hidden indictment of the oppressive laws which the Catholic population had to endure.

Such tendentious accounts of recent history form just one part of the political message. They are present throughout, making the view that the pastoral section is innocent of topical commentary impossible to sustain. In fact, *Windsor-Forest* deals with affairs of state at three different levels. There is a body of material relating to the immediate situation, including the recent creation by Oxford of the South Sea Company – a move, as we have seen, relevant to the precise terms of the peace treaty. Beneath this flows a current of allusion to the events of Pope's lifetime, including the Marlborough wars, evoked with sharp precision more than once, and extending to the famous visit of the Indian kings to London in 1710. At the furthest level we have a prolonged meditation on English history, from Saxon times onward. All three levels of reference are crucial to the overall argument, and all three have clear political implications.

At the poetic heart of the work lies a buried myth, taken from Book VIII of Ovid's *Metamorphoses*, adapted slightly through its use by Michael Drayton in his Jacobean epic of English topography, *Poly-Olbion* (1622). The story tells how Erisichthon violated a sacred grove in Thessaly by felling an ancient oak of massive proportions, despite a warning from the nymph who inhabited the tree. He destroyed the tree with heavy blows from his axe, so that blood flowed from wounds in its trunk, and as it toppled the oak brought down a great part of the grove. The dryads complained to Ceres, and asked for the wrongdoer to be punished. Ceres assented with a nod of her head, and as she bowed her head the grain in the fields, ready to be harvested, bowed too. This is a key poetic source for *Windsor-Forest*: 'Here Ceres' Gifts in waving Prospect stand, / And nodding tempt the joyful Reaper's Hand' (*TE*, vol. 1, p. 152). In this way Pope links the idea of rape of an innocent landscape with the preservative role of Ceres, something achieved by his use of Ovid's story. Erisichthon's fate was decreed by the goddess; he would suffer from the pangs of an unquenchable appetite, and famine would constantly ravage him. What would have been enough for an entire city or a nation did not suffice to appease his hunger. The political import seems clear: the warmongers and contractors abet Marlborough in his endless desire for ever more victories, ever more conquests, ever more blood.

Pope's own Ovidian myth follows a different trajectory, but it is of imagination compacted with Drayton's tale of a grove desecrated by an impious and brutal male. According to the inner logic of *Windsor-Forest*, the sacred oak groves of England are protected by Ceres = Anne. Condign punishment should be visited upon Pan (or Erisichthon), that is Norman/Williamite rapists. Similarly, earlier in the same section of his poem, Drayton narrates the rape of Sabrina's nymphs by satyrs in the Forest of Dean. Sabrina appeals for aid to 'her Sire', Neptune, much as Lodona appeals to Father Thames, a river god with Neptunian attributes in Pope's myth. As the editors explain, Drayton here 'poeticizes the robberies for which the Dean forest was notorious into rapes by the satyrs'.[9] It is all too plausible that the ravisher in *Windsor-Forest* might have a modern equivalent too – the incomers and carpet-baggers of the Whig oligarchy, who were displacing residents and following Cromwell's earlier example by rooting out the oaks.

What, then, of the supposed Jacobite colouring of the poem? The elaborate rhetorical engineering that went into its construction precludes an easy answer. Some facts are plain. One thing that contributes to the stylistic unity of *Windsor-Forest* is the use throughout of motifs and devices associated with Stuart art-forms such as masque. The verbal texture is fixed with a high gloss, deriving from the word-hoard of chivalric and heraldic discourse. Pope's most immediate model in formal terms was *Cooper's Hill* (1642) by Sir John Denham, which celebrated another Thames-side shrine in undeniably royalist terms. An edition of the work came out in 1709: Pope owned a copy and conducted a careful analysis of the changes Denham made to his poem in successive versions. But none of this fully settles the matter, since you could be an admirer of the Stuarts without wanting to see James Edward on the throne. This was the position of many Protestants, who constituted after all the majority of the Tory party. It may have reflected Pope's own views.

In addition we need to consider the identity of the dedicatee. Granville was a suitable choice in many ways. For one thing, he had known Pope for several years, and as early as around 1706 he had written to a certain 'Harry', who might be Henry St John, of 'a young Poet, newly inspir'd, in the Neighbourhood of *Cooper's-Hill*... he is not above Seventeen or Eighteen Years of Age, and promises Miracles'.[10] He was a competent poet and dramatist whose works had occasional relevance to Pope's subject-matter. Moreover, he made a feasible candidate for the Order of the Garter, a promotion that is envisaged in the text when it reaches the home of the order, St George's Chapel at Windsor. And centrally, of course, he was a leading figure at court who had served under Oxford as War Minister. In reality, he played no serious part in the peace process: Bolingbroke had taken full control of the negotiations, and in that respect *Windsor-Forest* contains a hidden complaint to Pope's friend. Finally, he had been elected to the 'Society', or Brothers' Club, in 1711. We get some hints of what this body stood for from references by Swift, one of its members along with wits and writers such as John Arbuthnot and Matthew Prior. The core of the club was made up of leading politicians such as Bolingbroke, the Duke of Ormonde and Sir William Wyndham. Others were the sons of ministers, notably Simon Harcourt, who would become a close friend of Pope. Another invitation to join had gone out to Bathurst, but this mainly because he was young and a Tory, not necessarily because he harboured Jacobite leanings.

That much provides straightforward evidence. What complicates matters is the circumstance that Lord Lansdowne, to give him his new title, acted as one of the leaders of the western rising when the rebellion broken out in 1715. He was arrested on a charge of high treason and sent to the Tower. Eventually he gained his release, but he continued to assist the Stuart cause, serving as secretary to the Pretender and taking a minor role in the Atterbury plot. We ought not to use this evidence *ex post facto* to determine the nature of Lansdowne's views in 1713; but the date is uncomfortably close to the moment when he organized a major sector of the Jacobites' invasion in 1715. We cannot afford to dismiss as a mere contingency of chance the fact that Pope dedicated the poem to such a man, and took occasion in its course to suggest the rewards in store for his patron. Everybody knew that when George I came to the throne, Lansdowne would be among the last in line for a place on the honours list. Just weeks into the new reign he was dismissed from the post he held at court. Little remained for him but to chase the mythical titles bestowed by the Pretender. He ended up as Duke of Albemarle, Marquis Monk, Earl of Bath, Viscount Bevil and Baron Lansdowne. Only the last of these counted – the rest brought with them pretend diplomas, like mail-order degrees.

Although Pope designated Lansdowne as his sponsor, this may have been to avoid an embarrassing choice between the two leaders of the ministry. Self-evidently, the real hero of *Windsor-Forest* is Anne herself. But implicitly the poem endorses three more tutelary figures. For recent events, this is Oxford, whose conduct of affairs is celebrated in the second half the poem, culminating in a vision of triumphs as a result of the foundation of the South Sea Company. For the intermediary period, Pope singles out Trumbull on account of his Scipio-like qualities of simple virtues, exercised in retirement after he had been rejected by the power elite. After the poem came out, Pope expressed his gratitude to Trumbull and wondered if he might have done better to remain in the forest, 'learning from one Man, than in London exposing my self perhaps to a hundred'.[11] Despite a measure of studied flattery in the compliment, the remark is not affected. At some level of his being, Sir William exhibited an almost Jeffersonian faith in simple country virtue as against the corruption of urban high society. This tended further to align him ideologically with the Tories, who represented for the most part the values of the landed gentry in parliament.

From a long historical perspective the doomed hero of *Windsor-Forest* is Charles I, whose execution supplies the most heartfelt moment in the entire text: 'Make sacred *Charles*'s Tomb for ever known, / (Obscure the Place, and uninscrib'd the Stone) / Oh Fact accurst!' *Fact* here means 'crime'. The passage continues:

> What Tears has *Albion* shed,
> Heav'ns! what new Wounds, and how her old have bled?
> She saw her Sons with purple Deaths expire,
> Her sacred Domes involv'd in rolling Fire,
> A dreadful Series of Intestine Wars,
> Inglorious Triumphs, and dishonest Scars.
> At length great *ANNA* said – Let Discord cease!
> She said, the World obey'd, and all was *Peace*!

(*TE*, vol. 1, pp. 180–1)

This verse paragraph can have only one meaning. In his original manuscript version Pope had gone even further: he wrote that a 'sacriligious Brood / Sworn to Rebellion, principl'd in Blood' had dominated the nation, until Anne with her godlike fiat quelled the 'Furies'.[12] But even as the printed passage stands, we get a clear statement: the killing of Charles by the republican forces had undammed a torrent of disasters, including the Plague of 1665, the Great Fire of 1666, the bitter battles during the reign of James II and the 'inglorious' British victories during the Marlborough wars. It makes for an extremely partial account of the course of history – but one that many on the Tory side of the fence would have accepted, regardless of their stance on the Protestant succession.

Events would soon falsify the sanguine hopes Pope expressed. The poem envisaged a time when 'The Trumpets sleep, while chearful Horns are blown, / And Arms employ'd on Birds and Beasts alone' (*TE*, vol. 1, p. 187). Symbolically, the final paragraph returns to a pastoral idiom, where 'listning Swains' drowse to the lulling sound of anodyne verses. This was the prospect that Richard III so despised in Shakespeare's play. By tradition, the soothing pipes of Arcady replaced the martial blast of the trumpet. What actually happened, of course, was that within eighteen months the administration had collapsed, the Tory party suffered a compound fracture which would not heal for a generation, and the Queen died quite suddenly in the midst of political chaos. Oxford would face impeachment on a charge of treason, and spend two years in the Tower of London; Bolingbroke would flee to the court of the Pretender, and many of Pope's allies would join one or the other either in jail or in exile. In 1715 the Pretender launched his ill-fated invasion of Britain, and once more 'intestine war' would split the nation.

This was just the first of a number of bitter controversies that passed before Pope's eyes in the next decade. Some of them even reached the heart of the forest, to catch up his own immediate family. In retrospect the poem serves as a threnody at once for a dynasty, a government, a circle of friends and a set of ideals that were shattered in 1714.

Windsor-Forest concludes with the prospect of a peaceful world order underwritten by Britain's naval supremacy. As we should expect, this aspect of the poem has received considerable attention of late from critics with strong views on the history of imperialism. We need to understand first that when Pope composed his poem, the British Empire was in its infancy. It covered an area less widely extensive than those of Spain, Holland and Portugal. The most important element among the possessions was formed by eleven colonies in North America: the Carolinas were not yet divided, and Georgia not yet founded. In the Caribbean the main British foothold lay in Jamaica, along with a few small islands including half of St Kitts. The East India Company had a strong commercial hold on the subcontinent, but no organized military or administrative presence. Beyond this, we can point to nothing more than a handful of tiny trading posts, scattered across South Asia and West Africa.

To put it shortly, Britain, or England until 1707, was chiefly a European power, with no naval strategy on an oceanic scale. Most Tories, as it happened, wanted to keep things that way, harbouring doubts about the benefits of rapid expansionism. However, one of the aims of the War of the Spanish Succession had been to resist the dominance of France and Spain in the world order. By the Treaty of Utrecht, as we have seen, some significant gains were made: Britain acquired Newfoundland, Nova Scotia and the Hudson Bay territory, but this still left Canada largely in the hands of France, who also maintained control of the huge Louisiana territory stretching from the Mississippi delta to the Canadian border. Although Britain had compelled France to cede the lucrative asiento contract, it failed to establish a footing in Spanish America, a region on which Whigs like Defoe cast an envious eye, as ripe for commercial exploitation. In the event, the South Sea Company delivered on none of its promises regarding trade to the western hemisphere. Not until the Peace of Paris in 1763 were the foundations of the later British Empire properly laid.

At the end of *Windsor-Forest*, Father Thames envisions a global system opened up by voyages of trade and discovery. Peace will bring about a world where 'Conquest [shall] cease, and Slav'ry be no more' (*TE*, vol. 1, p. 192).

Within the Spanish Empire, there will be a resurgence of the native civilizations of Peru and Mexico. This was not exactly the course imperial history would take over the next two centuries, but we have no reason to doubt the sincerity with which Pope set out his outlook for humanity, or the brilliant imaginative resources with which he gave utterance to this prospect of universal harmony. The entire peroration draws on an eloquence that he never surpassed in his most mature works on public affairs:

> The Time shall come, when, free as Seas or Wind,
> Unbounded *Thames* shall flow for all mankind,
> Whole Nations enter with each swelling Tyde,
> And Seas but join the Regions they divide;
> Earth's distant Ends our Glory shall behold,
> And the new World launch forth to seek the Old.
>
> (*TE*, vol. 1, pp. 190–1)

Maynard Mack called the lines here 'a kind of vision of Paradise Regained'.[13] This description of *Windsor-Forest* rightly identifies its underlying theme, as it moves from local beauties of the forest down the river to the concluding vista on an oceanic scale. Its sense of the future resembles not the crude forecasts of a contemporary astrologer, predicting the death of a monarch or the approach of a natural disaster, but rather the scenes foretold by an impassioned Old Testament prophet.

At the age of twenty-five, Pope had demonstrated his ability to confront the largest political issues of the day. *Windsor-Forest* enlisted all the technical skills he had been developing in his years at Binfield, and utilized for its ideological underpinning many of the notions and prejudices of the friends he met there. However, the next segment of his career drew him more and more into the group of new acquaintances he encountered in London. His work moved in two fresh directions: towards 'urban' themes and social satire, and towards the epic. As it happens, his masterpiece *The Rape of the Lock*, soon to reappear in a significantly expanded form, shows the impress of both areas of interest.

3

Two days after the work came out, Swift wrote to Stella in his most peremptory manner, 'Mr Pope has publishd a fine Poem, called Windsor Forrest: read it'.[14] The phrasing may indicate that the two men were already acquainted, but if so they had not known each very long. Soon they would become fast friends, and despite the usual ups and downs they remained close literary allies for almost thirty years, a bond broken only when the Dean fell victim to senile dementia. Moreover, Swift belonged to a group of bright people, and unlike Pope's former mentors they included individuals not much older than himself. This alliance helped in the formation of the Scriblerus Club, with Pope and Swift at its centre. At the same time it hastened Pope's exclusion from a rival set of Whigs, headed by Joseph Addison and Richard Steele, on the edge of whose circle he had recently hovered.

When Pope began to spend more time in London after the appearance of his *Pastorals*, Addison and Steele were embarking on a spell of immense influence in the literary world. The *Tatler* ran from 1709 to 1711, and became hugely popular. While Pope arrived on the scene too late to contribute, as Swift did, he obviously read the paper as closely as everybody else. Traces of its influence can be detected more than once in *The Rape of the Lock*. The authors followed up with daily numbers of the *Spectator* from March 1711 to December 1712. No organ had ever exercised quite such a hold on English public discourse. The essays covered a wide range of social and intellectual topics, from serious criticism and aesthetic analysis to light jocular commentary on fads and fashions of the day. Steele had initially taken the leading role on the *Tatler*, but Addison came to the fore on the *Spectator* with his delicate wit and good-tempered appraisal of men and manners. Some people today find his attitude towards women patronizing, and the journal no longer has the sort of renown that it carried through to the end of the nineteenth century. But at the time Pope could only relish the kind things said about his work in its columns, and he was glad to contribute material of his own, including *Messiah*, a sacred eclogue based on the book Isaiah.

In the week that *Windsor-Forest* came out, Steele set up another periodical called the *Guardian*. He seems to have hoped that Pope would become a regular contributor, and indeed at least seven papers came from this source – perhaps as many as twelve. The most famous items in this collection were an essay on gardening and one on pastorals, mocking the inept efforts of Pope's rival, Ambrose 'Namby Pamby' Philips. The incensed Philips is said to have 'hung a *Rod* over the Chimney at *Button's Coffee-House*, and declared he would take down our little Poet's breeches and whip him in Publick, the next Time he caught him there; – which obliged *Pope* to leave the House'.[15] Certainly by this date Pope was beginning to distance himself from the coterie which met at Button's coffee-house near Covent Garden, and included members of a strongly Whig parliamentary ginger-group called the Hanover Club.

For a short while he belonged to the coffee-house culture, seen by Jürgen Habermas and others as vital to the evolution of an emerging civil society in Britain, but he never became a true habitué of such resorts.[16] In this he was unlike Swift, who asked Stella to direct her letters to St James's coffee-house, and sometimes in the evening had 'loitered till nine' in the company of Whigs. 'Mr. Addison and I meet a little seldomer than formerly', he had written in November 1710, 'although we are still at bottom as good friends as ever; but differ a little about party'.[17] By 1713 these convivial cross-party meetings were a thing of the past, and with the political split went a cessation in social contacts.

One thing made the difference here: the *Guardian* took a clearly Whiggish line on topical events, a reflection of the increased politicization of all public discourse. In truth Addison and Steele had now begun to make their way as career politicians, and each had entered parliament in opposition to Oxford's ministry. Steele showed himself as more of a zealot, to the point that he was expelled from the House of Commons for alleged seditious remarks in his pamphlet *The Crisis*. In essence this was revenge by the government for the effective propaganda Steele had been conducting against the ministry's campaign, masterminded by Swift. All the same, Steele would have the last laugh. After the Hanoverians swept in, he gained a knighthood, as well as a post as governor of Drury Lane theatre. During the brief window of their friendship, Pope and Steele got along together very well: the young man found Steele, sixteen years his senior, agreeable company with his sense of fun and casually irresponsible ways. But eventually the 'curse of party' severed their relations permanently, and their collaborations on literary projects came to an abrupt end.

It was not quite like that in the case of Addison. Political issues mattered here too, for Addison devotedly followed the party line. Although he seems to have lacked strong ideological convictions of his own, beyond a default adherence to Protestant and Hanoverian causes, he showed unfailing loyalty to patrons such as Lord Halifax. Ultimately he would climb almost to the top in the public service, with a spell as Secretary of State under George I. This elevation owed more to his willingness to take on dogsbody work and his fame as a writer than to any striking talents as a politician: he flopped badly when he tried to address the House of Commons. But there are other reasons that occasioned a remark Pope made to Joseph Spence, 'He was very kind to me at first but my bitter enemy afterwards' (*Anecdotes*, vol. 1, p. 67). Faults on both sides led to a growing feeling of mutual suspicion. Pope did not show quite the expected degree of enthusiasm for Addison's tragedy *Cato*, which proved a blockbuster hit at Drury Lane in April 1713. The play, full of noble eloquence but dramatically dull, remained on the boards in England and America for more than a century, as it came to be seen as a prime statement of the benefits of liberty. On the other side, Addison shifted his support for Pope's translation of the *Iliad* to a much less talented acolyte named Thomas Tickell who was projecting a rival version.

In 1715 Pope made a brief attempt to mend fences, but it was already too late. Soon he started to draft his harshly critical lines on 'Atticus', which form the basis of a character sketch in the *Epistle to Arbuthnot*. Here the main thrust has little to do with politics. Pope attacks his adversary's personal character, accusing Addison of being jealous, small-minded, vengeful, vain and susceptible to flattery. Some of the phrases in this portrait have passed into the language:

> Damn with faint praise, assent with civil leer,
> And without sneering, teach the rest to sneer;
> Willing to wound, and yet afraid to strike,
> Just hint a fault, and hesitate dislike ...
>
> (*TE*, vol. 4, p. 110)

The drift of this entire passage corresponds to something that Pope told Spence, concerning the way Addison behaved when not surrounded by his friends: 'With any mixture of strangers, and sometimes with ... any man he was too jealous of, he seemed to preserve his dignity much, with a stiff sort of silence' (*Anecdotes*, vol. 1, p. 62). It looks as if Addison got to see an early draft of these verses, perhaps by Pope's deliberate instigation. In later years Pope would become known for his bitter quarrels as well as for his warm friendships. None of the broken relationships is as sad as that with Addison, for both men recognized the literary gifts of the other, and Pope knew that he had once enjoyed the support of a man of 'true Genius', who was 'Blest with each Talent and each Art to please' (*TE*, vol. 4, p. 109). On the surface, such enmities made for a quixotic rejection of opportunity thrown his way: he could scarcely afford to go on offending those who carried so much clout.

However, another dynamic came into play here, which helped to cause the break with Addison and Steele, but also served to mitigate its bad effects. A different set of alliances grew up as Pope entered the so-called Scriblerus Club and developed literary friendships which would have long-lasting significance for his career.

The club comprised an informal group of like-minded friends who collaborated on a range of satiric projects. They met regularly for a few months in 1713–14, before the course of events separated its members when the Queen died. However, some of the Scriblerians continued to work on literary projects in the following years, and something of a revival occurred briefly between 1715 and 1718. The visits of Swift to England in 1726 and 1727 prompted another resurgence of interest in older schemes. Along with Swift and Pope the membership included Dr John Arbuthnot, John Gay, Thomas Parnell and the Earl of Oxford. Meetings seem usually to have been held on Saturdays, often at Arbuthnot's grace-and-favour lodgings in St James's Palace. Some accounts suggest that Gay acted as secretary, perhaps because of his junior status – for only Pope among members of the group was younger. Part of the inspiration for the club may have come from a proposal that Pope had floated in the *Spectator* on 14 August 1712, in which he announced his plan to publish every month '*An Account of the Works of the Unlearned*'.[18] Apart from a few trifles in verse, such as rhymed invitations to dinner, nothing survives from this original phase of activity; but there is good reason to believe that a start was made on a number of satiric works that appeared in later years, notably the *Memoirs of Martin Scri-*

blerus. With the death of Anne and the fall of Oxford's ministry, Arbuthnot lost his place at court, while Swift was condemned to permanent exile in Ireland, where Parnell soon followed. Even Gay found his hopes disappointed after he returned from a diplomatic mission to Hanover. Odd as it might seem, Pope was least directly affected by the sudden turn in events, in part because his religion and his health had precluded official advancement. Thus it happened that he became the guardian of the club's conscience, as well as its archives.

Offshoots of the Scriblerian enterprise first came in front of the public with items such as the collaborative drama *Three Hours after Marriage* (1717) and a number of short squibs in prose. Later full-length works such as *Gulliver's Travels*, *The Art of Sinking* and *The Dunciad* had significant roots in the club's early project. In addition, the publication of the *Miscellanies* of Pope and his friends from 1727 allowed several of the smaller items to appear in print, usually some years after their composition. As the years took their toll on members of the group, Pope was left by 1735 as the only active and competent individual with a stake in preserving the club's memory. It fell to him to superintend release of materials in successive editions of the *Miscellanies* and to contrive the long-delayed publication of the *Memoirs of Martin Scriblerus* in 1741. Most of these items appeared anonymously, and few of the shorter works can be attributed with certainty to any one individual. Over the course of time, Pope stood out as the leading presence within the club, and he may well have edited the works of his colleagues with a degree of freedom before they appeared in print. Scriblerian satire belongs to a tradition of learned wit, which satirizes pompous and pretentious writing, bogus scholarship, trifling and word-chopping criticism, and other kinds of *déformation professionelle* in the world of letters. Its inspiration comes from older writers such as Erasmus, Rabelais and Cervantes, although Swift's own *Tale of a Tub* can be viewed as a pre-Scriblerian example of Scriblerus humour.

Some have doubted whether the club constituted a going entity in any real sense. This question arises more acutely in the light of their brief and intermittent existence as a collective group after 1714. While the individuals certainly held different ideas on many topics, and never surrendered their independence as writers, they left enough evidence to show that they did share a programme, if not a precise manifesto. Most coteries are made up of people with diverging goals who agree on loose objectives and engage in mutual support: we might think of the Barbizon school of artists in nineteenth-century France. The readiness of the Scriblerians to collaborate also helped to meld them as a group. And if the club had not had any other reason for being, the members clearly enjoyed each other's company in a convivial setting. Whatever we think of the literary outcome, we can hardly doubt that they formed a happy combination of men during their brief existence as a dining club. One reason must lie in the fact that

Swift, Gay and Pope were all unmarried, while Parnell lost his much-loved wife in August 1711. Even Arbuthnot had a kind of bachelor pad at St James's, to carry out his duties as physician to the Queen. For Oxford the meetings clearly served as a distraction from the responsibilities of government, which by this stage had almost overwhelmed him. Beyond that, he was able to display his wit and cultivation in a group of learned men, and thus gain the kind of respect that politicians sometimes crave. 'He used to send trifling verses from court to the Scriblerus Club almost every day', Pope reported, 'and would come and talk idly with them almost every night, even when his all was at stake' (*Anecdotes*, vol. 1, p. 95). It does not sound as if high matters of state took up much of their time.

Most Scriblerian satire lacks overt political content. Targets were chosen because the victims displayed pedantry, intellectual arrogance or incompetence, not on grounds of their political allegiance. However, the jokes generally rest on conservative prejudice – such as a tendency to regard scientific experiments or innovations as automatically funny. The comedy often proceeds from a feeling that anything in the world of learning not sanctioned by ancient authority is liable to go badly wrong. Moreover, we cannot blink the fact that the group had, as its link with power, the Prime Minister of a Tory government. Two of the other members belonged to what can loosely if unhistorically be called a rightwing association, namely the 'Society'.

No one among the Scriblerian writers had a stronger partisan commitment than Swift, a recent acquaintance of Pope, and he probably exercised the greatest influence on the younger man. A former supporter of Godolphin, Swift had turned to Harley and St John, as they were then styled, when he came to England in 1710 as an emissary of the Church of Ireland. Soon he had become the ministry's chief publicist and the most valuable writer in its campaign to blacken the reputation of the previous government. He took over the essay-paper the *Examiner* soon after its inception, and followed up with a series of excoriating pamphlets, notably *The Conduct of the Allies* (1711). In addition he composed some vitriolic onslaughts on men like Godolphin in verse 'lampoons' such as *The Virtues of Sid Hamet's Rod* (1710). In these works Swift hammered away against Whig policies and personalities. He proclaimed the need to end an expensive war, and attacked the moneyed men of the City for their attempts to defer the process. The Duke of Marlborough is portrayed as an obstacle to peace, and as a man with no heart who could bear to see thousands die in his quest for self-aggrandizement. Such rhetoric inflamed Swift's opponents, and led to a total estrangement with his former friends Addison and Steele. These worsening relations mirrored, and perhaps helped to cause, a similar cooling in Pope's friendship with his Whig colleagues.

For more than two years Swift and Steele berated each other's views in a succession of scathing tracts. For example, Steele produced *The Importance of*

Dunkirk Considered in late 1713, emphasizing the need to strengthen provisions in the Utrecht settlement with regard to the dismantling of fortifications. Immediately Swift came back with *The Importance of the Guardian Considered*, a political response that contained much *ad hominem* abuse on a personal level:

> To take the height of his [Steele's] Learning, you are to suppose a Lad just fit for the University, and sent early from thence into the wide World, where he followed every way of Life that might least improve or preserve the Rudiments he had got.[19]

And so on, at great length. The breach had already widened to an irreparable extent by the time that Steele was called to account by the House of Commons in March 1714 for alleged sedition in his pamphlet *The Crisis*. Tory members, led by Edward Harley and Thomas Foley (one a brother of the Lord Treasurer, the other a relative by marriage), contended that the offending passages 'were seditious and scandalous, injurious to her Majesty's government, the Church and the universities'.[20] The handsome Tory majority in the Commons meant that Steele had no chance, and he was duly expelled. Pope never got embroiled in quite such naked fist fights, preferring to undermine his opponents by more feline means. But even if he witnessed the contest between his old friends and his new ones with mixed emotion, his loyalties were now settled. Henceforth he would come down on the side of Swift, and Lord Oxford would become one of his most revered allies.

Some regarded Dr John Arbuthnot as the leading spirit of the club, especially in its early days. He had studied medicine at St Andrews before moving to London to teach mathematics. Before long he had been elected to the Royal Society, and in 1709 at the age of forty-two he was appointed physician to the Queen. With a nature at once humorous and humane, and articulate, John Arbuthnot became one of Pope's most respected friends soon after they met, as well as his trusted medical advisor. A genuine polymath, he was a man of broad cultivation who wrote on many subjects. He published works on probability, ancient units of measure, mathematics, diet, geology and other topics. In addition he had a strong interest in music and served as one of the directors of the Royal Academy of Music, which brought him into close contact with Handel and the Duke of Chandos at Cannons, the Duke's palatial residence near Stanmore in Middlesex. His main literary forte lay in satire and witty polemics, which led to controversies with men like the physician and antiquarian John Woodward. In 1712 he produced his best-known work, *The History of John Bull*, as well as a shorter piece, *The Art of Political Lying*, both of which were much admired by his friend Swift, whom he met about 1711.

In politics Arbuthnot seems always to have followed a Tory line. His father, a minister in Kincardineshire, was ejected for resistance to the Presbyterian orthodoxy that came in after the arrival of William III. His brother Robert, based in

France, took an important role in the financial affairs of the Pretender, acting as banker for the Stuart cause; while another brother, George, took part in the Jacobite rising. However, the doctor remained aloof from the movement, and his precise sympathies are hard to gauge. In all probability, Pope was introduced to Arbuthnot by Swift in 1713. At the outset Arbuthnot seems to have been the most active member of the group in prosecuting their main enterprise, the composition of what was to become the *Memoirs of Martin Scriblerus*: indeed, his colleagues sometimes addressed the doctor under the name of Scriblerus. Much of the medical and scientific satire in this work can be attributed with confidence to Arbuthnot, though finally it was left to Pope to put the material into shape and publish it. In addition, Arbuthnot wrote some of the shorter Scriblerian items, some printed in the group's *Miscellanies* several years later. He had a hand in the collectively written farce *Three Hours after Marriage* (1717) along with Gay and Pope. Quite apart from anything else, the poet's friendship with Arbuthnot extended his social contacts. The doctor had known individuals such as the virtuoso George Clarke, the mercurial Earl of Peterborough and the great antiquarian Sir Hans Sloane before they had come into the poet's orbit. It is not surprising that Pope addressed one of his most personal and heartfelt poems to his long-time friend. His famous *Epistle to Arbuthnot* chiefly celebrates the physician, whose 'Art and Care' had prolonged the poet's life, but as the work ends it movingly evokes the frail human being, whose last days will, Pope hopes, be 'social, chearful, and serene' (*TE*, vol. 4, p. 127). This phrase precisely captures some of the most noteworthy qualities of the doctor, who survived publication of the *Epistle* by no more than eight weeks.

John Gay had been known to Pope for about two years when the club held its first meetings. He came from quite modest origins, and at eighteen he moved to London from Devon to take up an apprenticeship to a silk mercer. This career evidently did not suit the young man, who returned to Barnstaple after being released from his articles. At first connected with the Whigs, Gay had shifted his ground by the time he published a georgic under the title *Rural Sports* in early 1713. Soon after he wrote a mock-heroic poem called *The Fan*. Obviously he and Pope were shadowing one another in their choice of genres at this stage. In 1714 Gay dedicated a comic version of a pastoral, *The Shepherd's Week*, to Bolingbroke and took Pope's side against Ambrose Philips when the two men contested supremacy in bucolic verse. This may have helped him gain a minor diplomatic post that summer; but the death of the Queen and the fall of Oxford's ministry left him out in the cold, a condition only too familiar to Gay as the years passed. The growing intimacy between the two men had one other important consequence for Pope's career: it was almost certainly through this agency that he met Gay's schoolfellow, the lawyer William Fortescue, who would later play a major role as a friend and a legal advisor (see Chapter 8).

The last member of the group, Thomas Parnell, descended from an Anglo-Irish family. Like Swift he studied at Trinity College, Dublin, and like Swift he took orders in the Church of Ireland. Through his fellow countryman, who was twelve years older, he was introduced to Oxford and Bolingbroke, to whom he dedicated a poem in March 1713. He also contributed occasionally to the *Spectator*, but along with his colleagues in the club he quickly moved away from Addison's set at Button's coffee-house. Depressed by his wife's death, he spent increasing periods of time in England, and when he went back to Ireland in 1714 it seems to have been no more than a dutiful resignation to the inevitable. Though he paid only one more visit to England, shortly before his death in 1718, he left his papers to his friend Pope, who had enlisted his knowledge of classical literature to provide material for the translation of Homer.

The five writers in the Scriblerian circle formed a tight-knit group for a crucial period lasting for about one year. Though events split them apart, with two members exiled to Ireland and their patron Oxford consigned to the Tower, the after-effects of these convivial gatherings lasted very much longer. Between them the members produced many of the greatest works of Augustan satire. If they had never even met, they would have become significant figures in literary history; but it was their good fortune to come together at a crucial stage of their careers, and to spark one another into even more creative activity.

4

What Pope came up with next had nothing much to do with the Scriblerus group, and indeed little obvious relevance to the great events that were convulsing the nation. In March 1714 Lintot published a much-expanded version of *The Rape of the Lock*, now running to five cantos as against the two-canto text of *The Rape of the Locke* which had appeared two years before. Of course, the new work remained a miniaturized cameo, with a mere 800 lines – no more than a single book of the traditional epic. Yet with its range of allusion, its density of witty implication and its multi-layered allegories, the *Rape* made a substantive contribution to English literature. If we exclude *The Faerie Queene*, *Paradise Lost*, *Don Juan* and *The Prelude*, it outdoes any of the 'serious' epic poems written in the language since the medieval age.

Most readers familiar with Pope will know the broad outline of the story behind the work. In the summer of 1711 Pope's friend John Caryll had been staying at Ingatestone, Essex, the presumed site of the main action of the poem. His host was the seventh Baron Petre, for whom Caryll had acted as guardian during the peer's minority. It may have been here that news came to light of a quarrel that had recently broken out, after a rash act by the young Petre had offended another long-standing Catholic family. He had cut off a lock from the hair of a reigning beauty, Arabella Fermor, whose roots were in Oxfordshire and who was probably already known to Pope through the Blount sisters. As the poet later recounted, Caryll had asked him 'to write a poem to make a jest of it, and laugh them [the feuding parties] together again'. According to this story, the work had its desired effect and the two families were reconciled (*Anecdotes*, vol. 1, pp. 44–5). Then, on 21 September 1711, Pope sent Caryll the *Rape* as 'a little Poetical Present'.[21] In the usual way, copies of the poem began to circulate in the world, and the author decided to publish the short form of the poem in Lintot's miscellany. In Pope's lifetime, the dedicatory address to John Caryll was disguised by the form C—l, although the poet told his friend as early as 1714 that he had wanted to print the name in full (*Corr.*, vol. 1, p. 210). The opening line also contains a concealed allusion to a verse written by John's uncle, the Jacobite courtier John, Lord Caryll.

After the appearance of this initial version came a hardening in family attitudes. Tight genealogical coils unwound as a defence strategy emerged. The bride and groom were in fact connected a couple of generations back: Arabella's great-great-aunt had married William Petre, great-uncle both of the baron and of John Caryll. At this point her first cousin once removed, Sir George Browne who figures in the poem as the blustering 'Sir Plume', began to make vague threats to the poet. Worse, Arabella herself, who had previously seemed well disposed, began to realize the full scandalous implications of the work, which may have been concealed from her by the elaborate compliments built into the verse. Possibly, the marriage of Lord Petre in March 1712, just before the poem first appeared, may have contributed to her vexed feelings. These developments may have been part of the reason that Pope embarked on his expanded version of the *Rape*, which would enable him to equivocate more genteelly (see *Corr.*, vol. 1, p. 350), in other words to surround the main plot with mythical and supernatural materials that would help to obfuscate the hero's responsibility for any of the actions in this risqué narrative. Moreover, it gave Pope the chance to write an introduction which would pretend, at least, to make some amends to the offended young lady. Addison is said to have tried to deter Pope from meddling with the 'delicious little thing' he had created (*TE*, vol. 1, p. 121); understandably the author considered this ill judged, if not ill willed, and went ahead regardless. Others such as Samuel Garth had a much more positive attitude to the changes.

By the end of 1713, Pope had completed the augmented work and decided to inscribe the new version to Miss Fermor by name. At one stage he had also contemplated a preface 'which 'salv'd the Lady's honour, without affixing her name', but he dropped this plan. Instead he used the dedication, where he claimed to have taken 'the best advice in the kingdom, of the men of sense' – including even that of the Lord Treasurer, Lord Oxford. The young lady herself, we are told, approved of the dedication. In the event, this teasing address doubtless spread the scandal as much as it worked to silence gossip, and we cannot take at face value Pope's boast that he had 'managed the dedication that it can neither hurt the lady, nor the author' (*Corr.*, vol. 1, p. 207). At a distance of three hundred years, it is hard to see how the *Rape* could have done anything but reopen fresh wounds.

That was bad enough, potentially, but the aftermath of the episode made things worse. The first version had not been published long before the Baron found a more suitable bride than Arabella, whom some now regarded as damaged goods. In her place he married a fifteen-year-old heiress from a Jacobite family in Lancashire. Twelve months later he was dead from smallpox, followed within weeks by his only sister. This all happened before the new *Rape of the Lock* came before the world. The Baron's mother, the dowager Lady Petre, and his young widow behaved well towards Pope even after their loss. As for Arabella, she made a much less grand marriage with a Berkshire squire, Francis Perkins, whose own family was just beginning to feel the effects of the squeeze exerted on Catholics. She had six children, who gradually frittered away what was left of the Perkins' fortune. Her husband died in 1736, when one of the trustees of his estate was Sir Henry Englefield of Whiteknights – she herself, we recall, was a granddaughter of Elizabeth Englefield. Arabella died two years later, having lived an unobtrusive and blameless life since the episode with Lord Petre. Nobody would know or care anything about her today, if Pope had not immortalized her as the heroine of his poem, the resplendent Belinda.

Still, most people in the recusant community probably wished that whole idea had never occurred to him. The bulk of the audience for *The Rape of the Lock* had, of course, little or no interest in these family secrets. But for those in the know, the poem must have been troubling as well as amusing. More than just exposing a localized scandal, it brought into play many of the stratagems that the community used to keep its identity intact. Pope can never have seriously believed that the poem's mock-heroic form took off all the implicit mockery of the families involved. For Caryll, a particularly close friend, who was related to the Petres, the *Rape* would call into question his guardianship of the Baron and his wife. For the child-widow, it meant constant reminders of a desperately short marriage. For the dowager Lady Petre, the glittering social world evoked in the poem brought up images of a life her recently deceased daughter would never now experience. For Arabella, it gave a public airing to events which had foreclosed the possibilities of a really grand marriage. Even if she herself had no regrets, the Fermors collectively would have deplored the loss of a dynastic connection.

Some might argue that the poem did no lasting harm. Pope remained on good terms with Caryll as long as the older man lived. Two years after Lord Petre died, his widow and mother showed some magnanimity in subscribing to the poet's translation of Homer: Catherine wrote to Caryll expressing her readiness to contribute. The two had most likely been recruited by a priest named Thomas Southcott, a resourceful Jacobite fund-raiser who could have used the *Iliad* as a blind for his larger task. In 1718 Caryll was still visiting the Petres at Ingatestone (*Corr.*, vol. 1, p. 518). Sir George Browne may finally have got over his pique, and the Fermors went on their quiet way, drifting into social obscurity. But members of the faith must have found it uncomfortable to read a text which so insistently drew attention to the little manoeuvres that sustained the marriage market. The affair sent ripples out over the entire community: after all, the Petres were 'the one family of cast iron landed magnates to remain invincibly Catholic from the sixteenth century onwards'.[22] Thanks to the hugely increased publicity that the *Rape* had brought to the episode, a small tempest in a domestic teapot had become almost a public event.

Within the first few lines Pope sets up a sly hint that Belinda's resistance to the Baron had been part of a calculated strategy:

> Say what strange Motive, Goddess! cou'd compel
> A well-bred *Lord* t'assault a gentle *Belle*?
> Or say what stranger Cause, yet unexplor'd,
> Cou'd make a gentle *Belle* reject a *Lord*?
>
> (*TE*, vol. 2, p. 145)

The tone seems genial enough, with the intimate flash of punning wit on Belle's name. Yet behind the smiling exterior hides a cruel accuracy. Here Pope uncovers the imperatives of a community in danger of losing its battle for survival. Artistically the poem needed all of the poet's tact, but in social matters it show itself as extraordinarily tactless. In so far as *The Rape of the Lock* has a political meaning (most of its concerns lie elsewhere), this lies in the exposure of the Catholic marriage market. A few genial thrusts at the fatuity of the *beau monde* have led some to look for a thoroughgoing attack on upper-class manners; but neither the Petres (for all their wealth) or the Fermors had any standing at court because of their religion. Pope himself satirized the urge to find hidden meanings beneath the text in 1715, when he produced a burlesque interpretation entitled *A Key to the Lock*. This ridiculous pamphlet, claiming to be the work of an apothecary and astrologer named 'Esdras Barnivelt', affects to uncover the 'dangerous Tendency' of the poem. The writer offers a reading of the *Rape* as an allegory of the War of the Spanish Succession with the object of promoting the papist religion. We can see that this ingenious decoding of a secret message barely exaggerates the many serious onslaughts on Pope's loyalty in years to come. As often, he got in his pre-emptive blow before his enemies had mustered their forces.

Hostile squads were beginning to draw up their lines. The blame for this must fall partly on Pope, owing to his willingness to allow manuscript copies of indiscreet ballads to get abroad. A number of unscrupulous publishers lay in wait for scraps from his writing table. Most notorious among these was Edmund Curll, a scavenger with a fine eye for saleable material. The bookseller had already offended Swift by producing an illicit edition of *Miscellanies* and a moderately well informed *Key to a Tale of a Tub*. He had also pirated works by Matthew Prior and Nicholas Rowe, who became friends of Pope. In 1714 Curll and his allies in the Grub Street trade produced some risqué items from Pope's hand, including 'An Epigram upon Two or Three', a salacious seven-line poem that had come out anonymously in Lintot's miscellany but was now attributed to Pope. There were some naughty lines, too, 'On a Lady who Pisst at the Tragedy of Cato'. Most of these items could not have reached print without tacit connivance at least on Pope's part. Sometimes he overreached himself, and Curll was master of extracting maximum embarrassment from such episodes. The minor affrays that took place at this time were the harbingers of a much more lasting contest in future years, where Pope received almost as many bruises as he delivered.

What really changed the course of his career, however, was a sequence of events in the summer of 1714. The fraying coalition of Oxford and Bolingbroke came to the point of no return. Swift fled to a remote village on the Berkshire Downs as his great friends split apart and the ministry lost all its credibility. The Scriblerus Club too started to unravel, when John Gay left as secretary to a mission sent to Hanover in the wake of the death of the Electress Sophia of Hanover. It had become clear to all that the government desperately needed to build bridges with her son and successor, the Electoral Prince George. But these diplomatic efforts were too little and too late. On 27 July the Queen forced Oxford to resign as Lord Treasurer, and a new administration was organized under the titular leadership of the moderate Duke of Shrewsbury. At this juncture the Queen's health deteriorated with dramatic speed, in spite of the efforts made by her doctors, including Arbuthnot. In the early morning of Sunday, 1 August 1714 she died and overnight the political world underwent a huge upheaval. 'I beleive', Arbuthnot told Swift, 'sleep was never more wellcome to a weary traveller than death was to her'.[23] Unlike many of his friends, Pope had nothing to fear regarding his personal safety, but he knew that his chief patrons faced death or disgrace. The future belonged to men like Addison, Steele and of course the Electoral Prince – now to be formally installed as George I of England, Scotland and Ireland.

PART II: GEORGE I, 1714–27

4 CIVIL AND RELIGIOUS RAGE

> Born to no Pride, inheriting no Strife,
> Nor marrying Discord in a Noble Wife,
> Stranger to Civil and Religious Rage,
> The good Man walk'd innoxious thro' his Age.
>
> *Epistle to Arbuthnot* (*TE*, vol. 4, p. 126)

At first it looked as if the Hanoverians had taken over at the cost of scarcely anything by way of blood, sweat or tears. With remarkably little fuss they had dislodged the Stuart family, who with one brief interregnum had occupied the British throne for more than a century. Of course many people saw the change in a different light – especially in Scotland, where Stuarts (or Stewarts) had reigned since the 1300s. A few riots broke out across the entire country, but nothing on the scale of the protests that had followed the trial of Sacheverell. In earlier centuries, from Saxon times onwards, it had needed civil war, invasion or outright murder to topple a dynasty, and so the legendary importance of battles such as Hastings, Bosworth or Marston Moor. Now in 1714 George I succeeded Anne without any effective resistance in the political class. One tale has it that the High Church Bishop Francis Atterbury (later to become a close friend of Pope) offered to go to Charing Cross in full episcopal regalia, with the intent of proclaiming the Pretender, but most scholars today discount this story. A reputed cabinet in waiting with Sir William Wyndham and other known Jacobites among its number turned overnight into a creation of pure fantasy, about as close to real life as the court of Ruritania.

1

For Oxford's government and its supporters, the sudden transformation took on an aspect both tragic and surreal. 'The Earl of Oxford was remov'd on tuesday, the Queen dyed on sunday', Bolingbroke informed Swift, who was still hiding away in Berkshire. 'What a world is this, and how does fortune banter us?'[1] As we have seen in the previous chapter, Pope was by now on intimate terms with the upper crust of the Tory party. By comparison with most of his friends, he emerged unscathed from the crisis: he had no official post to lose, and no valuable source of income dried up, since he had taken care not to accept large subsidies from the heads of the ministry – which he could certainly have engineered if he had wanted.

As the events unrolled, he redoubled his protestations of neutrality. On or about 25 July 1714 he wrote a letter to John Caryll:

> I find by dear experience, we live in an age, where it is criminal to be moderate; and where no man can be allowed to be just to all men. The notions of right and wrong are so far strain'd, that perhaps to be in the right so very violently, may be of worse consequence than to be easily and quietly in the wrong. I really wish all men so well, that I am satisfied but few can wish me so; but if those few are such as tell me they do, I am content, for they are the best people I know: While you believe me what I profess as to Religion, I can bear any thing the bigotted may say; while Mr. Congreve likes my poetry, I can endure Dennis and a thousand more like him; while the most honest and moral of each party think me no ill man, I can easily support it, tho' the most violent and mad of all parties rose up to throw dirt at me.
>
> (*Corr.*, vol. 1, pp. 238–9)

Perhaps as a mode of evasion, he now turned to his main obsession, the translation of the *Iliad* which he had begun earlier in the year. With affected disdain, he wrote three days later to another new friend, Charles Jervas: 'While you in the world are concerned about the *Protestant* Succession, I consider only how *Menelaus* may recover *Helen* ... I never inquire if the *Queen* be well or not, but heartily wish to be at *Hector*'s funeral' (*Corr.*, vol. 1, p. 240). Jervas, a sociable Irish painter, had studied with Sir Godfrey Kneller. His home close to St James's Palace became Pope's favourite *pied à terre* in London over the next couple of years. He had started to give the poet lessons in his art, and would produce two of the most famous images ever made of Pope, along with portraits of Swift, the Blount sisters, Arbuthnot and Prior. The ambition which his lodger harboured to excel as an artist soon got squeezed out, but it was Homer that did this, not politics. At this moment, indeed, Jervas was sketching the design of a frontispiece for the first volume of the *Iliad*.

In reality, Pope felt more anxious than he let on about what was happening, particularly as far as events affected his own community of Catholics. His next letter to Caryll, written from Binfield on 16 August, sets out some of his worries:

> I could not but take a trip to London on the death of the Queen, moved by the common curiosity of mankind, who leave their business to be looking upon other men's. I thank God that as for myself, I am below all the accidents of state-changes by my circumstances, and above them by my philosophy. Good will to all, are the points I have most at heart; and I am sure those are not to be broken for the sake of any governors or government. I am willing to hope the best and that I more wish than my own or

any particular man's advancement, that this turn may put an end entirely to the divisions of Whig and Tory, that those parties may love each other as well as I love them both, or at least hurt each other as little as I would either; and that our own people may live as quietly as we shall certainly let theirs, that is to say, that want of power itself in us may not be a surer prevention of harm, than want of will in them. I am sure, if all Whigs and all Tories had the spirit of one Roman Catholic that I know, it would be well for all Roman Catholics; and if all Roman Catholics had ever had that spirit, it had been well for all others; and we had never been charged with so wicked a spirit as that of persecution. It is indeed very unjust to judge of us in this nation by what other members of our communion have done abroad. Our Church Triumphant there is very different from our Church Militant here (if I may call that a Church Militant which is every way disarmed).

An even more striking passage follows, which draws attention to the ways in which legislation from the Williamite era might be reactivated:

> The greatest fear I have under the circumstances of a poor papist is the loss of my poor horse; yet if they take it away, I may say with the resignation of Job, tho' not in his very words, Deus dedit, Diabolus abstulit, I thank God I can walk. If I had a house and they took it away, I could go into lodgings; if I had money and they took it away, I could write for my bread (as much better men than I have been often suffered to do); if my own works would not do, I could turn writing master at last and set copies to children.

(Corr., vol. 1, pp. 241–2)

The fears that lay behind all those confident prophecies in *Windsor-Forest* have now come to the surface. It had taken little more than a year for the sylvan idyll to dissipate, as the realities of the new Hanoverian world began to emerge.

Less than two weeks later, Jervas received another message, in which Pope thanked his friend for attempting to heal the breach with Addison. He goes on to describe his obligations to Swift:

> The engagements I had to him were such as the actual services he had done me, in relation to the subscription for Homer, obliged me to. I must have leave to be grateful to him, and to any one who serves me, let him be never so obnoxious to any party: nor did the Tory-party ever put me to the hardship of asking this leave, which is the greatest obligation I owe to it; and I expect no greater from the Whig-party than the same liberty. – A curse on the word Party, which I have been forc'd to use so often in this period! I wish the present Reign may put an end to the distinction, that there may be no other for the future than that of honest and knave, fool and man of sense.

(Corr., vol. 1, p. 245)

Similar views are expressed in a letter to Edward Blount, a distant relative of the Mapledurham family, and a member of the Catholic gentry in Devon. He was one of those active in promoting subscriptions for the new version of Homer, and as will appear in a moment the campaign took up much of Pope's time at this juncture.

The Scriblerus project now stuttered to a halt, for reasons outlined in the last chapter. Swift left for Dublin in the middle of August, and would not see his colleagues again for more than a decade. His hopes of a fat English bishopric had disappeared forever: the future stretched ahead of him in the form of a long exile as Dean of St Patrick's cathedral, stuck in a country he despised even while he fought for its beleaguered political rights. Parnell paid a brief visit to Bath with Pope, but he too departed for Ireland in November. Gay had come back to England without a job or any prospects. On 23 September Pope sent him an intriguing welcome-home message:

> Whether returned a triumphant *Whig* or a desponding *Tory*, equally All Hail! equally beloved and welcome to me! ... If you are a *Tory*, or thought so by any man, I know it can proceed from nothing but your Gratitude to a few people who endeavour'd to serve you, and whose Politicks were never your Concern. If you are a *Whig*, as I rather hope, and as I think your Principles (as Brother Poets) has ever a Byas to the Side of Liberty, I know you will be an honest man and an inoffensive one. Upon the whole, I know you are incapable of being so much of either Party as to be good for nothing.

It may be true that Gay had shown no strong party loyalty to this point, but Pope's identification of poetry with whiggery sounds too much like John Dennis to represent a fully serious equation for a nuanced thinker to offer. The letter goes on,

> The late universal Concern in publick affairs, threw us all into a hurry of Spirits; even I who am more of a Philosopher than to expect any thing from any Reign, was born away with the current, and full of the expectation of the Successor.

(*Corr.*, vol. 1, p. 254)

If this was a sincere account of Pope's instant reactions, his honeymoon with the Hanoverian regime did not last long.

Arbuthnot faced as severe a backlash as anyone: he had to quit his apartment in the palace once he lost his post at court, and took up a much more modest role at Chelsea Hospital, the home for army veterans – there were plenty of those, of course, as a result of the wars under William and Anne. But the new regime also turned him out from unpaid offices that had no obvious link with politics, such as his place on the board of commissioners supervising the construction of the new 'Queen Anne' churches in London. By now almost everything had a party-political side to it somewhere.

Early in September, Arbuthnot suggested to Pope a way in which the aborted Scriblerian enterprise might be turned to a new purpose. He deplored the fact that the drafts of their satires had not been sealed up as had recently happened to Bolingbroke's papers by government order:

> Then might Scriblerus have pass'd for the Pretender, and it would have been a most excellent and laborious work for the Flying Post [a Whig newspaper] or some such author, to have allegoriz'd all his adventures into a plot, and found out mysteries somewhat like the Key to the Lock.
>
> (*Corr.*, vol. 1, p. 251)

Byplay of this sort cannot mask the worries that people like the doctor were now experiencing, as the ruling powers began to close in on the old administration and its servants. For the moment, Oxford retained his liberty, as did Bolingbroke – though he quickly lost his post as Secretary of State. However, no one knew how long this situation would last. Pope sent off some cheerful and easy-going letters to the Blount sisters, and joked about Gay's uncertainties in a message to Charles Ford, a likeable Irish friend of Swift who had come to live not far from Jervas. For a brief spell Pope was in Bath: 'If he [Gay] is afraid of corresponding with Tories, tell him I am a Whig, and he may write to me hither, till the end of next week, by which time I will be at London or in Berkshire' (*Corr.*, vol. 1, p. 259). The jocularity helped to defuse a situation fraught with all kinds of embarrassment. Ford himself had served under Lord Oxford as gazetteer, in effect the government's public relations officer. He must have expected that he would be hauled in to give evidence before the upcoming commissions of inquiry, and at worst that he would be named among the guilty men.

On 20 October the coronation of the new King took place at Westminster Abbey. Pope could hardly have expected an invitation, but he seems to have stayed in London until returning to Binfield after the ceremony. Unfortunately Martha Blount fell victim to one of the scourges of the day, smallpox, a few years before Lady Mary Wortley Montagu helped to popularize the new technique of inoculation. She soon recovered but may have been left with scars. At this stage Teresa still exercised the greater sexual magnetism over Pope, and it was probably the elder sister whom he addressed in his *Epistle to Miss Blount, on her Leaving the Town, after the Coronation*, written shortly afterwards. This is the finest of all his short poems, composed with a Mozartian deftness and precision. Within its short compass it versifies the round of a young lady of fashion, now condemned to tedious rural life, with the same brilliant economy of means as *The Rape of the Lock*. Like a skilled novelist, Pope had the knack of entering into the feelings of other people; and of course the partial feminization of his upbringing, as a result of his ill health, may have helped him to understand more fully than his male contemporaries the daily course of women's emotional lives.

Late in the year, shortly after he had paid a visit to Mapledurham, Pope dispatched one of his courtly yet jocose letters to Martha Blount. As usual, the political and religious references nearly all take a comic tone:

> Every one values Mr Pope, but every one for a different reason. One for his firm Adherence to the Catholic Faith, another for his Neglect of Popish Succession, one

for his grave behavior, another for his Whymsicalness. Mr Tydcomb for his pretty Atheistical Jests, Mr Caryl for his moral and christian Sentences, Mrs Teresa for his Reflections on Mrs Patty, and Mrs Patty for his Reflections on Mrs Teresa.

The next comment harks back to the heroine of *The Rape of the Lock*, and her recent marriage to Francis Perkins:

> My Acquaintance runs so much in an anti-Catholic Channel, that it was but tother day I heard of Mrs Fermor's being Actually, directly, and consummatively, married. I wonder how the guilty Couple and their Accessories at Whitenights look, stare, or simper, since that grand Secret came out which they so well concealed before.
>
> (*Corr.*, vol. 1, p. 269)

This passage occurs in the middle of a resolutely facetious message, and we should not put too much weight on it. Nevertheless we cannot miss Pope's determination to present himself as a citizen of the political world with ecumenical leanings. However, his correspondence shows that he retained contact with his old friends, most of them (apart from Trumbull) members of the Catholic gentry. It is not that his protestations are wholly without foundation, but they reveal less than the full truth.

2

In the early months of 1715, the forthcoming appearance of the first volume of the *Iliad* translation dominated Pope's mind. If he had known what was to follow in this momentous year, he might have found it more difficult to keep his full concentration on the matter in hand, but it is unlikely he would have allowed affairs of state wholly to distract him. Technical problems meant that publication could not take place until early June. When it did appear, the translation evoked a variety of responses – many of them, both for and against, coloured by political and religious prejudice, strange as such a thing may seem to us today.

The strenuous campaign to garner subscriptions in advance has become famous in literary history. This is mainly because of the financial success that Pope achieved, which in turn enabled him to acquire an unprecedented degree of independence for the rest of his career. He had made himself the first true professional poet, that is to say the first major English writer who made his way without support by means of patronage, official appointments or a private fortune. Nor, though he utilized the modern instrument of the book trade, was he reliant on publishers in the way that most authors would be from this time onwards. Over the years he came in effect to employ men like Bernard Lintot as sub-contractors, while retaining the valuable rights to his works. In one way this behaviour represented a blow in the battle to gain independence for authors generally, but it must be admitted that Pope's motives were largely self-interested.

Very few of his colleagues could hope to make the same sort of deal that he did, and hardly anybody until the nineteenth century enjoyed the same degree of freedom within the profession of letters.[2] As for Pope, the Homer translations gave him something more than an assured income not dependent on the fluctuations of power at Westminster. Equally important was the prestige in society which came with this. Increasingly he moved among the elite of the nation, paying extended visits to the country houses of the aristocracy, and advising their owners on the layout of their estates. We cannot claim that he lived on terms of complete equality with dukes and duchesses, counts and countesses. The social gap was simply too wide to bridge in this way, even after he set up his genteel residence at Twickenham. At the end of his visit to a stately home everyone knew that Mr Pope, for all his eminence and cultivation, would be returning to a modest villa with a postage-stamp garden.

As soon as he embarked on his work, Pope saw the need to rustle up a sufficient core of subscribers. He had the help of Swift, who was lobbying on his behalf by late 1713, soon after proposals were issued. On 19 November he could inform Trumbull that 'almost all the distinguished names of Quality or Learning have subscribed to it',[3] though this was of course an exaggeration. Others who aided in the campaign were John Caryll, John Gay and Matthew Prior. The deal for the buyers was that they should pay one guinea (£1.05) for each of the six volumes, with two guineas down at the start, and then a guinea each for the second, third, fourth and fifth instalments. In the end Pope procured 575 subscribers, with multiple copies bringing the total up to 654 sets. Among these multiple subscribers were peers known to Pope, such as Bolingbroke, Buckingham, Caernarvon (later Duke of Chandos), Halifax, Harcourt and George, Lord Lansdowne. It made up a large list by the standards of the time, although not extraordinarily so. Its particular distinction lay in the great names Pope had attracted. The average age came out around 39; some 8 per cent were women – about the norm for such books – and the only member of the royal family present was the Princess of Wales, later Queen Caroline. Lintot paid Pope 200 guineas (£210) for each of the volumes at dates between 23 March 1715 and 26 February 1720. In addition, Pope had the proceeds of the subscription volumes, and he cleared an estimated £5,000 overall. Financially it was the turning point in his career, and it enabled him to move to Twickenham.

The subscription list offers a fascinating insight into the market for Pope's translation. Of course we must not confuse subscribers with readers, and the poet obviously could not claim personal acquaintance with everyone whose name appears. Nevertheless, used with care, the list does reveal some important facts. Students of Pope have been misled by the presence of many government ministers and Whig potentates, along with a few courtiers – even the King's mistress. Naturally the poet needed to get as many leading figures in the state as possible to enhance the prestige of the venture. The fact that Whig politicians such as Walpole, Stanhope, Townshend and even the Duke of Marlborough appear on the list can largely be explained in these terms. So, too, in view of their high cultural visibility, can the presence of Addison, Rowe, Steele and other well-known writers. Moreover, many of the most prominent literary patrons belonged to the ruling party, among them peers such as Halifax, Somers and Sunderland. Equally crucial was the suffrage of James Brydges, later Duke of Chandos, who could afford to enter subscriptions for multiple copies (in effect an outright gift). A savvy political operator, he was in the process of disengaging himself from an alliance with the Harley faction and making friends with the new regime. The roll of subscribers records him as having ordered twelve copies of the *Iliad*.

What these facts conceal is the heavy Tory bias of the list as a whole, something that becomes apparent if we move down a notch or two on the social scale. Consider, for example, the tally of members of parliament. At least 75 MPs elected in 1715 figure on the roster, almost one seventh of the total count of members. Many others were Tories who had held a seat when the subscriptions were collected, but lost it at the general election. Even among sitting MPs, however, a large group belonged to the Tory rump. Jacobites are heavily represented, including the Duke of Berwick (natural son of the deposed King, and thus half-brother to the Pretender), Bolingbroke, Lansdowne, Mar, Ormonde, Strafford and Wyndham. Less prominent supporters of the cause include Pope's close ally Father Thomas Southcott, as well as Arbuthnot's brother Robert. Several individuals took up arms for the Stuarts – we have incidentally two natural sons of Charles II and a grandson – and were arrested for their pains. By far the most striking case is the Earl of Derwentwater, who ended up headless on Tower Hill only months after the first volume of the translation came before the public. The High Tory pressure group known as the October Club supplies at least fifteen names. Naturally the Scriblerus group and their friends in the Harley circle all show up, including Lord Bathurst and Matthew Prior. Some thirty Roman Catholics can be identified, with an especially intriguing batch from the Petre family. Arabella Fermor and her kinsfolk do not put in an appearance.

All these figures represent abnormally high tallies, if we compare the spread with a typically Whig list such as that mounted for Addison's collected works in 1721. The same difference emerges if we turn to the university background of subscribers. Alumni of the proverbially Tory Oxford supply a full hundred names, not including ten institutional subscriptions. By contrast traditionally Whig Cambridge provides only thirty such names. The most striking feature here is the presence of thirty individuals from Christ Church, the epicentre of High Church ecclesiology and High Tory politics, followed by Trinity and Magdalen. For Cambridge the only comparable return comes from Trinity, a large but now bitterly divided college under Richard Bentley. It should be added that the two most distinguished persons on the entire list, along with Marlborough, are Sir Isaac Newton, a product of Trinity, and Sir Christopher Wren, who had designed its noble library.

What does all this tell us? Pope reached a total of 575 subscribers, large but not unprecedentedly so. More impressive was his coverage of the good and great, including the reigning Whig potentates. The spread as regards age and gender came to about the average. However, the most distinctive feature of the *Iliad* list beyond doubt lies in its Tory bias, and its unmistakable whiff of Jacobite sympathies. Of course, this does not establish anything definitive about the poet's own beliefs or attachments. It does however provide concrete evidence which strongly suggests that Pope had come into contact with a disproportionate number of people who might have looked favourably on the Stuart cause. This may simply derive from his religion, or from the kind of persons he had encountered through living in a recusant family within the Thames valley basin, where many of the Catholic gentry had retired. It may also reflect the views of those who worked most ardently to promote his campaign on behalf of his translation.

As he laboured to get the subscriptions off the ground, Pope received the offer of a pension from Lord Halifax, who had supported him earlier. A leading figure in national affairs under King William, he served as an MP, Chancellor of the Exchequer and First Lord of the Treasury. As a member of the Whig Junto, he was involved in the foundation of the Bank of England and in the recoinage of the 1690s. From 1695 to 1698 he served as President of the Royal Society. He was created a baron in 1700, and an earl in 1714. At the time of the Hanoverian accession he was again appointed to the head of the government, but his health did not allow him to take an active share in power. Halifax had been a supporter of Matthew Prior, his schoolmate, and also of Joseph Addison, his protégé; but the reputation he acquired suggests that he was sometimes a distant and condescending patron, even though he received an impressive barrage of tributes from aspiring authors. A minor poet in his own right, he earned a small niche in the *Lives of the Poets* by Samuel Johnson. Halifax was appointed First Lord of Treasury to head the new Whig administration, and this prospect of official patronage evidently tempted Pope, at least for a short time.

In the preface to the *Iliad*, Pope acknowledged the kindness of Halifax, who 'was one of the first to favour me'.[4] But even before these words appeared in print, the Earl, who subscribed for ten sets, had died. Despite his public tribute, Pope referred privately to Halifax in somewhat equivocal terms. He told Joseph Spence that 'the famous Lord Halifax was rather a pretender to taste than really possessed of it'. As proof, he recounted the episode when Halifax asked him to read the early books of the *Iliad* at his house, with Addison, Congreve and Garth in attendance After asking for small changes, Halifax showed delight at the 'revisions' shown to him, when Pope brought the original text back a few weeks later

(*Anecdotes*, vol. 1, pp. 87–8). It is possible that 'Bufo', the complacent patron of the *Epistle to Arbuthnot*, is based in part on Halifax. On the other hand the reference in the *Epilogue to the Satires* is a kind one, augmented by a note reading 'A peer no less distinguished by his love of letters than his abilities in Parliament' (*TE*, vol. 4, p. 317). Perhaps the decision Pope took to reject the offer was influenced by the cool and dilatory response he received from the minister. Nevertheless, it marked a crucial moment in his career, and helped to define his relation to the political world for the rest of his life.

Afterwards Pope would insist on his personal stance of moderation, expressed in the first and arguably the best of his *Imitations of Horace*:

> My Head and Heart thus flowing thro' my Quill,
> Verse-man or Prose-man, term me which you will,
> Papist or Protestant, or both between,
> Like good Erasmus in an honest Mean,
> In Moderation placing all my Glory,
> While Tories call me Whig, and Whigs a Tory.

(*TE*, vol. 4, p. 11)

Was it really possible for him to listen to the promptings of his head, and quell the feelings that may have welled up in his heart during the tumultuous events of 1715 and 1716? No definitive answer emerges, but the evidence suggests it was extremely hard for him to stand on the sidelines and watch with cold detachment. However strong his reservations about the Pretender, he must have found it insufferable when his religion was decried so vociferously as the agent of treachery and sedition. The fate in store for so many friends who had unwisely enlisted under the banner of James VII would have crushed a less sensitive spirit than his own. Apart from that, it was a time when men and women of good will from all parties had trouble in detecting an honest mean to which they could cling.

At the start of 1715 Pope may have believed that his prospects were good, with the *Iliad* on its way, and his accomplished rendition of Chaucer, *The Temple of Fame*, issued by Lintot in February. That same month he could rejoice in the success of Gay's 'tragi-comi-pastoral' *The What d'ye Call It*, which pleased all sections of the town. He perhaps contributed to the play, though not as much as critics of the day supposed. By April he felt confident enough to bring out *The Key to the Lock*, written a year earlier, with its straight-faced reading of the *Rape* as a Catholic allegory of the recent war. In this account, the lock itself represents the Barrier Treaty, a convention of mutual support to which the British and the Dutch signed up in 1709. Belinda is Great Britain itself, while the Baron is the Earl of Oxford; Clarissa is the Queen's confidante Lady Masham, the virago Thalestris is the Duchess of Marlborough, and the foppish Sir Plume is absurdly cast as one of the leaders of the alliance, grim Prince Eugene of Austria. The boat trip down the Thames in Canto 2 is interpreted as the foundation of the

South Sea Company, and Belinda's lapdog Shock stands for Dr Sacheverell. The mythological machinery satirizes the negotiations conducted by the ministry, and the whole poem 'has a Tendency to Popery'.[5] Preposterously, but somehow almost plausibly, the smallest detail is made to fit the theory: Belinda's bodkin can become Anne's sceptre, the lines about the fall of the towers of Troy can refer to the destruction of the Dunkirk defences – and so on. This ingenious misreading by the putative author, 'Esdras Barnivelt', demonstrating Pope's secret message, exaggerates only by a shade many serious onslaughts on his loyalty and morality. The *Key* ends by recommending that the authorities should take into custody Bernard Lintot, who had published the poem, and interrogate him as to what he knew. It sounds absurd; but many hapless booksellers and printers found themselves subjected to precisely this treatment. For all its sparkling comedy, we can hardly fail to recognize that the pamphlet taps into some deep anxieties.

Soon the outlook began to darken for Pope and his closest friends. A general election early in the year saw an almost total reversal in the make-up of the new parliament, which met in March with a Whig majority of well over one hundred. On 26 March Bolingbroke fled to France and joined the court of the Pretender. As one story has it, Marlborough had tipped him off that his arrest was imminent. It seemed a precipitate act to many, and his unhappy spell as Secretary of State for the Jacobites' shadow administration would soon end ingloriously, meaning that he slunk back home to ask for a pardon. But, in harsh reality, parliament was going to impeach him if he stayed behind. As the leading architect of the peace process, he would have found it more difficult than anyone else in the outgoing government to ward off the charges. Meanwhile the net closed in on Oxford, as well as Bolingbroke's chief operative during the peace negotiations, the poet Matthew Prior. The government put its fairly primitive intelligence agency to work in the hope of hauling in more evidence: censors opened up the Irish mail and searched Swift's correspondence for damaging material. However, the Dean proved canny enough to avoid any obvious sign of guilt.

Throughout the summer, things continued to get blacker. A parliamentary committee was set up to investigate the misdeeds of the former ministers, with a rising star among the Whigs, Robert Walpole, at its head. When the committee instituted a series of interrogations, Oxford and Prior received some rough handling by an old enemy of the ex-Prime Minister, Thomas Coningsby, whose family had battled with the Harleys for control of Herefordshire over several generations. This inveterate persecutor would continue his private vendetta in years to come, and would earn some scornful references in the poetry of Pope. A major fear of the Tories was that Prior, a man who knew too much, would capitulate in the face of the inquisition. Luckily for them he refused to spill the beans. Meanwhile Oxford obstinately refused to save himself by decamping to the Continent, a course of action that the ministry would have been quite happy to see him take as an admission of guilt. Early in June, Coningsby proposed to the House of Commons that Oxford should be arraigned along with Bolingbroke. Parliament agreed, and on the 16th the Earl was dispatched to the Tower of London. Prior was also committed to custody, as was another key player in the peace negotiations, Lord Strafford. In his periodicals Steele kept up an unceasing barrage against his opponents, collecting post and pensions as he did. At the same time Addison, as a senior functionary, helped to implement government policy: the breach with Pope had now grown irreparable. So began the protracted effort of the Whigs to bring Oxford to book on a charge of high treason – the last such impeachment of an ex-minister in British history, paralleled in the United States only by the two instances of Andrew Johnson and Bill Clinton.

Amid all the pressures of the moment Pope found time to write a characteristic short ballad under the title of *A Farewell to London*. It describes the lively dissipations of the town, which the poet is now about to quit for the 'sober, studious Days' (*TE*, vol. 6, p. 130) he will pass in the country in order to complete the second volume of his *Iliad*. The form allows Pope to pay generous tributes to patrons such as the recently deceased Halifax and friends such as Gay and Arbuthnot, with his 'raillery' on pretentious fools. It also reveals that he had made the acquaintance of Lord Burlington, a young architect earl who had just returned from a Grand Tour of Italy, unusually disciplined and educative at an age when many peers simply took the chance to fly the coop and taste the pleasures of the senses under the undemanding guidance of a hired tutor. This meeting had consequences both in the short and the long term. Soon afterwards Pope would settle with his family near Burlington's home at Chiswick, and he would find a congenial neighbour in the cultivated Earl. Later Burlington became a supporter of Pope's experiments in garden design and would receive the homage of a noble verse epistle which singled out his friend as the embodiment of good taste in the arts.

But such relaxing moments proved hard to find, as tensions continued to mount. Street protests by Jacobites caused enough alarm for the government to introduce the famous Riot Act in early July, imposing tough penalties on anyone who failed to disperse when required. If twelve persons or more were deemed to be assembling for an unlawful purpose, they faced arrest if they did not immediately break up when a justice of the peace proclaimed the act 'in a loud voice': it was not necessary for a riot actually to take place. The measure (1 Geo. I, c. 5, s. 2) still makes for instructive reading. Pope witnessed these events mainly from Binfield, but he came up to London at intervals. On 23 July he wrote a long and informative letter to the Blount sisters, which modulates from sober fact to a desperate kind of comedy. He commends the behaviour of Lord Oxford: 'The utmost Weight of Affliction from Princely Power and Popular Hatred, were almost worth bearing for the Glory of such a dauntless Conduct as he has shown under it'. He notes the departure from England of another Tory champion, the Duke of Ormonde, who had followed Bolingbroke into exile: '[He] is retired and become a Rival of the Courage of that other Noble Lord'. His account of the Pretender's rumoured arrival takes a deliberately facetious tone:

> You may soon have your Wish to enjoy the Gallant Sights of Armies, Campagnes, Standards waving over your Brother's Cornfields, and the pretty windings of the Thames about Mapledurham, staind with the blood of Men. Your Barbarity which I have heard so long exclaim'd against in Town and Country, may have its fill of destruction.

In expectation of this assault, the authorities had set up a military camp in Hyde Park. Once more Pope treats this ominous development in an apparently casual air, suggesting that the young ladies at Mapledurham would be erotically gratified by a glimpse of so many dashing young soldiers:

> Those Eyes that care not how much Mischief is done, or how great Slaughter committed, so they have but a fine show; those Very-female Eyes will be infinitely delighted with the Camp which is speedily to be form'd in Hyde park. The Tents are carried thither this morning, New Regiments ready rais'd, with new Clothes and Furniture (far exceeding the late Cloth and Linnen designd by his Grace for the Soldiery.) The sight of so many thousand gallant Fellows, with all the Pomp and Glare of Warr yet undeformed with battle, those Scenes which England has for many years only beheld on Stages, may possibly invite your Curiosity to this place.

The next sentence reads, 'My Lady Lansdowne held her *Last* Assembly yesterday', and there follows a list of social junketings. It would be hard to deduce that the lady's husband, Pope's patron for *Windsor-Forest*, was busy at this very moment helping to organize the rising on behalf of the Pretender: or that Pope most likely suspected, if he did not know for certain, that this was the case. After this comes a mock newspaper story, concerning the Catholic gentleman Thomas Gage, who had been stripped of his Flanders mares and in despair had taken the oath abjuring the Stuart cause. The passage ends, 'The poor distressed Roman Catholicks, now Un-hors'd and Un-charioted, cry out with the Psalmist: Some in Chariots, and some in Horses, but We will invocate the name of the Lord' (*Corr.*, vol. 1, pp. 307–9). This flippant turn of phrase, utilizing Pope's own translation of Psalm 20 in the Vulgate, can be seen as one sort of response to the desperate circumstances. A week later the poet wrote again to the sisters, this time from Binfield, as the ten-mile Act had been reactivated on 27 July and papists had been ordered to quit the capital. He even included a bitter little joke about the Riot Act. He had been planning a trip to Devon with Arbuthnot, Jervas and another friend, the playboy 'Duke' Disney, but events caused them to postpone this – the party had hoped to stop at Sir William Wyndham's seat near Taunton in Somerset.

Unfortunately Sir William was up to his eyes in the conspiracy and it would have been a very inopportune moment to call at Orchard Wyndham.

The shockwave many people had been dreading for months finally struck on 6 September. That day the Earl of Mar sounded the 'trumpet blast' in the north, when he raised the banner of James VII at a specially convened hunting party held near Braemar. This ushered in the contest which had been simmering in one way or another for a quarter of a century, ever since William and Mary had arrived to oust the Pretender's father from the throne. We do not know Pope's immediate reactions, since his correspondence goes into something of a lull around the date. By the time that normal service was fully resumed, the rising was all but spent. On 13 November the Jacobites met with a double blow: the progress of the Highlanders under Lord Mar was arrested by the Duke of Argyll's army at Sheriffmuir, near Stirling, while the invading force of Lowlanders and northern recusants was brought to a halt at Preston in Lancashire, with many of the leaders captured. Pope received a gloomy letter from his friend in Devon, Edward Blount: 'What a dismal scene has there been open'd in the North? what ruin have those unfortunate rash gentlemen drawn upon themselves and their miserable followers, and perchance upon many others too, who upon no account would be their followers?' (*Corr.*, vol. 1, p. 320). Blount could write of peace and quiet in his own part of the country, but only because the south-western invasion by the Duke of Ormonde had been aborted. Promptly the authorities took up the two commanders who had stayed in England, Lord Lansdowne and Sir William Wyndham. Pope could not pretend any longer that events were unrolling at a safe distance. Even Blount, who opposed the rising, felt compelled to leave the country a year later and move to Bruges. At this fraught time it was not enough for a Catholic to be less than an active Jacobite.

So the inglorious rebellion stuttered to its close. The Pretender himself delayed his arrival in Scotland until just before Christmas, and after a certain amount of marching up to the top of the hill and marching down again he slunk back to France with Mar in early February. There followed a process of rounding up as many as possible of those involved in the rising, at whatever level. The government dispatched the principal leaders, mostly captured at Preston, to await their trial in the Tower of London. When they came before the court little mercy was shown, though in the end only three rebel lords were beheaded. By an act of official mercy, they were spared on account of their rank the ritual drawing and quartering that should have befallen a traitor. The severed heads were nailed up on Temple Bar – a message intended, as far as the behaviour of the Catholic population went, *pour encourager les autres*. Of the remaining Jacobite leaders, some got away with a milder sentence and some managed to escape, perhaps with the connivance of the authorities. Through the summer of 1716 a stream of lesser figures who had taken up arms passed through the courts, as a rabble of dispirited prisoners were dragged through the streets amid derisive hoots from the populace.

By far the most important of the Jacobite martyrs was James Radcliffe, third Earl of Derwentwater. This arose partly from his youth and good looks (he was only twenty-six when he went to the executioner's block), but it owed much also to his connections and to the eloquent speech he made on conviction, refusing to disavow his beliefs. It so happens that he had a number of close links with the Pope circle. The Earl came from an old Catholic family in Northumberland. His mother was a natural daughter of Charles II, and so he was a first cousin once removed of the Pretender, with whom he passed his boyhood at St Germain. In February 1716 Derwentwater faced a charge of high treason as one of the leaders of the Jacobite rising. Before his trial he had received advice from the Catholic barristers Nathaniel Pigott, who came to be one of Pope's most trusted counsellors, and Henry Eyre, whose mother was a member of the Bedingfield family. In addition the Earl's wife, formerly Anna Maria Webb, was a relative of John Caryll. She accompanied her husband into his lodgings in the Tower and campaigned to have him released. After his conviction, she went with a number of peeresses on 22 February to lobby both houses of parliament. Anna Maria and her supporters still held high hopes of a reprieve, but when Robert Walpole told the Commons that Derwentwater's friends had offered him a bribe of £60,000 – an immense sum in those days – the house voted to defer the issue.

It was now too late for the government to change course. In his last days the Earl sent Anna Maria a moving letter that repeated his enduring love for her. The execution took place on 24 February, when Derwentwater together with Lord Kenmure stepped out onto a special platform erected on Tower Hill and covered with black serge. A large crowd mustered, as it did at most state executions, to see 'what was at its core a grisly morality play'.[6] It would be a day long remembered in Stuart mythology. Much later Pope reflected on the mutability of things when his carriage happened to be drawn by a horse which had borne the Earl at the battle of Preston, an event that marked the end of the Jacobites' hopes (*Corr.*, vol. 2, p. 513). James Radcliffe's brother Charles, who had also been taken at Preston and condemned to death, managed to escape from Newgate prison to the Continent – not the only fugitive at this time from that leaky fortress. (Charles did not learn from his experience: after the second rising he was beheaded in 1746 on his return to England, a sign that memories were long.) Some years after the execution of the Earl, his daughter Maria Barbara went on to marry the son of Robert, seventh Baron Petre, whom we have encountered as the original of the character in *The Rape of the Lock*. Crucially, from Pope's point of view, Derwentwater had an affectionate relationship with Lady Swinburne, whose father Anthony Englefield was an early friend of the poet, and who was thus an aunt of the Blount sisters. In addition her husband, one of the twenty-four children produced by Sir John and Catherine Swinburne, was a first cousin of the Earl. Several of these intricate patterns of kinship can be traced in the subscription list for the *Iliad*, where Derwentwater's name appeared less than a year before he was beheaded.

The case of Derwentwater marked only the most conspicuous of many stories, involving families such as the Swinburnes. Edward and James Swinburne, sons of Pope's friend, the former Mary Englefield, were both captured at Preston, and each was sentenced to death on 4 June. James had suffered a mental breakdown while confined in the Fleet prison (called in as an emergency overflow jail), and though his plea of insanity at his trial was rejected, he was subsequently described as 'quite and clean out of his wits, and stark-staring mad'. According to a press report,

> Swinburne (who is a Lunatick) has renew'd his Outrages; he broke out of the Castle into the Press-Yard [in Newgate], knock'd down two of the Centinels, and 'twas long before the Turnkeys could master him; he is since plac'd under a more strict Guard, at a doctors.[7]

Within a few weeks James managed to escape, but he does not seem ever to have recovered his sanity. We can easily imagine the pain with which his mother and her friend Pope received this news.

Meanwhile his brother Edward died before sentence could be carried out. His estates were 'sold for the use of the public' in June 1719, with a price of £5,000 set by the Commissioners for Forfeited Estates, who in the aftermath of the rising had carried out reprisals of considerable savagery. Lady Swinburne entered a petition in which she claimed that some of the lands belonged to her grandson, Sir John, who was a minor, and should not have been taken; but the Commissioners turned a deaf ear.[8] Pope cannot have failed to learn of the travails of Mary Swinburne, whose husband had been arrested at the start of the rebellion, and had been forced to send the eldest son and heir John abroad for protection with his priest-tutor. However, two of the daughters acted as dispatch-riders for the rebels in Northumberland.[9] Few families in the entire land can have been so extensively implicated in the Jacobite insurrection. Hardly had the rebellion been quelled, and the rebel lords executed, when Sir William died, shortly after he had been released from custody.[10]

Just how wrapped up in this affair did Pope and the Blount sisters become? We get important clues from an unusually candid passage in the poet's letter to Caryll on 10 January 1716:

> I have made several offers of visiting Lady Swinburne, but herself and her friends [are] somewhat delicate as to my waiting upon her in the place where she now is. I have given them to understand, however, how desirous I should be of any occasion of testifying for her that benevolence and regard, which both her own merit, misfortune,

and, added to those, your friendship for her, challenge from me. The Mapledurham ladies (if they be any longer called so, since their brother makes so much haste to an alienation of his affections another way) are not so unfortunate in particular, but sensible enough (I can assure you) to be very much so in partaking the afflictions of others: Their behaviour is generous and exemplary on this occasion. I question whether, the time considered, their sorrows are not more seasonable than their brother's loves?

(*Corr.*, vol. 1, p. 427)

This significant message gives a better idea of the situation of the Catholic gentry than anything else in the poet's correspondence. We need first to remark that on the previous day Derwentwater and the other rebel lords had been carried from the Tower to the House of Lords to undergo formal impeachment for high treason. Mary Swinburne appears to have followed her husband to jail: a newsletter reported on 14 January that Sir William had been taken into custody (again?), but did not say where he was confined. Understandably Mary's 'friends' – probably meaning here 'relatives' – did not wish Pope to visit there. The Blount ladies behaved with sympathy and affection. Meanwhile Michael seems to be obsessed with his private emotional affairs, not altogether surprising perhaps since his marriage to Mary Agnes Tichborne had taken place only a few months before. For a reason not specified in Pope's letter, the Blount family had some special connection to events – one that we shall explore shortly.

Worse would befall poor Anna Maria Radcliffe, who made a similar claim to that of Lady Swinburne. This was on behalf of her infant children John and Anna Maria, stating that they had been denied necessary support and maintenance. She contended that though John's peerage had been surrendered by the act of attainder against her husband, the boy was entitled to the estates since he had inherited them 'in tail male' (that is, by an entailment) rather than by fee simple or freehold. Since the Commissioners had assessed her husband's estates at well over £6,000, the loss was obviously immense. Initially her appeal was brusquely refused by the Commissioners.[11] In due course her father Sir John Webb spent over £1,000 on legal fees in attempting to recover the property.

Her story is a pathetic one. She had met her future husband while still a girl at the Ursuline Covent in Paris. At this time the nuns bore some renowned Catholic names familiar to Pope like Petre, Englefield, Fermor, Perkins, Gage, Howard – not to mention those that recalled Jacobites caught up in the 1715 rebellion, such as Towneley and Widdrington. The couple married in 1712, when the bride brought with her a splendid dowry of £12,000, to be paid at stated intervals. On 13 July the Earl wrote to Mary Swinburne, 'I was married to great content on Thursday last. My dear wife, her father and mother, charm me more and more.'[12] The full dowry would never become due, and the marriage would last less than four years. Anna Maria was just twenty-two at the time of the rebellion, and pregnant with her daughter, born after her husband went to the block. For a period she relied for support at her father's home in Gloucestershire: he at first retired to the Continent after the Earl's execution, but afterwards came back to act as guardian to her children. In 1720 her little boy was finally restored to the family estates. Next year Lady Derwentwater moved to Brussels to give her children a Catholic education. Sadly she fell victim to the great scourge of those times, smallpox: her burial took place in August 1723 at the convent at Louvain, where Mary and Catherine, her husband's aunts, were both nuns. Again Sir John had to pay for the funeral and discharge the debts that his daughter had incurred. After her death parliament passed a law retrospectively amending the Naturalization Act of 1708, to ensure that any child born abroad whose father had been attainted of high treason should lose rights of citizenship. The obvious aim was to exclude the Earl's son from his inheritance, so that the Derwentwater properties would revert to the Crown. As it happened, young John Radcliffe died shortly afterwards at the age of only eighteen, following an unsuccessful operation to remove kidney stones carried out by William Cheselden, a close friend of Pope who later performed surgery on the poet. The kind of treatment meted out to the Radcliffes makes it hard to resist the conclusion of some historians that the English Catholics had been chosen as scapegoats for the rising.[13]

One more circumstance, missed by all students of Pope, makes it clear why the fate of the rebels had an immediate interest to the poet and his circle. It now turns out that Martha and Teresa were, as these things were defined then, sisters-in-law of the Earl and Anna Maria. To see this, we have to follow a chain of intermarriages within the same generation which would have hardly any significance today, but which in earlier times (especially inside the close-knit Catholic community) meant very much more. The line of connection is this. Michael Blount married Mary Agnes, who was the daughter of Sir Henry Tichborne, a member of a very long established recusant family in northern Hampshire, best known today because of the story of the Tichborne claimant in the Victorian age.[14] One of Mary Agnes's sisters, Frances, married George Brownlow Doughty, of Beenham in Berkshire, while another, Mabella, married John Webb, brother of Anna Maria Radcliffe. Thus the catena extended in a horizontal line across the family tree, reaching from the Blount girls to the Earl. People *routinely* described such relatives as brothers or sisters, meaning of course in-laws. We know that these family links were well preserved: for example, Michael mentions Doughty in his will. He is probably the 'Mr Dowty' who, according to gossip passed on to the Blounts, had professed that he did not have 'any designs' upon the young Belle Fermor.[15]

We can summarize the relationships in diagrammatic form like this:

Blount	Tichbornes	Webbs	Radcliffes
Martha, Theresa, Michael	Mary Agnes, Marbella	John, Anna Maria	James (Earl of Derwentwater)
→	→	→	

Moreover, it is possible to trace immediate links between members of this genealogical chain and Pope, who wrote to Caryll of services his friend had rendered to 'Sir H: T: and Mr B:' at the time of Michael's wedding in 1715 (*Corr.*, vol. 1, p. 313). In the same year Sir Harry Tichborne subscribed to the *Iliad*, although he was later among the few defaulters, as Pope told Caryll in 1718 (*Corr.*, vol. 1, p. 464). After Tichborne's death the baronetcy passed to his grandson, also named Henry, who married Michael Blount's daughter Mary. As for Sir John Webb, he too contributed to the Homer subscription. He named in his will his 'kinsman' Edward Webb, thought to be Pope's schoolmate under Thomas Deane. When Catherine Englefield, widow of Pope's friend Henry, married Edward Webb in 1732, the marriage settlement named John Caryll and Michael Blount as trustees.[16] Generally Sir John kept a low profile, but he declared his readiness to subscribe the tidy sum of £500 when the rising was being planned.[17] By themselves such facts may appear trivial or unrevealing. In combination they help to show that Pope and his immediate circle were more closely involved with the rebellion than has ever been properly appreciated. Many figures implicated in the rising were people they knew well, and one – the most conspicuous of those flaunted before the public in the trial of the rebel lords – was actually 'family' for Martha and Teresa.[18]

Yet, if we can trust the published correspondence, Pope maintained an attitude of studied neutrality, as when he printed a letter to Sir William Trumbull dated 16 December 1715 which contains this passage:

> I heartily joyn with you in wishing Quiet to our native country: Quiet in the state, which like charity in religion, is too much the perfection and happiness of either, to be broken or violated on any pretence or prospect whatsoever: Fire and sword, and fire and faggot are equally my aversion. I can pray for opposite parties, and for opposite religions, with great sincerity. I think to be a lover of one's Country is a glorious Elogy, but I do not think it so great an one as to be a lover of Mankind.
>
> (*Corr.*, vol. 1, p. 324)

However, we now have the opening fragments of this letter and a reply from Trumbull, and it is pretty clear that the printed letter was stuck together in the 1730s from other messages written at a slightly different date, as often happened.[19] If we could see all the originals, we might find that Pope took a less guarded line to his friends in 1715/16 than it was necessary for him to claim later in life. Arbuthnot makes an interesting observation in a message from the group to Parnell: 'Mr pope delays his Second Volume of his Homer till the Martial Spirit of the Rebells is quite quelld, it being judgd that his first part did some harm that way' (*Corr.*, vol. 1, p. 332). The poet needed to tread cautiously.

It is natural to ask what difference it would have made if the Pretender had succeeded and – an unlikely thought – managed to get an effective hold on all the machinery of government. This was after all a dynastic struggle from start to finish: it did not concern economic policy, the structure of society or other ideological issues which have come to dominate modern politics. Obviously a different scenario would show the new King James reliant on the Tory party. Of course the Whigs harboured not a single Jacobite, even though a few of their number such as Lord Sunderland might have been persuaded to come over to the winning side. The chances of such a switch rose if their only other option was to trust their fortunes to an exiled Georgite faction with a shadow court at some tinpot town on the plains of Brunswick. A restored Stuart monarchy would have had to reach out to moderate Tories to get business done in parliament. As for policy, we might expect that the government would have been less interested in overseas commercial expansion, and would certainly have kept out of European quarrels implicating the electorate of Hanover. It might initially have supported the cause of the ambitious Charles XII of Sweden. At home, we could look for a less cosy relationship with the city financiers, and more propitious days for the landed gentry. But these speculations can only make up the unreliable narrative of alternative history.

We can be sure of just one thing: civil disabilities would have been removed from the Catholic population. In real life, precisely the opposite happened. The government strengthened the old measures and brought in new Acts to curtail what it perceived as the threat from Romish dissidents. Some provisions look like reprisals in the wake of the rising. One statute set up a panel of commissioners, 'to inquire of the estates of certain traitors', official double-talk for a scheme to compel papists to register their estates as a prelude to jacking up the land-tax on this class. Pope's correspondence shows some anxiety on this score, for reasons his editor George Sherburn helps to explain:

> In anticipation of this device to increase tax on Catholics and possibly because of questionable title to the house and land at Binfield (for Catholics were not allowed to buy land, and the Popes had a sort of concealed ownership of the place at Binfield) the Popes had sold out and moved to Chiswick, there renting a new house.
>
> (*Corr.*, vol. 1, p. 344)

Once again the law had forced the family to move on like the merest vagabonds. For one so immersed in filial piety as Pope, the psychic effect must have been incalculable. Finally came one more law, 9 Geo. I, c. 18, by which taxes were yet further stepped up. 'If this Bill passes', wrote Pope at the time, 'I shall lose a good part of my income... I know I wish my country well and if it undoes me, it shall not make me wish it otherwise' (*Corr.*, vol. 2, p. 173). The bill did pass. Later in life it seems that Pope had to vacate his house at Twickenham when the court moved to Hampton Court, and that in his final illness he was deterred from receiving medical attention in London by a royal proclamation occasioned by the first stirrings of the 1745 rebellion (*TE*, vol. 4, pp. 168–9).

3

The public alarms of this time had a direct effect on Pope's private life. Rocked by the failure of the Jacobite incursion, especially the episode of Derwentwater which came so close to home, he had another major worry. Early in 1716 the family gave up their home and moved to Chiswick, outside London. They had two possible motives. First, the government was threatening to levy an additional property tax on Catholics to defray the cost of putting down the rebellion. Second, the title by which the Popes held Whitehill House amounted to nothing more than a legal fiction, and strict enforcement of the law would have led to their dispossession. On top of all that, Catholics now needed to take an oath of loyalty as part of the new system of registering estates. Documents survive in the National Archives to show how carefully the commissioners went about their business as they quizzed the papist community. Alexander senior, now a man of seventy, probably thought it best to make a strategic withdrawal.

For the younger Pope, the move from his childhood home had huge implications. In early February he spent a week in the forest with Nicholas Rowe, when memories flooded back. 'Binfield, alas! is no more', he wrote to Parnell in March,

> and the Muse is driven, from those Forests of which she sung, the Day may shortly come, when your Friend may too literally apply *nos Patriae fines, & dulcta linquimus arva* when he may look back with regret, on the Paradise he has lost, and have only the consolation of poor Adam[,] 'The world lies all before him, where to chuse / His place of rest, and Providence his Guide'.[20]

The quotation from the close of Milton's great epic is still a familiar one, but readers today may not easily pick up a reference to the start of Virgil's first eclogue. It was a favourite passage for Pope, who regularly turns to the language of classic pastoral when exploring his feelings about the forest. The line may be roughly translated, 'We leave the confines of our native country and our delightful fields'.

The same mantra turns up in a letter to John Caryll on 20 March, at the end of a particularly heartfelt paragraph:

> I write this from Windsor Forest, of which I am come to take my last look and leave of. We here bid our papist-neighbours adieu, much as those who go to be hanged do their fellow-prisoners, who are condemned to follow 'em a few weeks after ... I parted from honest Mr Dancastle with tenderness; and from old Sir William Trumbull as from a venerable prophet, foretelling with lifted hands the miseries to come upon posterity, which he was just going to be removed from.

In the same letter his thoughts reverted to the Blounts, and the misfortunes they had suffered along with their family connections:

> This brings into my mind one or other I love best and among those, the widow and fatherless, late of Mapledurham. As I am certain no people living had an earlier and truer sense of others' misfortunes, or a more generous resignation as to what might be their own; so I earnestly wish, that whatever part they must bear of these, may be rendered as supportable to 'em, as it is in the power of any friend to make it. They are beforehand with us in being out of house and home, by their brother's marriage: and I wish they have not some cause already to look upon Mapledurham with such sort of melancholy as we may upon our own seats when we lose them.
>
> (*Corr.*, vol. 1, pp. 336–7)

Over the next couple of years Pope would make occasional returns to his old home, and always he adopts the same elegiac tone.

News of the next development in his life emerges from an account that he gave to Caryll on 20 April:

> My father and mother having disposed of their little estate at Binfield, I was concerned to find out some asylum for their old age; and these cares, of settling, and furnishing a house, have employed me till yesterday, when we fixed at Chiswick under the wing of my Lord Burlington.
>
> (*Corr.*, vol. 1, p. 339)

The new base for his family stood in what was then an outlying village, on the north bank of the river about six miles west of London. It was located in Mawson's New Buildings, on the corner of Chiswick Lane and Mawson Lane, standing near the spot where today the Great West Road meets the Chertsey Road at the Hogarth Roundabout. The setting was no more than two hundred yards from the Thames, and Pope could easily travel up and down the river on trips to the city. Close at hand stood the parish church, where in due course the remains of Pope senior would lie. This was only a mile from the Popes' earlier home at Hammersmith, and about six miles from central London. The spot may have been chosen for this reason, or because of the proximity of Chiswick House, where the poet's friend and patron Lord Burlington was in the process of updating his house and garden. The Earl had just begun to remodel the old Jacobean house he had inherited, and eventually it would become the pattern of an English Palladian villa. With a judicious application of honeyed praise to his noble friend, Pope called the place 'the finest thing this glorious Sun has shin'd upon' (*Corr.*, vol. 3, p. 313). The language hints at a pertinent fact: the resplendent Belinda would have sailed by this very site on her sun-drenched passage down the Thames in *The Rape of the Lock*.

On top of all the upset caused by his move, Pope had to deal with his first serious brushes with the disreputable publisher Edmund Curll. As we saw in the last chapter, bad blood had been stirring since 1714, but it was only now that their major quarrels began. Curll had acquired a reputation for a total lack of scruples, but no one could deny that he was also a resourceful operator. His business lay chiefly around Fleet Street and the Strand, where he brought new advertising skills and modes of self-publicity to the relatively conservative book trade. His specialities included scandalous memoirs, instant biographies of the famous dead, unauthorized editions of major writers and obscene or risqué items, although he did publish serious works on antiquarian and legal topics. More than once he found himself under arrest, and in 1728 the King's Bench court sentenced him to stand in the pillory at Charing Cross. That event certainly did not escape Pope, who referred to it a year later in the *Dunciad Variorum*.

Recently Curll had squeezed out some more illicit items by Pope into print, after which pamphlets and poems on one side or the other jostled each other in quick succession. The most lasting product of this vigorous exchange came with two prose works that illustrate the range of Pope's comic invention, even when he did not have the resources of poetry to help him. These are *A Full and True Account of a Horrid Revenge by Poison, on the Body of Mr. Edmund Curll, Bookseller*, published at the very end of March, and *A Further Account of the most Deplorable Condition of Mr. Edmund Curll*, which followed perhaps around August or September. On the surface the battle between poet and publisher had little or no connection with politics. Curll favoured the Tory side during the Sacheverell affair, but since then he had taken steps to placate the ruling party. In later years he volunteered to act as a spy for Walpole and professed great loyalty to the incumbent ministry: however, analysis of his voting records in elections for the City of London shows that he usually cast his ballot on the opposition side. Many of Curll's hacks who turn up in *The Dunciad* were available for hire from the government, and in this sense the satire aligns the bookseller with rampant commercialism – coded by the Tories as a product of Whig ideology. It was not wholly just of Pope to depict Curll as a lackey of Walpole, who in any case had ignored the publisher's offer to serve as a press censor. But fairness did not have much to do with this bare-knuckle fight between two combative personalities.

In June, when he wrote to Caryll, Pope reverted to the great transformation that his life had undergone. This time he tried to make light of things:

> Tho' the change of my scene of life, from Windsor Forest to the water-side at Chiswick, be one of the grand Æra's of my days, and may be called a notable period in so inconsiderable a history, yet you can scarce imagine any hero passing from one stage of life and entering upon another, with so much tranquillity and so easy a transition, and so laudable a behaviour as myself. I am become so truly a Citizen of the World (according to Plato's expression) that I look with equal indifference on what I have lost, and on what I have gained.
>
> <div align="right">(<i>Corr.</i>, vol. 1, pp. 343–4)</div>

It looks suspiciously like a pose, and a message from Edward Blount would soon bring him back to reality, as it reminded him that a new anti-Catholic bill had gone through parliament. This empowered the commissioners to seek out the whereabouts of 'certain traitors, and of Papist recusants, and of estates given to superstitious uses, in order to raise money out of them severally for the use of the public'. On 9 July Pope told Jervas with bitter sarcasm, 'I pay a double Tax, as we Non-Jurors ought to do' (*Corr.*, vol. 1, pp. 344–7). Meanwhile his messages to women, notably Lady Mary Wortley Montagu and Teresa Blount, took a different turn, adopting a literary, flippant and comically flirtatious manner. He embarked on a ramble in the summer, a holiday custom preserved until almost the end of his life. This time he made a journey by horseback to Oxford, much of it in company with the rough-mannered publisher Bernard Lintot, as he described in a virtuoso letter to Burlington. On 14 December Sir William Trumbull died at the age of seventy-seven and a week later he was buried at Easthampstead church. Some time afterwards Pope wrote a heartfelt verse epitaph on his old mentor, and in this context such a tribute to a man of principled loyalty takes on a topical meaning. It was an intimation of mortality to follow, and another reminder that the formative days in the forest would not quickly pass from the poet's mind.

On another front some better news came for Pope. The split in the Whig ministry had accentuated over recent months. Sensing an opportunity to embarrass the ruling faction of Sunderland and Stanhope, Robert Walpole had joined with the Tories and other dissidents in his party when the long-postponed impeachment of Lord Oxford came before parliament in the early summer. Despite a number of procedural devices, the government failed to gain enough support to carry through a conviction on the most substantive charges. For years Oxford's enemies had confidently expected that he would be found guilty. The outcome would have meant banishment at least, and even at worst execution. Once the Earl was acquitted in the House of Lords, his release after two years in the Tower prompted a recrudescence of the bitterly divided debates of 1714. Among those who rejoiced were the loyal band of Tories including Swift and Prior, who had obtained his own freedom a year earlier. By contrast the ministry's supporters felt rage and bafflement, especially those like Lord Coningsby who had stood brandishing the executioner's axe at the start of proceedings against Oxford. It marked a turning point in British politics: no outgoing prime minister would ever again face in such a naked form the retribution of his opponents.

In August Joseph Addison, who had seen his fortunes rise ever since the Hanoverians made their entrance, further enhanced his social position when he married a widow of high birth, the Countess of Warwick. Rumour had it that 'Mr. Addison and the rest of the rhiming gang have dropt their resentment against the Lordlike Man', that is Pope.[21] The truth is probably that Addison now had better things to do than keep up the quarrel about Homer, in view of his political responsibilities and his marriage. Pope did not soften his attitudes and brushed off a mild attempt on Addison's part to heal the division in one of his essays in *The Freeholder*, a strongly Whiggish journal which lambasted the Jacobites in the wake of their failed rising. Gossip suggested that Addison had started to drink too much, and Pope is unlikely to have done much to refute the story: he later told Joseph Spence that his opposite number 'ate full and drank his two bottles a day'. He also intimated maliciously that Addison had made a bad marriage and 'took to drinking more' as a refuge, which may or may not be true (*Anecdotes*, vol. 1, pp. 78–9). A relationship of warm friendship had broken down irretrievably in the face of literary and political disagreements.

After his summer jaunts, Pope spent the remaining months of 1716 settling down in Chiswick. He had started work on *Eloisa to Abelard*, while his witty short poem *Moore's Worms*, first published by Curll, would become his most popular single work in his lifetime, if we judge by the number of editions. But soon it was time to return to the main business of his life, the translation of Homer. That monumental task remained to be completed, in order to satisfy the subscribers anxiously awaiting the next volume, and to cement the poet's reputation. Despite all the distractions and the tumults in his life during 1716, he managed to make good progress on the third instalment. He had reasonable grounds to look forward to 1717 in the hope that it would prove less disruptive.

5 TOIL, TROUBLE, SOUTH SEA BUBBLE

As things turned out, 1717 would mark an important stage in Pope's private life and in his literary career. For the next two years he consolidated his position in the world of letters and prepared for the move to Twickenham, by which he finally signalized his independence at the age of thirty. A necessary but not sufficient condition before he could take this step was to achieve financial stability by means of the *Iliad*. Here he benefitted not just from the subscriptions, but also from a deal he had made with Bernard Lintot over the proceeds of a trade edition for the general public.

1

By this time he had made friends at court. That is a misleading statement, for his contacts nearly all lay in what increasingly became an alternative court headed by the Prince and Princess of Wales. Pope enjoyed lightly flirtatious relations with some of the maids of honour to the Princess, and wrote a number of verses satirizing their foibles. Once, in September 1717, he sent the Blount sisters an amusing account of a day spent with these women. He went by water to Hampton Court (again his life seems to have been prefigured by Belinda's story in *The Rape of the Lock*) and commiserated with his hosts on their miserable existence:

> I met the Prince with all his Ladies ... on horseback coming from hunting. Mrs Bellendine and Mrs Lepell took me into protection (contrary to the Laws against harbouring Papists), and gave me a Dinner, with something I liked better, an opportunity of conversation with Mrs Howard.
>
> (*Corr.*, vol. 1, p. 427)

Here we encounter two names significant for the poet's later biography: Mary 'Moll' Lepell, who three years afterwards married the courtier John Hervey, immortalized by Pope as 'Sporus', and Henrietta Howard, mistress to George II and a key contact for politicians of all stripes.

One poem from this period, little known to everyone outside specialists, illustrates the way in which Pope had taken on board the major political issues now simmering to the surface. Originally titled *The Court Ballad*, it was issued on 31 January 1717 by Rebecca Burleigh, in effect a front for Curll. The background to this work relates to three crises identified by Ragnhild Hatton that attended the early years of the Hanoverian regime.[1] The first was the 1715 rising, and in particular its diplomatic aftermath, which hovers above the actual words of the text but sets the scene for its poetic activity. The second came in the shape of a ministerial breakdown which lies at the very heart of the ballad. The third is a quarrel in the royal family, only beginning to emerge in early 1717 but in full swing by the summer of that year. This dispute centred on the relations of the King with the Prince and Princess of Wales, and the poem keeps up a constant hum of allusion to the Prince and his circle. Not that Pope employs an especially oblique method at all points: his title names the court, and through various modes of innuendo – some of them conspicuously indecent – he drives home the very particular application of his wit.

The shadow of one further event hovers behind the text, the production of an uproarious farce called *Three Hours after Marriage* at Drury Lane on 16 January. Seven performances in quick succession provoked a good deal of audience participation, both pro and con the show, and a hostile campaign was waged in newspapers and pamphlets. This comedy seems to have been chiefly the work of John Gay, but contemporaries rightly grasped that he needed a little help from his friends Pope and Arbuthnot. The details of its plot do not concern us here, as they involve a typical Scriblerian assault on pretentious scholars, critics (represented by John Dennis), learned ladies and foolish men of the theatre – here the actor-manager and future poet laureate Colley Cibber had his first brush with Pope. A tale often told has it that the two leading ladies refused to go on stage after they had been given a rowdy reception on the first night, and that it took a timely gift of 400 guineas (£420) from three maids of honour to rescue the play. In the ballad Pope does mention these three maids, but it is doubtful whether this episode truly inspired the poem, as used to be suggested.[2]

However, the main basis of the poem lies in the ministerial crisis which had become acute in the autumn of 1716. The Secretary of State for the Northern Department, Viscount Townshend, was increasingly at odds with the King and with leading colleagues, including his opposite number for the Southern Department, James Stanhope, and the Lord Privy Seal, the Earl of Sunderland. The arguments concerned the Great Northern War, the degree of support to be given to Hanoverian military and diplomatic ambitions, and the balance of power in the wake of James Edward Stuart's rising a year before. Over the course of the next few months this quarrel continued to simmer: Townshend was finally dismissed on 12 December, and things grew steadily worse in the New Year. It was not until April 1717 that a full-scale split in the Whigs occurred, partly owing to interventions by the Prince of Wales, which saw Townshend and Walpole going into a kind of opposition. A subsidiary consequence of the split was the appointment of Joseph Addison as Secretary for the Southern Department, a post for which he was little equipped even without the bad health which increasingly dogged him in the last phase of his life.

The disputes among the ministry involved some questions of personal ambition, but at root went back to divisions over foreign policy. It did not altogether help that the King was in Hanover from late July 1716 to January 1717: when anyone visited him there, as Stanhope did in the autumn, suspicions grew at home, and on the other side the King may have harboured fears as to the activities of the Prince, whom he had left in London. It was on the King's return on 18 January that some of these suppressed anxieties came to the surface. As Norman Ault recognized, one line near the end of the ballad, 'God send the K[ing] safe landing' looks forward to his arrival as imminent, and this supplies a *terminus ad quem* for composition.[3] This date holds some significance, for it is a highly topical poem, up to the day and the week if not to the minute. The third stanza suggests that Townshend has already been dismissed, though the 'ado' over his position in the ministry started some weeks earlier than that event. All the signs thus far point to the fact that composition took place only shortly before publication, most likely well into the New Year of 1717.

Such was the general situation when Pope wrote his ballad. But there existed a more simple and direct trigger for its composition. Just before he left for Hanover, the King had forced the Prince to dismiss his groom of the stole, the Duke of Argyll, who had hoped to be appointed Commander in Chief of the army after his modest success in putting down the rebellion in Scotland. At this moment Pope had begun a long-lasting friendship with the Duke, who was also a great favourite with the entourage of the Princess. In the previous month he had dined with Argyll in company with John Campbell, a cousin of the Duke and much later a successor to the title, who married Mary Bellenden, one of the court ladies Pope knew best. John Gay, he reported in the same letter, 'dines daily with the Maids of honour' (*Corr.*, vol. 1, p. 379). There was more to it than that, though: Argyll had been carrying on an affair with another of the maids, Jane Warburton. Earlier in January, just before *The Court Ballad* came out, the Duke's estranged wife died. Before long Jane quitted her post at court to become Argyll's second wife. The dates fit perfectly. They indicate that Pope wrote his poem immediately after the return of the King and the death of the Duchess: Curll then rushed the item into print, unquestionably with Pope's connivance.

The ballad runs to eight stanzas, each of six lines. It alludes to high jinks in the playhouse, as well as the divisions between Townshend and Sunderland, the doings of the Hanoverian matrons George I had brought with him, and the risqué behaviour of ladies in high society such as Lady Rich. Pope may have become acquainted with some of the participants through Lady Mary Wortley Montagu, although by now she had embarked on her famous embassy to Constantinople with her husband. She knew almost everybody mentioned in the text. But at the heart of the poem Pope constructs an allusive history of the Whig split, focused by the recent developments concerning Argyll. It is an intensely political work despite its broad humour and seemingly offhand manner. The lines rehearse some of the criticisms most commonly voiced by the opposition party grouped around the Prince and Princess. These include the King's unduly long absence in Hanover, seen as symptomatic of his true loyalties, and his refusal to trust the Prince as his regent in this period. Equally the verses underline popular objections to the maintenance of a standing army to defend Hanoverian interests on the Continent. One phrase seems to refer to the delivery of a stillborn child to the Princess in the previous November. Overall *The Court Ballad* gives implicit support to the activities of the royal couple in their struggle with the King, despite some gentle mockery, and it clearly proceeds from the Argyll camp. The last line, 'And take off Ladies Limitations', has a rich array of connotations, stretching from the restrictions of court life to the period of recovery after childbirth and perhaps even the limitations imposed by parliament on the King's own movements. In his ballad Pope wittily, not to say licentiously, exploits the tensions and embarrassments of the situation. It makes for one of Pope's most effective sorties into topical satire, and it deserves to be much better known.

He now had another major literary undertaking on his hands, the first such since he embarked on the *Iliad* three years before. It was an innovatory project: Pope decided to bring out a collected edition of his works up to this point. Subsequently this would become a normal procedure on the part of an established poet, but it is hard to think of earlier precedents from a major English author. It made up a handsome and impressive volume, available in folio quarto editions, each running to more than 400 pages, and it carried at the start a folding portrait of the author by Charles Jervas. Within the text are nine ornamental headpieces by Simon Gribelin, a Huguenot artist who had previously illustrated *The Rape of the Lock*. It was printed by the leading printer William Bowyer senior and published by Lintot. The volume contains all of Pope's significant works so far published, omitting the early instalments of the Homer translation. He added an important preface, which sets out the poet's considered view of his career and his role as a poet. Among the contents were familiar items such as the *Pastorals*, *An Essay on Criticism*, *Windsor-Forest*, *The Rape of the Lock* and *Messiah*. But eleven pieces which had not previously appeared in print also found a place in the collection, most notably *Eloisa to Abelard*, the somewhat Gothic elegy *To the Memory of an Unfortunate Lady* and the charming epistle to Miss Blount after the coronation. Obviously the book represented Pope's effort to define his achievement to this point and to proclaim his credentials as a writer of 'classic' status. Such volumes typically celebrated a major Greek or Latin author, whose life's work had gone down in history as a key datum in the literary past. For such a young man of relatively humble English origin to present himself in this way must have seemed an act of arrogance to many.

The *Works* appeared on 3 June, at the same time as the third volume of the *Iliad*. A month later, there followed a completely different enterprise which also involved Bowyer and Lintot. This was an anthology entitled *Poems on Several Occasions*, although today it has become better known as 'Pope's Own Miscellany'. It is believed that he contributed up to twenty poems anonymously. Other writers include Thomas Parnell; Wycherley, who had died in late 1715; and Garth, who would follow him to the grave in 1719. An interesting name is that of the Duke of Buckingham, a minor poet and early supporter of Pope. He had been a courtier under Charles II, a patron of Dryden and a favourite of Queen Anne. Since the Hanoverian accession he had stood on the margins of politics, a belated Restoration Tory with some suspect connections to the Jacobite faction. His wife was Kathleen Darnley, a natural daughter of James II who did not try very hard to conceal her loyalty to her half-brother, the Pretender. A few years later Pope would edit the Duke's works, which contained some materials deemed subversive by the government (see Chapter 6). The Duchess lived with enough style and freedom to be dangerous company for the poet, who had certainly met her by 1720, and perhaps much earlier. Since Pope concealed his responsibility for this collection, it did not figure in the public sense of his standing. However, both the *Iliad* and the collected *Works* did much to establish his position at the head of English letters. Collected volumes by Matthew Prior and John Gay within the next three years did not overturn this judgement. Addison's works were delayed until after his death, while Swift's oeuvre at this stage appeared before the world mainly through the shabby made-up miscellanies put out by Edmund Curll.

2

While his career prospered, Pope continued to face difficulties in private life, some of them partly conditioned by wider social circumstances. In particular, he devoted considerable effort to the problems of the Blount sisters, even as his relationship with Teresa gradually deteriorated. The battle with Curll thrust him into greater public prominence: one of the retorts to *Three Hours after Marriage* depicted him as a toad and a monkey. Lady Mary Wortley Montagu, still a close friend, had now reached Constantinople, and sent back to him some of her famous accounts of the Ottoman Empire. In return Pope kept her up to date on the social round, describing the inanities such as the high jinks at the newly fashionable masquerades held in the Haymarket theatre. They had been organized by the Swiss-born impresario Johann Jakob Heidegger – his other enterprise centred on the operas of George Friderick Handel, whose immortal Water Music received its premiere on the royal barge on 17 July. 'The K[ing] and P[rince] continue Two Names', Pope told Lady Mary, 'there is nothing like a Coalition, but at the Masquerade; however the Princess is a Dissenter from it, and has a very small party in so unmodish a Seperation' (*Corr.*, vol. 1, p. 407).

He could snatch only occasional visits to Binfield, and mused nostalgically to Thomas Dancastle,

> The Memory of our old neighbors yet lives with me; I often give a Range to my Imagination, and goe a strolling with one or other of you, up and down Binfield Wood, or over Bagshot Heath. I wish you all health, not you only, but your Horse, your Dog Lilly, &c.
>
> (*Corr.*, vol. 1, p. 393)

In the summer he was planning a round of visits: 'I expect this instant Mr Harcourt, who is to pass some days with me. Mr Edw. Blount and Sir H[enry] Bedingfield follow next: I am engag'd to Mr Stoner's afterwards (there you have all my Catholics at once, except Mrs Blounts who have me always' (*Corr.*, vol. 1, p. 411). Early in August he reported to Caryll on his own rambles:

> After some attendance on my Lord Burlington, I have been at the Duke of Shrewsbury's, Duke of Argyle's, Lady Rochester's, Lord Percival's, Mr Stonor's, Lord Winchelsea's, Sir Godfrey Kneller's ... and Dutchess Hamilton's ... Then am I obliged to pass some days between my Lord Bathurst's, and three or more on the Windsor side. Thence to Mr Dancastle, and my relations on Bagshot Heath. I am also promised ... to the Bishop of Rochester for 3 days on the other side of the water.
>
> (*Corr.*, vol. 1, p. 418)

Nobody can miss a sense of pride as Pope recites this list of the good and great. By far the most significant literary consequence of all these wanderings was a wonderful letter to the Blount girls, describing with almost exaggerated romantic feeling his visit to Stonor Park, the home of an ancient recusant family set in woodlands north of Henley, from where the poet moved on to Oxford. In another letter he sent the sisters a plangent 'hymn' written in Windsor Forest, recalling the place as the scene of his 'youthful Loves, and happier Hours'. With a kind of playful solemnity he gave some advice to the pair – but mainly, we may suspect, Teresa:

> Take all thou e're shalt have, a constant Muse:
> At Court thou may'st be lik'd, but nothing gain;
> Stocks thou may'st buy and sell, but always lose;
> And love the brightest eyes, but all in vain!
>
> (*Corr.*, vol. 1, p. 429)

In reality, the fortunes of Teresa and Martha continued to occasion their friend a good deal of anxiety. Their brother Michael had inherited an already encumbered estate at Mapledurham on the death of Lister Blount in 1710. Five years later, as we have already seen, he married Mary Agnes Tichborne and took possession of the house. After the marriage the sisters were forced to leave their home and moved to London with their mother, the former Martha Englefield, now in her sixties. Pope told John Caryll, Patty's godfather, that he did not consider London the right place for her at this time, owing to her health, but there was nowhere else for her to go. The brother was dilatory in paying their allowances as stipulated by a legal settlement, and Pope became irritated by what seemed to him Michael's lack of care for the family property, as well as his unkindness to his mother and sisters. He appears to have been addicted to the pleasures of the town, and once a companion was killed in a street brawl after a night out in London. In the year of his death Blount calculated that he had overspent his income by £2,500 over time; it would have been more, had his wife not consented to go without 'Diament Earings'. The impact of double taxation under the penal laws continued to ravage the family finances in the time of his son and successor, also named Michael (1719–92).

The money troubles of the Blount family remained a major concern for some years, although Pope did all he could to put their affairs on a more stable basis. In December 1716 he wrote to Martha about investing in South Sea stock: he was expecting the price to fall and planned to buy £500 when it reached 103, 'which you shall have if you have a mind to it' (*Corr.*, vol. 1, p. 379). The poet continued to dabble in the stock almost up to the moment that the Bubble burst, with mixed results. To be fair, Pope does quote the opinion of a broker to Patty, but we cannot have very much confidence that the advice he gave her was always reliable. He had now made friends with the politician James Craggs junior, a figure at the centre of relations between the government and the South Sea Company. It looks as though Pope was trying to get Caryll to nudge Michael to take better care of his mother and sisters, but since he had his own financial anxieties and needed to ask Caryll for a loan, it may have been difficult for him to raise this matter. In addition he enjoyed less close contacts with a new generation of the Englefield family at Whiteknights, following the death of old Anthony, and they too faced a bleaker future as a result of government measures.

What made things worse was the growing estrangement between Pope and Teresa. Several short letters survive, written in a nervous and constrained style. They refer to unnamed disagreements and offence taken on either side: unfortunately, the exact basis of the quarrel cannot now be unravelled, although Teresa appears to have let out some romantic secret of the poet and spoken inopportunely behind his back. For his part, Pope grew increasingly unhappy with the young woman's behaviour in society, perhaps suspecting that she was chasing a well-heeled husband or, more disquietingly, protector. This did not prevent him from acting as a stockbroker when she sent him money to invest on her behalf.

A very strange development took place in March 1718. On that date Pope signed a document in which he pledged to pay Teresa an annuity of £40 for a period of six years, with two curious conditions. The first was that if Teresa should die within this space of time, all the money she had received up to then should be repaid to Pope. The second was that if Teresa should marry, the annuity would be void. It looks as if neither Martha nor Mrs Blount would benefit in any way from the agreement. Since Teresa did not countersign the document, which survives among the Mapledurham archives, we do not know if she was willing to take the money on these possibly humiliating terms. Maynard Mack has speculated that a mysterious letter, undated, in which Pope offers an apology to Teresa may relate to this affair, but we cannot be sure.[4] All that can be said for certain is that Pope continued to befriend Martha even while the family struggled financially and the obscure breach with Teresa steadily grew wider. While the situation of the Blounts had causes specific to their family history, it reflects a more general malaise within the recusant community. Private lives among the Catholic gentry often went through sharply different phases according to the political climate of the day.

Pope had enjoyed unusually good luck with his parents. Not only had they given him an exemplary upbringing: they remained generally in good health even as he approached the age of thirty. This was rare at a time when comparatively few people had both father and mother living when they reached adult years. On 23 October 1717, however, Pope suffered his first great loss. Magdalen Rackett gave an account of the circumstances:

> Mr. Pope's father died of a *Polypus* [i.e., blood clot] on the Heart; was very Well the Day before, and never known Pain. In the Night told Mrs *Pope*, He had a touch of her Disorder, shortness of Breath; took a little Mint-Water, Syrrop, and Brandy, and settled to Sleep; in an hour wak'd, and said He was Worse; she rose and rang for Pope's Nurse, who always Liv'd with them, and as she rais'd him in the Bed, He fell back, and Dyed.[5]

The son versified the event in his *Epistle to Arbuthnot*: 'His Life, tho' long, to sickness past unknown, / His Death was instant, and without a groan' (*TE*, vol. 5, p. 126).

As was natural, the passing of the elder Pope affected his son deeply. On the following day he wrote a short note to the Blount sisters: 'My poor Father dyed last night. Believe, since I don't forget you this moment, I never shall'. To John Caryll he added: 'His death was the happiest to himself, imaginable; but I have lost one whom I was even more obliged to as a friend, than as a father'. From his neighbour Lord Burlington he begged the favour of hartshorn drops, used as smelling salts, for his mother. He told John Gay that he had been 'upon the Ramble most part of the Summer, and have concluded the Season in Grief' (*Corr.*, vol. 1, pp. 447–9). On 26 October Alexander senior was buried in Chiswick parish church.

The event had wider consequences, financial and religious. Bishop Atterbury soon sent a message of sympathy which also gave his friend a somewhat crude invitation to join the Church of England and thus contribute to his own 'ease and Happiness'. Pope replied politely, setting out in detail his reasons for rejecting this step. While he acknowledged the temporal advantages which would come with a conversion to the Protestant faith, he held fast to his principles:

> I am not a Papist, for I renounce the temporal invasions of the Papal power, and detest their arrogated authority over Princes, and States. I am a Catholick, in the strictest sense of the word. If I was born under an absolute Prince, I would be a quiet subject; but I thank God I was not. I have a due sense of the excellence of the British constitution. In a word, the things I have always wished to see are not a Roman Catholick, or a French Catholick, or a Spanish Catholick, but a true Catholick: and not a King of Whigs, or a King of Tories, but a King of England. Which God of his mercy grant his present Majesty may be, and all future Majesties!
>
> (*Corr.*, vol. 1, pp. 451, 453–4)

His main concern, as this same letter reveals, was to look after his ageing mother, and she would have found such an abandonment of his hereditary religion hard to accept.

Some urgent problems faced Pope, as he reminded Edward Blount on 27 November: the death of his father had left him 'to the ticklish Management of a narrow Fortune, where every false Step is dangerous' (*Corr.*, vol. 1, p. 455). Since he received a substantial legacy from Pope senior, and had already obtained worthwhile income from the Homer enterprise, this may appear a cautious judgement. But it was a volatile financial climate, with speculative fever starting to mount in the lead-up to the pair of great crashes that would shortly rock Western Europe, the Mississippi and South Sea 'bubbles' – as it happened, some of the Popes' fortune was invested in Paris, and besides this the poet was not immune from the mania. As an independent agent for the first time, he had to find a suitable place to live along with his mother and his almost equally aged nurse. He planned at first to build a house on some land behind Burlington House off the east side of Bond Street. It would have been an agreeable place to settle, and if he had gone ahead in years to come he could have enjoyed the convivial company of Arbuthnot, very close at hand in Cork Street. It would only be a short step down the road to the Misses Blount, too. But the old ban against Catholics residing in central London still held on. Lord Bathurst, an increasingly close friend, advised him against going ahead with a scheme using the Scottish architect Colen Campbell, a client of Burlington and a *pur-sang* Palladian. In the end the costs turned out to be prohibitive and Pope had to look elsewhere.

Meanwhile the year 1718 went on in a relatively quiet way, despite some bouts of ill health. The publication of the fourth instalment of the *Iliad* in June encouraged the poet to push ahead with the last portion of his work, much of it undertaken at the country houses of wealthy friends. Before that, he had become embroiled in the controversy surrounding a comedy by the prominent actor-manager Colley Cibber. *The Non-Juror* premiered at Drury Lane in the previous December, an adaptation of Molière's *Tartuffe*. It came out, of course, in the aftermath of the Jacobite rising in 1715–16 and featured a Jesuit named Dr Wolf who clearly represented the nonjuring clergymen involved in the rebellion. The play enjoyed great success, and the King gave Cibber £200 in return for his dedication. At the same time it inevitably distressed Catholics who felt that the portrayal of Wolf as an evil conspirator traduced their faith. In a letter to Robert Digby on 31 March, Pope wrote bitterly, 'The Stage is the only place we seem alive at; there indeed we stare, and roar, and clap hands for K. *George* and the Government' (*Corr.*, vol. 1, p. 473).

In February a new pamphlet emerged from the shop of Edmund Curll, ever on the look out for juicy bits of scandal in the world of literature. It bore the title *A Clue to the Comedy of the Non-Juror*. Curll advertised this in the press with the words,

> The manuscript of this Pamphlet was sent to me on Tuesday last, and I was this Morning given to understand that this signal Favour was conferr'd on me by Mr. Pope, for which I hereby return my most grateful Acknowledgment for the same. E. Curll.

A second edition of the *Clue* appeared on 18 March with several alterations to the text. On the back of the half title Curll printed a quatrain urging Pope to be generous enough to admit responsibility for the work. In the event Pope remained quiet and the item only recently became established in the canon. Much later, after Pope had installed the dramatist as hero of the revised *Dunciad*, Cibber accused Pope of writing the *Clue* as an attempt to prove that it was 'a closely couched Jacobite Libel against the Government'.[6] A reply issued under the title of *A Blast upon Bays* probably came from Pope himself. In it he effectively admitted that this was the design of the *Clue*, but added – what should have been obvious to any competent reader – that the work was a 'Frolick'. It is indeed a characteristic example of Pope's humour, exhibiting many close similarities to his earlier *Key to the Lock*.

Pope spent much of the summer at Cirencester, the seat of Lord Bathurst, and Stanton Harcourt near Oxford, a house belonging to Viscount Harcourt, the Tory lawyer who had helped to manage the defence of Sacheverell and served as Lord Chancellor in the Harley administration. At Stanton Harcourt the poet worked on his translation in the old manor house, which was almost abandoned, and in one of the finest of all his letters he sent a vivid account of the romantic medieval buildings, especially 'Pope's Tower'. This edifice, still standing, goes back to 1470 and contains the Harcourt family chapel, by this date used for Protestant rites, along with a priest's room and a 'squint' which allowed a glimpse of the altar below.[7] Pope described it as 'a very venerable Tower, so like that of the Church just by, that the Jackdaws build in it as if it were the true Steeple' (*Corr.*, vol. 1, p. 505).

More significant in the long term were his visits to Cirencester, which became a home from home for the poet. Here Bathurst began to implement the landscaping programme that Pope set out in the *Guardian* in 1713. The peer had acquired a large portion of land to the west of his historic property, and began extensive plantations that created a forest interspersed with rides and glades. Pope made his first visit in the summer of 1718, and on his return sent its master an effusive account of his stay and of the attractions of Oakley Wood, as it was still known. He included in the letter some verses on the plantation scheme (*Corr.*, vol. 1, pp. 476–8; *TE*, vol. 6, pp. 195–6). Thereafter Pope often came back to Cirencester, helping to create an oasis of elysian scenery that survives today. He was there in 1721, 1728, 1733, 1734, 1737 and 1743, and probably at other times. Various items of garden ornament were installed, including substantial structures such as the Wood House of 1721, transformed by 1732 into one of the earliest Gothic folly-type ruins. In addition, Bathurst constructed the Hexagon at the junction of three rides, Ivy Lodge and a Doric column, erected in honour of Queen Anne in 1741 near a newly created lake. There was also 'Pope's Seat', a small classical temple, with a pediment and a niche on each side of the entrance, which stood near the far end of the park. Pope made numerous references to the park in his poetry and correspondence. He sees himself comically as a 'magician' appointed to guard 'that enchanted Forest' (*Corr.*, vol. 2, p. 115).

In some ways Bathurst served as a substitute for the recently departed Trumbull, although he had more of a bluff, no-nonsense character. He made an ostentatious virtue of retirement, shunning the court while taking an active role in parliament. Meanwhile Lord Oxford retired to Herefordshire after his release from custody, while Bolingbroke endured gloomy exile in France despite having broken with the Pretender – his enemies in the Jacobite entourage had helped to persuade James Edward to fire him as Secretary of State. Sir William Wyndham remained in the wings as a power of West Country Tory politics, but he had lost most of his parliamentary influence. It was Bathurst who became the focus for many party loyalists. The peer had lent discreet support to the 1715 rebellion, and then made a gift of £1,000 to a planned rising three years later. Pope cannot have been unaware of these things, and the growing intimacy of the two men drew on more than a shared interest in architecture and gardening. In a way the deep woods of Gloucestershire replaced the groves of Windsor, and Pope relished the comparative solitude which enabled him to get on with his translation: 'It is as fit for me to leave the World, as for you to stay in it', he told the Blount sisters (*Corr.*, vol. 1, p. 490). As we shall see in the next chapter, Bathurst had close relations with Lady Scudamore, his opposite number in the society of the next-door county, Herefordshire. Together with Robert Digby, a nephew of Frances Scudamore, Pope was able to build up a phalanx of like-minded devotees of landscaping in the Welsh border country.

At the same time, for Pope to associate himself so closely with the affable, worldly Bathurst – who also became a good friend of Swift, Arbuthnot, Gay and, still one of Pope's allies, Lady Mary Wortley Montagu – had distinct political overtones. Whenever measures came up in the House of Lords regarding topics such as the conduct of the former ministry, the fate of Lord Oxford or the treatment of the captured rebels, Bathurst inevitably spoke and voted as one of the limited bloc of Tories. Like Pope's closest contact in the Church, Bishop Atterbury, he sought ways of prising gaps in the splintered Whig ranks at Westminster. Pope kept one or two associates within the government, notably James Craggs, who supplanted the ailing and ineffective Secretary of State, Joseph Addison, in March 1718. By way of compensation Addison received a life pension of £1,600. During the course of this year Pope lost his most esteemed colleagues in the Whig literary fraternity, Samuel Garth and Nicholas Rowe, and now there was no remaining writer on the other side of the political divide whom he could trust. Any writer chosen by the government to take over as poet laureate could expect a less gentle ride than the Scriblerians had given to the agreeable Rowe.[8] Now that the Whig power elite was firmly entrenched, Pope began willy-nilly to identify himself with the opposition.

One other death that year caused him a deeper sadness. In the summer of 1718 Thomas Parnell made a long awaited visit to England, but on his return trip to Dublin he died suddenly at Chester. Pope would serve as his literary executor. During his spell in London Parnell had taken part in a brief recrudescence of the Scriblerus Club. Lord Oxford, now safely restored to his friends, also joined the party along with Pope and Gay. A notable absentee was Arbuthnot, the keenest among all the group: he may have been away in France. But although the Club was effectively no more, Scriblerian satire lived on. *Three Hours after Marriage* had displayed the dramatic face of Scriblerus, and several short pamphlets around this period represent the more traditional satiric side. In *Memoirs of P. P. Clerk of this Parish* (1718), Pope cast a sportive eye on Bishop Gilbert Burnet's self-obsessed and unreliable *History of his own Time*. In the years to come Arbuthnot and Pope would keep the flame alive, with occasional contributions by Gay. Bubbling beneath were some distillations of the original Club activity, yet to reach the surface, including the *Memoirs of Scriblerus*, *The Art of Sinking*, *The Dunciad* and, more distantly, *Gulliver's Travels*.

3

The History of my Transplantation and Settlement which you desire, would require a Volume, were I to enumerate the many projects, difficulties, vicissitudes, and various fates attending that important part of my Life: Much more should I describe the many Draughts, Elevations, Profiles, Perspectives, &c. of every Palace and Garden propos'd, intended, and happily raised, by the strength of that Faculty wherein all great Genius's excel, Imagination. At last, the Gods and Fate have fix'd me on the borders of the Thames, in the Districts of Richmond and Twickenham. It is here I have passed an entire Year of my life, without any fix'd abode in London, or more than casting a transitory glance (for a day or two at most in a Month) on the pomps of the Town.

Pope to Jervas, *c.* 1720 (*Corr.*, vol. 2, pp. 23–4)

Now Pope came up with a solution for the problems about his new home. He decided to move to a riverside site at Twickenham, up the Thames to the west of London. Here he was able to rent a property that would adequately house his mother, his old nurse and himself. This step marks his full independence as a man and a writer. He would live there for the rest of his life, and 'Alexander Pope of Twickenham in the County of Middlesex Esquire' became his official title to genteel status from now on. To his enemies the address became a ready-made label: it did not take long for a legend of the wasp of Twickenham to evolve.

The historic neighbourhood where he now settled had grown up on a small rise near the medieval church, where the Middlesex bank of the Thames takes a pronounced curve to the right as the river flows down towards Richmond. Twickenham village stands on a low gravel shelf. Pope's villa was located a short way to the south of the centre of the village, along the road to Teddington and Hampton Court.[9] At this date Twickenham stretched no further than Cross Deep, the bounds of which were marked by a stream running into the Thames just above Pope's home and which gave its name to the surrounding area. (Cross Deep refers to the stream, a crossing, the road, the district and a house.) South of this stream, from 1747, Horace Walpole created his fanciful residence, Strawberry Hill, on the site of a dwelling formerly known as Chopped Straw Hall. This was a small house built in 1698, once occupied by Colley Cibber. Downstream the village extended in the direction of Mrs Howard's home at Marble Hill. Other important mansions stood near the river bank, including Orleans House, Lebanon House and Radnor House. The chief road leading westward from the centre of the village to the Common was Heath Lane, which branched off from King Street at its junction with the Hampton road (known here as Cross Deep). Among those with homes located near Heath Lane was Lady Mary Wortley Montagu. On the corner of Cross Deep and Heath Lane stood the Grove, rented in turn by James Craggs junior and the Duke of Wharton. East of the church, in the direction of Orleans House, was Mount Lebanon, where the Earl of Strafford had a residence. In the years following Pope's death the area became still more fashionable, but even in the course of his lifetime it was a distinctly genteel and desirable neighbourhood.

Much of the life of the village revolved around the Thames. The river provided a beautiful setting, especially with the picturesque islets and the attractive Hamwalks on the Surrey bank, about which Pope often rhapsodized. It also afforded a transportation link and a commercial artery. Pope would regularly travel to and from London by boat; his boatman was one Bowry. A ferry had existed from the middle of the seventeenth century, crossing the river below Eel Pie island, then known as Twickenham ait: Pope would have used this conveyance often to get to Richmond and other places. A crucial stage in the evolution of this area came in 1718 with the arrival of the Prince and Princess of Wales at Richmond Lodge, a short way downstream, leased to them after it was sequestrated from the Duke of Ormonde following his flight to the Continent. Not far off the Princess had the handsome terrace called Maids of Honour Row built to house her ladies in waiting. In years to come she would turn Richmond Park into a scene of vaunting ideological claims, with a hermitage and a horticultural folly called Merlin's Cave, designed by William Kent. This edifice made strenuous efforts to forge a link between the Hanoverian line and earlier British monarchs and heroes, to the extent that it could be seen as an above-ground riposte to Pope's grotto and other landscaping sites of the opposition. The poet's circle found the whole place altogether risible. However, the presence of the royals undoubtedly drew men and women of consequence to the area. No one less than Walpole, whose son was Ranger of the Park, had a lodge there. Even the Blounts, with their straitened means, occupied a small house in Petersham, a short way up the river opposite Twickenham.

In nearby villages such as Whitton many other individuals known to the poet made their home. Among them was 'learn'd Pigot' (*TE*, vol. 6, p. 255), as Pope described the Catholic barrister Nathaniel Piggot (1661–1737), whom we have encountered through his involvement in the trial of Lord Derwentwater. He became a trusted legal advisor to the poet and would also come to the rescue when Pope had a coaching accident nearby. The minister in the adjoining parish of Teddington was Stephen Hales (1677–1761), an important early biologist, and a respected friend until Pope discovered that Hales was using animal vivisection in his experiments. Joseph Spence asked if Hales cut up rats, and Pope replied 'with emphasis and concern' that he did, 'and dogs too' (*Anecdotes*, vol. 1, p. 118).

Pope's own villa occupied a plot of land on the road to Hampton. The house was built on two strips of land, one freehold and one copyhold, and each containing a cottage when Pope acquired the lease. Not long before the plot and adjoining land had been acquired by an MP and army contractor named Thomas

Vernon. Separately, on the side of the road furthest from the river, lay the garden, containing barely five acres in all. In the following year, perhaps as early as April or May, Pope moved into the property with his mother and nurse. One of the two existing cottages was demolished or totally transformed in the reconstruction. The other may have stood in some form, probably on the southern side of the villa, and could be used as a guest annex. Pope's landlord seems to have provided a separate free-standing cottage. It is just possible that Edith Pope lived in this.

Soon after his arrival Pope began to remodel the house with the help of the architect James Gibbs, and he was able to report progress to friends by the summer of 1720. In the following year he described it as 'quite finished' (*Corr.*, vol. 2, p. 77). What emerged was a symmetrical structure of three stories, with a basement standing above ground on the river frontage and containing the entrance to Pope's celebrated grotto. The design conformed to the fashionable style of Palladianism. Since the frontage consisted of only three central bays plus a single bay on each wing, it was little more than a cut-down version of the mansions that the poet had seen at the homes of his aristocratic friends, and it represents a typical piece of Popian miniaturization. A lawn sloped down to the Thames in front of the house: the formal garden lay on the other side and was reached by a subterranean passage. In the basement were small chambers whose use is not totally certain; one may have served as a wash-house. The first floor probably contained a hall, together with rooms fronting the river: the great parlour, the small parlour and a private retiring room for Pope. In the back may have been some offices such as the kitchen. On the second floor were three major rooms overlooking the river and, it is likely, Pope's library behind. The garret floor was confined to the central block and contained three rooms, probably bedrooms. There were cottages and outhouses of indeterminate character near to the villa, as well as a rented boathouse. In later years extensive remodelling was carried out and eventually demolished by Lady Howe, known as 'Queen of the Goths', who laid waste to the garden and stripped the grotto. This act incensed the artist J. M. W. Turner so much that he produced a painting of the desolate scene as well as drafting a fragmentary poem on the subject.[10]

The most famous aspect of the villa could not be seen from the road: it lay underground in the shape of a grotto. Its origin lay in the fact that the villa faced towards the river and away from the road, Cross Deep, which divided the house from the main garden. A passageway was needed to form a connection and here in this space under the house Pope constructed his grotto. It was no more than part of the basement through which visitors could have access to the garden, with a view back towards the Thames opening up as they went. In October 1720 Pope was granted a license by the Manor Court to undertake the work. He worked on the tunnel and its growing assemblage of contents for the rest of his life. It was four feet wide and six feet six inches at the highest point, stretching for twenty-two feet from the rear of the house and culminating in a lobby of seven feet in length. Later it was extended to a length of sixty-three feet. The passage rose about two and a half feet as it made its way up a slight natural gradient into the garden. There may have been statutes along some of the walls, as well as busts and urns. To that extent the place had at first an element of a cabinet of curiosities, that is an assemblage of diverse natural phenomena and *objets d'art*. Around 1739 Pope became passionately involved with geology and mineralogy, and the contents of the grotto took on a specialized character, when he acquired a large collection of marbles, crystals, ores and other rocks.

Pope's grotto was less spectacular than some, and it did not celebrate the taste for the 'grotesque' as openly as some later creations in this vein. Rather, it expressed his own identity, as a writer, a Catholic, a devotee of the classics, a lover of natural beauty, a gardener, a connoisseur of artistic and scientific objects, a refugee from the city and a disciple of the past masters of 'retirement' in its psychological and political senses. Swift was told of Pope's work by their common friend Charles Ford and wrote to congratulate him on his 'Subterranean Passage to your Garden whereby you turned a blunder into a beauty which is a Piece of Ars Poetica' (*Corr.*, vol. 2, pp. 325–6), a nicely turned comment on the ingenious contrivances that went into the grotto. From the start Pope saw his creation as a place of retreat and reflection – he seems to have had a table and chairs in place. The cave with its spring resembled some of the scenes in classical literature that the poet knew so well. Over the garden entrance was set a marble plaque, bearing the inscription 'Secretum iter et fallentis semita vitae': the source is one of the epistles of Horace (I.18), with the sense, 'a solitary journey down the path of a concealed life'. Pope selected a variety of items to endow the location with a sense of privacy and to create emblems of retirement.

The poet now had a firm base from which he could launch his varied undertakings. Surrounded by the good and great, he had finally achieved his own great good place, halfway between Plough Court and Binfield. But if he thought his home on the banks of the river would mean his life would be all plain sailing, events would prove otherwise before very long. Most of 1719 passed in a reasonably tranquil manner, with what must have seemed to Pope the endless task of the *Iliad* finally drawing to its conclusion. Back in Berkshire, Thomas Dancastle remained a devoted amanuensis on this work. In June Sir Godfrey Kneller told Pope of a house he had rented not very far from the villa for the use of Lady Mary and her husband, now back from the embassy to Constantinople. In the same year Matt Prior's sumptuous collected poems were issued by the firm of Tonson, modelled on the *Works* Pope had published in 1717. They contained a major new poem named *Alma, or The Progress of the Mind*, a comic epic of neuro-physiology composed while its author languished in custody around the time of the rising. Pope admired the work above everything else from the hand of Prior, and its witty octosyllabics rivalled anything produced by Swift. Relations with Teresa still had their tricky moments, but he saw something of the Blount girls on his trips up to town. On the family front there was a misfortune when his sister Magdalen lost a new baby girl to a fever. Throughout the year Pope kept up relations with Lord Burlington and, in a more relaxed mode, with Lord Bathurst.

On 17 June Joseph Addison died after a long illness involving at least one stroke. His body lay in state at Westminster Abbey and was buried in King Henry VII's chapel, next to that of Lord Halifax, his own patron as well as Pope's. It fell to Francis Atterbury, Dean of the cathedral as well as Bishop of Rochester, to conduct the service, a task he managed to perform despite an undisguised lack of sympathy with the government which the deceased man had served. Pope left no comment at the time. The lasting expression of his feelings was reserved for the scarifying lines on 'Atticus', which first appeared in a newspaper three years later and soon found in a place in one of the agglomerative miscellanies of Edmund Curll.

For a short time, Pope had managed to put day-to-day politics on the back seat. Even a feeble attempt at a further incursion by Jacobite forces passed without comment. It took the form of an expedition backed by Spain and led by George Keith, tenth Earl Marischal, who had suffered an attainder following the 1715 rising. A body of men landed on the Hebridean island of Lewis and made their way to the mainland. Here on 10 June 1719 they were met and defeated by the Hanoverian forces near the pass of Glenshiel, across the water from Skye. The Highlanders fled and the Spanish troops surrendered. Pope was of course perfectly aware of these happenings, but out of discretion or embarrassment he kept quiet about it. These things all changed in the course of the following year.

4

A single event dominated the attention of people in Britain during 1720, and it was one whose shadow would lie over politics for a decade and more. The great Bubble formed a recurrent theme in Pope's later work, especially during the 1730s, and like most contemporaries he viewed it as a turning point in the self-awareness of the nation.[11]

The formation of the South Sea Company, we recall, went back to 1711, with Robert Harley, Earl of Oxford, serving as its chief promoter and first governor. Quite openly, the Tories had designed it as a counterforce to a Whig creation, the Bank of England. However, it never managed to operate at any serious level in the trade of Spanish America, despite confident claims at the outset, and it became in effect a stock-jobbing operation. After the collapse, it emerged that corruption had existed at the top of the company (with the King himself now serving as governor) and that many leading politicians had bought and sold stock in return for favours or influence. Swift was an early investor in the company and seems to have escaped without a major loss, although he railed bitterly against the course that the company had pursued under the Hanoverian regime. By contrast, John Gay lost most of the profit of £1,000 he had just gained by his subscription volume of *Poems*.

The crisis was brought about by the giddy inflation of stock prices and then their collapse over the summer of 1720. Prices had risen to 1,050 on 24 June but rapidly plummeted in September and October, falling below 200 by the end of the year. Thousands of investors, as well as annuitants and creditors, lost heavily in the process. As panic set in, rumours of bankruptcies and suicides filled the newspapers. Stories appeared about a glut in second-hand carriages. The authorities belatedly mounted a rescue operation and made an example of a few guilty directors who lacked political shelter in the storm; but others escaped, and Robert Walpole soon took advantage of the confusion to achieve unchallenged power.

Amid the general carnage one hammer blow struck Pope personally. This was the sudden death on 17 February of James Craggs junior, the Secretary of State, who had been heavily implicated in the corrupt dealings of the company, notably tranches of stock made available to figures at court and in the government. He had encouraged Pope to invest in the South Sea. To make matters worse, his father, the Paymaster General, also died a month later, probably by his own hand. Pope commemorated his close relations with the younger Craggs in an epistle written when his friend became Secretary of State in 1718 (*TE*, vol. 6, pp. 209–10). Another warm commendation comes in a letter to John Caryll soon after the death of his friend:

> There never lived a more worthy nature, a more disinterested mind, a more open and friendly temper than Mr Craggs. A little time I doubt not will clear up a character which the world will learn to value and admire, when it has none such remaining in it.
>
> (*Corr.*, vol. 2, p. 73)

Pope kept a portrait of Craggs in his house at Twickenham. He appears as 'bold, gen'rous *Craggs*' in Gay's poem *Mr. Pope's Welcome from Greece* (1720).[12] This may not seem surprising in view of the fact that Craggs entered his name for ten copies of Gay's *Poems* in that year – but the poem was written some time earlier. Pope recorded his verdict on Craggs in his memorial list: 'a man of liberal and upright character, a resolute friend, of fondest memory'.[13]

Throughout the course of the year Pope followed the market with great interest. For example, he wrote to his broker James Eckersall around February,

I daily hear such reports of advantage to be gained by one project or other in the Stocks, that my Spirit is up with double Zeal, in the desires to enrich ourselves. I assure you my own Keeping a Coach and Six is not more in my head than the pleasure I shall take in seeing Mrs Eckersall in her Equipage. To be serious, I hope you have sold the Lottery orders, that the want of ready money may be no longer an Impediment to our buying in the Stock ... I hear the S. Sea fell since, and should be glad we were in.

(*Corr.*, vol. 2, p. 33)

In March he told Teresa, 'I have borrowed mony upon ours and Mr Eckersals Orders, and bought 500ll stock S. Sea, at 180. It has since risen to 184.' As the price continued to rise during the summer, Pope and his friends kept watch. He even contemplated buying an estate in Devon for himself and Gay, and asked William Fortescue, Gay's friend and fellow West Countryman, to explore the possibilities. He sold some stock before prices started to fall, but he was not immune from the crash when it came in the early autumn: Atterbury wrote in commiseration on his losses on 28 September, but added that he believed that 'had that project taken root and flourish'd it would by degrees have overturn'd our Constitution'. This was the base Tory position on the entire South Sea episode. Reflecting on the affair to John Caryll at the end of the year, Pope observed, 'The vast inundation of S. Sea has drowned all, except a few unrighteous men (contrary to the deluge), and it is some comfort to me I am not one of those, even in my afflictions' (*Corr.*, vol. 2, pp. 38, 56, 60). Caryll knew all about this: his own family had lost money in John Law's Mississippi Bubble, since like many Catholics they found it more convenient to invest in French funds.[14]

Not until 1733 did Pope confront directly the issues raised by the South Sea episode. His *Epistle to Bathurst* deals at length with the Bubble and its aftermath, as will become clear in Chapter 8. Its cast list includes the chief promoter of the scheme, Sir John Blunt, who figures in a significant section of the poem beginning, 'Much injur'd Blunt! Why bears he Britain's hate?' (*TE*, vol. 3.ii, p. 104). This was a real question for Pope, who disliked the current administration, but could not forget Lord Oxford's association with the South Sea Company. In some ways the *Epistle* seems to harbour the greatest resentment against those who went after the South Sea directors in an often sanctimonious witch-hunt, rather than the 'culprits' themselves. The poem ends with the ineffable Thomas Coningsby 'haranguing' parliament to impeach the guilty men. To a dyed-in-the-wool Whig like Coningsby everything seemed black and white. The corrupt City financiers had joined wicked ministers like Aislabie to impose a cruel fraud on the public. Even friends and allies of Coningsby in the ministry, such as Lord Sunderland, shared in the blame. By contrast, a hidden sympathy for Blunt lurks in Pope's text, if not for the crooked company accountant Robert Knight

The Bubble sent an enormous shockwave across the nation. Pope too went through a chastening experience, and with the last instalment of the *Iliad* now published he needed a fresh source of income, especially in view of his increasing outlay on the villa at Twickenham. Although people on both sides of the party war had found themselves implicated in the Bubble, the dramatic events it spawned would continue to polarize Britain. As for Pope, he still had some friends among the Whigs, but the politician within the ministry to whom he was closest, Craggs the younger, died at the height of the crisis. Now the rise of Walpole ushered in a period of greater stability in political and economic affairs, although no one of course could ever have guessed just how long the great man's hold on power would last. New challenges awaited the country and Pope himself.

6 A DULL DUTY AND A PUBLIC CAUSE

It was partly fortuitous circumstances that brought Robert Walpole to eminence. As Britain tried to regroup after the traumas of the preceding year, the ruling Whig oligarchy suffered a succession of reverses. The first of the leading ministers to depart was James Stanhope. On 4 February 1721 the opposition, led by the mercurial Duke of Wharton, grilled a principal architect of the scheme, Sir John Blunt. Members of the Lords also had Stanhope in their sights, partly because his own cousin was deeply implicated in some shadier dealings. The minister made a spirited defence, but after his speech he collapsed and had to be carried out of the chamber unconscious. Three days later, he died from a brain haemorrhage. It struck a grievous blow against the administration. Only ten more days passed before Pope's friend Craggs, the Secretary of State, succumbed to smallpox. The Earl of Sunderland was obliged to rejig his cabinet, and brought in Lord Townshend, Walpole's brother-in-law, as one of the new secretaries. At the start of April Sunderland had to accept the inevitable and gave way as Walpole took over as First Lord of the Treasury – a position he would hold for an extraordinary spell of twenty-one years. Meanwhile suspicion still dogged Sunderland for his part in the government's involvement in the South Sea affair, and within twelve months he died too, in circumstances thought by some a little suspicious. The field was left clear for Walpole, but the Tories now had more room to manoeuvre than at any time since the Hanoverian regime began.

However, Pope held his hand at first. He would not involve himself directly in politics until the arrest of his friend Atterbury in late 1722. Even an unfortunate episode that saw his own in-laws, the Racketts, dragged into the criminal court did not spur him into a response – actually he never made any open reference to the affair in his published writings. We can locate the chief explanation for his silence at this juncture in two circumstances. The first concerns his need to get settled at Twickenham. The second relates to the 'secondary' work of translating and editing to which he had now committed himself.

1

It took time for Pope to establish himself at his new home. For a while he continued to feel a sense of impermanence, as though the place might be snatched from him at any moment. In 1725 he wrote to his friend Hugh Bethel, 'I am but a *Lodger* here: this is not an abiding City. I am only here to stay out my lease, for what has Perpetuity and mortal man to do with each other?' (*Corr.*, vol. 2, p. 387). A decade later he would adapt Horace to a slightly altered effect: 'My lands are sold, my Father's house is gone; / I'll hire another's, is not that my own / And yours my friends?' (*TE*, vol. 4, p. 67). Behind the autobiographic reference lies a whole topic in philosophy, to which Pope alluded in a later poem that took Bathurst's grand possessions at Cirencester as a test case: 'The Laws of God, as well as of a Land, / Abhor, a *Perpetuity* should stand' (*TE*, vol. 4, p. 183).

James Gibbs had carried out much of the original renovation needed on the house, and Pope made further improvements over the next few years, such as a portico added to the river frontage after consultations with Kent and Lord Burlington in the early 1730s. In his early days at Twickenham he had occasional house guests and kept up his own routine of annual rambles, such as a trip to Oxford en route to Cirencester and Edward Blount's home in Gloucestershire during the summer of 1721. Nearer home there were musical activities after the composer Giovanni Battista Bononcini arrived in Twickenham and collected a group of local supporters. His operas gained the favour of a number of prominent men and women, mostly either Tories or opposition Whigs, who often had links to the Prince and Princess of Wales – now settled, we recall, just across the water at Richmond. Among those who subscribed to his *Cantate* (1721) were the Duke of Argyll, Alderman John Barber, the Duke of Chandos, Lord Cobham, Lady Hervey (formerly the court lady Molly Lepel), Mrs Henrietta Howard, William Pulteney, the Duke and Duchess of Queensberry and Lord Radnor – all connected with Pope in one way or another, not to mention his intimate friends Arbuthnot, Bathurst, Bethel, William Congreve and Charles Jervas, together with the Wortley Montagus. The last couple had now made their home in Twickenham, and many others on the list were local residents. Pope dared to enter the name of the grand Duchess of Buckingham among the subscribers, as he told her in a letter surprisingly lacking in the obsequious tone to which her grace must have grown accustomed (*Corr.*, vol. 2, pp. 99–100). This short passage of events shows that Pope had not entirely withdrawn from cultural politics, and had even attached himself more securely to the trends of the day when he went to live in Twickenham.

The partisan activity of Bononcini's supporters brought Pope one more significant contact. This was with the singer Anastasia Robinson (*c.* 1692–1755). Born in Italy, the daughter of an English painter, she had started out as a soprano and joined the opera company at the Haymarket Theatre in 1714. She later sang for the Royal Academy of Music (another operatic company) as a contralto, where she earned the remarkable salary of £1,000. She retired two years after making a secret marriage in 1722 with the Earl of Peterborough. The couple did not set up home together, and from 1723 she continued to live near to the Earl's house at Parson's Green, Fulham, with her mother and sister. Lady Mary Wortley Montagu unkindly described Anastasia as at once 'a prude and a kept Mistriss'.[1] The sister, Margaret, was married in 1728 to George Arbuthnot, half-brother of Pope's friend the doctor, but she died in 1729. Around 1722 Pope was told that 'Mrs Robinson haunts Bononcini' (*Corr.*, vol. 2, p. 123). Indeed, she was closely associated with the group of devotees at Twickenham supporting Bononcini. Some had Italian connections and several, like Anastasia, were Roman Catholics. She was instrumental in gaining a pension for Bononcini from Henrietta, Duchess of Marlborough, the eldest daughter and heiress of the great Duke. Pope had probably known her for some time before her marriage. Shortly before his death in 1735, Lord Peterborough finally acknowledged the union (see Chapter 9). Pope continued to visit the widow at her home, Bevis Mount, near Southampton.

One occasion that typifies her role in the circle occurred in January 1723, when a musical soirée was held in honour of the young Duke of Buckingham, who had succeeded to the title on the death of his father in February 1721. It took place at Buckingham House, later developed as Buckingham Palace, and featured Anastasia with the opera orchestra under the direction of Bononcini singing a then unpublished version of *Julius Caesar* by the late Duke. He had supplied two choruses, and two more were provided by Pope. It may be no coincidence that Bononcini's rival Handel produced one of his own great operas, *Giulio Cesare*, just a year later, though this deals with a different episode. Unquestionably Pope was nailing his colours to the mast when he took an active part in this affair: the noble Brutus could be read all too easily as a heroic Atterbury-like figure, punished for his resistance to the tyrannical Walpole. Among all of Pope's Catholic friends, Anastasia stands out as perhaps the most devout. Her close relations with him, both before and after her marriage to the Earl, indicate that the poet harboured a continuing urge to associate with those who, like himself, went on quietly keeping the faith.

Despite these various claims on Pope's time, his major distraction lay elsewhere: it came as a result of the commissions he had accepted and the work he had taken on as editor and translator. Later he spoke of 'the dull duty of an editor', and his feelings about his new Homer undertaking are expressed graphically, if a little sarcastically, in *The Dunciad*: 'Hibernian Politicks, O Swift, thy fate, / And Pope's, whole years to comment and translate' (*TE*, vol. 5, pp. 190–1).[2]

Soon after the last instalment of the *Iliad* appeared in 1720, Pope borrowed a copy of Chapman's Homer from Bishop Atterbury. While the impact of the volume cannot have been on a Keatsian scale, bearing in mind his early exposure to the version by John Ogilby, he evidently felt the need to refresh himself by reading the classic English version of Homer's second epic. (The word 'second' here refers of course to the chronological order of events within the story, since we cannot know the order of composition.)

Why did Pope embark on this renewed heavy labour, in view of the time and trouble that the *Iliad* had cost him? The most obvious, and probably the most adequate, answer has been supplied by Maynard Mack:

> To have taken up again so exacting a task after so short an interlude argues, one is bound to suspect, a financial pinch. The building and gardening he was busy with at Twickenham must have called for considerable outlays and had come, moreover, just at a time when he may have lost part of his earnings from the *Iliad* in the widespread bankruptcy following the collapse of the South Sea Bubble.[3]

We know that this was the opinion of John Gay, from a letter he wrote to Swift, intimating that the venture was undertaken 'rather out of a prospect of Gain than inclination', occasioned by financial losses.[4] However, it would not be too rash to speculate that other factors may have influenced Pope. At some level he seems to have been holding off from original poetry, maybe in part because like others he had not yet come to terms with the new Britain that was emerging in the aftermath of the great crash.

Daunted by the scale of this enterprise, he secretly invited two lesser poets, William Broome and Elijah Fenton, to take a share in the translation. Broome was a clergyman of about Pope's own age who had been educated at Eton and Oxford. With two collaborators he had composed a prose version of the *Iliad* (1712), which probably led to his employment by Pope on the poet's own translation, to make extracts from the commentary of Eustathius used in the notes. Broome served as a rector in Suffolk before he gained a Crown living and other clerical posts in Norfolk. In 1727 Lintot published his *Poems on Several Occasions*, possibly on the recommendation of Pope. After his work on the *Iliad*, Pope hired Broome to translate eight books of the *Odyssey*. Broome came to feel that his work had not been recognized at its full worth, and a coolness developed between the two men: 'He has used me ill, he is ungrateful', Broome told Fenton, his fellow collaborator on the project, in 1728 (*Corr.*, vol. 2, p. 489). He actually figures as one of the hopeless poets in chapter 6 of *The Art of Sinking*,[5] and Pope could not resist an unkind thrust in *The Dunciad*: 'Hibernian Politicks, O *Swift*, thy doom, / And Pope's, translating three whole years with Broome' (*TE*, vol. 5, pp. 190–1). As we have just seen, he afterwards removed the allusion, and the pair came to a truce.

Elijah Fenton, a slightly older man, graduated at Cambridge but he stymied his own career in the Church by refusing to take the prescribed oaths. Partly through the influence of Pope, he was given the task of instructing James Craggs in polite literature in the summer of 1720; Craggs took a house at Twickenham close to Pope's home for this purpose. However, the bursting of the Bubble distracted the student, who was heavily involved in the scandal. After this Fenton became tutor to William, the son of Sir William Trumbull, and he remained at Easthampstead for the remainder of his life. His works included *Oxford and Cambridge Miscellany*, edited for Lintot in 1708; *Poems on Several Occasions* (1717), also published by Lintot; *Mariamne*, a five-act tragedy in verse, successfully presented at Lincoln's Inn Fields theatre in 1723; an edition of *Paradise Lost* by Jacob Tonson junior in 1725, for which he wrote a life of Milton; and an edition of the poems of Edmund Waller (1729), again for Tonson. However, he is remembered today chiefly for his collaboration with Pope in the shape of four books that he contributed to the translation of the *Odyssey*. Unlike Broome, he stayed on good terms with Pope after the nature of his work was uncovered. Fenton also assisted on the Shakespeare edition. Pope regularly spoke of him with a degree of affection: 'Fenton is a right honest man. He is fat and indolent; a very good scholar: Sits within and does nothing but read or compose' (*Anecdotes*, vol. 1, p. 213). Along the same lines, Samuel Johnson related a story that he would 'lie a-bed and be fed with a spoon'.[6] When Fenton died he was buried at Easthampstead, and Pope wrote an epitaph for his monument that still survives in the church. On the list of his deceased friends, Pope noted, 'Elijah Fenton, an honest man, and by no means a bad poet'.[7] In such contexts 'honest' is almost always code for a supporter of the Stuarts.

As time went by Pope came bitterly to regret his decision to employ Broome and Fenton. He kept the lid on what he had done for as long as he could, and when suspicions began to come to the surface he prevaricated in a shameful way. His conduct not only led to a breach with his collaborators, Broome in particular, but also alienated some of the good will within the public that the *Iliad* had brought him. Worse, it provided a ready handle for his critics. For the rest of his career he had to put up with a series of barbs directed against him by hostile pamphleteers, and naturally it was not the sort of thing Grub Street hacks – let alone Edmund Curll – would forget. A sharp attack in 1734 entitled *An Epistle to the Egregious Mr. Pope* even linked the way that the poet behaved badly to the notorious scams of the South Sea episode: 'Thou undertak'st the *Odysssy*, dost not write, / Pope jobs imaginary Stock – a Bite'.[8] The word 'bite' here means a swindle.

Once more the first necessity was to drum up enough subscribers. This time Pope enjoyed the help of Mary Caesar, the fiercely Jacobite wife of one of the doughtiest of all Jacobite MPs, named Charles Caesar. She obtained an astonishing total of seventy subscribers, and this fact among others lends credence to the suspicion that the campaign was in part a cover for Jacobite fund-raising, around the time of the Atterbury plot and its aftermath. Between April 1724 and February 1725 she obtained more than fifty, an outstanding promotional feat. In the printed list Pope put an asterisk with her name and thus 'made a Star of Mrs Caesar, as well as of Mrs Fermor' (*Corr.*, vol. 2, p. 293). This usage unwittingly anticipates the modern sense of 'star', identified in the *OED* as a nineteenth-century theatrical coinage.

Compared with the *Iliad*, the subscription reveals about the same number of Jacobites, declared or reasonably presumed, although some of the leaders of the earlier group have gone missing – dead, disgraced or exiled. Not surprisingly, the constituency that Pope reached averages a little older than before: the median age was 43, as against 39. There are more dukes and duchesses, but fewer of the Whig peers. The biggest jump occurs in the number of sitting MPs in 1725, with 120 making up almost a fifth of the total and no less than 22 per cent of the parliamentary body. (This count omits former members and the twenty-odd future members.) Another advance came in the tally of multiple subscriptions by individuals, although the Duke of Chandos, his wings clipped by the South Sea Bubble, entered his name for only ten copies, as against the fifty he had ordered for Gay's *Poems* in 1720. College affiliations (past and present, not future) show that Oxford maintained a strong hold in the list: Christ Church and New College have gone up, Magdalen declined. The King is present, along with the Prince and Princess of Wales – a real coup, as he did not commonly engage in such ventures. This served as a prelude to the award of a grant of £200 from the Civil List in April 1725, in recognition of the translator's work on the *Odyssey*. Pope made the reasonable claim that, unlike some writers, he could never 'Expect a Place, or Pension from the Crown' (*TE*, vol. 4, p. 227). But if his enemies had heard of this grant, they would certainly not have let him forget it.

Homer did not occupy all of Pope's time. Ever since the death of Thomas Parnell in 1718, he had been assembling the materials for a posthumous edition of his friend's works. In a letter to Jervas somewhat later he linked the recently departed Garth and Rowe with Parnell, 'to whose Memory I am erecting the best Monument I can' (*Corr.*, vol. 2, p. 24). The volume came out in December 1721 from Lintot's shop as *Poems on Several Occasions*, and it contained the best of what Pope's old Scriblerian colleague had left behind – indeed, few works of any substance have been added to the canon in later times. Most significantly, at the head of the volume stood a new poem by the editor, dedicating the enterprise to the Earl of Oxford. On 21 October 1721 he wrote to the Earl, requesting permission to include the verses, and on 6 November his old patron replied expressing his gratitude. 'I look back, indeed', he remarked, 'to those Evenings I have usefully and pleasantly spent with Mr Pope, Mr Parnel, Dean Swift, the

Doctor, &c. I should be glad the World knew you admitted me to your Friendship' (*Corr.*, vol. 2, pp. 90–1).

In fact the poem goes beyond its declared purposes as a remembrance of Parnell and a tribute to the Earl. Its forty lines constitute a hymn to retirement, depicted as a valiant counter-measure against the corruption of powerful men at court.

> In vain to Desarts thy Retreat is made;
> The Muse attends thee to the silent Shade:
> 'Tis hers, the brave Man's latest Steps to trace,
> Re-judge his Acts, and dignify Disgrace.
> When Int'rest calls off her sneaking Train,
> When all th' Oblig'd desert, and all the Vain:
> She waits, or to the Scaffold, or the Cell,
> When the last ling'ring Friend has bid farewel.
>
> (*TE*, vol. 6, pp. 240–1)

These lines have an astonishingly prescient ring, for within two years much of what is said came to apply to another of the Tory stalwarts, Francis Atterbury – once a coadjutor of Robert Harley, and promoted to the bishops' bench through his influence. Like Oxford, Atterbury would be arrested, publicly arraigned in parliament and sent to the Tower of London. Unlike Oxford, he would not escape the reprisal of baying Whigs, and while he avoided the scaffold he would be forced to retreat into exile. As for Oxford, he spent his few remaining years in Herefordshire, seldom coming up to sessions of the Lords – 'Desarts' is a nicely couched hyperbole. Those involved in the Atterbury plot had wanted the Earl to act as their *éminence grise*, but he preferred to stand on the sidelines. He died in 1724 and was succeeded by his son Edward, previously known as Lord Harley. Pope and the new Earl formed an equally close relationship, even though Edward was not greatly interested in politics, taking a sort of default Tory stance. In addition there was a little friction with his wife Henrietta: the marriage of this pair had taken place with great pomp in 1713. Bolingbroke observed with some bitterness in his *Letter to Sir William Windham* that the principal objective in the Lord Treasurer's mind had been to achieve this dynastic union.

We could reasonably call the *Epistle to Oxford* the most overtly political poem that had come from the hand of Pope since *Windsor-Forest*. As Rachel Trickett observes, 'The Muse shares the purpose of history – reflecting and distinguishing, giving praise to the truly great and blame to the vicious'.[9] The key phrase is perhaps 'dignify Disgrace': Pope wanted to remind the Whigs that, while they had brought down Oxford, they had failed to finish him off in 1717 as they had wished. Their conduct, so the poem implies, had been born of a desire to revenge themselves on a discarded statesman, apparently with the monarch's blessing. Now the verdict of history has come in with a resounding 'not guilty', and it is the persecutors of Oxford who merit disgrace. These ideas will re-echo in the political poetry of the 1730s, when part of the opposition plan was to remind the government of their savage treatment of those who had stood against them. The poem in effect rubs the Whigs' noses in the dirt, something Swift attempted shortly afterwards in his epistle to Charles Ford, who was a friend and ally of the Scriblerians.

By the time that the volume of Parnell came out, Pope had already embarked on two other projects. In May 1721 he signed a contract with Jacob Tonson, nephew of old Jacob, to produce a subscription edition of the plays of Shakespeare. On this occasion the venture was designed to make a profit for the publisher, and Pope received a straight fee of little more than £200, far less than he had earned from his work on Homer. He accordingly went about his business with a certain lack of enthusiasm. The subscription went rather lamely. While the ultimate tally of 411 names was moderate in size, it was far lower in social distinction than the lists for Homer translations, as well as smaller by about one third in number. There were also fewer multiple subscriptions entered by individuals. Among other things this reflects some unwillingness on Pope's part to mount the intense personal campaign that he had waged on behalf of his own ventures. Overall the list bears a far more Whiggish colouring, with a substantial presence of Tonson's old friends in the Kit-Cat Club. Interestingly, the median age is lower than usual, with a substantial block of 'new men' in their twenties whom Pope had not reached in his Homer campaigns. They perhaps represented an emerging meritocracy who would come to the fore in the post-Bubble years. All the evidence points to the fact that the undertaking had much less connection with the poet and his personal milieu.

It is true that Pope had taken a great interest in Shakespeare from an early age. He embarked on the work around 1721 and placed an advertisement in the *Evening Post* on 21 October of that year, requesting that anyone with 'old Editions' would get in touch with Tonson. On 18 November Mist's *Weekly Journal* carried a statement that 'The celebrated Mr. Pope is preparing a correct Edition of Shakespear's Works; that of the late Mr. Rowe being very faulty'. Pope's friend Nicholas Rowe had produced his pioneering edition in 1709. This had been the first independent effort to produce a critical edition and text, and it contained the fullest biography of Shakespeare up to that date. From Pope's correspondence it is clear that he set out with the intention of producing a scholarly performance. He consulted his friends, sought out the advice of interested persons such as the cultivated surgeon William Cheselden, and reclaimed an early copy (perhaps the third folio of 1663–4) he had lent to Francis Atterbury. However, he had other irons in the fire. Finding 'the dull duty of an editor' a restricting task, he went to others for help. His friend John Gay and his collaborator on the Homer translation, Elijah Fenton were both paid sizeable sums by Tonson for their aid, while

Pope recruited an unknown 'man or two here at Oxford' to ease him of 'part of the drudgery of Shakespear', at a cost of £35 (*Corr.*, vol. 2, p. 81). By October he could report to William Broome that 'Shakespeare is finished. I have just written the preface', and he anticipated speedy publication (*Corr.*, vol. 2, p. 270) – but more delays followed. As it turned out, the preface was the best thing in the entire production.

When the edition finally appeared in 1725, a far better scholar, Lewis Theobald, pointed out the defects of Pope's performance in a book with the aggressive title, *Shakespeare Restored*. Theobald had several advantages: he knew more of the background in Elizabethan drama than did Pope, and was more accurate in his references. In fact, Pope set out the duties of an editor reasonably well in his preface: unfortunately he was more capricious in his handling of textual matters than his claims would suggest. Moreover, on the biographic side he had little to add to Rowe. Ultimately he had to acknowledge the justice of many of Theobald's points, and without much grace he adopted some of the improvements in a second edition, which came out in 1728. But he possessed a more effective way of humiliating his critics. It was in the same year that the first version of *The Dunciad* appeared, with 'Tibbald' enthroned as the principal laureate of dullness. Even though Theobald brought out his own, rather better, edition of Shakespeare in 1733, much of the damage had been done, and it has taken him almost three centuries to regain some part of his reputation.

Pope had one more literary project under way, and this caused him considerable trouble. As we have just seen, the elderly courtier and poet John Sheffield, Duke of Buckingham, had died in early 1721. Although Pope did not think very much of his writing, he was unable to resist when the imperious widow invited him to edit the works. This was a touchy affair, as some of these works carried a distinct Jacobite flavour. In September 1721 Pope wrote to the younger Tonson that he wished to remove himself from 'the business of the impression', and to take no share in the profits (*Corr.*, vol. 2, p. 81). These would be left to the printer Alderman John Barber, who was granted a royal licence in April 1722 and supervised the publication. All the same, Pope had not heard the last of the affair.

While all this was going on, news came in June 1722 of the death of an erstwhile hero, the Duke of Marlborough. He had suffered at least two strokes and his final days had seen him reduced to something approaching total dementia. A spectacular funeral was mounted at the Abbey, with an astonishing display of the accoutrements of mourning. As Dean it fell to Atterbury to conduct the service, a task which must have seen much gritting of teeth on his part. Shortly before the ceremony Pope wrote to him, 'At the time of the Duke of Marlborough's funeral, I intend to lye at the Deanery, and moralize one evening with you on the vanity of human Glory' (*Corr.*, vol. 2, p. 127). Again this has a prescient ring. In his greatest poem, *The Vanity of Human Wishes*, Samuel Johnson would muse on life's last scene: 'From *Marlb'rough*'s Eyes the Streams of Dotage flow, / And *Swift* expires a Driv'ler and a Show'.[10]

The Tory party in general had never forgiven the Duke for his part in events during the days of Queen Anne. They accused him of deliberately prolonging the war; of allowing City financiers to enrich themselves at the expense of the hard-done taxpayers; of neglecting the suffering of his troops; of exerting undue pressure on the Queen through his wife; of personal misconduct involving graft; and of profiting from the erection of the vast pile at Blenheim Palace at the cost of the public purse. In addition they resented his popularity among the masses, which helped to bring about the downfall of the Oxford ministry.

Pope went along with most of these adverse judgements, no doubt under the influence of Swift's vicious hatred for the Duke. However, he did recognize that Marlborough was an extraordinary figure. He once wrote that the 'Great General ... has meaner mixture [*sic*] with his great Qualities', and that his 'real Merit' and 'shining Virtues as a Public Man' had not been sufficiently transmitted to posterity (*Corr.*, vol. 4, p. 36). He praised Marlborough's courage but deplored his parsimony, relating a number of stories on this theme (*Anecdotes*, vol. 1, pp. 162–4). Most of the references in Pope's poems and correspondence take a negative turn, though often veiled. His most direct assault on the Duke comes in a character sketch originally written around 1731 for *An Essay on Man*, but omitted from the printed text. He considered it 'one of the best I have ever written' (*Anecdotes*, vol. 1, p. 162). The lines refer to almost every one of the charges just listed, and hint at Marlborough's adulteries, a topic that had not surfaced much since his marriage to Sarah Jennings (*TE*, vol. 3.i, p. 155; vol. 6, pp. 358–9). In fact, Pope had already put much of the critique in place at the time of the Duke's fall in 1711. Though he is not mentioned in *Windsor-Forest*, the poem obliquely replays the familiar criticisms. The character sketch also points towards the old man's last years, a scene brilliantly evoked in another damning portrait, Swift's 'Satirical Elegy on the Death of a late Famous General'.

2

With the help of his friends, Pope managed to make steady progress on the *Odyssey*. 'We are but auxiliars', Broome wrote to Fenton in May 1722, 'yet I hope we shall behave so valiantly as to secure Mr. Pope on this throne on Parnassus' (*Corr.*, vol. 2, p. 121). The edition of Shakespeare also advanced, with Fenton especially involved. Tonson arranged for a start to be made on printing what would ultimately be six volumes: the individual title pages bear the date '1723'. However, two major crises intervened in 1722 and 1723. One affected Pope in his personal family life, while the other was a public issue of national importance. But both were ultimately political, and each related to Walpole's efforts to clamp down on dissidents. So, for that matter, did a third uncomfortable passage for Pope regarding the edition he had assembled of the works of the Duke of Buckingham.

The first blow struck with bemusing speed late in the summer of 1722, very soon after the funeral of Marlborough, and a chatty letter in which Atterbury regaled Pope with talk of gardens, gout and Lord Bathurst. On 24 August government messengers arrived to arrest the prelate and carry him off to the Tower. Simultaneously raids were made on the Deanery and the Bishop's country home ten miles south-east of London at Bromley. It quickly emerged that the Secretary of State's office had been keeping a close eye on Atterbury, and with the help of informers had already built up a damaging case against him. A key part of the evidence came from an obscure barrister from Norfolk, who had visited the Pretender at Rome, and now received the offer of a plea bargain. Embarrassingly for Pope's friend John Caryll, his own first cousin, Philip, had gone to the authorities and implicated his Sussex neighbour, Sir Henry Goring, in the plot.[11] Others caught up in the affair were simply riff-raff, career criminals and professional snitches. The omens did not look good, and Pope knew immediately that he himself might be implicated. We can see, too, the beginnings of a growing paranoia about state surveillance, partially justified but exploited for their own ends by those in opposition to Walpole.

The Atterbury plot consisted of a scheme to invade Britain and instal the Stuart claimant on the throne. In the course of 1721 a group of English Jacobites drew up extensive plans for a rising, and sent a list of likely participants to the Pretender. This formed a blueprint for the so-called Atterbury plot. The document set out the strengths of the cause county by county, and named individuals capable of mounting the insurrection, with a suitable 'chief' specified in each case. The West Country and the Welsh border supplied one of the main concentrations of support. First comes Cornwall, with the politically influential Lord Lansdowne as leader. Dorset, in an assignment of more dubious accuracy, was to be commanded by Lord Digby. In nearby Somerset Earl Poulet and Sir William Wyndham headed the list. For Gloucestershire the unquestioned chief was Lord Bathurst. Meanwhile Lord Strafford figures as chief in Northamptonshire, but more crucially through his interest in Yorkshire he became recognized as the overall commander in the north of England. Yorkshire appeared especially promising, since it offered 'the generality of the gentlemen even the whiggs whom Aislaby [John Aislabie, the corrupt Chancellor of the Exchequer, a renegade ex-Tory] drew into the S.S. scheme and ruined'.[12]

The compilers of this list took an unduly sanguine view about some of those they included. For the most part it accurately registered the grandees and upper gentry with clear-cut Tory views, and in an ideal world most would almost certainly have preferred to see a Stuart on the throne. But that does not mean that they were all eager to risk everything on a rebellion whose outcome no one could foresee with confidence. Neither Lord Oxford's brother, Auditor Harley, nor his cousin Thomas appears on the list, and his relatives the Foleys are absent from the entry for Worcestershire. Atterbury may not have been involved in the preparation of this document, but he must have known of its existence. Plans then went ahead for 'A Scheme for a General Rising in England': again, it is uncertain how large a share the Bishop took in composing this. Some of the Stuart supporters urged rapid implementation of the plan, among them two prominent Tory peers, the Earl of Stafford and Lord North and Grey. On the other hand Bathurst and Orrery both considered the scheme a rash one, but expressed a willingness to back a more prudent version.

In the run up to the plot, as we have seen, Pope's friends were busy organizing the subscription to the *Odyssey* translation. Among the subscribers there figured many prominent individuals known personally to Pope, most relevantly Oxford and his son, Auditor Harley, Thomas Harley, Lady Scudamore, Lord Digby, Robert Digby, Lord Strafford, Lord Foley and of course Bathurst. Matthew Prior had died in 1721. At this juncture came the exposure of the whole Jacobite intrigue, as Walpole's informants shopped a number of those implicated, both in England and France. Most of those arrested turned out be low-life characters, and leading supporters among the upper class, for instance the Duke of Norfolk, Lord North and Grey, and the fashionable physician Dr John Freind, spent only a brief period in prison. The government cipherers had little trouble decoding the laxly encrypted correspondence which passed across the English Channel. As often a trivial event helped to break the case: here, a spotted dog called Harlequin given by Lord Mar to Mrs Atterbury, which figured in an intercepted letter. The Tories who had survived so many threats in 1715 once more found themselves exposed to severe peril, as the government went looking for the usual suspects. But among their number only the Bishop of Rochester faced the full blast of retribution.

The conspirators had devised a plan, and to be fair it made sense on paper. According to their scheme, the Duke of Ormonde, still languishing on the Continent after his previous failures, would lead an expeditionary army and would be met by groups of forces organized around the country. Unfortunately leaders of the Jacobite movement as usual were riven by disagreements, which meant they were prone to disastrous failures in planning and execution. The invasion had to be postponed, and in any case Walpole's rudimentary intelligence service had proved up to the job of watching every move the plotters made. Across the water Lord Lansdowne had added his not very extensive strategic talents to the attempt. The Jacobite command had wished to enroll Lord Oxford, at least as a figurehead, but he prudently kept aloof, even though he would most likely have been called up as an elder statesman if the Pretender had succeeded. Bathurst also harboured serious doubts over the entire business, but to his credit he made no effort to conceal his support for those arrested when the plot was busted.

After the Bishop was seized, Pope wrote to John Gay expressing concern at the treatment he was receiving in custody:

> Pray tell Dr. Arbuthnot that even Pigeon-pyes and Hogs-puddings are thought dangerous by our Governors; for those that have been sent to the Bishop of Rochester, are open'd and prophanely pry'd into at the Tower: 'Tis the first time dead Pigeons have been suspected of carrying Intelligence. To be serious, you, and Mr. Congreve (nay and the Doctor [Arbuthnot] if he has not dined will be sensible of my concern and surprize at the commitment of that Gentleman, whose welfare is as much my concern as any Friend's I have. I think my self a most unfortunate wretch; I no sooner love, and, upon knowledge, fix my esteem to any man; but he either dies like Mr. Craggs or is sent to Imprisonment like the Bishop. God send him as well as I wish him, manifest him to be as Innocent as I believe him, and make all his Enemies know him as well as I do, that they may love him and think of him as well!
>
> (*Corr.*, vol. 2, pp. 133–4)

While we can understand his sense of outrage, the poet's sympathy for his friend and his own increasing isolation led him to turn a blind eye to the many signs of guilt. It is true however that letters between Atterbury and Bathurst had been intercepted and vetted for some time, and that the Bishop's enemies remained bent on his destruction. Moreover, Arbuthnot also had his own reasons for anxiety, since an intercepted letter examined by the committee investigating the plot had mentioned his brother Robert, a banker in Rouen and a suspected Jacobite.

Certainly the man in charge of Atterbury in the Tower, Colonel Wilkinson, saw no occasion to use kid gloves. Once the two men came to blows in the cell, and subsequently the only contact allowed by the colonel involved the Bishop shouting down to his children from a window on the top storey, around one hundred feet up. Pope contrived to visit him in his remote quarters and spoke to him through a grill.

The trial started in Westminster Hall on 6 May 1723. A little while before Atterbury had warned Pope that he might need his friend to appear as a witness on his behalf: 'I know not but I may call upon you at my Hearing, to say some what about my way of Spending my Time at the Deanery, which did not seem calculated towards managing Plots and Conspiracys' (*Corr.*, vol. 2, p. 165). On the tenth day of the hearings, Pope's turn came to make his testimony. He did not have a very difficult task, but he obviously felt considerable anxiety about appearing in public. Most observers put this down to simple stage fright, but he may have worried that the prosecution would bring up his religion in irrelevant ways, and that he would give away more than he realized. At all events he worked himself into enough of a state to consult Lord Harcourt, who had led Oxford's defence in 1717:

> Your Lordship gave me a Hint, in relation to what I was to say before the Lords, and to the proper manner of answering, which I thought would be of great service to me, as well as extreamly obliging in your Lordship. I shall certainly to the best of my memory observe it. But I have chanc't to drop a paper in which I had sett it down, and where I had enterd another memorandum to ask you about. Which makes me wish I had found an opportunity this day, or early to morrow, to talk further to your Lordship hereon. I resolve to take any opportunity of declaring (even upon Oath) how different I am from what a reputed Papist is. I could almost wish, I were askd if I am not a Papist? Would it be proper, in such case, to reply, That I dont perfectly know the Import of the word, and would not answer any thing that might for ought I know, be prejudicial to me, during the Bill against such, which is depending. But that if to be a Papist be to profess and hold many such Tenets of faith as are ascribd to Papists, I am not a Papist. And if to be a Papist, be to hold any that are averse to, or destructive of, the present Government, King, or Constitution; I am no Papist.

He added, 'I very much wish I had your Lordships opinion a little more at large, since probably I may not be calld upon this day or to morrow' (*Corr.*, vol. 2, pp. 171–2). Such were the crises of conscience that political intrigues stimulated at this juncture.

The best record we have of the poet's appearance on the witness stand comes from one of the Bishop's counsel. He reports what ensued in this way:

> We have likewise shewn your Lordshps by Mr. *Pope*, who has been for these two or three Years last, the most constant Companion of his Lordship's Hours; Two or Three Days, he says, almost in every Week, and an Hour or two almost in every of those Days: that his Lordship generally sat in one Room which I think was his Bed-Chamber; that he was admitted to him at all Hours, and into all Companies, and never found the Discourse change at his coming in. That his Lordship never in the least discover'd any Thoughts or Intentions like those now charged upon him; but had heard occasionally many Things drop from the Bishop, of a Tendency directly contrary: And to this we might have called many others, if it were necessary.[13]

Either Pope was naive, or he chose to indulge in what he elsewhere called genteel equivocation to save Atterbury's bacon (*Corr.*, vol. 1, p. 350). On balance the second explanation seems more likely. Even though he had nothing to do with the plot, Pope clearly felt that his avowed intimacy with the leading figure in the case had made things uncomfortably hot for him.

The Bishop's speech in his own defence prompted elaborate, maybe excessive, praise among the Tories. According to Neddy Harley, Lord Oxford's nephew, his words left scarcely a dry eye in the House of Lords:

> The Defense was clear Strong and well put together, It took in all the Heads of the Accusation against Him, but He was most particular upon those which his Counsel had not touched upon, And I think He gave a full, clear and Distinct Answer to them all, and with great fairness proved that He was not guilty of any of Those Facts which

they had charged Him with. And I am certain an unprejudiced Person upon Hearing the Accusation and the Defense would have instantly pronounced Him not Guilty.

As to that part of his Speech which related to the Severity of his Punishment, He mentioned it in the most moving expressions, and which drew Tears from Many even from some of the most relentless, Yet these were soon wiped away, and the Violence of their Nature returned strong again, but none appeared so Hardned as his Brethren to whom He applied Himself in a very severe as well as a moving manner, which at least might have awakened them, if it had not any other consequence.[14]

Atterbury spoke for more than two hours, but his famed eloquence could not save him. 'You have met with the fate frequent to great and good men', Pope told the bishop unctuously, 'to gain applause where you are denyed justice'. He added with only a little self-dramatization, 'I must and will correspond with you, till the very moment that it is Felony' (*Corr.*, vol. 2, p. 168).

When Atterbury died in 1732, Pope composed a solemn epitaph on the Bishop. The lines on Atterbury, touching in their simplicity, took this form:

EPITAPH, for Dr. Francis Attterbury, Bishop of Rochester, who died in Exile in Paris, in 1732.
(His only Daughter having expired in his arms, immediately after she arrived in France to see him.)

Dialogue

SHE. Yes, we have liv'd – one pang, and then we part!
May Heav'n, dear father! Now, have *all* thy Heart.
Yet ah! How once we lov'd, remember still,
Till you are Dust like me.
HE.　　　　　Dear Shade! I will:
Then mix this Dust with thine – O spotless Ghost!
O more than Fortune, Friends, or Country lost!
Is there on earth one Care, one Wish beside?
Yes – *save my Country, Heav'n,*
　　　　　– He said, and dy'd.

(*TE*, vol. 6, pp. 343–4)

The die was cast, and Atterbury had to make preparations for his lifelong banishment. Pope visited him on the eve of his departure, when the Bishop presented him with a Bible, published in 1676, to which the poet added a proud inscription commemorating the gift.[15] On 18 June Williamson escorted the prisoner out of the Tower and put him on board the man of war which was to carry him down to the Thames and on to Calais. For the first stage of his journey he had the Duke of Wharton on board with him, to lend moral support. Along the banks of the river many people stood in respectful silence. By now they had grown accustomed to the sight of the Stuarts and their followers leaving for an indefinite term of exile.

One last glint of irony emerged as Atterbury left. Lord Bolingbroke, having relinquished his ties to the Pretender, was granted a partial pardon by Walpole and allowed to return to England. However, he was not permitted to resume his seat in the House of Lords. In effect he was stripped of his political peerage, but not of his social standing. An old story has it that he crossed Atterbury's outward journey at Calais, and observed grimly. 'So we are exchanged'. The detailed timeline makes this unlikely, although Bolingbroke had arrived back on English soil just two days after the Bishop began his passage to France. *Se non è vero, è ben trovato.* Pope was happy to see his friend restored, and wrote to thank Lord Harcourt for his part in bringing this about, speaking of his 'personal Esteem for and Obligation to my Lord Bolingbroke' (*Corr.*, vol. 2, p. 175). The two men resumed their former good, if not wholly intimate, relations, and when Bolingbroke took up residence at Dawley, near Uxbridge to the west of London, regular social meetings became possible. In addition the death of Lord Oxford in May 1724 lessened the pull of conflicting loyalties for Pope. However, many had still not forgiven Bolingbroke for his disloyalty to Oxford, for his supposed cowardice when he fled in 1715, or for his break with the Pretender (it was possible to hold all three things against him at once). Over the next decade Bolingbroke played an important role in the emergent opposition to Walpole, and clearly he hoped to have a major influence on politics despite his neutered condition. Pope admired his philosophy, if not his way of life. But by 1735 the would-be philosopher of opposition had grown disillusioned by his failure to enthuse his old allies, and left again for retirement in France.

Another blow struck just as Atterbury passed out of Pope's life for ever. He refers to the two concurrent events in a letter of 2 June:

> I have not wanted other Occasions of great melancholy, (of which the least is the Loss of part of my Fortune by a late Act of Parliament). I am at present in the afflicting Circumstance of taking my last leave of one of the truest Friends I ever had, and one of the greatest men in all polite learning, as well as the most agreeable Companion, this Nation ever had.

(*Corr.*, vol. 2, p. 174)

The government introduced a vindictive new measure to impose an added burden on Catholics, with 'An Act for granting an Aid to His Majesty, by laying a Tax upon Papists; and for making such other Persons as, upon due Summons, shall refuse or neglect to take the Oaths therein mentioned, to contribute towards the said Tax, for reimbursing to the Public Part of the great Expences occasioned by the late Conspiracies'.[16] The bill passed through all its stages in parliament during the second half of May, despite a protest entered by leading Tories, including Bathurst and Strafford, and some now disgruntled Whigs like Lechmere. Immediately Pope consulted Caryll about the possibility of buying an annuity as a hedge against what could prove to be an impoverished future.

3

Throughout his travails in the midst of the Atterbury affair, Pope had to deal with problems caused by the *Works* of Buckingham. He tried to keep the project at arm's length, as we saw, allowing the printer John Barber (who owned the rights) to micromanage the edition. But Barber had himself become a suspect person at this date as a result of his involvement with the Jacobite movement. He played an important role in the careers of both Pope and Swift, as he provided a link with the politics of the City of London. As will emerge in the next two chapters, this connection provided a significant background to *The Dunciad* and the Horatian imitations of the 1730s.

Barber was born in London, a godson of the writer Elkanah Settle, who figures so prominently in Pope's satire as the forefather of the dunces. Under the Harley administration, Barber had served as official government printer. Now, as the Atterbury plot dominated public attention, he went on a visit to Naples and Rome. It looks very much as if the aim of this trip was not just to recoup his health, as he claimed, but to carry to the Pretender the huge sum of £50,000 (worth millions today) that English Jacobites had raised to support the cause. A good chance exists that he was sent on this mission by the Duchess of Buckingham. On his return he was briefly detained by the authorities and agreed to give up his printing business, perhaps to escape punishment for his political activities. In 1725 he became Sheriff of London, where one of his tasks was to supervise the management of the corrupt Newgate prison. Some of the things he learned in this capacity seem to have ended up with John Gay and found a place in *The Beggar's Opera* a few years later.

If Pope did not realize that the works of Buckingham might involve some risky elements, he soon would. The signs emerged when Edmund Curll announced the appearance of his own unauthorized version of the Duke's works, to be garnished with a life by none other than Lewis Theobald, later cast as the original hero of *The Dunciad*. A formal complaint was made to the House of Lords, and on 23 January 1723 Curll admitted that he had no permission for his proposed work. In a fit of high dudgeon the august members ordered Curll to apologize on his knees before the bar of the House, as well as forbidding publication to go ahead. Moreover, the Lords issued a ruling on 30 January, stating that it was a breach of privilege for anyone to print the works, life or will of a deceased peer – these of course formed Curll's stock in trade. The response was characteristic.

Curll simply removed the life and the will, adding a note that the Duke had revised the works himself and given them to a minor writer named Charles Gildon to publish. Otherwise, the works, backdated to 1721, soon found their way on to Curll's shelves again, probably much in the state they always been.

Meanwhile the Barber version, of which Pope remained the clandestine editor, appeared on 24 January. It ran into immediate trouble. Three days later, the King's messengers (officers employed by the Secretary of State) carried out a search of Barber's printing shop and seized copies of the work as 'a seditious and scandalous Libel'. One press story claimed that Pope himself had been taken in for questioning, but no evidence has emerged to show whether or not this happened. Pope seems to have thought that his old enemies in the Whig circle at Button's coffee-house were to blame, especially Thomas Tickell. In any case, he obviously had to tread very carefully at this juncture, since the government was just then setting up the prosecution of his friend Francis Atterbury. Delicate negotiations went on with the Secretary of State, Lord Carteret. On 9 March the *London Journal* reported that Pope was reediting the volumes in order to 'expunge all those Passages which have given Offence'.[17] The doctored book went back on sale, although several copies survive in which the suppressed portions are present. It was left for Curll to capitalize on events in his usual fashion. He issued a forty-page pamphlet, *The Castrations*, which printed the two offending essays in full. In 1726 the cuts were restored in the Barber edition. Also in that year came a piracy by a notorious fringe operator called T. Johnson in The Hague. Pope changed his mind about taking the profits and received about £200. Barber remained under suspicion by the ministry, and it was apparently Tonson who carried the publication through.

As a result of the actions of the Lords, Pope had to adopt a more cautious policy with regard to his Homer campaign. As he wrote to Lord Harley on 13 February 1723, 'I find such a Cry upon me, however unreasonable, about the Duke's Books … that I am advisd by Lord Harcourt, to defer pushing this Subscription till a more seasonable time'. He acceded to this suggestion, and even proposed writing to the Lord Chancellor, 'proposing to resign my Design on the Odysses to Tickell … and at the same time to vindicate myself from the notion of being a Party man' (*Corr.*, vol. 2, pp. 159–61). The somewhat desperate tone of these letters indicates how anxious Pope was to undo the damage caused by his association with Buckingham's works. Pope had always known that this enterprise, which he had been reluctant to take on, might be dull and laborious. He can scarcely have realized that it would land him in such embarrassments at this fraught juncture.

Worse was to come, involving the family of Pope's sister Magdalen. On 20 May 1723 Charles Rackett and his son Michael, together with two servants, were arrested and charged with deer-stealing in Windsor Forest. Charles was bailed on a large recognizance of £500 to appear in court at the King's Bench a few days later. This was where major state trials were held, and the legal documents suggest Rackett was thought to have taken part in Jacobite, if not treasonable, activities. For some reason the case never went forward. It may have been transferred to Reading assizes, but if so there is no trace there either. This is puzzling since the authorities seemed to have good evidence – a keeper had seen the family at work poaching royal deer. Ultimately Charles escaped punishment: Michael fled the country and received a sentence of outlawry, and his father may have followed him into exile. Charles's death occurred in 1728, and by that time the previously affluent family fortunes were much impaired. The long-term effects on Magdalen Rackett and her children were disastrous, and Pope later had to expend a lot of energy on his attempts to keep them afloat. Although the public at large was unaware of this skeleton in his closet, he had to live with some consequences of the affair for the rest of his days.

The background to this episode concerns the introduction of the notorious Black Act (9 Geo. I, c. 22), passed in the very month that the Racketts fell into the clutches of the law. It was extended for five years in 1725 (12 Geo. I, c. 30), amended in 1754 and made permanent in 1758. Effectively the law survived for a century, until Peel took it off the statute book, despite opposition mounted even at this late date by the *Quarterly Review*. The Act's main provisions were directed against 'wicked and evil-disposed Persons going armed in Disguise, and doing Injuries and Violences to the Persons and Properties of his Majesty's Subjects'. It became a felony without benefit of clergy to go abroad into woods in any form of disguise or with a blackened face. Commission of a specific act of destruction or larceny was not necessary for a prosecution to lie.

The trouble blew up in late 1720, and it had run its main course by the end of 1723. In fact the deer-stealers who came to be known as 'Blacks', from the disguise they sometimes adopted, were operating during this period in two contiguous regions. One group based itself in Hampshire, and drew its members chiefly from the Portsmouth area. It was active in the Woolmer Forest district, together with the Forest of Bere, one corner of which forms Waltham Chase itself. Another group surfaced around the same time in Windsor Forest, principally the Easthampstead-Bagshot portion. The first group reached as far north as Farnham, and some contact may have existed between the two areas of operation, although the evidence on this point is inconclusive. The Rackett affair relates to the Windsor Forest sphere of activity.

National politics had some bearing on the episode, even though at a local level the main cause of disaffection was the existence of harsh forest laws dating from medieval times. Some of those involved may have lost money in the South Sea Bubble. Others were possibly Jacobites and using the occasion to strike at the Hanoverian establishment. In any case the Prime Minister, Robert Walpole, began an energetic exercise to crush the Blacks, allowing the impression to get about that they were linked with the ongoing Atterbury plot. Eventually the government mounted some prosecutions, but only a few convictions were obtained, and sporadic outbursts of Blacking broke out in the forests for years to come.

Pope had further reasons to take notice of what was going on, since as we have seen his mentor Sir William Trumbull had long served as a Verderer, helping to administer forest law. Some of the major activity took place within close range of Easthampstead, where Sir William was lord of the manor. Although Trumbull was dead by this time, his family remained. Again, Pope's patron Viscount Cobham held the office of Constable of Windsor Castle, and as such he stood at the head of the administration of law within the forest. Other issues came up to draw the poet and his friends into the imbroglio. An *agent provocateur* used by the government in Berkshire was Rev. Thomas Power, the curate of Easthampstead and son of the absentee vicar. In 1725, to get him out of the way, he was given a living in Ireland, and there he fell foul of Swift. The Dean wrote contemptuously of 'a certain Animal called a Waltham black ... It is a Cant word for a Deer stealer. This fellow was Leader of a Gang, and had the Honour to hang a half a dozen of his Fellows, in Quality of Informer.'[18] Among those in Berkshire for whom the activities of Power caused great embarrassment was Lady Trumbull, the widow of Pope's mentor. We recall that Philip Caryll, the first cousin of Pope's close friend John Caryll, got himself mixed up in the grubby relations of Jacobite conspiracy and Blacking, emerging as a government informer in 1723. As it turned out, Pope had contacts with many of those who lived in the neighbourhood, including some who were the victims of Blacking. He referred disparagingly to some of the Whig grandees affected (notably Lord Cadogan) and also officials seeking to enforce Walpole's measures. There may well be further undiscovered links between the poet and the principal actors in the affair of the Waltham Blacks. For all these reasons, the episode casts retrospective light on the forest as Pope had portrayed it in the time of Queen Anne.

The question remains as to the exact relationship Pope had to the events, and his precise attitude to them. By far the most searching analysis of the general situation has been made by E. P. Thompson in his brilliant book *Whigs and Hunters*. Thompson presents a theory that the case against the Racketts was 'not quashed but held in suspension'. He argues that Walpole may have held this charge over their heads as a hostage for 'the good behaviour of Alexander Pope'. This was useful, because Pope had seemed in early 1723 to be 'moving towards open criticism of the Walpole regime'. For one thing, 'He had given testimony on behalf of his friend Francis Atterbury, the Jacobite Bishop of Rochester, when on trial before the House of Lords; and his correspondence with the imprisoned Bishop was well known. So also was his friendship with Bolingbroke.' While the charge was impending, it is argued, Pope was forced to 'tread very warily'. Thompson adds, 'It is my impression that for several years, he did'.[19]

In support of this reading of events, Thompson alludes to various passages in Pope's correspondence. One case in point is a letter to Lord Harcourt on 21 June 1723: 'You have done me many and great favours, and I have a vast deal to thank you for' (*Corr.*, vol. 2, p. 175). Thompson thinks this may relate to what he calls Pope's 'great application' at the end of May 1723 to save his brother-in-law from immediate prosecution.[20] It should be emphasized straight away that the phrase 'great application' comes from a press report and is there used without reference to any individual, let alone to Pope himself. The passage in Applebee's *Weekly Journal* on 25 May reports in a gossipy fashion that 'great application is making to men in power in [Rackett's] favour'. The *application* to Pope of this phrase is Thompson's own.

Also cited are a number of passages in the correspondence which show Pope in a sombre mood in the summer of 1723. These contain explicit references to the taxation of Catholics; to 'the ocean of avarice and corruption' in post-South Sea days; to Bolingbroke, Atterbury and Peterborough. What they do not mention is the Blacking episode, at least in any transparent way. Thompson detects a covert allusion: an expression used to Swift around August ('all those I have most lov'd and with whom I have most liv'd, must be banish'd') might 'carry a reference to the Racketts'. In any case, the text comes from a transcript among the Cirencester papers: it might always (we are to suppose) have been doctored. A month or so later, Swift replied. His response at this point reads: 'I have often made the same remark with you of my Infelicity in being so Strongly attached to Traytors (as they call them) and Exiles, and State Criminalls' (*Corr.*, vol. 2, pp. 184, 198). This passage was excised when Pope printed the letters, and the source is again a transcript: but, Thompson assures us, a 'more reliable' one.[21]

Thompson reached the conclusion in what is conceded to be 'a matter of speculation' that the Blacking affair turned Pope 'decisively' from the pastoral mode, and 'directed him more urgently towards satire'. Of course, the shock was postponed:

> Yet, though evidently working inside him, the satire was delayed expression for several years. It is customary to attribute this to his preoccupation with the work on his Homer. But if we recall the earlier suggestion that – at least until Charles Rackett's death – Pope remained in some way a hostage to Walpole's favour, one may see his predicament in a different way.[22]

The problem here is that the argument disposes of the most sustained labour of Pope's life as a seminal force, and explains by a single obscure incident a creative process which began very much earlier in the poet's life.

Naturally Thompson provides a sophisticated argument, based on his detailed gasp of local and national politics. He also makes some interesting observations on Pope, especially with regard to *Windsor-Forest*. But his case neglects some key facts, such as Pope's continuing good relations with Lord Cobham. At times it seems to eschew any directly literary or aesthetic concerns which are likely to have governed the poet's choice of words. For example, Thompson cites the insertion of two new lines in *Windsor-Forest* on its publication in 1713: 'Fair Liberty, *Britannia*'s Goddess rears / Her cheerful Head, and leads the golden Years'. The copy of the poem Pope made in 1712 had four different lines at this point, alluding to the wrongs endured under 'a foreign Master's Rage' – formally, anyway, relating to the treatment of New Forest by William I. These four lines were printed in a note when Pope revised the text for editions from 1736 onwards. It is quite clear that the revised version is more discreet: we should, however, note that this discretion was exercised before the Hanoverians came to the throne, and may well have to do with its offensiveness concerning William III – *not* the future George I. Second, Thompson calls the revised couplet 'more gummy' than the material it replaces. The verses are also poetically superior, surely; more economical, more apt to the stylistic decorum of the work as a whole, more resonant for the total allegory. The mention of Britannia cements a theme later developed. One phrase introduced ('the golden Years') has often been quoted as a 'key image', central to the imaginative design of *Windsor-Forest*. Such aesthetic concerns plainly occupied a large part of Pope's attention when he revised the manuscript for publication. They do not enter at any point into Thompson's calculations.

Whatever the truth about these matters, no one can doubt that the affair of the Blacks in some sense poisoned the golden glades of Windsor. At the heart of Pope's work had lain a certain imaginative centre that went beyond the pastoral to a kind of ecological or 'green' quality, whereby the health of the nation was guaranteed by the protection of a sylvan fastness (see Chapter 3). This could be violated by an intruder such as William I, Cromwell, William III – or Walpole. Events in 1723 may not have exactly shattered the dream, but Pope found it hard to hold on to his faith in these historic values. It was not the only force impelling him towards resuming his career as a satirist, but Thompson is right to see it as one of the factors that pulled the poet in this direction.

4

Most of 1725 was taken up with the business of getting into print both the Shakespeare edition and the first instalment of the *Odyssey*. This involved much toing and froing with Pope busily networking among publishers and subscribers. His regular trips to London left his spirits somewhat depleted, to judge by the weary air of his letters. A foolish controversy over the monument in Twickenham parish church to Sir Godfrey Kneller cost him further energy. The artist had died in 1723 and was succeeded as official portrait painter to King George by Charles Jervas. There was no let-up in the stream of abusive pamphlets from Curll, while the *Odyssey* enjoyed a mixed reception, partly as a result of Pope's use of hidden assistants in Fenton and Broome. Occasional trips to the houses of friends like Lord Oxford and the Duchess of Buckingham gave him some relief, while gratifying news came when Swift announced his intention of visiting England for the first time in over a decade. But Pope was plunged into grief by the death of his old nurse, Mary Beach, who passed away in November aged about seventy-seven. This must have thrust further responsibility on to Pope with regard to the care of his mother, now frequently ailing – no surprise, as Edith had now entered her eighties.

The big event of 1726 came with the arrival of Swift in March, bringing with him a time-bomb in his luggage – the manuscript of *Gulliver's Travels*. He spent some time with Bolingbroke at Dawley before moving a few miles to Twickenham. Throughout the summer Swift spent much of his time with old friends such as Pope, Gay and Bathurst. A newer acquaintance was Voltaire, currently exiled from France after a spell in the Bastille as a result of unwisely free speech at the expense of a nobleman. He was impressed by Swift, and in a more qualified way by Pope: a section of his *Lettres philosophiques* (1733) is allotted chiefly to Pope, described as 'the most elegant, the most correct Poet; and at the same Time the most harmonious ... that *England* ever gave birth to'.[23] In August the Dean left to return to Dublin, having finalized arrangements for the publication of *Gulliver* with the bookseller Benjamin Motte, delighting in some preposterous mystifications over the book's origins. It made a tremendous impact on the reading public when it appeared at the end of October. 'There has been a vast demand for Gulliver', Arbuthnot told Lord Oxford: the Princess of Wales burst out laughing when she came to one episode.

> Minesterial folks say the book is a pleasant humorous book and it was pity he descended so low, as some Little satyr, that is too particular some Folks that I know went immediately to their Maps to look for Lillypott, and reckond it a fault in their Maps not to have sett down. Lord Scarborrow Mett with a Sea Captain that Knew Guliver but he said the bookseller was mistaken in placing his habitation at Rothereth [Rotherhithe] for he was sure he livd at Wapping. in short the Book has made very good diversion to all the town.
>
> (*Corr.*, vol. 2, p. 411)

As a whole, the establishment decided to close ranks. Shrugging off the harsher implications of the work, they sought to rejoice in the common opinion of the *Travels* as a harmless diversion. 'Gulliver is a happy man that at his age can write such a merry book', Arbuthnot wrote to the author with a degree of irony that it is hard to calculate.[24]

On 16 November Pope took up the issues in a letter to Swift:

> I congratulate you first upon what you call your Couzen's wonderful Book which is *publica trita manu* [heavily read by the public] at present, and I prophecy will be in future the admiration of all men. That countenance with which it is received by some statesmen, is delightful; I wish I could tell you how every single man looks upon it, to observe which has been my whole diversion this fortnight. I've never been a night in London since you left me, till now for this very end, and indeed it has fully answered my expectations.
>
> I find no considerable man very angry at the book: some indeed think it rather too bold, and too general a Satire: but none that I hear of accuse it of particular reflections (I mean no persons of consequence, or good judgment; the mob of Critics, you know, always are desirous to apply Satire to those that they envy for being above them) so that you needed not to have been so secret upon this head. Motte receiv'd the copy (he tells me) he knew not from whence, nor from whom, dropp'd at his house in the dark, from a Hackney-coach: by computing the time, I found it was after you left England, so for my part, I suspend my judgment.
>
> (*Corr.*, vol. 2, p. 412)

How far does *Gulliver's Travels* offer a direct political commentary on its times? This question has excited debate ever since the book first came out, and no definitive answer has ever proved to be possible. The Lilliputian part certainly gets in some sharp digs at George I and Walpole, and arguably a more pervasive thread of reference develops to events such as the impeachment of Oxford, the Bubble and the trial of Atterbury. In the third voyage, which has always been the least popular, Swift devotes a lot of space to the lunacies of contemporary science, as he judged them when he perused the columns of the Royal Society *Transactions*. But even here much of the satire appears to relate to the South Sea affair. One thing can be said with confidence: the book breathes an air of traditional humanism, and has little time for the trappings of power or the ambitions of *conquistadores*. That does not constitute a party manifesto in the narrow sense; but there is little doubt that Pope and the other Scriblerians expected the book to offer Walpole and his allies absolutely no comfort.

At the moment when *Gulliver* appeared, Pope had just suffered a serious injury. In September, when he was returning from a visit to Bolingbroke at Dawley, his coach was overturned while descending a steep bank near the River Crane. Pope found himself trapped in the partially submerged coach until one of Bolingbroke's footmen broke a window and pulled him out. He was taken to the nearby home of the Catholic lawyer Nathaniel Pigott. In the process he received a bad cut to his right hand, which threatened to result in the loss of two fingers. Fortunately he got by without permanent damage, although for a time he had to use John Gay as an amanuensis. The event became a widely known story, and Voltaire wrote to commiserate with the poet. Years later Pope wrote to beg a place for the footman, a Belgian named Philippe Hanaus, who had saved his life.[25]

Among the sadder events of 1726 came the death of Robert Digby, one of Pope's most valued friends. His father was William, fifth Baron Digby (1662–1752), who as an Irish peer with a base in the town of Coleshill served as MP for Warwick. However, his High Church principles and alliances (including friendship with the saintly Bishop Thomas Ken and the philanthropist Thomas Bray) pushed him towards the nonjurors, and he spent most of his time living a quiet country life at his seat, Sherborne in Dorset. Two sons and a daughter died in young adulthood. One of these was Robert, Pope's great ally in gardening projects. Another son, Edward, was known to Pope and helped to distribute copies of *The Dunciad* in 1729. The great fondness Pope had for the family is shown by the epitaph that he wrote for Robert and his sister Mary, who died from smallpox in 1729, which was placed in Sherborne Abbey by their father. Robert worked obsessively on the fine gardens at his family estate, which Pope visited in 1724 and where his advice obviously came in useful. In turn, Digby stayed with the poet at Twickenham. About twenty letters survive from the correspondence of the two men, who had met by 1717. Robert had long suffered from ill health, but his death on 21 April 1726 came as a considerable blow (*Corr.*, vol. 2, pp. 375–6). In *An Essay on Man* the poet mused on Robert's early death:

> Say, was it Virtue, more tho' Heav'n ne'er gave,
> Lamented DIGBY! Sunk thee to the grave?
> Tell me, if Virtue made the Son expire,
> Why, full of days and honour lives the Sire?

(*TE*, vol. 3.i, p. 138)

Such thoughts often have a hidden partisan basis: an equally apt question might be why men like Coningsby, singularly bereft of these virtues, were also fated to live on to a good old age. Robert Digby subscribed to both the *Iliad* and the *Odyssey*. In one of his brief obituaries, Pope described him as 'endowed with the ancient moral qualities of his father',[26] and he kept a portrait of his departed friend in his house at Twickenham. Together with Lord Bathurst, and his own cousin Viscountess Scudamore, Robert formed a tight network of Pope's supporters active mainly in the border country. Frances Scudamore was a daughter of the fourth Lord Digby and had married James, Viscount Scudamore, a member of the most important Tory family in Herefordshire, and went to live in their impressive home outside Hereford. There she conducted a prolonged battle over local spoils with her neighbour, the intransigent Whig Thomas Coningsby. Digby often visited his cousin at Holme Lacy, and Pope is thought to have done so on more than one occasion. He had met Lady Scudamore, probably through

Charles Jervas, around 1715, and their friendship ripened over the succeeding years. The main common element that united this gang of four was undoubtedly their love of landscape gardening, but there was a deeper cultural attachment, too, which was expressed in their Tory attitudes and outrage over the treatment of Atterbury in 1723.

As with the South Sea episode, Pope would use the *Epistle to Bathurst* to construct a profound mediation on earlier personal and public history involving his western alliance. In part the *Epistle* may serve as a memorial to Lady Scudamore, who had also died of smallpox in 1729, just five weeks after Mary Digby. The poem sets up a neat symmetry between the Scudamore-Digby domain of Herefordshire and Bathurst's sphere of influence in the adjoining county of Gloucestershire, symbolized by the Wye and the Severn: 'Pleas'd Vaga echoes thro' her winding bounds, / And rapid Severn hoarse applause resounds' (*TE*, vol. 3.ii, p. 114). Not enough attention has been paid to this dimension of the *Epistle*, which lays over the discussion of city politics a vision of the rural, centring on Bathurst, the second Earl of Oxford and the Herefordshire philanthropist John Kyrle, known as 'the Man of Ross'. Pope does not mention Digby and Lady Scudamore by name, but as we shall see in Chapter 8 their ghosts haunt the text of this poem.

With the publication of the last instalment of the *Odyssey* in June, Pope was at last free from an undertaking which had absorbed most of his energies for all of thirteen years. While we can seek out occasional passages in the translation which cast an oblique light on contemporary events, the task had largely removed Pope from the *va et vient* of everyday politics. By now he had been forced to acknowledge the collaboration first of Broome and later of Fenton, a circumstance that overshadowed the publication of the last volumes. Even more embarrassment came as a result of a typical piece of opportunism on the part of Edmund Curll. For a price of ten guineas the scallywag bookseller had bought a packet from letters from a poet named Elizabeth Thomas, who had fallen on hard times and was trying – without success, as it turned out – to stave off incarceration in the Fleet debtors' jail. She had formerly been an acquaintance and possibly mistress of Pope's friend from his youth, Henry Cromwell. The packet included a large cache of Pope's early letters to Cromwell. They contained nothing much in the way of libel or sedition, luckily, but they did show the young man as coltish and irresponsible, with a taste for smutty jokes. Curll made the most of his find, setting them at the head of the first of two volumes called *Miscellanea, Never before Published*. The contents of this production were like Curll's usual fodder, in other words a ramshackle collection of literary bric-a-brac scavenged from any available source. But it was the first eighty pages, where the Cromwell material appeared, which caused all the fuss. The publisher regularly advertised the work as *Mr. Pope's Familiar Letters*, with occasional variants. Pope retaliated against Thomas in *The Dunciad*, giving her an undignified part in the action as 'Curll's Corinna'. She retorted in 1728 with a stinging mock-biography entitled *Codrus*. As for Curll himself, he would face many more rough blows from Pope; but this must count as one of his better days in the long contest between the poet and the publisher.

So the new year of 1727 dawned, with the possibility of a repeat visit from Swift. It may have been these contacts with his old colleague and club-mate that inspired Pope to go ahead with a Scriblerian poem he had been contemplating for some time. Allegedly, the first sketch of this work 'was snatch'd from the fire by Dr. Swift, who persuaded his friend to proceed in it' (*TE*, vol. 5, p. 201). By 1725 Pope could quote to the Dean a few lines of what became *The Dunciad* (*Corr.*, vol. 2, p. 332). Another spur to action came when Lewis Theobald produced *Shakespeare Restored* in 1726, offering the poet a model for what he portrayed as intrusive and wrong-headed scholarly commentary. So the possibilities were opening up for Pope to resume his stalled career as a major satirist. With a fresh access of energy and confidence, he had already embarked on a collection of the Scriblerians' earlier work, to appear as the first two volumes of *Miscellanies* – in part as a riposte to Curll's *Miscellanea*. On 17 February 1727 he announced that publication was imminent:

> Our Miscellany is now quite printed. I am prodigiously pleas'd with this joint-volume, in which methinks we look like friends, side by side, serious and merry by turns, conversing interchangeably, and walking down hand in hand to posterity; not in the stiff forms of learned Authors, flattering each other, and setting the rest of mankind at nought: but in a free, un-important, natural, easy manner; diverting others just as we diverted ourselves. The third volume [not yet ready] consists of Verses, but I would chuse to print none but such as have some peculiarity, and may be distinguish'd for ours, from other writers. There's no end of making Books, Solomon said, and above all of making Miscellanies, which all men can make.
>
> (*Corr.*, vol. 2, p. 426)

Three months late, John Gay produced his politicized *Fables*, his first substantial composition for a long time, which were to make a great splash. The Scriblerians were queuing up with satires of the first magnitude ready for the press. All looked set fair for a great renaissance for the group, who could hope to walk down to posterity in the aftermath of the huge success enjoyed by *Gulliver's Travels*.

But before all this came to fruition, there would be further developments in the outside world which made a heavy impact on the new work Pope had planned.

PART III: GEORGE II, 1727–44

7 DUNCE THE SECOND REIGNS

> How will you pass this Summer for want of a Squire to Ham-common and Walpole's lodge; for, as to Richmond lodge and Marble-hill they are abandond as much as Sir Spencer Compton.
>
> Pope to Martha Blount, 1728 (Corr., vol. 2, p. 476)

In the spring of 1727 Swift obtained leave for six months from his post in Dublin and travelled once more to England, on what proved to be his last visit. He arrived at Twickenham around 21 April. After spending a week there, he went up to London for a short stay with Gay at his lodgings in Whitehall, leaving Pope to care for his sick mother. He soon returned to the villa along with Arbuthnot. In May the second edition of *Gulliver* appeared, with some amusing verses by his friends added. The associates were already busy with the third volume of *Miscellanies*, intended chiefly as a collection of poetry, with Swift, Pope and Gay all well represented. Their correspondence that summer included amiable letters between themselves and their allies, including Bolingbroke, Oxford, Mrs Howard and even Voltaire, who finally met Swift in May and offered to help him with a planned visit to France.

Suddenly this scheme was put on ice. George I had set out for his beloved Hanover on 3 June. A week later he was travelling by coach towards Osnabrück when he suffered a stroke. A surgeon in the party ordered immediate bleeding, the best recourse that the basic medicine of the time could offer. But all efforts proved in vain, and the King died on 10 June. On the afternoon of the 14th the news reached London, when Walpole dashed out to Richmond to summon the Prince and Princess of Wales back to the capital for their proclamation at Leicester House. Everything in the political world had entered a state of total flux. Immediately Bolingbroke advised Swift to defer his Continental jaunt, as there might now be better prospects for him in England. Along with everyone else, Pope and his friends waited to see what developed at this critical moment. Some, like Gay, had particularly high hopes. Bolingbroke, who had made an inept attempt to get the old King in his last days to dismiss Walpole, now felt that the tide might finally have turned for his party, after their long spell in the wilderness.

The confused scenes that followed have often been described. If Thackeray provided the most graphic narrative in *The Four Georges*, a somewhat more reliable account comes from Lord Hervey in his memoirs. When Walpole got to Richmond he found the heir to the throne in bed taking an afternoon siesta. As Hervey relates, 'Whatever questions Sir Robert asked him with regard to the council being summoned, his being proclaimed, or other things necessary immediately to be provided, the King gave him no other answer than "Go to Chiswick and take your directions from Sir Spencer Compton".[1] Walpole rightly took this as a notice of dismissal, as the new King had never much trusted him. Compton seemed much better placed, as he held the office not just of Speaker in the Commons, but also of Treasurer to the Prince of Wales. Throughout the reign of George I, dissident Whigs along with Hanoverian Tories had placed their expectations on what was called the reversionary interest, that is the prospect of favour and employment when the new monarch took over. These men had assiduously courted the Prince and Princess, and now looked to Compton to clear out the old ministry in return for their steadfast conduct in opposing almost everything that Walpole had done.

They could scarcely have made a worse choice. Compton, a member of the Sussex gentry in his early fifties, showed himself quite unequal to the task. He had sat in parliament for thirty years, latterly as Speaker, without reaching high ministerial office. A dependable Whig, he took part in Sacheverell's trial, speaking with such passion that at times he 'trembled in every joint and almost foamed at the mouth'.[2] He had also held the remunerative job of Paymaster-General for some time. But none of his experience as a busy House of Commons man prepared him for the leadership role he now needed to play. In the words of Hervey:

> Sir Spencer Compton was at this time Speaker of the House of Commons, Treasurer to the Prince, and Paymaster to the army. He was a plodding, heavy fellow, with great application, but no talents, and vast complaisance for a Court without any address. He was always more concerned for the manner and form in which a thing was to be done than about the propriety or expediency of the thing itself; and as he was calculated to execute rather than to project, for a subaltern rather than a commander, so he was much fitter for a clerk to a minister than for a minister to a Prince.[3]

Edith Pope drolly called him 'the Prater' (*Corr.*, vol. 2, p. 303). The urgent need at this point was to draft a suitable speech for the new King, as well as to prepare a budget to provide for royal expenses: but Compton jibbed at the task, and when Walpole arrived at his house he had to ask the former First Lord to prepare a draft that he could copy out.

The Privy Council had now assembled at the Prince's home in Leicester Fields, as Hervey again relates with malicious glee:

> Sir Robert, retiring into a room by himself, went immediately to work, and Sir Spencer Compton to Leicester Fields, where the King and Queen were already arrived, and receiving the compliments of every man of all degrees and all parties in the town. The square was thronged with multitudes of the meaner sort and resounded with huzzas and acclamations, whilst every room in the house was filled with people of higher rank, crowding to kiss their hands and to make the earliest and warmest professions of zeal for their service. But the common face of a Court at this time was quite reversed, for as there was not a creature in office, excepting those who were his servants as Prince, who had not the most sorrowful and dejected countenance of distress and disappointment, so there was not one out of employment who did not already exult with all the insolence of the most absolute power and settled prosperity.

Everyone sought out the presumed favourite:

> As soon as Sir Spencer Compton had been with the King in his closet, he returned to his coach through a lane of bowers in the ante-chambers and on the stairs, who were all shouldering one another to pay adoration to this new idol, and knocking their heads together to whisper compliments and petitions as he passed.[4]

For a few days Compton basked in his fresh glory, and the outlook remained promising. Tories who had pointedly absented themselves from court for more than a decade suddenly showed up again. People started giving Walpole a wide berth. A few tentative approaches were made to the more moderate Tories. But it took George II very little time to discover that Compton lacked the qualities he was looking for, particularly on the crucial point of getting an adequate maintenance from the Civil List approved, something that parliament had to settle before it went on recess. As the days went by, the fact grew more obvious to the King that he would do better to stick with Walpole, despite his personal antipathy for the minister. In this he had the support of Caroline, who with her usual shrewdness in these matters had recognized that the most promising way of cutting a favourable deal with the Commons on the royal allowance would be to keep the present minister in power. In turn Walpole had rightly seen that Caroline, rather than the King's official mistress, Henrietta Howard, provided the best avenue to pursue when he wanted to influence George's decisions.

By the time that parliament was dissolved in August, Compton's incompetence had become clear to all, and he could expect nothing better than a peerage and a few stately posts on the fringe of government. The general election which followed immediately afterwards consolidated Walpole's position. This time the Tories gained only about 130 seats, an even lower number than their previous results under George I. Equally, the opposition Whigs led by William Pulteney attracted minimal support. The great majority of the Commons, over 400 members, was made up either of placemen who owed their living to the Prime Minister or else independents who willingly allowed him to get on with governing the country, so long as he did not disturb their settled ways or intervene in their local dominion. Compton was replaced as Speaker by Arthur Onslow, who would serve for a record thirty-three years. The new man contrived to keep a reputation for integrity in his post while never seriously rocking the ministerial boat.

This train of events quashed any hope that the Scriblerian group would find greater favour at court, even though Pope and, especially, Gay had taken pains to support the Prince against his father. In the event Gay received nothing more than the offer of a position as gentleman usher to Princess Louisa, the royal couple's two-year-old daughter, at a salary of £150. As he told Swift, 'upon account that I am so far advanc'd in life, I have declin'd accepting'. Pope wrote him a long letter commending his friend on this principled decision, and declared him 'a free-man' rather than a slave at court (*Corr.*, vol. 2, pp. 453–4). Meanwhile Swift had taken himself back to Dublin in a state of depression, stating on his return that he was sure Gay had 'a firm Enemy in the Ministry', that is Walpole.[5] In addition to his blighted hopes of preferment in England, Swift had another reason for dreading to go back to the Deanery: it lay in the failing health of his 'most valuable friend', Esther Johnson, known to posterity as 'Stella'. She lingered on until January 1728, when Swift through some mixture of embarrassment, cowardice and *amour propre* could not even bring himself to attend her funeral.

In 1731 Swift gave literary expression to all the disappointment he and his friends had felt at the time of the old King's death. He had heard a mistaken story that Gay was to become steward to his patrons the Duke and Duchess of Queensberry. Gay wrote to tell him that this was untrue, but his friend took the chance to write a blistering attack on the other 'manager', that is Walpole. Swift's poetic epistle 'To Mr. Gay' casts the Prime Minister as an unjust steward, making obvious use of Christ's parable in Luke 16:1–18: as we shall see in the next chapter, Pope would invoke the same text in his satires of the 1730s. Near the end of Swift's poem occurs this passage:

> I knew a *brazen* Minister of State,
> Who bore for twice ten Years the public Hate.
> In every Mouth the Question most in Vogue
> Was, *When will* THEY *turn out this odious Rogue*?
> A Juncture happen'd in his highest Pride:
> While HE went robbing on, *old Master* died.
> We thought, there now remain'd no room to doubt:
> *His Work is done, the Minister must out.*
> The Court invited more than One or Two:
> Will you, Sir *Spencer*? or will *you*, or *you*?
> But not a Soul his Office durst accept:

The subtle Knave had all the Plunder swept.
And, such was then the Temper of the Times,
He owed his Preservation to his Crimes.
The Candidates observ'd his dirty Paws;
Nor found it difficult to guess the Cause:
But, when they smelt such foul Corruptions round him;
Away they fled, and left him as they found him.
Thus, when a greedy Sloven once has thrown
His *Snot* into the *Mess*; 'tis all his own.[6]

The bitter tone is understandable. If Walpole had lost power when the 'juncture happened' in 1727, as his enemies had so confidently predicted, the new reign might have followed a quite different course. Pulteney could have been brought into the government, perhaps, and the Pelham brothers (Thomas, Duke of Newcastle, and Henry) might have been sent out to pasture. Lord Carteret, with whom Swift at least was on good terms, could have risen to the post of considerable power he always threatened to attain, but to which he never clung for very long. Conceivably, the government would have granted Bolingbroke a full pardon and allowed him back into the Lords. But once more these amount only to the flimsy speculations of alternative history. The reality was that Walpole had managed to ensconce himself in authority, and not for another fifteen years would his grip loosen.

1

The first two volumes of the Scriblerian *Miscellanies* were published by Benjamin Motte around 22 June 1727. Pope's main contribution to the first volume took the form of a preface, jointly signed by Swift and himself, and dated from Twickenham on 27 May. This offers a halfway plausible justification for the enterprise:

> Having both of us been extreamly ill treated by some Booksellers, (especially one *Edmund Curll*), it was our Opinion that the best Method we could take for justifying ourselves, would be to publish whatever loose Papers in Prose and Verse, we have formerly written; not only such as have already stolen into the World (very much to our Regret, and perhaps very little to our Credit,) but such as in any Probability hereafter may run the same Fate, having been obtained from us by the Importunity, and divulged by the Indiscretion of Friends, although restrain'd by Promises, which few of them are ever known to observe, and often think they make us a Compliment in breaking.
>
> But the Consequences have been still worse: We have been entitled, and have had our Names prefixed at length, to whole Volumes of mean Productions, equally offensive to good Manners and good Sense, which we never saw or heard of till they appeared in Print.[7]

These statements contain only a limited amount of truth. Spurious works had been foisted on to both men, Swift especially. Unscrupulous operators like Curll had obtained some of their works by groping around the trash-can of celebrities, but in most cases the author had permitted the item to reach the public through carelessness or deliberate connivance. Clearly Pope had wished for some time to bring out a selection of his own uncollected works, and persuaded Swift during his trips to England to allow his writings to appear, as a counterblast to the illicit edition of his miscellaneous works that Curll had produced in 1711, 1714 and 1721. The project also embraced works by Gay and Arbuthnot, as acknowledged at the end of the preface. A few relatively unimportant items now came before the public for the first time. Obviously the team wished to assert, or reassert, their copyright in the various contents.

The first volume is made up entirely of Swift's compositions. Apart from the early 'Contests and Dissentions' (1701), a Whiggish take on the disputed partition treaties at the end of King William's War, the contents largely eschew direct political comment. None of the excoriating pamphlets that Swift had written in support of Oxford's ministry during the peace process gained admission. The second volume reprints at the start all five parts of Arbuthnot's 'History of John Bull', still pointed in its satire but not quite so explosive as it had been fifteen years earlier. More puzzling at this date was Swift's 'Famous Prediction of Merlin' (1709), a mock-prophecy with the full Scriblerian apparatus of pseudo-learned notes. Pope included three of his own minor prose works, none of them likely to arouse charges of scurrility or libel. The hotter properties he kept back for later instalments of the series.

Before that happened, he made considerable progress on *The Dunciad*, with the coronation of George and Caroline on 11 October offering up new possibilities for satire. Today, the best remembered feature of this occasion comes with the 'soaring drama' of four new anthems provided by Handel, notably 'Zadok the Priest', still performed each time a coronation takes place.[8] Pope noticed delicious absurdities in the somewhat ill-managed ceremonial, apt to his satiric purposes. On the first day of 1728 he wrote to Swift about the imminent appearance of the *Miscellanies*, adding that the doctor (Arbuthnot) had 'grown quite indolent in it'. As for the other major work in hand: 'It grieves me to my Soul that I cannot send you my Chef d'oeuvre, the Poem of Dulness, which after I am dead and gone, will be printed with a large Commentary, and lettrd on the back, *Pope's Dulness*'. He did however send the opening invocation to Swift, famous lines addressed to his friend under 'whatever Title please thy ear, / Dean, Drapier, Bickerstaff, or Gulliver' (*Corr.*, vol. 2, pp. 468–9). This tribute carried an impolitic reminder of Swift's efforts under the guise of a Dublin draper to resist the English government's attempts to foist a shoddy coinage on the Irish in

1724. For prudential reasons, Pope omitted the lines in the first edition and they saw the light only in the variorum edition a year later.

By this stage Gay had completed *The Beggar's Opera* and following its rejection by Colley Cibber and the managers of Drury Lane theatre he began to ready the play for its premiere at Lincoln's Inn Fields. The first night on 29 January 1728 attracted a fashionable audience, including Pope and his many of his friends, headed by the Duke of Argyll. At first the success of the piece hung in the balance, but gradually the house warmed under some encouragement by the Duke, and the final curtain brought 'a clamour of applause', as Pope noted (*Anecdotes*, vol. 1, pp. 107–8). After this the play enjoyed a phenomenal run, with royal command performances and proceeds of £700 or more for Gay in the first few weeks. In the end he probably made something like £2,000 all told. The *Opera* was among the most popular plays on the English stage in the eighteenth century and it is still regularly revived in the theatre, quite apart from performances on film and television

The play has its roots in Scriblerian ideas of generic transformation. Swift wrote to Pope in 1716, suggesting that a 'Newgate pastoral' might form a possible subject for Gay's dramatic talents (*Corr.*, vol. 1, p. 360). Pope stressed that Gay was the sole author of the play, though he admitted that appearances were against this, 'for 'twas writ in the same house with me and Dr. Swift. [Gay] used to communicate the parts of it, as he wrote them, to us, but neither of us did more than alter an expression here and there' (*Anecdotes*, vol. 1, p. 57). As the play headed towards its premiere, Pope and Gay kept Swift apprised of its progress. The great coup came in finding suitable words to match both the storyline and the music of some familiar tunes, principally ballads, which were set by the Prussian-born composer Johann Christoph Pepusch. The play initiated a taste for ballad opera, which lasted for decades to come. Subsequent arrangements have been made by Benjamin Britten and others, while Kurt Weill supplied original music for Bertolt Brecht's topical adaptation *Die Dreigroschenoper*, or *Threepenny Opera* (1928).

In the course of the play, the author has fun with many contemporary topics, including the current rage for Italian opera and the cult of superstar performers like the two bickering *prime donne* Cuzzoni and Faustina. Ever since the comedy first took to the stage it has been accepted that the key figure in the action, the thief-taker Peachum, stands for both the gang boss Jonathan Wild and the Prime Minister Robert Walpole. Legend has it that Walpole attended the show one evening, and loudly encored one of the numbers that had been seen as critical of his government; but no one has managed to authenticate this story. Through the medium of the jailer Lockit, who perhaps represents the keeper of Newgate, William Pitt, the *Opera* strikes at the corrupt workings of the prison system – not least the mismanagement and deliberate sloppiness which had allowed so many prisoners to make their escape, including a number of Jacobites after the rising. As for the nominal hero Macheath, with his timely reprieve from the gallows at the finale, he bears a striking resemblance to Roger Johnson, the serial escapee whom Henry Fielding would later use in his fictional rendition of Jonathan Wild.

Another curious coincidence lies in the fact that the disreputable poet Richard Savage, later befriended by both Pope and Samuel Johnson, was sentenced to death at the Old Bailey in late 1727. He had been convicted for his part in a tavern brawl that left a man named Sinclair fatally stabbed. According to Edward Young, a writer well placed to know the truth, Pope asked him to forward five guineas to the inmate at Newgate prison: 'Mr. Pope afterwards told the Doctor [Young] that if he should be in want of necessaries, he had five more ready for his service' (*Anecdotes*, vol. 1, p. 216). Friends of Savage mounted an energetic campaign to gain a reprieve, and in February this was granted by the intercession of the Queen. Audiences at the *Opera* could find another basis for the throwaway ending. Seemingly Pope had not dealt much with Savage prior to this event, but soon after he became marked as the poet's man in Grub Street, always prepared to sniff out information on Curll and his hack writers. As a result the authors pilloried in *The Dunciad* regarded him as a turncoat, while Pope arranged for a pension of £50 to be paid to Savage each year, £20 of this from his own pocket.

Up to this time Gay had tended to write only obliquely of the government: his *Fables* exploit an abstract technique that lampooned generic cut-out courtiers and politicians. With the *Opera* he moved into a harder-edged form of satire, equating politics and crime. At almost the same juncture, Swift began to write more openly on public themes, with poems such as 'A Libel on Dr Delany' (1730). Equally Pope embarked on his last great phase as a writer: almost all his substantial works during the remaining years of his life would include some overt political content. The Scriblerians had not made Walpole their prime target during the reign of George I. From now on, however, the King and his chief minister would stand at the heart of some of their most incisive works, including Swift's poem 'On Poetry: A Rhapsody' and Pope's 'Epistle to Augustus'. The new King's decision to hold on to Walpole in 1727 had sealed his own fate.

On 8 March, with the *Opera* still wowing the entire town from the literati to the general theatre-going public, Motte published the so-called 'Last Volume' of the *Miscellanies*. Pope had originally meant to include *The Dunciad* as the opening item, but the poem outgrew this narrow compass and he substituted a mock rhetoric called 'The Art of Sinking'. The rest of the volume is taken up by miscellaneous poems written by Swift, Pope and Gay. We know that Swift for one thought this commingling a good idea, as he told Pope: ' I have reason to chuse the method you mention of mixing the several verses, and I hope thereby among the bad Critics to be entitled to more merit than is my due' (*Corr.*, vol. 2, p. 420).

The contents include some of Swift's best-known poems, some of which had appeared in earlier collections, authentic or clandestine. Here we come on some of the birthday poems to Stella, as well as 'Cadenus and Vanessa', 'The South Sea' (sometimes known as 'The Bubble'), 'The Progress of Beauty', 'The Petition of Frances Harris' and very many more. Gay is represented by some of his most popular items, including 'Molly Mog' and 'Newgate's Garland', a pendant to *The Beggar's Opera*. As for Pope, he let out for publication a number of small items written in previous years, of which the best is 'Sandys's Ghost', dating from about 1716. More important, he effectively admitted to several works that had crept into print already, but that he did not care to acknowledge at the time. Among these come the often reprinted lines on John Moore's worm-powder; the verses 'On a Lady who Pisst at the Tragedy of Cato'; the short and naughty poem 'A Receipt to make a Cuckold'; and the jaunty verses inspired by *Gulliver's Travels*. Strictly speaking, no one could positively identify these as works by Pope, since the different items are not attributed to any single writer among the group, and they do not follow any chronological or topical arrangement. None the less, it marked a departure for the Scriblerian group to put quite so many of their productions on show all at once. The other contributors, including Arbuthnot, may well have thought that this would prove to be the final instalment; but Pope had other ideas.

One work takes up a substantial portion of the volume, namely 'Peri Bathous, or Martinus Scriblerus His Treatise of the Art of Sinking in Poetry'. This treatise most likely has its origins in the schemes of the Scriblerus Club around 1713–14, when the members projected 'an account of the works of the unlearned'. Each of the group contributed something to the work in its infancy. However, nothing emerged for the next fifteen years; and Pope was unquestionably the main author of the book in its published form. Some sketchy evidence, produced by opponents of the poet, suggests that Swift never saw the item before publication and that Arbuthnot wished to reduce the amount of personal satire in it (see *TE*, vol. 5, p. xvi).

'The Art of Sinking' amounts to a cod version of a familiar Augustan genre, the 'art' or guide to a given subject. Specifically, it parodies the influential Greek treatise *Of the Sublime*, attributed to an unidentified author of the first century AD known as Longinus. Since a translation into French by Boileau in 1674, this had become a classic work of criticism and provided a touchstone for impassioned or emotional writing of all kinds. Pope does not follow the organization of the Greek work very closely, but he systematically undercuts its definition of the 'profound' (deep, in the sense of lofty, exalted) by describing the way to achieve 'profound' effects in literature (abysmal, obscure, anti-climactic). The work consists of sixteen chapters. Of these the first twelve constitute the direct parody of a rhetorical treatise along the lines of Longinus. The remaining four represent more general advice on how to produce bad literature. Chapter 13 embodies 'A Project for the Advancement of the Bathos', suggesting some institutional ways of promoting bathos in the nation. Chapter 15, 'A Receipt to Make an Epic Poem', is taken almost whole from an early essay Pope had written for the *Guardian* in 1713. The last chapter contains 'A Project for the Advancement of the Stage', in which Pope airs some of his prejudices on theatrical matters. The earlier chapters provide amusing illustrations of bad writing, produced by pretension, ignorance, bad taste and general ineptitude. Pope divides the 'profound' authors into various classes, distinguished by their characteristic failings, for example, parrots (plagiarists) and porpoises (clumsy authors addicted to big words). Abundant quotation is provided to illustrate the ways in which poets can fall into bathos, in the modern sense, and the use of initials purposely fails to disguise the identity of Pope's favourite butts, such as the maker of pompous epics Sir Richard Blackmore; the testy critic John Dennis; the hopeless laureate Laurence Eusden; and the envious poetaster Leonard Welsted. All these writers will turn up again in *The Dunciad*.

Pope must have released the treatise as a trial balloon to test the winds before the appearance of his great work. Certainly the two works have some common themes and, as just mentioned, they share some of the same individual targets. However, the differences are more marked. *The Dunciad* has a full mock-epic action, a closely described setting in London, an extended social register and a wider basis in ideological issues of the day. 'The Art of Sinking' deals mainly with localized examples of bad writing, regarded as a vice worthy of exposure. In *The Dunciad* literary incompetence becomes an emblem of a general cultural malaise. It is in fact a more political text.

So Pope had set the stage for the appearance of his most controversial work. All London was agog, with writers attempting to get in pre-emptive strikes to combat the flak that they knew lay in store for them. Other journalists issued spoilers, by which they tried to lessen the impact that the poem would have. Curll had already made his intentions clear, telling Motte that he meant to 'reclaim' items in 'The Art of Sinking' which he had published in the past – he certainly had done as much, but whether he ever had any right to do so is another matter. Obviously something could be expected from this quarter as soon as *The Dunciad* made its appearance. In Dublin, Swift was growing impatient. 'Why does not Mr Pope publish his dullness', he asked Gay, 'the rogues he mawles will dy of themselves in peace, and So will his friends, and So there will be neither punishment nor reward'. On 28 March he wrote more cheerfully, 'The Beggers Opera hath knockt down Gulliver, I hope to see Popes Dullness knock down the Beggers Opera, but not till it hath fully done its Jobb' (*Corr.*, vol. 2, pp. 475, 484).

At the same moment he was trying to persuade Martha Blount to get Pope to make a joint visit to Dublin:

> Since I can never live in England, my greatest happiness would be to have you and Mr Pope condemned during my life to live in Ireland, he at the Deanery, and you for your reputation Sake just next door, and I will give you eight dinners a week, and a whole half dozen of pint bottles of good French wine at your lodgings ... and every year a suit of 14 penny stuff, that should not be worn out at the right side; and ... you shall have catholicity as much as you please, and the catholick Dean of St Patricks, as old again as I, to your Confessor.
>
> (*Corr.*, vol. 2, p. 477)

The letter shows that the Dean had become almost as fond of Patty as even Pope was, for he only allowed himself such teasing with those to whom he felt close. Yet Swift's message contains strange depths, not least the idea of resurrecting for his friends almost the same arrangement as the one he had enjoyed with Stella. Obviously neither Pope nor Patty could take up such an offer. Behind the badinage we can trace a yearning together with a melancholy recognition that the old friends would never meet again on this earth. From now on, their alliance took the virtual form of literary collaboration.

2

> Behold the fatal day arrive!
>
> *Verses on the Death of Dr Swift*[9]

At length, on 18 May 1728, an otherwise unremarkable Saturday, people woke up to find the capital struck by a strange type of guided missile. While most papers advertised the usual clutch of sermons, or else *Onania: The Heinous Sin of Self-Pollution*, the event was primly announced in the *Daily Post*: 'This Day is publish'd, THE DUNCIAD. An Heroic Poem. In Three Books. Dublin, printed, London reprinted for A. Dodd, 1728.' Unfortunately this minimalist statement, which does not even follow convention in citing the price, contains more than one misleading claim. In fact the small duodecimo volume of about fifty pages, costing one shilling (5p), was printed in London by James Bettenham, a nonjuror. The advertisement uses the name of Anne Dodd (*c.* 1685–1739) simply as a convenience: she was a leading mercury, or distributor of pamphlets and newspapers, but though she would have been happy to sell as many copies of this hot item as she could, she had certainly acquired no rights to it. Within days a pirate version came out, sometimes attributed on dubious grounds to Edmund Curll.

Immediately a furore grew up in the literary world as its members scurried around to discover in just what ways the poem libelled them, or if not why Pope had chosen to ignore them. We must remember that the work did not contain the elaborate apparatus to which we have grown accustomed in recent editions, and while some of the prefaces and notes later introduced serve to obfuscate certain issues, they do explain pretty well who is who. At first the shock of recognition mingled with a degree of puzzlement, as contemporary readers made their tentative approaches to this strange new thing. Pope had concealed many of the names in blanks, so that an early reference in Book I reads like this: 'Hence springs each weekly muse, the living boast / Of *C—l's* chaste press, and *L—t's* rubric post' (*TE*, vol. 5, p. 64). That is not a hard one. Most of the public would have been able to decipher the lines without difficulty, and thus to spot jokes involving Curll's licentious publications and Lintot's fondness for red-letter title pages, displayed on boards at the front of his shop. But what to make of a couplet like '*Mears, Warner, Wilkins* run: Delusive thought! / **, **, and **, the wretches caught' (*TE*, vol. 5, p. 111)? You had to be up on the book trade to make an instant identification of Mears and his colleagues, and who on earth was in Pope's head when he composed the second line? All we can be sure of is that their names contain two syllables. Even the (officially) third edition, later that year, did not make it a lot easier when replacing the stars with 'B—B—B'. Only when the *Dunciad Variorum* appeared in 1729 would relative clarity emerge: 'Breval, Besaleel, Bond'. The text still left plenty of wiggle-room for making good or bad guesses, and that was all part of the fun, unless your name happened to be William Bond or Bezaleel Morrice.

We get some idea of what went on during these first tumultuous days from a pamphlet that later appeared under the title *An Author to be Lett*, written by the disreputable Richard Savage, now recruited to Pope's cause. In a dedication that Pope may well have written himself, this passage occurs:

> On the Day the Book was first vended, a Crowd of Authors besieg'd the Shop; Entreaties, Advices, Threats of Law, and Battery, nay Cries of Treason, were all employ'd to hinder the coming out of the *Dunciad:* on the other Side, the Booksellers and Hawkers made as great Efforts to procure it. What could a few poor Authors do against so great a Majority as the Publick?

(*TE*, vol. 5, p. xxii)

In the ensuing weeks and month came a rash of editions, accompanied by a huge tide of hostile responses, welling out through every aperture in the popular press. Predictably we find Curll among the quickest off the mark, with a helpful 'Key' that he managed to get out within a fortnight. He kept up his attacks for several years. But this time he was by no means alone, and by the end of the year at least sixteen separate replies in pamphlet form had hit the streets, not to mention many columns in the daily and weekly press. Half a dozen of these came from Curll's shop, with *The Popiad* and *Codrus* – the latter co-written by Elizabeth Thomas – dealing some of the sharper blows.

The Dunciad has its roots in the projects of the Scriblerus Club, when the idea of a poem on the progress of dullness probably first evolved. At the heart of this design lay the traditional mode of learned wit, as employed by writers such as Rabelais and Cervantes (both named in the tribute to Swift at the start of Book I), in which pedantry and the jargon of professions were exposed to ridicule. Pope had started to collect materials to launch an attack on his opponents at any early date, but the work itself took shape only in the mid-1720s. Swift's first return visit to England in 1726 gave the author further impetus, while the caustic response by Lewis Theobald to his edition of Shakespeare provided one basis for the satire. In fact many other aspects of his victim's career gave Pope a handle by which to dramatize his conception of dullness. Theobald had combined high-minded Shakespearian scholarship with the composition of pantomimes for the populist theatrical entrepreneur John Rich. He would attempt to revive work by Jacobean authors such as Beaumont and Fletcher, whom Pope and his contemporaries – unlike modern critics – regarded as best left in obscurity. Furthermore, he had got involved with Curll in projects such as the cut-price version of Buckingham. Worse, he had brought out an unauthorized edition of Pope's boyhood friend Wycherley. All in all, he represented the things that the poet considered the essence of dullness. 'Tibbald', as the narrative styles this construct, comes over as a barren pedant, a baseless pretender to polite literature, and a coadjutor of low Grub Street hacks. This hardly qualifies as a fair statement of Theobald's attainments, but it holds a certain symbolic truth, and that was enough for the purposes of the poem.

In this earliest incarnation, *The Dunciad* comprises three books of unequal length. The only ancillary material came with a preface labelled 'The Publisher to the Reader'. Hardly any notes were added to the text. Everything changed when the *Variorum* edition came out in April 1729 – previous to this a special advance copy was presented to the King and Queen on 12 March by Robert Walpole, a bizarre circumstance which has never been satisfactorily explained. Pope had assigned the copyright to three noble lords, Bathurst, Oxford and Burlington, to serve as a protection against any retaliation by his victims, whether through the law or through physical assaults. In effect this was a new work, even if most of the lines were much the same. The elaborate apparatus includes lengthily imperceptive notes by foolish commentators, some attributed to Martinus Scriblerus. These underline the satiric points made in the text: Pope got much of his information from the works of the dunces themselves, and he also raided Curll's Key. A series of prefatory documents and damaging appendices culminate in a wickedly detailed index. And of course the blanks are filled in, so that the dunces were no longer anonymous, even if some of them would remain no less obscure to most readers with their names spelled out.

The new guise of the poem made its wider social critique more obvious. Inevitably, a fresh deluge of replies emerged. Among those in pamphlet form the most vicious is perhaps the *Remarks upon ... the Dunciad*, a root and branch assault by John Dennis that seeks to counter any epic pretensions on Pope's part. 'P. is so far from singing an Action, that there is no such Thing as Action in his whimsical Rhapsody'.[10] All the old charges against the poet come in for recycling, and the pamphleteers frequently reminded us once more of his deformity and of his Catholic religion. Some are funny, some are informative at times; *The Curliad*, published around 27 April, achieves both things.

However, the responses fall down in one crucial respect. Their basic mode of operation amounts to a simple *tu quoque*. The respondents try to show that Pope is just as bad as they are. He too writes for money, while he inhabits his own Thames-side Grub Street. He uses tricks and subterfuges in publishing his works, and hides behind pseudonyms. He attacks his social betters and he pours flattery on his friends. He indulges in smut and blasphemy. He employs the harshest terms of abuse. He is actuated by party motives and he spies for the Tories. His knowledge of grammar is defective and he can hardly spell. And so on. All these charges, except the last, hold some truth. Yet in the end the syllogism will not stand up because, however just the premises, the conclusion is vitiated by a fatal flaw in the argument. Pope is *not* as bad a writer as his critics, because he implants his attack in verse of stunning invention and outstanding linguistic verve. Where he writes with delicate precision, subtle allusiveness and learned wit, they seek to match him with clumsy abuse and jogging metres. The contrast shows clearly that the difference between crude lampoons and satire of timeless value does not lie in authorial motives, still less in the presence or absence of malice. It derives from the verbal and constructive power of the satirist, in controlling rhythm, sound, syntax, connotation and denotation. *The Dunciad* lives on, when the targets of its wrath are otherwise totally forgotten. This is because the work enlists supreme poetic skill, something that lay quite outside the reach of Pope's antagonists:

> Here to her Chosen all her works she shows;
> Prose swell'd to verse, Verse loit'ring into prose;
> How random Thoughts now meaning chance to find,
> Now leave all memory of sense behind:
> How Prologues into Prefaces decay,
> And these to Notes are fritter'd quite away.
> How Index-learning turns no student pale,
> Yet holds the Eel of science by the Tail.
> How, with less reading than makes felons 'scape,
> Less human genius than God gives an ape,
> Small thanks to France, and none to Rome or Greece,
> A past, vamp'd, future, old, reviv'd, new piece,

> 'Twixt Plautus, Fletcher, Congreve, and Corneille,
> Can make a Cibber, Johnson, or Ozell.
>
> (*TE*, vol. 5, pp. 90–1)

This passage strikes at several individuals, some particular plays, a number of editions. None of it strays far from the observable facts concerning the practice of men like Theobald. But it creates at the same time a mythical abstraction, pure duncehood. The victims were never able to respond in kind, despite their understandable resentment, because none of them could operate on this level of literary virtuosity.

3

Only in comparatively recent times have we begun to understand just how deeply political a poem *The Dunciad* is. Of course, some of the more obvious thrusts were there in plain sight, from the very start. A work which appeared in 1728 and began like this could hardly hope to conceal its animus:

> Books and the Man I sing, the first who brings
> The Smithfield Muses to the Ear of Kings.
> Say great Patricians! (since your selves inspire
> These wond'rous works; so Jove and Fate require)
> Say from what cause, in vain decry'd and curst,
> Still Dunce the second reigns like Dunce the first?
>
> (*TE*, vol. 5, pp. 59–61)

Pope's opening note to the *Variorum* text asserts that 'This Poem was writ in 1727', so he had no basis to claim that the reference preceded the change of monarchy in that year. Nor can the 'patricians' be other than the 'Great' in the land, a term substituted in 1742: it is they who have presided over the nation's decline under the Hanoverian regime.

At several other points Pope gets in a little dig at the monarchy. To take one very early example, in the 'argument' to the first book, he writes of the possible 'period', or end, of the empire of dullness 'from the old age of the present monarch *Settle*' (*TE*, vol. 5, p. 54). Every competent reader would insert the name of George I here. More widely, it has been suspected that Queen Dulness herself represents some facets of the real Queen. Members of the opposition convinced themselves that Caroline dominated her husband, and that Walpole ruled through her influence, although this is no more than a half-truth. We could also speculate on an innuendo in Pope's reference to the new Lord Mayor, Sir George Thorold. He is said like the Athenian general Cimon to have 'triumph'd, both on land and wave' (*TE*, vol. 5, p. 69). Up to this time the future George II had led a supine existence, with no military experience – later, admittedly, he would lead the British troops into battle at Dettingen in 1743, but this was a long way ahead. The comparison with Cimon would not help: even if Pope had been correct in supposing that Cimon triumphed in the naval battle of Salamis in 480 BC, the general later lost favour, underwent prosecution for bribery and suffered ostracism by the city-state – that is, banishment for ten years.

Such a reading implies that the Lord Mayor and the monarch merge at such a juncture. The evidence for this view derives initially from the coronation and surrounding events in late 1727. We shall review this case more fully in the pages to come. For the moment it is enough to point out that the installation of the new king of the dunces in Book I bears a close similarity both with the solemnities that consecrated George on the throne in October 1727 *and* with the ceremony which raised Thorold to the mayoral seat in October 1719.

Was Pope fair to the King? Obviously not: he had chosen to vent his disappointment with the non-events of 1727, and to blame the continuance of what he saw as Walpole's malignant reign on George himself. The new monarch was more than the uncultivated ninny that the opposition believed, or pretended to believe, him to be. His main offence lay in the fact that he was Hanoverian, and thus suspected of putting the interests of a foreign principality before those of Britain. In 1728 the opposition had not yet cemented a well-articulated case against the King and his ministers. At this stage their attacks often come across as the peevish complaints of those who had expected to come into their own again, now that the former incumbent of the throne had gone. Their diatribes against the court could have been written at any previous time since the Restoration. What marks off Pope's treatment is not any special insight into the constitutional or moral issues raised by the style of government George II adopted – even disregarding the fact that he had hardly got going at this stage. The greatness of *The Dunciad* lies in the range, particularity and precision of its targets.

Of course, the politics of the poem go well beyond the royal family. Theobald had been a candidate for the office of poet laureate in 1718, after the death of Rowe, but instead the post went to a booby named Laurence Eusden. In *The Dunciad* Pope allots the hapless Eusden only a minor role, befitting his literary stature: 'Mr. *Eusden* was made *Laureate* for the same reason that Mr. *Tibbald* was made *Hero* of This Poem, because there was *no better to be had*', as Pope scornfully noted (*TE*, vol. 5, p. 187). The Duke of Buckingham had written a satire on the jostling that went on over the appointment, cited by Pope in the same note, and this episode may have given the poet his first notion of a work on the succession of dullness, in the manner of John Dryden's *Mac Flecknoe* (*c.* 1680). In 1730 Eusden died, and the stage was set for the ineffable Colley Cibber to ascend to the bays. After this, as we shall see in the last chapter, Pope rewrote his work to make an exact equivalence between the court poet and the leader of the dunces. In all versions of *The Dunciad* the choice of a bad writer as laureate is attributed directly to the government and the court, with especial blame shovelled out on the Duke of Newcastle.

One way of bringing to light the submerged ideological bent of the work is to contrast it with Pope's earlier work. In many ways *The Dunciad* serves as an antitype of *The Temple of Fame*, by means of a systematic degradation of the candidates for honour and reputation as they had been portrayed by Chaucer. But a more sustained reductive process operates in the poem, that looks back rather to *Windsor-Forest*. Instead of an Arcadian landscape, we have a despoiled setting that exposes urban decay and eco-disaster. Instead of a limpid river, fed by transparent tributaries, we have a filthy waterway into which the Fleet Ditch deposits its foul contents. (This contrast is written into the text: 'The King of Dykes! Than whom, no sluice of mud / With deeper sable blots the silver flood' (*TE*, vol. 5, p. 133).) Instead of a noble castle with its grand park merging with the forest, we enter a bleak and claustrophobic cell located in a squalid part of London. Instead of hearty outdoor sports, we meet with obscene and debased games in which the participants suffer pain and humiliation. Instead of the distinguished authors who had celebrated the environs of Windsor in works of lasting literary value, we are surrounded by second-rate hacks and muck-raking journalists whose productions die within hours of their creation. And so on.

A case could be made that this contrast does little more than reflect the predominantly rural locale of *Windsor-Forest* as against the wholly urban milieu of *The Dunciad*. But that would move the argument only a short way forward. For Pope's decision to set his mock-epic in the capital carries its own political charge. Most traditional epics had celebrated the destiny of nations: even the *Iliad* is about a Greek struggle and not an Athenian one, the *Aeneid* a legend of the birth of empire rather than a history of the building of Rome itself. But in Pope's design London stands as something more than a synecdoche for England. In this city the destructive forces of modernity have concentrated, so that it represents the matrix of all the evil trends in social and economic life that Pope and his friends reviled. He has the metropolis specifically in mind – the geographical entity, but also the political organism that was the City of London.

Pope had every reason to take note of the politics of the City of London. We do not often think of him as primarily an urban writer, in the way of Ben Jonson, Baudelaire or T. S. Eliot. Yet, after all, his origins lay in the London mercantile community and he kept up contacts with this group more than has been realized, even when resident in Berkshire or at Twickenham. Evidence of this fact is sprinkled through his poems and letters. His City friends included men like Slingsby Bethel, a prosperous African merchant who in the years immediately following Pope's death became warden of a livery company, alderman, sheriff and finally Lord Mayor.[11] He enjoyed a particularly warm relationship with Lord Bathurst, an aristocrat whose father had been a prominent figure in the City: Benjamin

Bathurst had earned a knighthood for his extensive loans to the government, and ended up as Treasurer to Princess, later Queen, Anne.[12] We can detect a sign of the poet's continuing interest in London life in his portraits of Sir Balaam and Sir John Cutler in the *Epistle to Bathurst*. However, the most telling literary exploitation of his commercial heritage occurs in *The Dunciad*.

As we saw at the start of this book, Pope was born in the heart of the 'square mile', during the same year that his father retired from his business as a linen merchant, 1688. No evidence has come to light showing that the elder Pope served an apprenticeship or gained his freedom. Even if he did, as a converted Catholic, Alexander senior would have experienced great difficulty in swearing the oath of loyalty to the monarch, as freemen were required to do. Within six months of the birth of the Popes' new son, William of Orange had landed at Torbay and within three more he had accepted the throne along with his wife Mary. By that time Mr Pope had given up trade. Then, we recall, the Popes moved out to Hammersmith, later to Binfield, and ultimately back to Chiswick. They never again lived within the historic confines of the City. However, this does not mean that Pope forgot all about his first home or lost interest in the doings of his native city. Quite the contrary.

Consider some of the evidence. The plot and setting of *The Dunciad*, as just stated, both relate to the installation of a new Lord Mayor, identified by Pope as Sir George Thorold, who took office in 1719. A key role in the action belongs to Elkanah Settle, the last of the City poets whose job was to organize the municipal carnival on Lord Mayor's Day. Important figures in the politics of the corporation, such as the plutocrat Sir Gilbert Heathcote, make a prominent entrance into the narrative. Finally, Alderman John Barber, the Jacobite printer who had a long association with both Pope and Swift, played a major role in City politics.

The tradition of mounting the 'triumphs of London' in the form of allegorical carnival floats and pageants lapsed in the early eighteenth century. These events represent the final flowering of the old civic displays which Pope had witnessed as a boy, described in Chapter 1. The last known occasion when they took place was in 1702, when Elkanah Settle contrived a show in the hopes of bringing back to life a festival said to be 'almost dropping into oblivion'.[13] In fact Settle devised one more fully choreographed pageant in 1708, to commemorate the installation of a new Lord Mayor, Sir Charles Duncombe; but for various reasons the plan fell through. However, the idea of reviving the tradition continued to float in the head of Pope and in that of his friend, the incoming Lord Mayor, as late as 1732. On 24 August in that year Alderman Barber wrote to Swift:

> The mayor's day is the 30th of October ... It would add very much to my felicity, if your health would permit you to come over in the spring, and see a pageant of your own making. Had you been here now, I am persuaded you would have put me to an additional expense, by having a raree-shew (or pageant) as of old, on the lord-mayor's

day. Mr. Pope and I were thinking of having a large machine carried through the city, with a printing press, author, publishers, hawkers, devils, &c., and a satirical poem printed and thrown out to the mob, in publick view, but not to give offence; but your absence spoils that design.

As David Woolley comments, citing Aubrey Williams's study of *The Dunciad*, 'One recalls irresistably the *mise en scène* of Pope's great poem'.[14] Barber, we shall see, was Pope's closest contact among the top political brass of the City. The point about the machines is that they express a *company* identity, for Barber belonged to the Stationers' guild; and municipal politics in the City always had a great deal to do with the status of the livery companies. Equally, the progress of the Lord Mayor on his inaugural day was attended with the rites and symbols of the companies. But the most significant aspect of the letter lies in its reminder of Pope's continuing absorption in the choreography of City pageants.

When *The Dunciad* first came out, John Barber had already taken some part in the most recent show. Just after the accession of George II, the City fathers resolved to invite the entire royal family to the Lord Mayor's Day banquet. They also set up a small panel of aldermen and common council members to seek permission from the King to erect his statue in the Royal Exchange and also portraits of George and Queen Caroline in the Guildhall – actions which would collectively bestow a symbolic blessing on commerce and civic pride. We may wonder in what spirit three of the aldermen appointed – Barber, Humphrey Parsons and John Williams, strong Tories and probably Jacobites in every case – went about their task. All three men were also deputed to a larger committee to 'take Care of the Entertainment' on the day itself. The show duly took place in its accustomed fashion, with the new Lord Mayor, Sir Edward Beecher, a loyal acolyte of Robert Walpole, proceeding in the City barge to Westminster, 'attended by the several Companies in their respective Barges'. But the procession that year had a new feature: the aldermen and councilmen who had acted in this committee were directed to march that day, 'with Gold Fringes on their Gloves, and rich Favours upon their Hats'.[15] It all looks uncomfortably close to the 'Pomps' that Pope had described early in Book I of his poem.

Once the official party had done their business at Westminster, they made their way back down the river to Blackfriars, and thence to the City. Although there were no pageants, the royal family watched the procession from a balcony overlooking Cheapside. At Guildhall the City fathers entertained the royal family with considerable state, after a greeting had been delivered in a speech by Sir William Thompson. This man acted as Walpole's chief fixer in criminal matters, decided whether individuals such as Jonathan Wild should live or die, and exerted great influence both as a government MP and as recorder of the City of London. The feast was 'very magnificent', and so it should have been, as it cost the civic authorities almost £5,000, with not far short of 300 dishes consumed at the royal table alone. The table provided for the Lord Mayor and the aldermen got through only 130. During the meal the King proposed a toast to the health of Beecher, 'and Prosperity to the City of *London,* and the Trade thereof'. The Lord Mayor, aldermen and councilmen duly reciprocated.[16] Some of these goings-on are given a comic replay in *The Dunciad*, particularly during the episode in Book I which sees the new king of the dunces installed, although Pope has as his major target here the recent coronation of George and Caroline. At all events, 315 dozens of bottles of wine, including champagne, burgundy, claret, malmsey, madeira, moselle, port, canary and hock, went down the throats of the assembled guests at the Guildhall. This may have left them as stupefied as the dunces at the end of Book II.[17]

4

In 1735 Pope added to the preliminaries of *The Dunciad* a new 'Declaration' by the author, printed in black letter. This took the form of a mock-proclamation as issued by the King, and was sworn before 'John Barber, Mayor'. As we have seen, Barber had served in the office in 1732–3, and concerted plans with Pope for an imaginary Lord Mayor's procession featuring the Stationers. In some ways the document parodies the official licence granted by the Secretary of State in 1722, which permitted Barber to bring out Pope's edition of the works of the Duke of Buckingham. Given that the most notable aspect of the printer's term in office was his vigorous resistance on behalf of the City to Walpole's Excise scheme, we might anticipate that Pope would have held him in high regard – even more so, perhaps, because this activism did not prove enough in 1735 to gain Barber election to represent the constituency in the face of government pressure on floating voters. But the position is more complicated.

Scholars have not been able to work out the exact relations between the two men. Pope never became as close a friend of Barber as did Swift. He may even have written an unkind epigram, or more than one, on the monument which Barber erected to the memory of Samuel Butler in Westminster Abbey. This seemingly benevolent act would inspire a good deal of comment from satirists: and at least one versifier found a way to link Barber with none other than Elkanah Settle. The lines appear in the *Daily Journal* on 21 March 1722:

Castle Baynard's, March 20. 1721–2.

SIR, As I have lately set up a *Barber's* Shop, I beg your Recommendation as a young beginner.

The first Customer I *Trimm'd* was a new Alderman, and he has promis'd to recommend me for the Lightness of my Hand. Yours, *Andrew Shaveclose.*

AD[V]ICE.

Let not the *Golden Chain* thy *Neck* adorn,
While *Portland-stone* sinks *Butler*'s Name to scorn;
Rather let *Peru's Mines* his Ashes deck,
And hang the *Portland-Stone* about thy *Neck*.
Thy *grateful Bounty* let poor *Settle* share,
To whom *you owe* the *very Gold* you *wear*.

The point of the joke about Settle will emerge in a moment. The remaining context derives from the fact that Barber was currently engaged in an aldermanic election for Castle Baynard ward. Many people suspected that Barber had designed his gesture on behalf of Butler, coupled with a gift of £500 to found a charity school in the ward, to ease his passage in a contest against the ministerial candidate.

Here lie the seeds of some equivocal attitudes on Pope's part. Barber had become heavily involved in municipal affairs. From 1709 to 1724 he had been City Printer, as well as holding the reversion to the post of King's Printer, a right he would never get to exercise. He served as Sheriff in 1729–30, and went to Westminster for his installation attended by sixteen Stationers in a barge pulled by the company's watermen. During his tenure he gave the usual feasts, and John Gay attended one such function in March 1730, which as he told Swift incorporated 'a very fine dinner and a very fine Appearance of Company'.[18] When the City decided to build a grand new Mansion House in 1735, Barber was appointed to the committee to choose a site and obtain designs. Some of these events occurred just too late to have influenced the original *Dunciad*; but they show the way Barber's life was moving.

For one reason or another, a faint suspicion of coolness attends the relations of the two men, which makes Barber's legacy of £100 the more generous. Scholars have isolated one possible reason for this. The story allegedly goes back to a conversation between Pope and William Warburton:

> Mr. Pope never flattered anybody for money, in the whole course of his writing. Alderman Barber had a great inclination to have a stroke in his commendation inserted in some part of Mr. Pope's writings. He did not want money, and he wanted fame. He would probably have given four or five thousand pounds, to have been gratified in this desire: and gave Mr. Pope to understand as much, but Mr. Pope would never comply with such a baseness. And when the Alderman died, he left him a legacy only of a hundred pounds; which might have been some thousands, if he had obliged him only with a couplet.

(*Anecdotes*, vol. 1, p. 161)

Whether this story has any truth in it cannot be proved now. In any case, a more solid reason exists for any possible loss of cordiality – and this bears directly on *The Dunciad*.

All previous scholarship on Pope seems to have ignored one crucial issue – the nature of the relationship between Barber and Settle. In fact, the City Poet was godfather to the City Printer, and a friend of Barber's own father. According to a biography published by Thomas Cooper in 1741, just after the alderman died, Settle had taken the young boy into his home, clothed him and 'put him to School at *Hampstead*'. Through the influence of his mentor, together with a gift of twenty guineas, John got the chance to serve his apprenticeship in the Stationers' Company; and perhaps Settle brought him his first profitable job, a widely sold pamphlet by Dr Charles Davenant.[19] A different narrative appears in Edmund Curll's rival life, stressing the role of Davenant and not that of Settle; but the documents in the case establish that Cooper's account was right about the family link. In these circumstances, it is hard to imagine that Barber felt anything but gratitude towards his benefactor. If so, we can easily conceive what must have been his chagrin and distress when Pope allocated Settle such a key role among the dunces, and picked out details of the old man's career with such cruel accuracy. Pope seems not to have cared too much about Barber's feelings – if he had not got wind of the relationship with Settle, then his normal intelligence gathering had suffered a severe breakdown. The poet in the *Daily Journal* certainly knew all about it. Perhaps, despite the political sympathy he felt with Barber as a tribune of the opposition, Pope had come to associate the printer with the corporate activity of the City. The gold fringes in 1727 might almost prefigure an event in 1732, Barber's admission to the Goldsmiths' Company, to qualify as Lord Mayor.

Barber must have known of some of the adverse views his friends and fellow Tories harboured, after his advancement to the pinnacle of City affairs. At the time of the Excise crisis, Swift wrote to him, addressing him as 'My Lord', and mentioning 'our friend Sir Gilbert' as a byword for avarice: the Dean's protégé Matthew Pilkington had become chaplain to the Lord Mayor, at the request of Swift, and he had evidently been telling tales out of school. On 6 August Barber replied from Goldsmiths' Hall: 'I flattered myself with being very happy with you and some friends, on the important subject of the Cap of Maintenance, Custard, the Sword, and many more laudable things in the lord mayor's house'.[20] David Woolley suggests that Barber was remembering a plate to *A Tale of a Tub*, but the phrasing seems to indicate a more recent source – *The Dunciad*.

It sometimes looks almost as if Pope devoted his life to distancing himself from the mercantile background he inherited on his paternal side. He could do this without reneging on the intense family piety he always displayed: 'In a word, my Lord, I think it enough, that my Parents, such as they were, never cost me a *Blush*; and that their Son, such as he is, never cost them a *Tear*'.[21] His father spent his life in trade certainly, but not as the great princes of the City like Sir Gilbert Heathcote were in trade. The locus of *their* activities lay in the great public spaces of commercial London. They stalked the Royal Exchange, eulogized by Addison in the *Spectator*: 'I look upon High-Change to be a great Council, in which all considerable Nations have their Representatives'. They supplied the motor that powered 'the great Hall where the Bank is kept', where Addison was pleased to find 'the Directors, Secretaries, and Clerks, with all other Members of that wealthy Corporation, ranged in their several Stations, according to the Parts they act in that just and regular Oeconomy'. It is significant that contemporaries saw the figure of Sir Andrew Freeport, the 'Merchant of great Eminence in the City of *London*' who represents the acceptable face of trade, as based principally on Heathcote.[22] All around the Exchange stood the palaces of commerce, along with the solid brick mansions of the goldsmiths in Lombard Street. Nearby, we are unlikely to forget, ran the hidden back alley of Plough Court and the modest premises of Alexander Pope, senior.

Most scholars choose to analyse Pope's attitudes towards the moneyed interest in moral terms. They tend either to deplore his views on the financial revolution as backward-looking and snobbish, the product of a cultural ideology which has been described as the politics of nostalgia: or they applaud his principled denunciation of a corrupt and spiritually bankrupt ruling elite.[23] In both cases, we fail to see how much of the poet's outlook on such matters derived from his quarrels with the City of London in the narrow sense – in other words, how thoroughly his attitudes were shot through with intense personal feelings. His scorn for the burghers rested on something more particular than dislike of 'commercial values', or than opposition in terms of national politics – his treatment of the Tory grandee Sir Charles Duncombe and his warm relations with the Whig businessman Slingsby Bethel both point to this fact. Aldermen fall under the poet's obloquy because they rigged elections, not just because they embodied financial values. Mostly they kowtowed to Walpole, apart from one brief episode, and even then the leader of City opposition, John Barber, failed to get himself a seat at Westminster. The reason that Whigs formed Pope's chief target was that they occupied the key role in City affairs, and notoriously rode roughshod over the smaller businessmen – people just like Alexander Pope, senior, in fact. Among many other things, *The Dunciad* served as a long-delayed act of reprisal.

8 LIBELS AND SATIRES

Libels and *Satires*! lawless Things indeed!
The First Satire of the Second Book of Horace Imitated (*TE*, vol. 4, p. 21)

When the new decade began, Pope had reached the age of forty-one. All round the outlook seemed distinctly promising. *The Dunciad* brought him new confidence in his creative powers, and established him as the most dreaded satirist in the nation. The poem had revived his old enmities, and drawn in a fresh cadre of hostile critics, something he always needed for his art to function effectively. Meanwhile his contacts with friends and colleagues in the Scriblerian group remained positive, not least in the case of Swift, with whom his relations would begin to fray at the edges in later years. Equally he could count on the good will of aristocratic supporters like Bathurst, Bolingbroke and Oxford, together with a newer recruit, Lord Cobham. A serving general until he fell into disfavour on political grounds, and a member of the influential Temple family, Cobham had carried out extensive improvements to his house and garden at Stowe in Buckinghamshire. Over the course of time this site became a focus of opposition to Walpole, as the dissident group met there to forge mostly ineffectual plots against the ministry. Pope visited Stowe regularly from about 1724, and contributed his views on the gardens, which boasted the handiwork of the architects James Gibbs and John Vanbrugh, together with the landscape designers Charles Bridgman and William Kent. Once in 1731 he gave his opinion that 'If any thing under Paradise could set me beyond all Earthly Cogitations: Stowe might do it' (*Corr.*, vol. 3, p. 217).

Pope now gained support in his war with Grub Street. Encouraged by the example of *The Dunciad*, a new organ named the *Grub-Street Journal* began publication on 1 January 1730: it would appear every week for more than 400 issues until 1738. Pope's enemies claimed that he took a leading share in the operations of the paper. This does not seem to be true, although the main writers, a nonjuring clergyman named Richard Russel and a botanist named John Martyn, certainly looked to him for inspiration. Several of the poet's principal butts made regular appearances, including Cibber, Theobald, James Moore Smythe,

John 'Orator' Henley and Curll. The young dramatist Henry Fielding came in for his fill of abuse, too – a little surprisingly, as unlike those just named he was an adherent of the opposition to Walpole.

While most of the satire in the *Journal* took a literary rather than political form, the editors made no attempt to disguise their hostility to the court and its minions. This bias became obvious when Lord Hervey produced *An Epistle from a Nobleman to a Doctor of Divinity* in 1733, where Pope's recent epistles are scornfully treated:

> Had not his *Taste* and *Riches* lately shown,
> When he would talk of Genius to the Town,
> How ill he chuses, if he trusts his own.[1]

Immediately the *Journal* retorted with 'Advice to a Nobleman', an excerpt from the last act of Ben Jonson's *Poetaster* (1602). The lines are spoken by Horace, the dramatist's mouthpiece in the play, and addressed to the feeble writer 'Fannius' – a variant of Hervey's nickname Fanny, as used by Pope. This speech presents the writer as a viper who will 'bite and gnaw' his absent friends, will 'carry tales, and do the basest offices', and will reveal secrets entrusted to him.[2] Here we can see the germ of the famous portrait of Hervey as 'Sporus' that Pope gave to the world little more than twelve months later. It is likely, though not certain, that he was responsible for seeking out the passage from Jonson for the editors of the *Journal*.

Unavoidably his life had its darker sides. In 1729 his friend Lady Scudamore fell victim to smallpox, just four days after the death of her neighbour and antagonist Lord Coningsby. Together with the loss of her nephew and niece, Robert and Mary Digby, this meant the break-up of a congenial group in the Welsh border country, united on both horticultural and political matters. Now only Bathurst was left, and Pope felt an even stronger urge to spend part of the summer with his friend at Cirencester. Whilst in this tranquil setting he could distance himself briefly from the troubles stirred up by *The Dunciad*. Meanwhile things had not gone well for John Gay, whose less trenchant sequel to *The Beggar's Opera*, entitled *Polly*, ran into trouble with the government censors: the Lord Chamberlain banned performances of the new play when he saw the script. The Duke and Duchess of Queensberry, Gay's patrons, continued to support him, and as a result they were banished from court. Gay lost his grace and favour apartment in Whitehall. 'So, they have taken away your Lodgings', Swift observed. 'This is a sample of Walpole's Magnanimity'.[3]

In private life Pope found other worries distracting him. They arose from the fact that Teresa Blount, whose conduct gave rise to rumours on a previous occasion, had now embarked on an affair with a married man. 'The circumstances are very flagrant', he told Caryll. In addition she had behaved outrageously towards her mother, 'striking, pinching, pulling about the house, and abusing to the utmost shamefulness' (*Corr.*, vol. 3, pp. 40–1). Pope deplored the cavalier way in which she treated the pained reactions of her mother and her sister: he also thought that Mrs Blount was too easily swayed by her elder daughter, and that it might be best for Martha to move out of the family home. He hoped Caryll might use his good offices to do something to allay the 'general disreputation' that threatened the family (*Corr.*, vol. 3, p. 46). The leading scholar in this area, Valerie Rumbold, has stated the matter with startling accuracy: 'Like typical victims of domestic violence, mother and younger daughter strove to conceal their sufferings'.[4] By now Pope had reached a decisive view on the merits of the two sisters. As Magdalen Rackett succinctly put it, '*Patty Bl.* The fair one, Mr. *Pope*'s, the other he did not love, call'd Bitch. Hoyden'.[5]

The affairs of his sister Magdalen occasioned just as much concern for Pope. In 1728 her husband Charles Rackett died in mysterious circumstances, possibly even in exile. Once a man of substance, he left the family finances ruined. His two daughters had died young and Magdalen was left with five sons. The eldest, Michael, spent the rest of his life abroad as an outlaw after the Waltham Blacks episode. Another, Henry, tried to enter the legal profession, but he was unable to take the oaths because of his religion, and efforts by Pope to get special clearance for his nephew came to nothing. John, whom Pope regarded as a sober and industrious lad, went to sea but also ended up in debt around 1733. A further difficulty lay in Magdalen's inability to dispose of the family home at Hall Grove, where the young Alexander had so often visited. She spent the remainder of her days in London. Throughout the 1730s Pope kept up a stream of correspondence with the lawyer William Fortescue, seeking ways to alleviate his sister's money problems, and to sort out the affairs of her variously challenged offspring.

If all that was not enough, Edith Pope naturally grew a greater burden to her son as she aged and began to exhibit signs of dementia. The most worrying episode occurred in October 1730, as Pope related to John Caryll:

> My own poor mother is yet a partaker of her reason, which renders all other decays less grievous; but her memory is very near gone. She had within this month a very extraordinary escape from a terrible accident: She fell into the fire without touching her body, tho' it consum'd the clothes she had on, at least a yard about. Her back lay on the grate, but her head (tho' dressed in Musselin) reclining sideways was not burnt. The shock of the fall and blow has much hurt her, but after a week or two she recovered of all but her feebleness.

(*Corr.*, vol. 3, p. 142)

Of course the son could no longer look to his old helper, Mary Beach, whom he had described in a Homeric turn of phrase as 'the tender Second to a Mother's Cares'. That did not stop the press from spreading malicious gossip about his past conduct: 'That I have had criminal Correspondence with my old Nurse of 70, I have seen in Print', he once told Lord Oxford (*Corr.*, vol. 3, p. 84).

Looming behind these personal anxieties was the general malaise experienced by Pope and his friends as a result of the ongoing dominance of Robert Walpole. The Prime Minister seemed to have become immovable after the brief window of opportunity that the opposition had sensed in 1727. For a time Pope attempted to achieve some kind of rapprochement. The only tangible result came when he managed to ensure that Walpole did not block a proposal to advance his friend Thomas Southcott (1671–1748), a Benedictine father. Educated at Douai, Southcott spent long periods in England as an organizer of clandestine activity on behalf of his order, when he became a friend and mentor of young Alexander. Around the time of the Jacobite rising in 1715–16 he was sent on a mission to England, where he began to collect funds for the Stuart cause. He had again served as one of the principal agents raising money in the years leading up to the Atterbury plot. It is natural that Southcott took a leading share in the subscription campaign for Pope's translations of Homer since the two fundraising exercises seem to have overlapped. In 1728 he sought to become head of an abbey outside Avignon. Pope intervened on his behalf with Walpole, again using Fortescue as his avenue of approach, and the appointment was approved (*Anecdotes*, vol. 2, p. 615). This was surprising since Southcott had long caused embarrassment to the English government, because of his activities on behalf of the Pretender. Unquestionably Walpole, with his widespread intelligence system, knew all about this. He could have acted to stop the appointment, but it looks as if he used his contacts with the French court to facilitate its progress.[6] No one who has dipped into the ecclesiastical history of this period will find the eventual outcome at all shocking. Southcott held his Provençal post in absentia and spent the remainder of his career at Cambrai in Flanders as vicar of the English convent. That was the way things worked then.

Faced with these various issues, Pope took a remarkably bold step. He reconstituted his literary identity to forge an idiom adequate to the new political realities. In his *Epistle to Arbuthnot*, he would famously claim to have abandoned 'Fancy's Maze' and 'moraliz'd his song' (*TE*, vol. 4, p. 120). But this does not mean that that he suddenly discovered ethical issues for the first time in 1730, as a cursory glance at *An Essay on Criticism*, *The Rape of the Lock* and *The Dunciad* would show. The difference partly lies in a more aggressive tone, coupled with a heavy infusion of topical material. Like Yeats in his last phase, Pope adopted looser forms and a more insistent personal voice. Like Dickens, he abandoned conventional patterns of organization and substituted a richly dramatic manner of proceeding. Like Shakespeare, he replaced a smooth rhetorical style with abrupt, colloquial language that made use of jagged rhythms and denser syntax. In the 1730s he wrote more distinguished, and distinctive, poems than at any stage in his career. In quick succession he produced a group of *Moral Essays* on contemporary themes; a wide-ranging discursive work, *Essay on Man*, sufficiently different from his previous output in its form and content to fool many readers when it came out anonymously; and a set of *Imitations of Horace*, to which he added two versions of Donne's satires as well as the *Epistle to Arbuthnot* and a closing dialogue in two parts. Many of these items rank among his finest achievements, and all were completed by 1738. Nothing that he wrote in the last six years of his life resembles them very closely.

1

The series opened with the *Epistle to Burlington*, published in December 1731. As with much of the work that followed, the leading ideas go back to an overarching scheme for a large 'system of Ethics in the Horatian way' that he first planned around 1730. The project is generally known as his '*opus magnum*', from a reference in a letter to Swift (*Corr.*, vol. 3, p. 401). It proved too unwieldy, and perhaps too ambitious intellectually, ever to be realized, but its traces can be detected in much of the poetry from the following decade, and even as late as 1742 in Book IV of *The Dunciad*.

Pope had included in the programme for his great opus a contrast between prodigality and avarice. The former comes under review in the poem to Burlington; the latter in its successor, addressed to Bathurst. A marked disparity appears in the mode of writing used for each of the items. This discrepancy owes a great deal to the opposing character of the two peers, and hence to the different relationship they enjoyed with Pope. Burlington was a prim, dignified and rather self-contained individual, a virtuoso with great learning in the visual arts. Bathurst strikes us – the way he must have struck Pope – as much less formal: a breezy, congenial, worldly man, with a taste for good living. They were unlike in another respect, and one that matters here. Burlington, though he acquired a number of highly esteemed gongs, from the Garter downwards, never showed very much interest in politics. He took little part in the fractious debates that regularly divided the Lords, and seems to have taken a moderate Whig stance on most questions. (The story that he had crypto-Jacobite leanings has not been substantiated.) On the other hand Bathurst remained one of the most active Tories in the upper house. From his close dealings with these two men, Pope constructed two outstanding poems, each beautifully apt to the personality and interests of the dedicatee.

Both at one stage bore the same subtitle, 'Of the Use of Riches', but the similarities soon fade. The Burlington item had earlier been styled 'Of Taste', a more suitable label in view of the main drift of its contents. The full title of the earlier work reveals that Pope was celebrating the publication by the Earl of an edition of Palladio, entitled *Fabriche antiche disegnate da Andrea Palladio Vicentino*, whose first volume appeared in 1730. A second volume was planned, but never came out. In April 1731 the author sent Burlington a manuscript of the poem, though it was still in the process of revision, and made the slightly indelicate hint that his friend might wish to append it to the planned Palladio sequel (*Corr.*, vol. 1, p. 187).

The *Epistle* proved one of the most contentious and, partly as a consequence, most frequently reprinted items in the canon of Pope's works. This came about almost entirely because of a single long passage in the middle describing a visit to the residence of a showy vulgarian named 'Timon'. Very quickly people identified Timon with the Duke of Chandos, a story that Pope's enemies missed no chance to foment. It did not take much ingenuity to align the *nouveau riche* owner with the Duke, or to see his palatial house at Cannons near Edgware, to the north of London, as the model for the villa. In fact neither identification yields a perfect match, and Pope certainly had other houses and other individuals in mind – possibly including Houghton, Walpole's grand mansion in Norfolk. But repeated denials by the poet, including an open letter to Burlington in the third edition, failed to dispel the rumours. Pope also mounted a joking self-defence in *A Master Key to Popery*, a prose pamphlet written about 1732 but unknown until it was printed from a manuscript at Chatsworth in the 1940s.

The section of the poem devoted to Timon is full of comic invention and surreal details, as on garden ornaments: 'Here Amphitrite sails tho' myrtle bow'rs: / There Gladiators fight, or die, in flow'rs' (*TE*, vol. 3.ii, p. 149). However, it would be a mistake to allow ourselves to be distracted from the precepts on landscape gardening which provide the core of the work, emphasizing the need to consult 'the Genius of the Place' (*TE*, vol. 3.ii, p. 142), and holding out Stowe as a model. The poem ends with a sounding tribute to Burlington as architect, patron and cultural entrepreneur. But the finest verses in the *Epistle*, and some of the greatest in Pope's entire canon, come a little before this. They describe the undoing of all those costly improvements that Timon had undertaken with such vainglorious zeal:

> Another age shall see the golden Ear
> Imbrown the Slope, and nod on the Parterre,
> Deep harvests bury all his Pride has plann'd,
> And laughing Ceres re-assume the land.

(*TE*, vol. 3.ii, p. 154)

The companion poem to Bathurst was already well under way, but the public had to wait another year for its appearance. One reason for the delay lay in the continuing fuss over the character of Timon. Pope also wanted to make some revisions, including a check on some details with Jacob Tonson. The venerable bookseller had retired to Herefordshire and could monitor the treatment of a local worthy who figures centrally in the *Epistle*, the so-called 'Man of Ross'.

In the early part of 1732, Pope spent a great deal of time with his closest allies, including Gay, Burlington, Oxford, Fortescue, Bathurst and Bolingbroke. In this phase of his life he particularly enjoyed contacts with Lord Peterborough, the mercurial soldier and diplomat who had opted to grow old disgracefully, while keeping his marriage to Anastasia Robinson a secret from the world. On 4 March came the death of the exile Francis Atterbury, whose passing brought back many memories. His body was brought back to England for burial in the Abbey, where he had once governed the chapter with imperious authority. When the coffin arrived along with his effects, the government searched his papers for incriminating evidence, just to make sure. Just before his arrest in 1722 Atterbury had prepared a vault for himself and his recently deceased wife, at a spot near the west door of the Abbey, 'as far from Kings and Kaisers, as the space will admit'.[7] Among those to mark his death was Pope, though the epitaph he wrote for the Bishop (quoted in Chapter 6) took too personal and pointed a form to be used on the memorial in the church.

Nothing of substance came from Pope's pen in these months, until Benjamin Motte brought out the misleadingly named 'third' (really, fourth) instalment of the *Miscellanies* in October. Again Swift provided a major part of the collection, with a number of his best-known poems reprinted, including the birthday verses to Stella and the much-pirated 'Cadenus and Vanessa'. There were also several works in prose, most notably 'A Modest Proposal' – here, in effect, acknowledged for the first time. The verse that Pope culled from earlier publications included some short items that he had allowed to slip into the world without acknowledgement, as well as the two pamphlets on Curll from 1716 and a hilarious sequel, detailing the bookseller's inadvertent circumcision. Other squibs in the Scriblerian manner he may have concocted jointly with Arbuthnot. The best is a mock astrological prediction called 'Annus Mirabilis', dating from 1722, and attributed to a certain 'Abraham Gunter, Philomath'. It describes a sudden universal sex-change, providing abundant opportunities, gleefully accepted, for double entendre. Even in the very different atmosphere of 1732, with the palmy days of Tory satire under good Queen Anne long gone, the brio of early Scriblerus still comes through.

This time the *Miscellanies* contained no work that can safely be assigned to Gay. Sadly Pope's cherished companion in so many battles did not have long to live. In the summer he had gone to stay with the Queensberrys at Amesbury in Wiltshire, and worked on a new play called *Achilles*. In October he told Swift, 'I cannot so much boast of my health as before I went, for I am frequently out of order with my colical complaints, so as to make me uneasy and dispirited'. After he got back to London his condition declined rapidly, and on 4 October he died at the age of forty-seven. It came as a shock, as he succumbed with little warning to what may have been peritonitis brought on by an obstruction in the bowels.[8] Even in the 1730s it was considered a premature death. Any well-nourished child who survived into adulthood, and did not have to endure multiple pregnancies, had a fair expectation of life, commonly into the sixties and seventies. Edith Pope lived to be ninety, while the unsinkable Lord Bathurst would last until he was almost ninety-one, and while that was a long way above the average it did not count as freakishly abnormal among the prosperous classes.

Immediately Pope dispatched the sad news to Swift:

> One of the nearest and longest tyes I have ever had, is broken all on a sudden, by the unexpected death of poor Mr Gay. An inflammatory feaver hurried him out of this life in three days. He died last night at nine a clock, not deprived of his senses entirely at last, and possessing them perfectly till within five hours. He asked of you a few hours before, when in acute torment by the inflammation in his bowels and breast.

Arbuthnot added some medical details: 'Poor Mr. Gay dy'd of an inflammation, and I believe at last a mortification of the bowels; it was the most precipitate case I ever knew, having cut him off in three days' (*Corr.*, vol. 3, pp. 321, 324). The event prompted Pope to look forward to the death of his ailing mother, which could not be long delayed now, and characteristically turned to Patty Blount in his hour of need: 'Indeed I want a friend, to help me to bear it better. We want each other.' For understandable reasons, far from being able to provide the support he desired, she herself collapsed on learning what had occurred. On 14 December Pope gave Caryll a brief account:

> Your god-daughter has been very ill. I no sooner saw the death of my old friend Mr Gay, whom I attended in his last sickness ... but she fell very ill, partly occasioned by the shock his death gave her. Dr Arbuthnot who attended the one was constantly with the other, and has had better success with her. During her whole illness, the worthy family set open all their windows and doors, and washed the house and stairs to her very door twice in the week in which her recovery depended upon being kept warm; and had a constant clatter of doors, and removal of chairs, and all the noise that could possibly be made, while she was ordered to be composed to rest by the Doctor. This I saw and heard, and so did Dr. Arbuthnot, who very humorously asked, as he went up and down their stairs, why they did not sell and make money of their sashes, and leave the windows quite open?
>
> (*Corr.*, vol. 3, pp. 335, 337)

As sometimes happens with long-term invalids, Pope could find it hard to appreciate the sufferings of others around him until events forced them to his attention.

The burial of Gay took place at Westminster Abbey, where a monument by Michael Rysbrack was erected with an epitaph by Pope. One authority has objected to the lines inscribed on the tomb for setting up a 'childlike paragon' which unduly emphasized Gay's simple and gentle nature.[9] It is true that he had sought preferment as assiduously as any of his colleagues, and had a certain worldly ambition concealed behind his easy-going nature. But in many ways he lived the most unfulfilled life of any among the Scriblerus fraternity, if we except Thomas Parnell on account of his death so soon after the Club was instituted. Unlike Swift, Gay had not come to a final grudging acceptance that he would never attain the position he had hoped for. Unlike Arbuthnot, he lacked the social and professional skills to prosper even in a politically hostile climate. Unlike Pope, he had not contrived to turn his opposition to the powers that be into a principled refusal of patronage and favour.

Gay's passing meant that Pope grew to feel more and more isolated, and this may be one reason why in his later work he increasingly portrays himself as a lone champion of public virtue – supported, true enough, by a corps of like-minded aristocrats, but essentially standing by himself in the London literary world. This self-dramatization required him to ignore the work of Walpole's other critics, who included men of great talent such as James Thomson. But the pose did provide him with a satiric base and a political stance.

2

The year 1733 started out as an *annus mirabilis* for Pope himself. In the first five months of the year he produced three remarkable works, each of which exhibited his daring new approach. He began with the poem addressed to Bathurst. Next came the first item in his series of poems updating the satires and epistles of Horace. After that came the first three sections of *An Essay on Man*. Each has, in its different way, a substantial component of politics.

The roots of the *Epistle to Bathurst*, as has been suggested, go back to the idea of the *magnum opus*. By the time he drew up these plans, Pope was already contemplating using examples such as that of the Man of Ross, which duly figure in the poem as finally drafted. We know from Spence's recollections that Pope considered that this was 'as much laboured' as anything he had written (*Anecdotes*, vol. 1, p. 139). He told his friend John Caryll that it was 'the work of two years by intervals', and confirmed this information when he sent Swift a copy soon after publication: 'I never took more care in my life of any poem'. He regarded it as 'not the worst' thing he had written, a masterly understatement, even though Swift worried that some of it might be obscure to readers in Dublin (*Corr.*, vol. 1, pp. 340, 348, 353, 362). This actually could have occurred, because Pope had made a deliberate effort to name names more insistently, as he strove to avoid the problems caused by his caricature of Timon in the *Epistle to Burlington*. At one point he even planned to make some amends to Chandos by incorporating a complimentary reference into the new poem, but he later decided to confine the allusion to the second Earl of Oxford. After the debacle over Timon, he wrote an open letter announcing his intention to 'make use of *Real* Names and not of Fictitious Ones' in his next work (*TE*, vol. 3.ii, p. 132). Although at first he expected 'much noise and calumny' to greet the epistle (*Corr.*, vol. 3, p. 337), as it turned out the poem received a good reception.

The work is an intricately wrought tessellation made up of diverse materials. It features vivid character sketches, culminating in the brilliantly told moral fable of Sir Balaam, which concludes the poem. In particular Pope describes a number of vicious and grasping misers. Some are historic, like the Duke of Buckingham; some are topical, like the infamous Colonel Francis Charteris and the corrupt broker Peter Walter (who serves as an emblem of the unjust steward of scripture); and some are allegorical types, like 'Cotta'. A key figure in the design is Sir John Blunt, the chief architect of the South Sea Bubble. As a foil to this gallery of villains, comprising 'the Fool, the Mad, the Vain, the Evil' (*TE*, vol. 3.ii, p. 85), Pope offers the counter-example of John Kyrle, the Herefordshire philanthropist known as the Man of Ross, who fed the poor and relieved the sick out of a modest personal income. The poet also exempts Bathurst, and more briefly Lord Oxford, from his criticism as grandees 'unspoil'd by wealth' (*TE*, vol. 3.ii, p. 111).

The new *Epistle* runs to almost twice the length of its predecessor. Its unbuttoned style makes possible a more direct and impassioned tone. The Burlington poem had ended in a resonant passage lauding his lordship on his role as a kind of unpaid Minister of Culture, who promotes the national interest by sponsoring good works of engineering and architecture:

> Bid Harbors open, public Ways extend,
> Bid Temples, worthier of the God, ascend;
> Bid the broad Arch the dang'rous Flood contain,
> The Mole projected break the roaring Main;
> Back to his bounds their subject Sea command,
> And roll obedient Rivers thro' the Land;
> These Honours, Peace to happy Britain brings,
> These are Imperial Works, and worthy Kings.
>
> (*TE*, vol. 3.ii, p. 156)

But not, we are invited to conclude, works that the present monarch is likely to undertake. The entire passage has the air of rolling back the course of the past twenty years, reverting to the dreams of *Windsor-Forest*, and undoing the events of *The Dunciad*. It is magnificent, but not very human.

By contrast, the second poem gets close enough to Bathurst for Pope to indulge in some cheeky dialogue with his noble friend:

> Since then, my Lord, on such a World we fall,
> What say you? 'Say? Why take it, Gold and all'.
> What Riches give us let us then enquire:
> Meat, Fire, and Cloaths. What more? Meat, Cloaths, and Fire.
> Is this too little? would you more than live?
> Alas! 'tis more than Turner finds they give.
> Alas! 'tis more than (all his Visions past)
> Unhappy Wharton, waking, found at last!
> What can they give? To dying Hopkins Heirs,
> To Chartres, Vigour; Japhet, Nose and Ears?
>
> (*TE*, vol. 3.ii, pp. 94–5)

Significantly, this excerpt calls for quite a lot of annotation. Richard Turner, a miserly Turkey merchant, bore the nickname 'Plum', a slang term used to describe the sum of £100,000 and by extension plutocrats who could lay hands on such an enormous sum. Wharton refers to the mercurial Duke, a man of pleasure and a Jacobite who had abjured his father's doughty Whig politics. Hopkins was always known as 'Vulture', as Pope states in a note. His Jonsonian nomenclature came from his ruthless business methods and penurious treatment of his family. 'Chartres' fails to disguise the identity of Colonel Francis Charteris, an ageing rake who was the most notorious sexual addict of his time. He also had shady links to Walpole's information machine. Japhet Crook was a swindler recently sentenced to the pillory, where his ears and part of his nose were sliced off in a time-honoured punishment for offences deemed especially hateful. All these men had appeared in news stories within the past couple of years, and all were dead by 1734. They resemble modern celebrities, in that they had become famous for being famous. Pope dismisses them with a single verbal flick, knowing that their fame would last not much longer than fifteen minutes. (Charteris has enjoyed more of an afterlife, since Hogarth showed him hanging around for no good purpose at the start of *The Harlot's Progress* later in the same year.) The verse brims with conversational energy, while the victims are plucked from the most sordid courtroom narratives of that very moment.

A good case exists to regard the *Epistle* as the most successful work Pope ever wrote on an explicitly political subject. To go further: hardly any English poem from any period confronts so many aspects of social and economic reality. Its theme is the financial revolution, a term coined by historians to describe a large-scale process whose main impact coincided exactly with Pope's lifetime. The key developments include the foundation of the Bank of England; the incorporation and reconstitution of other great trading houses, such as the East India Company; the growth of public borrowing, with a huge leap in the national debt, a change which much increased the dependence of the Crown on City financiers; the evolution of the insurance market, both for lives and for property; a massive recoinage in the 1690s; a leap in the number of joint-stock companies. This era witnessed the birth of new institutions like the Bank, the Stock Exchange and Lloyd's, which stand at the centre of what we know today as the City of London. As noted at the start of this book, most of these innovative steps were taken around the area of Lombard Street, right on the doorstep of Alexander Pope senior, prior to his retirement.

Among the new organizations founded at this time, of course, was the South Sea Company, with its baleful outcome a crucial part of contemporary history – as we saw in Chapter 5. Pope had a tricky path to tread here. This was not just because his own fingers had been burnt: years later he wrote of himself, 'In *Southsea* days not happier, when surmis'd / The Lord of thousands, than if now *Excis'd*' (*TE*, vol. 4, p. 65). The last phrase puns on Walpole's Excise scheme, while the word 'surmis'd' nicely declines to confirm or refute the nature of his losses. On top of this, Pope's friend Robert Harley, later Oxford, had acted as the prime mover and first governor of the Company. The present King had also served in this role, and he is thought to have accepted clandestine allocations of shares. Courtiers attached to the then Prince and Princess of Wales had been given *douceurs*, and as we discovered earlier Pope enjoyed the company of this group during the period leading up to the crash. The poet maintained close contacts with many of those most heavily implicated in the fraudulent allotments, notably the Secretary of State James Craggs. Perhaps as a result of these circumstances the poem deals in a fairly kind fashion with Sir John Blunt, so widely reviled in the aftermath of the collapse. A share of the blame, we are clearly meant to feel, belongs to the monarchy, the court, parliament and the mercantile community at large – it ought not to be sprayed over a few rogue directors, plucked out for exemplary punishment in a series of show hearings before the House of Commons.

Just how widely the toxic effects spread, we can judge from an eloquent passage not far into the *Epistle*:

> Blest paper-credit! last and best supply!
> That lends Corruption lighter wings to fly!
> Gold imp'd by thee, can compass hardest things,
> Can pocket States, can fetch or carry Kings;
> A single leaf shall waft an Army o'er,
> Or ship off Senates to a distant Shore;
> A leaf, like Sibyl's, scatter to and fro
> Our fates and fortunes, as the winds shall blow:
> Pregnant with thousands flits the Scrap unseen,
> And silent sells a King, or buys a Queen.

(*TE*, vol. 3.ii, p. 93)

The last line could not be more brutally direct. It refers to a story that Caroline had taken a bribe from Robert Knight, the South Sea cashier, and the one individual among the Company's servants whom Pope probably looked on as an unmitigated villain. Whether or not the rumour had any truth in it, Pope was taking a huge risk in making such an open allusion. The general attack mounted in the poem on the power of money allows for few exceptions:

> Trade it may help, Society extend;
> But lures the Pyrate, and corrupts the Friend:
> It raises Armies in a Nation's aid,
> But bribes a Senate, and the Land's betray'd.
>
> (*TE*, vol. 3.ii, p. 88)

This passage exemplifies beautifully the capacity of antithesis, in the hands of a master like Pope, to dramatize a complex and conflicting set of facts.

The most richly ambiguous section comes at the very end, with the descent of a City magnate styled Sir Balaam. For a moment, the comic mode turns into something close to tragic farce:

> My Lady falls to play; so bad her chance,
> He must repair it; takes a bribe from France;
> The House impeach him; Coningsby harangues;
> The Court forsake him, and Sir Balaam hangs:
> Wife, son, and daughter, Satan, are thy own,
> His wealth, yet dearer, forfeit to the Crown:
> The Devil and the King divide the prize,
> And sad Sir Balaam curses God and dies.
>
> (*TE*, vol. 3.ii, pp. 124–5)

The rapid staccato narrative somehow implies a rush to judgement. Whatever his faults, Sir Balaam might deserve a bit more of a hearing. The last verse obviously harks back to the misfortunes of the prophet Job as he rails blasphemously at his fate. But at least God does listen to Job and allows him to repent. Here we feel that Sir Balaam has been subjected to an unfair process conducted by his very ungodlike accusers.

To make sense of this ending, we need to ask ourselves a number of questions. Who had been accused of illicit commerce with France, and sometimes even taking bribes? Not a City merchant, but members of the Tory party and especially Jacobites. Who had been impeached by parliament? Obviously, Oxford and, *de facto* if not *de jure*, Atterbury. Whom had the court forsaken? Most of the ministry's opponents, including the proscribed Tories and dissident Whigs, most recently the Duke and Duchess of Queensberry, sent packing because of their support for Gay. Whose possessions had become forfeit to the Crown? The leading Jacobites arrested in the wake of the Rising in 1715–16, with Lord Derwentwater the most conspicuous example from Pope's standpoint. While Atterbury retained a few temporal goods, he was stripped of all his valuable preferments, and the Lords laid down as part of the 'pains and penalties' inflicted on him that if he did not go into perpetual exile within a month he would undergo the normal punishment of a felon.

Evidently Pope has devised the tale as something more than a piece of cut-and-dried morality, along the lines of a medieval apologue. Instead he uses the fall of Sir Balaam as an allegory of political revenge. The incidents he has chosen irresistibly call up the recent political history of the nation. This becomes clearer if we pose one final question. Why does the poem invoke the name of Lord Coningsby, in view of the fact that he had been dead for almost four years after lapsing into severe mental derangement? There can be only one answer, or rather one set of related answers. The vehement peer led the drive against Oxford (he actually brought forward the motion for impeachment in parliament), Bolingbroke, Matt Prior, Atterbury and others. He stood out among the most virulent anti-Catholics in the Whig party, barely rivalled by Lord Lechmere, whom Pope had also mocked. He had spoken against measures that he considered a cover-up in the wake of the Bubble, and inveighed repeatedly against the guilty men, by whom he meant Blunt and the directors. Furthermore, he was the lone individual in either of the houses of parliament to oppose the safe return from exile of John Law, when in 1721 the government fixed a pardon for the impresario of the French bubble, to free him of an old conviction for murder. By a pleasant irony, Coningsby had himself undergone impeachment for corruption as a result of his conduct as hatchet-man for William III in Ireland.

A further aspect of Coningsby's career helps to cement the design of the poem, and makes its political slant more visible. For generations his family had wrestled with the Harleys for control of Herefordshire, a struggle that persisted in numerous elections held during Pope's lifetime. On numerous occasions Coningsby fought pitched battles over the local spoils with the rival family, at the hustings and in court. He made constant efforts to unseat his opponents from parliament, regional office or the magistracy: at the head of these men stood the first Earl of Oxford, his brother Ned, his son Edward and his cousin Tom. At the same time Coningsby kept up with equal energy one more ancestral feud with another neighbouring clan, the Scudamores. He had scarcely helped to build bridges when, in his youth, he attempted to elope with the wife of the second Viscount Scudamore – the father-in-law of the woman who became such a strong supporter of Pope and Bathurst, that is the former Frances Digby. Together this group formed an alliance based on shared horticultural interests and allegiance to the Tory cause (see Chapter 6 above).

It now becomes apparent that the latter half of the *Epistle* uses the political and social world of the border country as a local microcosm of the nation. The part in question begins when Pope celebrates the second Earl of Oxford together with Bathurst as models of benevolence. Oxford had been brought up at the

Harley family home in the Welsh Marches and knew this region intimately in his younger days. Though he took only a moderate interest in politics, his party recruited him to serve as MP for New Radnor – the chief town of an adjoining county where Coningsby regularly clashed with the Harleys – during the time that his father served as Lord Treasurer. In 1715 was ousted from his seat, largely through the efforts of his family's most bitter enemy, Thomas Coningsby. We recall that Pope had originally planned to graft on to this compliment another name, that of the Duke of Chandos, until embarrassments caused by the Timon episode ruled this out. Chandos, too, had his political base in Hereford, and he had taken over many of Coningsby's most treasured official posts after the old man degenerated into unmistakable lunacy around 1721.

At this juncture Pope introduces the famous portrait of the Man of Ross. Few commentators notice the precise way this is done:

> Rise, honest Muse! And sing the MAN of ROSS:
> Pleas'd Vaga echoes thro' her winding bounds,
> And paid Severn hoarse applause resounds.
>
> (*TE*, vol. 3.ii, pp. 113–14)

Only one good reason, appropriate to the aims of the poem, exists for linking the rivers Wye ('Vaga') and Severn in this way. These verses commemorate the friendship of Bathurst (whose estate lay close to the Severn), not with John Kyrle, whom he can hardly have known at all, but with the Scudamore and Digby families. Holme Lacy, the seat of the Scudamores, lies only a few miles from Ross, and it is generally believed that Pope acquired his knowledge of Kyrle – who was not a national figure – during a visit to the house, most likely made in conjunction with Bathurst and Robert Digby. We can add that Kyrle's relatives had held employment under the Harleys on several occasions, and that his own half-sister married into the Scudamore family. When she died in 1706, she left a legacy to her 'dear and loving brother', and much in the spirit of John Kyrle she bequeathed £3 to the poor of the parish of Ross.[10] She even specified that the alms should be distributed after her death 'in bread', reminding us of the very words of the *Epistle*: 'The MAN of ROSS divides the weekly bread' (*TE*, vol. 3.ii, p. 115). Such circumstances help to explain the 'Hereford' inflexion that the second half of the *Epistle* – unaccountably, otherwise – manifests. The Wye links Lady Scudamore – and by extension Bathurst, Digby and even Pope, who delighted in her estate – with John Kyrle, while it excludes Coningsby, whose seat lay on the river Lugg. Thus the poem capitalizes on old friendships and enmities in the circles Pope frequented. Coningsby, a villain in public life, also acts the part of a reprobate among the Herefordshire families whose private lives the poet shared.

More widely, the material just described enshrines the dedicatee of the poem as a surviving witness to the revenge that the Whigs had meted out to their rivals after 1714, in the border country and in the nation as a whole. Thus the *Epistle* serves as a belated act of reprisal on Pope's part. It enlists Kyrle as a paragon of provincial virtue, who 'baulks' the intent of courts and lawyers, a kind of wish-fulfilment expressing the urge of the poem to vanish away the ill-treatment that Pope's friends had received at the bar of justice. It includes an implied threnody to revive the memory of Lady Scudamore and the two Digbys, brother and sister, whose epitaph Pope had composed in 1730. It names Coningsby as the persecutor of Sir Balaam because he had been a main instrument of the revenge that had been wreaked on the Tories, ever since the Harley administration fell and the Pretender's rising came to grief.

3

We can place with unusual accuracy the moment when Pope's next series of poems, written in imitation of Horace, got under way. He wrote the opening item around late January 1733, when confined to his room for several days with a fever, and receiving a visit from Bolingbroke. As the poet later told Joseph Spence, Bolingbroke picked up a copy of Horace and happened to open it at the first satire of the second book. He remarked that it would fit Pope's present state if he were to imitate it in English. 'After he was gone, I read it over, translated it in a morning or two, and sent it to the press in a week or fortnight after. And this was the occasion of my imitating some other of the Satires and Epistles afterwards' (*Anecdotes*, vol. 1, p. 143). On 15 February the poem made its appearance as a folio, when the title page stated that the work was printed by ('for' would be more accurate) L.G., that is Lawton Gilliver, and sold by the mercuries Anne Dodd and Elizabeth Nutt along with the booksellers of London and Westminster – all designed to produce a mystifying and slightly clandestine air. The full title admits Pope's authorship in a roundabout way: *The First Satire of the Second Book of Horace, Imitated in a Dialogue between Alexander Pope of Twickenham in Com. Midd. Esq; on the one Part, and his Learned Council on the other*. This wording parodies the formula used in a legal suit, with the plaintiff's address couched in Latin. Latin and English texts were placed on facing pages.

Where Horace's satire consists of 86 lines, the version by Pope is almost twice as long, at 156 lines of heroic couplets. Perhaps the most brilliant of all his imitations, it shows a new colloquial freedom and a technical virtuosity barely apparent on this scale since *The Rape of the Lock*. Even the rendering of the same poem by Ben Jonson in 1616 seems quite rough-hewn by comparison. Horace sets up a consultation between himself and a noted lawyer, C. Trebatius Tesca. The discussion centres on libel and other aspects of free speech. This gives Pope a wonderful opportunity to play games with courtroom jargon, to pun and to dance around the terminology of the law. He uses as his interlocutor William

Fortescue, a daring choice in view of the fact that Fortescue was actually a part of the establishment. Since the poem makes bold references to the government and royal family, this was an extraordinary move on the author's part. Even though he is not openly named, Fortescue must have seen the potential for trouble when Pope wrote to him about the poem on 18 February (*Corr.*, vol. 3, p. 351). In the course of the poem Pope pays off a few old scores, reverts to the imbroglio concerning Timon's villa and nudges the Horatian text for his own purposes. As usual, the text contains tributes to friends such as Lord Peterborough and Bolingbroke. Just as habitual in Pope's work is an attempt to position himself in a centrist role:

> Papist or Protestant, or both between,
> Like good *Erasmus* in an honest Mean,
> In Moderation placing all my Glory,
> While Tories call me Whig, and Whigs a Tory.
>
> (*TE*, vol. 4, p. 11)

If this had ever been wholly true (and that is highly dubious), the *Epistle* as a whole undermines such a pose of neutrality. It depicts Pope as brave warrior for 'Virtue', a code-word for oppositional attitudes, in the face of corruption on high. The author portrays himself as 'Un-plac'd, un-pension'd, no Man's Heir, or Slave' (*TE*, vol. 4, p. 17), at once a boast and a rebuttal of the ministry with its hordes of willing lackeys. At the end Pope amusingly pretends to abjure '*Libels* and *Satires*' in favour of something less dangerous:

> But grave *Epistles*, bringing Vice to light,
> Such as a *King* might read, a *Bishop* write,
> Such as Sir *Robert* would approve ...
>
> (*TE*, vol. 4, p. 21)

It would take a very imperceptive reader to miss the fact that Pope's *Epistle* (far from grave, in its general colouring) struck directly at George II, his minister and the compliant bench of Whig bishops.

The most immediate response came from Lady Mary Wortley Montagu, now a confirmed enemy, and the courtier Lord Hervey. The former had been savagely lampooned by Pope, the latter only lightly touched on. We can well understand Lady Mary's chagrin when she encountered one passage that coupled her with two individuals – a dissolute court lady named Lady Deloraine, who had been accused of poisoning another maid of honour, and the fearsome Francis Page. A notorious 'hanging judge' and corrupt Whig MP, this was the man who had dispatched the Berkshire Blacks to death or transportation in 1723, and who later sentenced Richard Savage to the scaffold. He had earned a line in *The Dunciad*, and Henry Fielding would recall his fondness for brutal gallows humour in *Tom Jones*. Pope's verses are these:

> Slander or Poyson, dread from *Delia*'s Rage,
> Hard Words or Hanging, if your Judge be *Page*;
> From furious *Sappho* scarce a milder Fate,
> Pox'd by her Love, or libell'd by her hate.
>
> (*TE*, vol. 4, p. 13)

The cruelty of this last couplet derives from the malicious exactitude of its phrasing. Lady Mary had suffered a severe infection of smallpox over the New Year in 1716, which impaired her great beauty from this time onwards. The innuendo comes harshly from Pope, who at that time was just getting to know her well and developing some literary collaborations with her at this juncture. The words also hint at Lady Mary's campaign to introduce inoculation against smallpox after her return from the Turkish embassy. As to the benefits of this new medical treatment, the jury was still out; but many people had already found it efficacious in particular cases. The person most likely to be 'poxed' could be a French adventurer named Rémond, with whom Lady Mary had conducted an unwise liaison and who then made trouble for her, duly noted in a later poem by Pope. On the other hand 'Sappho' carries with it an undoubted implication that she might be more attracted to her own sex, even though the terms Sapphic and lesbian were not yet used in this context. As for the libels, Pope believed that she had written some of the savage attacks published by Curll and others after the publication of *The Dunciad*.

Nobody quite knows how, when and why the quarrel between these two formidable antagonists developed in the late 1720s.[11] At all events Lady Mary seems to have been chiefly responsible for *Verses Address'd to the Imitator of the First Satire of the Second Book of Horace*, which was published on 9 March.[12] While this retort may lack the finesse of the original, it is quite as vituperative as anything in Pope's satire and ranks as one of the most effective of the numerous attacks on him. Fortescue seems to have feared that there would be repercussions if any answer was issued to these verses, and Pope wrote to him promising to desist (*Corr.*, vol. 3, pp. 354–5). It was the first time that a serious threat of action menaced the poet as a result of his original writing. At least he could claim a minor victory in that he was now able to present himself as having been 'libell'd' by Lady Mary's hate, in exactly the way that the imitation had predicted. The *Verses* must have stung Pope, because he broke with his usual habits and wrote an answer to it in prose, called *A Letter to a Noble Lord*. This was completed in 1733, but it never appeared in Pope's lifetime. Hervey got wind of the response, and had heard it described as 'very low and poor'. The author's own account of the matter appears in some affectedly off-hand remarks to Swift on 6 January 1734:

> There is a Woman's war declar'd against me by a certain Lord, his weapons are the same which women and children use, a pin to scratch, and a squirt to bespatter. I writ a sort of answer, but was ashamed to enter the lists with him, and after shewing it to some people, supprest it: otherwise it was such as was worthy of him and worthy of me.
>
> (*Corr.*, vol. 3, p. 401)

It should be noted that the imitation provoked a few more rejoinders, the best of them a neat travesty in verse that seems to have come from the fluent pen of Edmund Curll.[13]

Almost immediately afterwards, on 30 February, the first epistle of *An Essay on Man* made its appearance. The second and third sections came out on 29 March and 8 May, with the last delayed until 24 January 1734. Each part was first issued with a subtitle indicating that it was part of a series of 'epistles to a friend'. It follows that we should not see the work as too remote in spirit from the other series on which Pope had now embarked, represented by the poems addressed to Bathurst and Fortescue respectively. Indeed, it can rightly be judged 'essayistic', in the sense that the text consists of a witty *causerie* rather than a solemn academic treatise. Like most of us, Pope did not possess a very solid grasp of the full range of philosophic topics. What he did have was an ability to join the dots in an argument, something not apparent in all philosophers. Nor is his thought unsystematic: indeed, it has a decisive cut-and-dried quality, shunning ambiguity, that can strike the modern mind as alien.

Pope issued all four items anonymously, with a misleading imprint. He had deliberately contrived this, so that he could enjoy the spectacle of widespread homage paid to the author of this noble and uplifting poem. Often these views were expressed most fervently by long-time enemies such as Leonard Welsted, a victim of *The Dunciad*, in ignorance of the truth. Pope did not reveal his hand until the poem went into his collected *Works* in 1735. But by then the authorship was an open secret, and Voltaire, who greatly admired the poem, soon learned the truth. In addition, the 'friend' on the title page had now been identified as Bolingbroke. The opening address had begun, 'Awake, my Laelius', a cover name taken from a Roman patron of Horace, but Pope subsequently replaced this by 'St. John', Bolingbroke's family name.

From the outset the *Essay* achieved great success in Britain and abroad. Translations into several languages soon followed. Just as promptly, the criticisms of a Swiss theologian named Jean-Pierre de Crousaz set off a debate over much of Europe on the orthodoxy of the author's religious and moral position. In this war of words a leading role fell to the poet's editor William Warburton, although his efforts to portray the poem as a coherent, rigorous and unimpeachably Christian document have not always been accepted. An equally fierce and latterly more vigorous controversy has surrounded the degree of Pope's debt to the ideas of his mentor Bolingbroke. Today scholars generally discount the claim that Pope used a lost dissertation by Bolingbroke as the framework of his argument. However, it is certain that he employed a summary in prose that he later put into verse, and we cannot rule out the possibility that Bolingbroke made some contribution to this. Commentators have detected a wide range of other influences, ranging from Plato to Leibnitz, but none of them seems to have been regularly enlisted as a controlling system of belief.

But what about politics? The crucial section from this point of view unquestionably comes in the third epistle, which from 1735 bore the subtitle, 'Of the Nature and State of Man with respect to Society'. Part of this composes an analysis of the origins of government, taking in such hoary concepts as the state of nature, as debated by theorists such as Hobbes, Locke and Sir Robert Filmer. Contemporary debate between rival schools of thought commonly reverted to this kind of issue, and Bolingbroke would enlist cognate ideas in his sustained attempt to provide an ideology for the opposition to Walpole. But near the end Pope lets loose a maxim dangerously close, in terms of political philosophy, to outright scepticism: 'For Forms of Government let fools contest; / What e'er is best administer'd is best' (*TE*, vol. 3.i, pp. 123–4). While Maynard Mack saw this as essentially an Aristotelian doctrine, it seems a recipe for a kind of pyrrhonism, making scrutiny of the beliefs and positions of those engaged in government a secondary matter, less important than the way in which those in power exercised their authority. Pope attempted to elucidate the proposition in a marginal comment he made on one of the numerous pamphlets which came out in rejoinder, but he made no public response.

Whatever his exact intentions here, it is clear that the text skates well over most of the matters that divided government and opposition, or Whig and Tory, in this decade. Overall Pope may be described as writing from a traditional humanist perspective, analysing social change only at a broad abstract level, and avoiding historically determined instances. Now and then there is a flash of something more precisely aimed, as with the couplet in Epistle IV: 'And more true joy Marcellus exil'd feels, / Than Caesar with a senate at his heels' (*TE*, vol. 3.i, p. 152). We shall not feel surprised to learn that an early manuscript draft reads 'W—' rather than 'Caesar' at this point.[14] Readers in 1733 would have easily formed a suspicion that the lines contrast Bolingbroke and Walpole. However, such moments occur seldom in the text. By comparison with the other poems Pope was writing at this time, *An Essay on Man* resolutely avoids the topical and declines to engage with particular individuals. That, of course, was one of the strategies that the poet had to adopt if he wished to conceal his identity on first publication, and it was one of the reasons that he managed to hoodwink so many of his earliest readers.

Pope chose to alienate himself from the court at a fraught moment. Walpole had for once miscalculated the mood of the nation, when in March 1733 he introduced measures to reduce the burden of the land tax, by replacing customs duty on tobacco and wine with a levy imposed when the goods were removed from bonded warehouses for sale to the public. This was the notorious 'Excise' which aroused so much hostility across the nation. In theory the scheme had many advantages. It would increase national revenue, eliminate inefficiencies in the customs system and deter smuggling. Above all it would shift some of the impact of taxes from landowners to the very group who had done well out of the Whigs' rise to power, the commercial class. 'Great towns and moneyed men pay little or nothing', the Prime Minister pointed out, while the landed gentry (who numbered less than half a million out of a population of eight million) bore the brunt of taxation. When the first measure went before parliament, it struggled through despite opposition from about a hundred Tories and almost as many dissident Whigs. But by the time that the full bill was introduced in the Commons at the start of April, a concerted body of opposition had grown up inside and outside Westminster, with the City of London among the most vociferous critics of the plan. Alderman Barber, now Lord Mayor, held a 'loyal' meeting at his house to concert opposition.[15] In a series of votes the government majority fell to an unprecedentedly low margin. Walpole realized that he would have to abandon the scheme, for all its demonstrable fiscal advantages.

The premier made an orderly retreat, prudent behaviour in view of the general election that was due the next year. In 1734 his opponents made the Excise scheme a target during the campaign, so that voters and non-voters were caught up in a mood of heightened political excitement. A few Tory diehards burned an effigy of the Prime Minister, the ultimate sign of hostility in age with no television, blogs or social networking sites. Many of the critics adopted a libertarian line, claiming that the new tax was aimed against basic freedoms and would lead to the growth of surveillance over ordinary citizens. These tactics resonated in some constituencies – William Pulteney, the leading dissident in the Commons, was returned for Middlesex, with its large and influential body of electors. But Walpole managed to prevail yet again, even though he had a much reduced majority. He could look forward to another seven years safely ensconced in power, while opposition looked on with bemusement. Once again they had seen their hopes dashed. It was only in 1735 that they made any real headway, with the coalition around the Prince of Wales of the group of 'Patriot' Whigs known as 'Cobham's Cubs' with the remnant of Tories led by Sir William Wyndham – a development to be explored in the next chapter. Only then, too, did Pope find genuine common cause with forces working in and out of parliament to achieve specific political ends. For the first time since 1714, his works reflected an identifiable agenda that his allies could put before the electorate. And for the first time ever he put some of his highest creative energy into propaganda.

4

Edith Pope had been sinking for a long time, and it came as no great shock when she died on 7 June 1733. She had lived to the age of about ninety. Her son Alexander had tended her devotedly until the end, although it appears that she may have been unaware of his presence in her last days. The burial took place at Twickenham parish church on the evening of 11 June. As we might expect, the ceremony was carried out with exceptional dignity and formality, with the elderly and the poor among parishioners selected to perform a role dressed in full mourning. Clearly Pope had arranged things in this way as a tribute to his mother's charity and piety. A more lasting commemoration came in the last epistle of the *Essay on Man*, published a few months later. After a heartfelt passage recalling Pope's lost friend Robert Digby, together with his still-surviving father Lord Digby, the poem continues:

> Tell me, if Virtue made the Son expire,
> Why, full of days and honour, lives the Sire? ...
> Or why so long (in life if long can be)
> Lent Heav'n a parent to the poor and me?
>
> (*TE*, vol. 3.i, p. 138)

This unquestionably ranked as one of the lowest points that Pope had ever experienced. Swift sent him a sincere but somewhat gruff letter of condolence:

> I must condole with you for the loss of Mrs. Pope, of whose death the papers have been full. But I would rather rejoice with you, because if any circumstances can make the death of a dear parent and friend a subject for joy, you have them all. She died in an extreme old age, without pain, under the care of the most dutiful son that I have ever known or heard of, which is a felicity not happening to one in a million.
>
> (*Corr.*, vol. 3, p. 378)

In reply Pope acknowledged the state of nervous exhaustion into which he had fallen, as the loss of his mother caused the events of the wider world to lose any interest they once had:

> I have every day wish'd to write to you, to say a thousand things; and yet I think I should not have writ to you now, if I was not sick of writing any thing, sick of myself, and (what is worse) sick of my friends too. The world is become too busy for me, everybody so concern'd for the publick, that all private enjoyments are lost, or disrelish'd ... I have written nothing this year: It is no affectation to tell you, my Mother's loss has turned my frame of thinking. The habit of a whole life is a stronger thing than all the reason in the world. I know I ought to be easy, and to be free; but I am dejected,

> I am confined: my whole amusement is in reviewing my past life, not in laying plans for my future.
>
> (*Corr.*, vol. 3, p. 383)

Gradually he found the strength to go on. Visits to the homes of Bolingbroke, Peterborough, Cobham and Oxford aided the process of recovery. By this time another member of his circle had lost favour at court. This was the King's official mistress, the Countess of Suffolk, formerly Henrietta Howard, whose home at Marble Hill stood less than a mile downstream from Pope's villa, and where according to Swift's *Pastoral Dialogue between Richmond-Lodge and Marble-Hill*, composed a few years earlier, 'Mr. *Pope* was the Contriver of the Gardens, Lord *Herbert* the Architect, and the Dean of St. Patrick's chief Butler, and Keeper of the Ice House'.[16] Pope continued to visit the house – now splendidly restored – along with luminaries of the opposition such as William Pulteney and William Murray.[17] After her separation from her charmless husband, she became mistress of the robes, more or less a sinecure; but in 1734 it was made clear to her that she was no longer *persona grata* with the royal family. Lord Hervey explains:

> Sir Robert Walpole hated Lady Suffolk, and was hated by her, but did not wish her driven out of St. James's, imagining somebody would come in her place who, from his attachment to the Queen, must hate him as strongly, and might hate him more dangerously.
>
> The true reasons of her disgrace were the King's being thoroughly tired of her; her constant opposition to all his measures; her wearying him with her perpetual contradiction; her intimacy with Mr. Pope, who had published several satires, with his name to them, in which the King and all his family were rather more than obliquely sneered at; the acquaintance she was known to have with many of the opposing party, and the correspondence she was suspected to have with many of them; and, in short, her being no longer pleasing to the King in her private capacity, and every day more disagreeable to him in her public conduct.[18]

All this rings fairly true. Henrietta had been one of Gay's most loyal supporters, and she had good relations with Arbuthnot, Peterborough and Martha Blount. If her defection did not strengthen Walpole's opponents in terms of hard politics, at least it stiffened their resolve and gave them another reason to band together.

In November Pope published his jaunty version of Donne's fourth satire, ascribed to 'an eminent Hand'. It is likely that this draws on work from a much earlier date, composed around the time of the Harley administration. In its denunciation of court life, the style of the imitation has much of the racy eloquence of the poems based on Horace. Thus, in one passage the importunate stranger who has buttonholed Pope's narrator tries to show off his knowledge of the world:

> When the Queen frown'd, or smil'd, he knows; and what –
> A subtle Minister may make of that?
> Who sins with whom? Who got his Pension *Rug*,
> Or quicken'd a Reversion by a *Drug*?
> Whose Place is *quarter'd out*, three Parts in four,
> And whether to a Bishop, or a Whore?
> Who, having lost his Credit, pawn'd his Rent,
> Is therefore fit to have a *Government*?
> Who in the *Secret*, deals in Stocks secure,
> And cheats th'unknowing Widow, and the Poor?
> Who makes a *Trust*, or *Charity*, a Job, –
> And gets an Act of Parliament to rob?
> Why *Turnpikes* rise, and now no Cit, nor Clown –
> Can *gratis* see the *Country*, or the *Town*?
> Shortly no Lad shall *chuck*, or Lady *vole*, –
> But some excising Courtier will have a Toll.
>
> (*TE*, vol. 4, p. 37)

The verses are stuffed with references to contemporary scandals, such as the fraudulent Charitable Corporation, whose directors had been convicted of embezzlement in the previous year. It is amusing to find Pope deploring the corruption involved in some turnpike trusts, when just ten years before Daniel Defoe had hymned these innovations in road transport as a mighty blessing to the nation. To match this topicality, Pope uses language dense with current slang and financial jargon: *rug* means safe, in the argot of gamblers, while *vole* comes from card games and *chuck* from a homely pastime. We have already discovered what 'excising' means.

By the end of the year he had completed the last portion of *An Essay on Man* and the *Epistle to Cobham*, ready for publication at the start of 1734. Most readers have always looked on the poem addressed to Cobham as the least successful of the four *Moral Essays*, mainly because its central idea of 'the ruling passion' seems a curiously simple-minded concept for Pope – very disparate forms of human activity are reviewed under this rather blunt rubric. Two striking portraits stand out in the text: one concerns the Duke of Wharton, a dissolute and vacillating Jacobite who frittered away his genuine talents, and the other dramatizes the life of a great actress, Anne Oldfield, in just six merciless lines. But the poem never quite comes to a concerted resolution, and its implicit ideological structure has surprisingly little to do with Lord Cobham, now emerging as a leader of the opposition. Nor does it connect with his well-wrought landscape at Stowe, a *paysage moralisé* dropped down into the English countryside to celebrate patriotic and patrician virtues. If we judge it by the highest standards we commonly apply to Pope's work, the *Epistle* must be regarded as something of an opportunity missed.

Two more new versions of Horace appeared during the course of the year. In early July Gilliver published the second satire of the second book, addressed to Hugh Bethel. This engaging work reflects Pope's long friendship with this country gentleman and one-time MP, who lent practical assistance on financial matters to Martha Blount as well as the poet. What complicates the matter is that Bethel had not shifted from the position of an unreconstructed Whig, while his brother Slingsby was an Africa merchant and a leading light in the City of London who ultimately achieved the highest dignity in the municipality as Lord Mayor. Bethel also took a keen interest in the visual arts, and belonged to a group of connoisseurs from East Yorkshire attached to the local magnate, Lord Burlington. The poem that emerged contains some neat adaptation of the praises of a simple life found in the original work by Horace, but it sedulously avoids direct mention of George II and Walpole. By comparison with Pope's other writings at this juncture, it goes remarkably easy on the failings of the ministry. However, it does launch some sharp arrows in the direction of the plutocrats benefitting from Walpole's stable reign, especially when they avert their eyes from the poverty around them, or ignore ways in which the infrastructure of the capital is falling apart:

> Oh Impudence of wealth! With all thy store,
> How dar'st thou let one worthy man be poor?
> Shall half the new-built Churches round thee fall?
> Make keys, build Bridges, or repair White-hall:
> Or to thy Country let that heap be lent,
> As M***o's was, but not at five *per Cent*.

(*TE*, vol. 4, p. 63)

These last two lines contain a dig at the rich but always money-conscious Duchess of Marlborough, while the previous couplet once more suggests that a job of civic reconstruction needs to be done, preferably by Bethel's friend Lord Burlington.

The remaining item came out as *Sober Advice from Horace* on 21 December, when it was said to be 'imitated in the manner of Mr. Pope' – a true but totally misleading claim. This uninhibited exercise in sexual innuendo derives from an early satire by Horace (the second in his first collection), and its freedom of speech so deterred later academics that it was always omitted from Pope's works by eighteenth and nineteenth century editors. Today we can see it as something more than 'a very indecent Sermon, after the *Essay on Man*', as he slily described it to Caryll (*Corr.*, vol. 3, p. 447). It shows that the poet had regained much of his bounce and élan, something that comes through in a letter from Bolingbroke to Swift in the summer of 1734:

> He is actually rambling from one friends house to another: he is now att Cirencester, he came thither from my Lord Cobhams; he came to my Lord Cobhams from Mr Dormers; to Mr Dormers from London, to London from Chiswick; to Chiswick from my Farm, to my Farm from his own Garden, and he goes soon from Lord Bathursts to Lord Peterborows, after which he returns to my farm again. The Daemon of verse sticks close to him. He has been imitating the Satire of Horace which begins Ambubaiarum Collegia, Pharmacopolæ, &c. and has chose rather to weaken the images than to hurt chaste ears overmuch. he has sent it me, but I shall keep his secret, as he desires.[19]

In fact, Pope was usually at his most slippery when he felt assured and confident. Even the references to Walpole, Lady Mary and Lord Hervey in *Sober Advice* have a good-humoured air. For the moment, comedy seemed a viable option.

9 FRIENDSHIP AND OPPOSITION

> Opposition is true friendship.
> William Blake, *The Marriage of Heaven and Hell*[1]

At the start of June 1735 Bolingbroke suddenly decamped and went to stay in France, where he would spend most of his time for the next decade. He had always been given to impulsive acts, but this step took his friends by surprise. Long afterwards an Edwardian biographer, Walter Sichel, neatly summed up the restless quality of Bolingbroke's life by the chapter titles he chose: Rebellion, Recoil, Retirement, Recall, Rebuff, Retreat, Return. This new departure from England did indeed amount to a retreat. Having lost his battles with Walpole, Bolingbroke now quarrelled with William Pulteney, nominally co-leader of the opposition. Besides, the long campaign he waged in the *Craftsman* had yielded few tangible gains. The Prime Minister had weathered the Excise crisis, got through the general election and rallied the court party once more. By now many of his adversaries had lost faith in both of the chiefs of their faction. They were not sorry to see Bolingbroke head off for a comfortable home at Fontainebleau, where he devoted himself to composing high-minded historical and philosophical works. The first fruit was a treatise *Of the True Use of Retirement and Study*, dedicated to Bathurst. In part it composes a *pièce justicative*, in part a self-consoling reflection by Bolingbroke on his own enforced idleness and political impotence. For Pope, who had always been an outsider, the tract needed little explication.

Paradoxically, just at this the moment, the opposition started to regain momentum. They selected Frederick, Prince of Wales, as their figurehead, in the hope that the notoriously bad relations between Hanoverian monarchs and their heirs would play into their hands – as did happen, for a while. The Prince scarcely fitted the role of the ideal 'patriot king', whose qualifications Bolingbroke would set out in his influential work published in 1739. But the treatise reflected the aspirations of the Prince's friends, among whom Pope figured at this time. The rhetoric of opposition demanded that the heir to the throne should espouse 'virtue', which in essence meant getting rid of Walpole and the machinery of government which kept him in office. The Prince visited Pope at Twickenham in October 1735, a symbolic gesture that was noted in the press. Thereafter their relations were cordial, but necessarily a little less than intimate. Pope presented Frederick with a puppy born to his dog Bounce, and in 1738 when the Prince stayed at Cirencester with Bathurst, Sir William Wyndham made efforts to enlist him in Pope's cause. For the time being at least, the poet agreed to go along with his royal highness, as a better alternative than his father George II, now seen by the opposition as hopelessly enmeshed in Walpole's corrupt management.

The real ideological thrust of the movement came from another quarter. In 1733, as part of his bid to stack the government with loyal followers during the Excise crisis, the Prime Minister had dismissed a number of office-holders, including men known to Pope such as Lord Chesterfield and Lord Marchmont. No individual suffered more than Cobham, who lost along with civilian places his colonelcy, which laid the basis for considerable power and prestige. He now set about forming a more coherent and effective party to stand against Walpole's never-ending hegemony. For this undertaking his circumstances gave him some huge advantages. He stood at the centre of a great family web composed of the Temple and Grenville clans together with their immediate kinsfolk. Cobham's nephew was the poet George Lyttelton, who would become one of Pope's closest allies in the group. His niece Hester Grenville subsequently married William Pitt, later the great Earl of Chatham. Both these men entered parliament in 1735, and formed the nucleus of 'Cobham's Cubs', a brilliant cadre of speakers and polemicists who transformed the stuffy atmosphere of an ageing House of Commons. Their other nickname, the Boy Patriots, reflected their youthful ardour along with the cult of 'patriot' virtue – a term connoting devotion to civic humanism as expressed in noble Roman republican heroes such as Cato and Brutus. Their ranks were swelled by George Grenville, best remembered as an ill-starred Prime Minister in the years leading up to the American revolution, but at this stage one of the most effective political operators in the group. On the fringe stood another of Cobham's nephews, the poet Gilbert West, who had made an early name for himself with his work *Stowe* in 1732, replete with paeans to Saxon liberty, a stock item in any denunciation of Walpole's oppressive rule. Pope evidently admired West's writing, but this may have had more to do with its politically acceptable content than its slender literary qualities.

As already mentioned, Stowe became the nerve-centre of activity for the new body forming the Patriot opposition. This fact helped to draw Pope into the circle, as he got to know Cobham mainly through their common interest in landscape gardening. Of course, he had taken an active share in advising on the layout of parks for several friends: Burlington at Chiswick, Bathurst at Cirencester and Riskins, the Digbys at Sherborne, the Dormers at Rousham, Bolingbroke at Dawley, Henrietta Howard at Marble Hill in Twickenham, and Peterborough at Bevis Mount. Gardening design and horticultural pursuits, Peter Martin has observed, 'became immensely reassuring to Pope', and compensated him 'for the physical limitations imposed on him by ill-health and a frail constitution'.[2] But, with the partial exception of Cirencester, these were private estates, expressing the cultivated interests of the owner, but not coloured directly by politics. Stowe had a different feel to it, and here Pope came to the fore as he was prepared by his early taste for landscape through all its emotions and moods to pioneer new elements in design, 'the associative, the iconographic, and the emblematic'.[3]

The gardens at Stowe constitute a physical embodiment of opposition ideology, stressing the historic values the group espoused, and scorning those of the ruling elite. They work both by commission and omission. Classical aspirations and patriotic clichés inspire some fancifully named groves and arbours. Almost every summer house is dubbed a Temple of Liberty, at the least; no item of garden furniture escapes its allotted place in the scheme. Cobham laid out his park as a moral exhibition: anyone visiting the place (and many did) was given a mythological tour of mankind and society. It was everything Pope would have liked to do, but could not, in his own pint-sized garden at Twickenham.

Cobham created many celebrated features in the landscape at Stowe. Along with James Gibbs's gothic Temple of Liberty, they included the Elysian Fields; the Temple of British Worthies, containing busts with inscriptions by George Lyttelton (after his death Pope himself was added to the gallery); and the Temple of Ancient Worthies. Nearly as renowned were the Palladian Bridge; a statue of Queen Caroline, possibly designed by Rysbrack; the Temple of Venus; the Temple of Friendship; and a monument to William Congreve. Also on show were a Doric Arch, a Chinese House, a Gothic Temple, a Hermitage, a Grotto and a Shell Bridge. Most of these survive in good condition. Features that have disappeared include the Temple of Modern Virtue, constructed as a ruin, with deliberate ironic intent; the Temple of Bacchus; statues of Saxon deities; and the Temple of Contemplation. For Pope the attraction lay chiefly on account of his architectural and gardening tastes, but he also went there as an adherent of the opposition, whose members sometimes gathered at Stowe to forge ineffective plots to bring down the Prime Minister. Many believe that Pope 'helped articulate the governing iconography' of the landscape;[4] and he may even have chosen the site of some features in the garden as deliberate allusions to the *Aeneid*.

It does not seem to have concerned him that the underlying ideology at Stowe was strongly Protestant, Whiggish and in an abstract way republican. He enjoyed the pseudo-antique ruins and modishly Gothic properties of the buildings, which reflected the antiquarian tastes common in this period: similarly at Cirencester he relished Alfred's Hall, otherwise called King Arthur's Castle. This was Bathurst's own preferred 'hermitage', set up in the heart of the home park where two of the broad walks through the woodland met. The structure had a mock-Tudor round tower at one side, abutting on some elderly yews. It has been described as 'the ancestor of Sanderson Miller's tower on Edgehill (which in Horace Walpole's words "preserves the true rust of the barons' wars," and has been held to be the archetype of all such castellated follies, although built twenty years after the Cirencester one was begun)'. Despite all the bogus pieces of historic kitsch, the hall 'remains transparently, delightfully sham'.[5] Pope shared in the aesthetic pleasures at Stowe while indulging in a few conspiratorial games with his hosts. We may feel that sometimes the unreality of their artistic projects crept into their political calculations. The Saxon constitution they used to prop up their attacks on Walpole had scarcely more bedrock to support it than the pasteboard battlements they put up on their toy castles.

1

The year 1735 began with the publication of the *Epistle to Dr Arbuthnot*, Pope's most autobiographic poem and one of his greatest. It gains added poignancy from the fact that he addressed its sober reflections on human mortality to a friend of such long duration, who was now mortally sick. Pope assembled the work from a cento of sketches he had been putting together for something like twenty years. He did not alter some lines at the end which events had now, in some sense, made obsolete:

> Me, let the tender Office long engage
> To rock the Cradle of reposing Age,
> With lenient Arts extend a Mother's breath,
> Make Languor smile, and smooth the Bed of Death.
>
> (*TE*, vol. 5, p. 127)

As Maynard Mack rightly observes, 'The patient momentarily becomes physician, possesses lenient, i.e., healing arts'.[6] While critics often read the *Epistle* as a renewed onslaught on Grub Street, a sort of postlude to *The Dunciad*, it actually contains a good deal by way of self-analysis and personal retrospection. The passage on the vain and complacent 'Bufo' contains a damning indictment of literary patronage, while the succeeding lines on Gay (one of several friends memorialized) provide a sharp rebuke to the treatment meted out to the dramatist and his protectors, the Duke and Duchess of Queensberry.

Most strikingly, Pope's famous depiction of Lord Hervey as the reptilian 'Sporus' is riddled with political innuendo. The allusions become explicit more than once:

> Whether in florid Impotence he speaks,
> And, as the Prompter breathes, the Puppet squeaks;

> Or at the ear of *Eve*, familiar Toad,
> Half Froth, half Venom, spits himself abroad,
> In Puns, or Politicks, or Tales and Lyes ...
>
> (*TE*, vol. 5, pp. 118–19)

Here the prompter is Walpole, urging Hervey to parrot speeches in his master's voice; while Eve, caught with the devil as Milton had described her, can be no one else but the Queen. The last couplet indicates that politics and scandal-mongering have merged – there is little difference between Hervey's backstairs activity as a courtier and his malicious gossip in poetry and pamphlets. Lady Mary Wortley Montagu got off lightly this time, but that did not stop her from coming to the aid of her collaborator in the *Verses* attacking Pope. Immediately after the new poem came out, she wrote to Arbuthnot, who had often attended her as her physician, disclaiming any recognition that the name 'Sappho' covered her identity:

> I have perus'd the last Lampoon of your ingenious Freind, and am not surpriz'd you did not find me out under the name of Sapho, because there is nothing I ever heard in our Characters or circumstances to make a parallel, but as the Town (except you who know better) generally suppose Pope means me whenever he mentions that name, I cannot help taking Notice of the terrible malice he bears against the Lady signify'd by that name, which appears to be irritated by supposing her writer of the verses to the Imitator of Horace, now I can assure him they were wrote (without my knowledge) by a Gentleman of great merit, whom I very much esteem, who he will never guess, and who, if he did know he durst not attack; but I own the design was so well meant, and so excellently executed that I cannot be sorry they were written; I wish you would advise poor Pope to turn to some more honest livelihood than libelling.

It is unlikely Arbuthnot would ever have done any such thing, but inside six weeks he was dead. Lady Mary got in one more shrewd retort to claims made in the *Epistle* before she closed her letter: 'As to Pope's being born of Honest Parents I verily beleive it, and will add one praise to his mothers Character that (tho' I only knew her very old) she always appear'd to me to have much better sense than himselfe' (*Corr.*, vol. 3, p. 448).

Naturally distraught by the death of his old friend, Pope wrote to George Arbuthnot, offering any help he could give to the doctor's son and daughter. He reported on the loss to Lord Oxford, mentioning his own bad health as well as many 'melancholy Circumstances ... The death, and the sickness, of Friends, particularly' (*Corr.*, vol. 3, p. 452). With Swift a permanent exile, he was now the lone survivor of the Scriblerus Club left in England. His worries also centred on Lord Peterborough, who was now seventy-seven and had to face an operation on his urinary tract, perhaps for an enlarged prostate. As it turned out the Earl lived long enough to acknowledge his secret marriage to Anastasia Robinson, before embarking on a journey to Lisbon in a vain quest for health. Before this

Peterborough asked Pope to make him a final visit at Bevis Mount, which the poet duly performed in late August. He thought the proposed trip was unwise, but could not prevail on Peterborough to change his plans. Soon after the Earl reached Lisbon he died – a fate almost identical to that of Henry Fielding, less than twenty years on. In a letter to Martha Blount, Pope described the touching scenes as he said goodbye to his rumbustious old friend, with whom he had spent many happy days in London and Southampton.[7]

In February, just before the death of Arbuthnot, Pope had issued the last of his four *Moral Essays*. It bore the title *Of the Characters of Women: An Epistle to a Lady*. Today this is one of the most intensely debated works in the canon, largely because of what now looks an unenlightened attitude in respect of gender politics. Certainly the lightning-quick sketches of fashionable ladies appear superficial and psychologically crude beside the subtle studies of humanity – mostly male – in earlier poems such as the *Epistle to Bathurst*. Only in the last fifty lines does the quality of the poetry rise to something approaching Pope's highest level. In one passage he evokes the sad state of ageing beauties, condemned to repeat endlessly their dreams of the pleasures they had known in their youth:

> At last, to follies Youth could scarce defend,
> 'Tis half their Age's prudence to pretend;
> Asham'd to own they gave delight before,
> Reduc'd to feign it, when they give no more:
> As Hags hold Sabbaths, less for joy than spight,
> So these their merry, miserable Night;
> Still round and round the Ghosts of Beauty glide,
> And haunt the places where their Honour dy'd.
> See how the World its Veterans rewards!
> A Youth of frolicks, an old Age of Cards,
> Fair to no purpose, artful to no end,
> Young without Lovers, old without a Friend,
> A Fop their Passion, but their Prize a Sot,
> Alive, ridiculous, and dead, forgot!
>
> (*TE*, vol. 3.ii, pp. 69–70)

It is not an altogether simple matter to define the tone of these verses. They convey a blend of emotions: pity, a degree of sympathetic fellow feeling, along with distaste and a kind of surreal pleasure in the grotesque images conjured up.

Pope did not name the 'lady' mentioned on the title page, but beyond a shadow of doubt he was addressing his closest woman friend, Martha Blount. In the closing sequence her 'mild' and 'serene' presence, as a model of feminine equanimity, contrasts sharply – perhaps too sharply, for the balance of the poem – with the capricious and emotionally violent behaviour of the other women whose portraits have been put on show during the tour of an imaginary gallery earlier on. The most vivid of these sketches include 'Sappho', one more brief and brutal onslaught on Lady Mary; 'Narcissa', based most likely on the Duchess of Hamilton, an imperious *grande dame* who had been married to a Jacobite leader, killed in a famous duel in 1712; and the conflicted and contradictory 'Atossa', who seems to be drawn chiefly from the Duchess of Buckingham. These bitterly satiric depictions have prompted charges of misogyny against Pope. The charge would probably surprise him. He feared that he was going to suffer some official sanction as a result of his plain-spoken comments on the state of the nation. The idea that he might come to be reviled more for his observations on the nature of women (just or unjust) would not have entered his head.

At this juncture he had something else on his mind, and the problems it raised were largely of his own making. For several years he had been planning to bring out an edition of his correspondence, and begged his friends to return letters he had written to them. Some complied, but Swift did not prove so willing. Pope then embarked on an elaborate scheme by which he manoeuvred Edmund Curll into issuing a 'pirate' edition. This involved clandestine contacts with the publisher under a disguised name, a cloak and dagger mission to Curll's shop from an actor got up in a clergyman's gown and a barrister's bands, and the delivery of bundles of ready-printed copies, carried on a horse accompanied by two porters. Pope now claimed that the Curll version was a fraud, and so he issued his own 'authentic' collection. Meanwhile a complaint was lodged in the House of Lords and Curll's impression was seized by Black Rod. On 13 May the bookseller was interrogated by the Lords, with Bathurst and Harcourt among those present, and on the following day he went before a committee of the House to explain his conduct. In the end members of the committee were unable to find that Curll had offended against the orders of the House, and specifically the ban on publishing the works of living peers without permission that had been promulgated in the wake of the Buckingham affair twelve years before.

Understandably Curll regarded this as one of his greatest triumphs, and issued advertisements crowing over the way in which he had outwitted Pope. On 26 July he inserted in the press an open letter to the public, reiterating his claims about the edition. After Pope consulted Fortescue the newspaper backed down and issued an apology:

> N.B. There having been inserted in our Paper of Saturday last a defamatory Advertisement signed, containing several Reflections on Mr. Pope, which we have since been inform'd from very good Hands are without Foundation, the Printer of this Paper is heartily sorry the same was inserted, and asks Pardon of Mr. Pope and the Publick.
>
> (*Corr.*, vol. 3, p. 477)

But it took more than this to shut Curll up. His cheeky verse recalled earlier clashes between the two men:

> The *Vomit* foul, the *Dunciad* keen,
> Vex'd *Curll* – but all admit.
> Tho' *Pope* twice *shew'd he had most Spleen*,
> *Curll* once *has shewn most wit*.

In the course of this episode Pope did achieve his larger objectives, and he was able to produce his own selection of letters, craftily edited, followed by four more volumes in the next two years. By this means he brought before the public some of his most finished exercises in the epistolary art, and demonstrated his friendship with major figures in contemporary literature, politics and society. But many observers got the idea that there was something underhand in his actions – an impression greatly enhanced when the full range of his subterfuges came to light in the nineteenth century. The suspicion grew that Pope had hidden behind his great protectors among the peers. The poet and the bookseller, they concluded, were 'akin by trade'. In the long run Pope's reputation has suffered as a consequence of this affair, strengthening the view of his critics that he deserved to undergo the same humiliations as his opponent – the 'plucky' and 'lovable' rogue Curll. And assuredly Pope had not yet seen the last of this determined adversary.

With his attentions so heavily distracted in the summer, it gives rise to some surprise that he managed to do anything else in 1735. In April he had seen through the press a second volume of his *Works*, to supplement the collection published in 1717, handsomely got out in folio, quarto and octavo editions. This publication constituted an important summation of his career to date, not least because it brought together for the first time the *Moral Essays* and the four epistles of *An Essay on Man*, along with the *Epistle to Arbuthnot* and shorter items such as the poem addressed to the first Earl of Oxford in 1721. The two imitations of Horace and one satire of Donne that had so far appeared also found a place, as did an early version of Donne's second satire previously unpublished. Finally there came *The Dunciad*, with a number of textual changes. This layout formed the basis for subsequent editions up to the present, with the arrangement necessarily adjusted to take account of some poems that did not yet exist in 1735. It ought to have been a moment of triumph. Yet Pope made a tactical error when he embarked on the correspondence at almost the same time, for the public were naturally drawn to the scandal and mud-slinging in the press that Curll helped to promote.

In the same year an enterprising bookseller named Charles Davis had the bright idea of bringing out a fifth volume of *Miscellanies* to supplement the earlier set. What this contains is a compilation of items from George Faulkner's edition of Swift, omitting those pieces that had gone into the previous series of *Miscellanies* published by Motte. Nothing by Pope appears. Davis did not mind raiding the Dublin texts, because no proper mutual arrangement existed to establish a common copyright between England and Ireland. It would have been a riskier business to infringe the rights that Pope held for works published in London.

2

On the surface the following year went a little more quietly. Pope did not produce anything new of importance and contented himself with bringing out new editions of his collected works. But this involved some work of revision and rearrangement, and naturally Curll did not let up. New volumes of *Mr. Pope's Literary Correspondence* issued by the enterprising bookseller contained less and less from Pope's hand, and so they had to be stuffed with materials with no relevance to the poet whatsoever. Still they could only stir up further troubles. In the fourth volume, which came out in the spring of 1736, Curll reprinted some of the earlier documents in the long-standing quarrel he had waged with Pope, including some embarrassing *Court Poems* from 1716, as well as a cheekily annotated version of *Sober Advice for Horace*. In addition Curll advertised a pamphlet called *The Honour of Parnassus*, said to contain 'a curious Draught and prospect of Mr. Pope's House and Gardens at Twickenham, with Verses describing the same; Mr. Pope's Method of Living, and Manner of treating his Friends. Written by Himself.' No copy appears to survive, but an engraving that has been preserved may come from this production. In the second volume of his series Curll had described how on 12 June 1735 he went to Twickenham with the artist Peter Andreas Rybrack, a brother of the famous sculptor, to take a 'full view' of the poet's property.[8] We may take it as certain that Pope had not sent out any invitation. By now it was clear that he just could not get away from his stalker.

Pope's shrinking group of friends was now augmented when Ralph Allen arrived on the scene. Allen (1693–1764) achieved prominence as a businessman and philanthropist, operating many postal routes across southern England. He also contributed to the growth of Bath as a fashionable resort by supplying building stone from his quarries, which were situated just outside the city on Combe Down, four hundred feet above the River Avon. In about 1734 he began work on his palatial mansion, which gave commanding views over Bath from the edge of town, with a fine Corinthian frontage and an extensive park sloping down the hill. Here Pope advised the owner on the proper disposition of greenhouses, grottos and sham castles. From this time onwards Allen proved one of the poet's most loyal friends, and one of his earliest acts of kindness was put up money to subsidize the publication of the 'authentic' set of correspondence. Pope spent long periods of time at Prior Park, with one visit in company with Martha Blount ending in an unpleasant scene prompted by suggestions of some kind of improper conduct. Martha never went back. Pope continued to visit Allen, and there he got to know William Warburton, the husband of Allen's niece Gertrude. Warburton, a determined ecclesiastical careerist, would end up as Bishop of Gloucester, but before that he had infiltrated himself into Pope's good graces and managed to take over the coveted role of literary executor. Meanwhile Allen remained a generous patron, and gave support to the novelists Henry Fielding and his sister Sarah. He served in part as a real-life model for the fictional Squire Allworthy in *Tom Jones*.

Other old acquaintances had passed from the scene, including the now prosperous publisher Bernard Lintot, who had done so much to set Pope's career in motion. In recent years the two men had quarrelled over financial arrangements, and the role Pope had given Lintot in his grotesque duncely games seven years before helped to confirm their alienation. A bigger loss came with the death of John Caryll in April 1736. The two men had forged a strong bond across more than thirty years, and Caryll provided a sterling example of loyalty to religious and political beliefs in the face of repeated setbacks:

> The virtue of constancy seems to have been what Pope finally most appreciated in Caryll, and most wished to display to him ... Fidelity to a principle professed, despite the consequences in the realm of practical life, was perhaps the most significant value which Pope learnt from his friendship with Caryll.[9]

By far the most attractive new item associated with Pope at this time is *Bounce to Fop: An Heroic Epistle from a Dog at Twickenham to a Dog at Court*, published by Thomas Cooper in May and attributed to 'Dr. SW—T'. The poem later went into the *Miscellanies*, shorn of a passage at the end lauding 'Master *Pope*'. Most scholars agree that the original idea belonged to Swift, probably when he visited England in 1726 and 1727, with Pope playing some part in revising the work. What remains uncertain is the extent of this revision. The verses are written in the voice of a dog named Bounce: Pope had more than one dog with this name, but in the poem's final state it can only refer to the bitch who gave birth to a puppy presented to the Prince of Wales in this year. Bounce addresses his remarks to a dog named Fop, who most likely belonged to Henrietta Howard. From the internal content, it appears that the main lines of the poem were laid down by 1732 at the latest, although Pope may well have tinkered with the text after this date. We can trace a large range of parallels with Swift's works, especially his satires in octosyllabic verse, strongly suggesting that his was the main hand in composition. In all likelihood Pope confined himself to preparing the manuscript for publication, certainly as regards the version in the *Miscellanies*. The work aims chiefly to make fun of courtiers and court life, with playful references to the Prince of Wales and leading aristocrats such as Bathurst, Burlington, Cobham, Oxford and Strafford. Its style has some of the easygoing swagger that

Swift had perfected many years before, and lacks the sharp intensity of Pope's work at this juncture.

3

Two events concerning the royal family in 1737 seemed to open up new possibilities for those ranged against Walpole. In July the Princess of Wales gave birth to a daughter at St James's Palace, after the King and Queen had made it clear that they wished the confinement to take place at Hampton Court. The political world rightly saw this as a bid for freedom, and observers braced themselves for a stronger clash. It duly came in September when George II ordered Frederick to quit the palace, leaving the Prince and Princess to set up their own separate court at Leicester House, a mansion on the north side of what is now Leicester Square. The gesture had a pleasing symmetry, because George himself when heir to the throne had used the very same site as a focus of his somewhat ineffectual opposition to the King. Frederick's declaration of independence proved rather more consequential. For the next few years a recognizable power block had its base here, as the Leicester House opposition – even after the Prince died, his widow the Princess Dowager and her son, the future George III, kept up the tradition of resistance on the same spot.

Not long afterwards Caroline expired at the end of a painful and protracted illness, regarded at the time as a constriction of the bowels or hernia. It may have been some kind of undiagnosed cancer. Her medical attendants tried everything: purgings and cuppings, blisters and clysters, and all the futile remedies of an age without anaesthetics or even effective palliatives. Finally her surgeons attempted to remove some of the mortification, but it was too late. The King, who had set up a cot by her bedside, dissolved into lachrymose self-pity. A month after her death she was carried to the Abbey for burial, but George still felt too badly stricken by his loss to make the journey of a quarter of a mile across the park from the palace.

Pope, who had always admired the Queen's strength of mind, now learnt of the courage she displayed in her final days. But her notice no longer flattered his vanity as it once had. He thought little of her cultural aspirations, such as the ponderous allegory of the Cave of Merlin she erected in Richmond Park; he regretted her deep hostility to her son Frederick; and above all he deplored her obstinate loyalty to Walpole. One result was a savage epigram 'On Queen Caroline's Death-bed', almost certainly Pope's handiwork, though never attributed to him with absolute security:

> Here lies wrapt up in forty thousand towels,
> The only proof that C*** had bowels.

(*TE*, vol. 6, p. 390)

In the wake of these events, the opposition sensed its chance to widen the split within the royal family and weaken the position of the Prime Minister. Bolingbroke soon addressed the Prince of Wales, urging him to stand up as the focus of resistance to the government.[10] External events also seemed to supply added leverage. In particular, a silly tale of the severed ear of a seaman named Captain Robert Jenkins, already seven years old, was cleverly spun to provide a *casus belli* for a conflict with Spain. Such stunts stirred up public indignation even more effectively than had happened during the Excise crisis five years before. The argument for war was especially popular with London merchants, who blamed the Spanish for attacks on their ships in defiance of the *asiento* agreement signed at Uretcht. Frederick had always made a point of associating himself with the trading community, and he implicitly gave his support to the hawks. At first Walpole stuck to his peace policy, but in the end the pressure overwhelmed him. Britain declared war in October 1739, to the jubilation of many. Allegedly the Prime Minister gave vent to his feelings with a glum comment, 'they are ringing their bells, soon they will be wringing their hands'. As often, he was right. The war dragged on in one form or another for almost a decade, morphing into the larger War of the Austrian Succession along the way. In the end, Britain proved incapable of preserving its hold on the *asiento*, which was sold to Spain for £100,000. Neither Pope nor Walpole survived to see this dubious outcome.

During the course of the year Pope produced a new version of his collected letters, promptly matched by a further volume of Curll's alternative series – again largely bereft of materials from the poet's own hand. In addition he published two more imitations of Horace, both epistles from the second book, both of the highest quality, and both exhibiting a significant level of political commentary. The earlier of the two, an imitation of the second epistle of the second book, appeared under the imprint of Robert Dodsley, one of Pope's major publishers from this time onwards. Dodsley was a former footman who had attracted notice by a poem called *Servitude*, and then set up as a bookseller. He became one of the most important figures in the trade in later years. As one of his first productions he issued a poem by the young Samuel Johnson, *London* (1738), a work quickly claimed by the opposition, and a decade later he acted as the main initiator of Johnson's great *Dictionary*, which finally appeared in 1755. Pope addressed his epistle to an unspecified 'colonel', who has usually been identified with a Surrey landowner named Anthony Browne. Another candidate is James Dormer, colonel of the foot and later general, who owned the splendid estate of Rousham, north of Oxford: Pope stayed at the house several times and may have helped William Kent to remodel the gardens.

In his imitation he sticks remarkably close to the original, choosing to bend its text only in small ways with pointed topical allusions. Two of the most striking passages come directly from Horace, with a personalized touch created by minimal changes. One excerpt, which concerns Pope's upbringing as a member of a persecuted minority, the Catholic community under William III, has already been quoted in Chapter 1 (see p. 20). The second is a close translation of Horace's reflections on the impermanence of ownership:

> The Laws of God, as well as of the Land,
> Abhor, a *Perpetuity* should stand:
> Estates have wings, and hang in Fortune's pow'r
> Loose on the point of ev'ry wav'ring Hour;
> Ready, by force, or of your own accord,
> By sale, at least by death, to change their Lord.
> *Man?* And for *ever?* Wretch! what wou'dst thou have?
> Heir urges Heir, like Wave impelling Wave:
> All vast Possessions (just the same the case
> Whether you call them Villa, Park, or Chace)
> Alas, my BATHURST! what will they avail?
> Join *Cotswold* Hills to *Saperton's* fair Dale,
> Let rising Granaries and Temples here,
> There mingled Farms and Pyramids appear,
> Link Towns to Towns with Avenues of Oak,
> Enclose whole Downs in Walls, 'tis all a joke!
> Inexorable Death shall level all,
> And Trees, and Stones, and Farms, and Farmer fall!
>
> (*TE*, vol. 4, p. 183)

This brilliant sequence refers to a plan Lord Bathurst had devised to join Cirencester House with another part of his estate by building a canal that would link the Thames and the Severn – a far from delusionary project, since it was actually accomplished only fourteen years after the death of the elderly peer.[11] Pope referred to this dream in a letter of 1722 to Robert Digby:

> The Palace that is to be built, the Pavillions that are to glitter, the Colonnades that are to adorn them: Nay more, the meeting of the Thames and the Severn, which (when the noble Owner has finer Dreams than ordinary) are to be led into each other's Embraces thro' secret Caverns of not above twelve or fifteen Miles, till they rise and openly celebrate their Marriage in the midst of an immense Amphitheatre, which is to be the Admiration of Posterity a hundred Years hence.
>
> (*Corr.*, vol. 2, p. 116)

It is not just the vulgar 'improvements' of new men like Timon which will revert to wilderness. Even Bathurst's noble designs will decay into ruin. We may recall what Robert Macfarlane has lately written, in his outstanding book on *The Wild Places*:

> The wild prefaced us, and it will outlive us. Human culture will pass, given time, of which there is a sufficiency. The ivy will snake back and unrig our flats and terraces, as

it scattered the Roman villas. The sand will drift into our business parks, as it drifted into the brochs of the Iron Age. Our roads will lapse into the land.[12]

As often, Pope anticipates the insights of modern ecology. In a very real sense, he was a green poet from his earliest years.

On 25 May came the second of the Horatian poems that year, devoted to the first item in the second set of epistles. It has acquired popularity as the *Epistle to Augustus*, since it is modelled on the famous survey of literature and patronage which Horace dedicated to the Emperor Augustus. The most risky manoeuvre on Pope's part was to replace the Roman emperor, with his immense standing and genuine interest in patronage, with the patently inadequate George Augustus – to cite the King's full name. It made for a steep contrast. Horace had been invited by the Emperor to accord him some favourable mention in his work, and at one point Augustus had suggested that the poet should make the official imperial residence his own.[13] Such an invitation from the King would not be coming Pope's way, even though Caroline had once made initial overtures to win him over to the side of the court. In an 'advertisement', or prefatory note, the author put in a double-edged justification for the tone he had taken: 'We may farther learn from this Epistle, that *Horace* made his Court to this Great Prince, by writing with a decent Freedom towards him, with a just Contempt of his low Flatterers, and with a manly Regard to his own Character' (*TE*, vol. 4, p. 192). Such a notion licences Pope to indulge in the heaviest irony, for example in a passage near the end where he laments his inability to find the right style of panegyric to laud the King and his government:

> Oh! could I mount on the Mæonian wing,
> Your Arms, your Actions, your Repose to sing!
> What seas you travers'd! and what fields you fought!
> Your Country's Peace, how oft, how dearly bought!
> How barb'rous rage subsided at your word,
> And Nations wonder'd while they dropp'd the sword!
> How, when you nodded, o'er the land and deep,
> Peace stole her wing, and wrapt the world in sleep;
> Till Earth's extremes your mediation own,
> And Asia's Tyrants tremble at your Throne –
> But Verse alas! your Majesty disdains;
> And I'm not us'd to Panegyric strains.

(*TE*, vol. 4, p. 229)

Readers would have had no difficulty at the time in decoding what this passage really says. It deplores the peace policy that Walpole had maintained over the years, pours scorn on the King's lack of influence in international affairs, casts doubt on the government's diplomatic measures (some implemented by Walpole's brother Horatio) and portrays the nation as sunk in lethargy as its institutions wither under the Prime Minister's relentless grip. We naturally think of the ending of *The Dunciad*, particularly in its expanded four-book version.

In the middle of the *Epistle* Pope inserted an eloquent tribute to Swift as the guardian of freedom in Ireland, and the enlightened benefactor of a proposed mental hospital in Dublin:

> Let Ireland tell, how Wit upheld her cause,
> Her Trade supported, and supply'd her Laws;
> And leave on SWIFT this grateful verse ingrav'd,
> The Rights a Court attack'd, a Poet sav'd.
> Behold the hand that wrought a Nation's cure,
> Stretch'd to relieve the Idiot and the Poor,
> Proud Vice to brand, or injur'd Worth adorn,
> And stretch the Ray to Ages yet unborn.
>
> (*TE*, vol. 5, p. 213)

The first reference points unmistakably to the episode of Wood's cheap coinage, countered by Swift in his persona as 'the Drapier'. Alarmed by this allusion to a touchy subject, the Privy Council went so far as to consider issuing a warrant for the arrest of the author.[14] Luckily it was possible to use a technical sleight to avoid this, so that Pope got away with his contumacious verses, although some hint of official disapproval may well have reached his ears. Swift felt flattered by the lines, and admired the poem as a whole when he received a copy shortly after publication. He told Pope,

> The curious are looking out, some for flattery, some for ironies in it; the sour folks think they have found out some: But your admirers here, I mean every man of taste, affect to be certain, that the Profession of friendship to Me in the same poem, will not suffer you to be thought a Flatterer. My happiness is that you are too far engaged, and in spight of you the ages to come will celebrate me, and know you were a friend who loved and esteemed me, although I dyed the object of Court and Party-hatred.
>
> (*Corr.*, vol. 4, p. 72)

During the summer Pope embarked on his usual course of 'rambles', stopping off to see Lord Peterborough's widow Anastasia at Bevis Mount, as well as Bathurst at Cirencester and Ralph Allen at Prior Park. His round of visits still coincided with a core of old friends who represented traditional values, and did not in every case associate themselves with the Patriot ideology. He had found a new ally in the Earl of Orrery, a member of a distinguished Irish family numbering the physicist Robert Boyle among his ancestors. Conveniently Lord Orrery, whose father had been implicated in the Atterbury plot, had homes in Dublin, London and Somerset. He served as an intermediary between Pope and the elderly Swift, who grew more recalcitrant as his health steadily declined. His symptoms, including deafness and giddiness, have prompted a posthumous diagnosis of

Ménière's disease, but he had also started to show signs of dementia. The Earl had undertaken a collection of Swift's manuscripts, preparing the way for what would eventually become the first proper biography, *Reflections on the Life and Writings of Dr. Jonathan Swift*, published in 1751. Elaborate negotiations went on until Orrery managed to get hold of Swift's letters, as Pope had long desired. By this time the long-awaited authorized edition of the letters had appeared, and Pope sent copies to Orrery and Swift amongst others. Even Curll's fifth volume, which followed within days, could not damp his enthusiasm.

4

The two final imitations of Horace came out in the early months of 1738. Neither contains much by way of direct political commentary: instead, they dilate on large social and philosophic themes. *The Sixth Satire of the First Book of Horace* was addressed to a young Scottish lawyer named William Murray, whom Pope had met not long before. Subsequently he became better known as Lord Mansfield, Lord Chief Justice in the second half of the century, when he delivered many groundbreaking verdicts on slavery, copyright and libel. At this date Murray had still not entered parliament, although he was in the process of forging links with Cobham's Cubs. This time the satire concentrates on standard topoi of satire, like the temptations of wealth, gluttony and lust – where Pope goes in for more explicit detail than Horace. At various points in the poem he lauds Murray as a budding Cicero, recalls his old friend James Craggs, belabours the hapless Colonel Charteris (no longer an immediate threat, since he had been dead for six years), and singles out for special mention Lord Cornbury, a rising star among the Boy Patriots. One short snippet near the end anticipates Pope's famous depiction of the effects of the Grand Tour on a young nobleman, which would form part of the expanded *Dunciad* in 1742. Are we, the poet asks, to act like the fashionable rakes:

> From Latian Syrens, French Circæn Feasts,
> Return well travell'd, and transform'd to Beasts,
> Or for a Titled Punk, or Foreign Flame.
> Renounce our Country and degrade our Name?

(*TE*, vol. 4, p. 245)

Soon afterwards Dodsley issued the last of the main series, *The First Epistle of the First Book of Horace Imitated*, addressed to Bolingbroke. Horace had addressed the original work, introducing the first set of his epistles, to his patron Maecenas. Pope omitted three lines from the middle of the Latin text in presenting his longer version. One striking passage in the English poem occurs in the concluding section, where Pope personalizes the Roman poet's depiction of the incongruities and inconsistencies of his character. The role of Maecenas is allotted to Bolingbroke, and indeed the poem neatly recalls a phrase Pope had used of his friend in *An Essay on Man*: 'Is this my Guide, Philosopher, and Friend?' (*TE*, vol. 4, p. 293). Although the imitation stays close to the host poem most of the way, it brings in a few allusions to contemporaries such as the composer of ponderous epics, Sir Richard Blackmore, and more tellingly Alderman John Barnard, the current Lord Mayor of London. Barnard led the opposition of the City to Walpole during the Excise crisis and afterwards. He is contrasted with a noisome courtier, the Duke of Kent, generally known as 'Bug':

> BARNARD in spirit, sense, and truth abounds.
> 'Pray then what wants he?' fourscore thousand pounds,
> A Pension, or such Harness for a slave
> As Bug now has, and Dorimant would have.
> BARNARD, thou art a *Cit*, with all thy worth;
> But wretched Bug, his *Honour*, and so forth.
>
> (*TE*, vol. 4, p. 285)

This highly elliptical style typifies the manner of Pope's late verse. A reference to the 'Screen' and 'Wall of Brass' clearly points to Walpole: 'His long record of screening peculators and embezzlers from parliamentary enquiries had early won him the title of "Screen" or "Skreenmaster general." His broad florid countenance, said to be incapable of a blush, invited allusions to brass and brazen.'[15] But this had become a stock mode of expression, found every day of the week in the public prints. All in all, the *Epistle* may be described as loosely oppositional in its outlook, but for the most part lacking in specifics.

The Horatian sequence ended with a bang, when Pope brought out an *Epilogue to the Satires* in two parts, each of which was separately published in the summer of 1738. The first appeared on 16 May, just before the poet's fiftieth birthday, while the second followed on 18 July. Although these items carry the imprint of Cooper and Dodsley respectively, Pope himself entered the titles in the register of the Stationers' Company, as a means of holding on to the copyright. Both are couched in the form of a dialogue between the author and an unnamed interlocutor. In the opening dialogue, the writer's friend complains that the earlier works in the series have been too bold and rough, in contrast to Pope's model Horace, with his 'sly, polite, insinuating stile' (*TE*, vol. 4, p. 298). The poet defends his practice and points to the urgent need for a public scourge of contemporary morals. This part reaches a climax in a coruscating attack on 'Vice', which as we have seen serves as a code word in opposition polemics for the government machine. The exchange continues in the second dialogue, with the satirist reviewing his career and setting out the moral basis for his writing: 'Ask you what Provocation I have had? / The strong Antipathy of Good to Bad' (*TE*, vol. 4, p. 324). Both poems, the first especially, have generally been regarded as outstanding examples of Pope's mature art. We know that he worked over the manuscripts with great care and revised almost every line. On 8 August 1738 Swift told his old friend that he thought the second dialogue 'equal to almost any thing you ever writ', while the writer Aaron Hill, who had often tangled with Pope, praised the way in which it united 'the acrimony of *Juvenal*' with the '*Horatian* air of ease and serenity' (*Corr.*, vol. 4, pp. 112, 115).

Nowhere does Pope identify himself more closely with the opposition than in these dialogues. The second in particular 'reads like a roll-call of Patriot worthies', including a tribute to the Prince of Wales.[16] It is true that that the poem finds room for a civil reference to Walpole personally, a fact to which Pope drew Fortescue's attention on 31 July (*Corr.*, vol. 4, p. 114). But for all the grace of these compliments, what comes across most strongly is the power and passion of Pope's vituperations. As for example:

> Let Courtly Wits to Wits afford supply,
> As Hog to Hog in Huts of *Westphaly*;
> If one, thro' Nature's Bounty or his Lord's,
> Has what the frugal, dirty soil affords,
> From him the next receives it, thick or thin,
> As pure a Mess almost as it came in,
> The blessed Benefit, not there confin'd,
> Drops to the third who nuzzles close behind;
> From tail to mouth, they feed, and they carouse;
> The last, full fairly gives it to the *House*.
> *Fr.* This filthy Simile, this beastly Line,
> Quite turns my Stomach – *P.* So does Flatt'ry mine;
> And all your Courtly Civet-Cats can vent,
> Perfume to you, to me is Excrement.

(*TE.* 4, pp. 324–5)

That Pope had it in him to match Swift's 'excremental vision', we could deduce from *The Dunciad*.[17] But this is almost the only occasion that he enlists coprophilia as part of an onslaught on the court, with Lord Hervey a prime target.

In the first dialogue, he reverts to the allies of the ministry, not so much City merchants as the brokers, money-men and crooked operators who moved between Westminster and the business world. Not for the first time he singles out individuals such as John Ward, Japhet Crook, Denis Bond and Peter Walter as the most egregious villains:

> Shall *Ward* draw Contracts with a Statesman's skill?
> Or *Japhet* pocket, like his Grace, a Will?
> Is it for *Bond* or *Peter* (paltry Things!)
> To pay their Debts or keep their Faith like Kings?

(*TE*, vol. 4, pp. 306–7)

In this gallery of crooks the land-agent, money-lender, marriage broker and tricky lawyer Peter Walter stands out as the best-known figure. One reason is that he owned an estate as lord of the manor of Stalbridge, very close to Henry Fielding's family home in Dorset, where he sat as MP for a borough, Bridport, that rarely saw an election conducted with clean hands. Pope gave his brutal mixture of fraud and extortion a roasting in the *Epistle to Bathurst*, while Fielding's *Joseph Andrews* immortalized him in the character of the grasping attorney Peter Pounce. Even Swift, who probably did not know Walter, bestowed a few choice words on this notorious rogue.

However, Denis Bond provides almost as interesting a case. He too represented compliant boroughs in Dorset before he got himself expelled from parliament. This came about as a result of his involvement in a notorious racket, the Charitable Corporation, but the immediate occasion for Pope's hatred lies in another fraudulent act, missed by previous students of the poet. In March 1732 Lord Gage, a Protestant convert known to Pope, initiated an enquiry into the activities of Bond and a lawyer named Birch in their capacity of commissioners for the forfeited estates of Jacobites caught up in the rising of 1715–16. We saw in Chapter 4 that the family of the Earl of Derwentwater had endured particularly harsh reprisals, as Pope well knew because of the contacts both Martha Blount and he shared with the Radcliffes. The *Parliamentary History* reports the facts brought before the Commons in 1732:

> Lord Gage had, before he was made a nobleman, been a Roman Catholic, which threw him into some connections with those families. Certain commissioners were appointed to sell the English estates forfeited by the rebellion of the year 1715, and among others the forfeited reversion of one that had belonged to the Derwentwater family, which actually brought in near 8,000*l*. a year, and was improveable to 9,000*l*. The commissioners employed in the sale of this reversion were sir John Eyles, sir Thomas Hales, Serjeant Birch, and **Dennis Bond**, esq. Birch and Bond were men of business, knowing in the ways of life, and therefore in person attended all the transactions of the commissioners ...

Now we come to the sneaky part of the operation:

> By a particular management, this sale was held in so clandestine a manner, though publicly advertised, that none appeared to bid but one Mr. Smith, who bought the reversion at the easy rate of 1,000*l*. At the time of this sale, the eldest son of the late earl of Derwentwater, who was but a stripling, was in a languishing state of health; and he actually dying soon after, the estate came to Smith and his associates, who had been concerned in the management of the sale: because Charles Ratcliffe, brother to the earl of **Derwentwater**, and next heir, was forfeited, and therefore could not enjoy. This event, however, opened both the eyes and mouths of the world; and by the indefatigable pains which lord Gage took, the whole mystery of iniquity was traced through all its labyrinths. Birch and Bond, who were members, were expelled the House.[18]

In the *Epistle to Bathurst* we have the line, 'Bond damns the Poor, and hates them from his heart', a saying that really was attributed to the MP during investigations of one scandal (*TE*, vol. 3.ii, pp. 98–9). In the light of what we know of the Derwentwater estates, it is not surprising that Pope wrote of Bond with such venom.

The epistle that Pope addressed to Bolingbroke marked the exile's temporary return to England in July 1738, in order to dispose of his now unwanted home at Dawley. He stayed with Pope at Twickenham for nine months, until he completed the sale and went back once more to France in the following April. During this period Pope's involvement with the Patriot group reached its most intimate point. He maintained his closest contacts with Lyttelton, who served as a conduit to the Prince of Wales. In early 1739 Frederick sent a message through Lyttelton, offering to donate urns to Pope's garden. Soon after he presented the poet with marble busts of Spenser, Shakespeare, Milton and Dryden, ultimately bequeathed to Lyttelton.[19] At this stage Pope still kept up some degree of involvement with leaders of the opposition, as emerges from a letter to Swift in the middle of May:

> You ask me how I am at Court? I keep my old Walk, and deviate from it to no Court. The Pr[ince]. shews me a distinction beyond any Merit or Pretence on my part, and I have receiv'd a Present from him, of some Marble Heads of Poets, for my library, and some Urnes for my Garden. The Ministerial Writers rail at me, yet I have no quarrel with their Masters, nor think it of weight enough to complain of them. I am very well with all the Courtiers, I ever was, or would be acquainted with; at least they are Civil to me, which is all I ask from Courtiers, and all a wise man will expect from them. The Duchess of Marlborow makes great Court to me, but I am too Old for her, Mind and body. Yet I cultivate some Young people's friendship, because they may be honest men, whereas the Old ones, Experience too often proves not to be so. I have droppd ten, where I have taken up one, and hope to play the better with fewer in my hand: There is a Lord Cornbury, a Lord Polwarth, a Mr Murray, and one or two more, with whom I would never fear to hold out against all the Corruption of the world.
>
> (*Corr.*, vol. 4, p. 178)

Here he refers to increasingly good relations with the elderly Duchess of Marlborough, actuated in part by a consuming hatred that the indestructible Duchess felt for Walpole. More significance attaches to an early mention of Lord Polwarth, later the Earl of Marchmont, who became one of Pope's favourites among the political class in his last years.

Soon after Bolingbroke went back to France, the ties began to weaken, and Pope's brief flirtation with the Patriot opposition soon drifted away. While he kept up good relations with Lyttleton, they gradually turned into something less warm and intimate. He looked to old friends such as Bathurst, Bethel and Allen for comfort and support, while continuing to help Martha Blount and the Rackett family. More and more and he retreated into his new obsession, that of improving the grotto. Once he had brought the Horatian series to a conclusion, he published nothing more of an explicitly political nature. The only attempt he made was a draft called *One Thousand Seven Hundred and Forty*, written in 1740 but left as an unfinished manuscript until it reached print more than half a century later. This draft contains a number of blanks, suggesting some measure of indecision on the part of the author. He writes in his late manner, which embodies a challenging style of outright brutality:

> Can the light packhorse, or the heavy steer,
> The sowzing Prelate, or the sweating Peer,
> Drag out with all its dirt and all its weight,
> The lumbr'ring carriage of thy broken State?

(*TE*, vol. 5, p. 336)

The following lines celebrate Marchmont and commemorate the Tory leader Wyndham, who died in June 1740. Not enough remained of the old spark for Pope to carry through this promising work. Nor, as we shall see, did he get very far with a projected epic on Brutus that would have put some of the Patriot shibboleths into an epic form.

Two questions arise. First, what attracted Pope to the Patriot cause in the first place? Second, why did his enthusiasm ebb away so quickly? Both questions demand a mixed answer, since a range of political, cultural and personal factors underlay the choices Pope made in the later 1730s. As to his recruitment to the Patriot group, he obviously enjoyed the society of its leading members, and shared with the nominal head of the faction, Lord Cobham, a deep interest in all aspects of landscape design, as this gained expression in so spectacular a form at Stowe. He could reasonably believe that the key ideas of the opposition at this stage derived from his 'guide, philosopher and friend', Bolingbroke. For a time, he may well have thought that the Prince of Wales would live up to the exalted standards demanded of the patriot king. He may have thought that it was worth signing up to almost anything to get rid of Walpole: the brief rapprochement in the early 1730s had faded away and the two 'mighty opposites' were openly at war once more.[20] By now the Jacobite cause had fallen into a period of quiescence, at least among its English followers, and would not revive until the desperate final throw by Bonnie Prince Charlie in 1745, a year after Pope died. Former adherents of the Stuarts like Bolingbroke, Bathurst, Wyndham and Orrery had given up on the Old Pretender, who lived out the last thirty years of his life in gloomy seclusion at Rome, despairing over his son's military defeat and subsequent defection from the Catholic Church. Finally, on a personal level, Pope needed to find what substitutes he could for those he had lost: Atterbury, Gay, Arbuthnot, Peterborough, Caryll and others. The old guard had gone: symbolically Lord Oxford, drowning in debt and perhaps in drink, eventually had to sell his seat at Wimpole, and to get rid of the fine collections of books and manuscripts assembled by his father, the first Earl. If nothing else, Cobham's Cubs offered youth and optimism.

All along, though, there were difficulties. We could sense as much from the iconography at Stowe. As Christine Gerrard has written, 'There is something incongruous about finding a Catholic poet's bust enshrined in Stowe's Whiggish Temple of British Worthies alongside Milton, Hampden, Locke, Algernon Sidney, William III (Pope's unfavourite king), and an Elizabeth, who had "restored Religion from the Corruptions of Popery"'.[21] In truth Pope could never have bought into large parts of the Patriot ideology, except ideas loosely drawn from Bolingbroke. Admittedly, their republicanism was academic and shallow enough to allow them to rally round the Prince as the embodiment of the once and future king that their ideology craved. True, also, that their cult of Queen Elizabeth took a strongly literary turn – it found expression in a revival of the Spenserian stanza, rather than in a recrudescence of the militant Protestantism that had dragged heretics like Thomas Campion to the scaffold. What may have saved the day is the fact that their embellishments of a Gothic constitution, and their idealization of the Saxon kings, stood at a remove from recent politics: anyone from any party could buy into this woolly alternative history. In the end, though, Pope must have seen how thin a core of humanism underlay Patriot thinking. It became obvious that he had comparatively little in common with the group, apart from shared aesthetic tastes and a dislike for Walpole's brand of government. Moreover, he did not enjoy close relations with most of the writers who produced material on behalf of the opposition, apart from an on/off friendship with Aaron Hill. His own vein was satire, and he had little desire to work in the high-sounding style of James Thomson's *Liberty* (1735–6), a repository of the clichés of orthodox Whig panegyric verse.

In any case, the opposition remained frequently divided and tactically naive. In January 1739 the government negotiated the convention of Pardo, which attempted to settle the differences between Britain and Spain over trading rights, especially the alleged depredations on shipping. The King's speech at the opening of parliament set out the advantages of this agreement, but opposition peers thought they had a chance of defeating the government on the issue. Considerable outrage had been fomented in the community of merchants within the City, with Sir John Barnard taking a leading part. When the matter came before the Lords in February, it fell to Lord Hervey to defend the measure against the attacks of Carteret and Argyll among others. For the first time the Prince of Wales exercised his right to attend proceedings at the chamber and cast his vote against the ministry. Despite all their efforts, the opposition fell short when the House divided, losing the vote by 71 to 58. The government also managed to maintain a slender majority in the Commons. Later that year it grew clear that no progress had been made on a wide-ranging new treaty with Spain, and hostilities became an inevitability. When Walpole reluctantly conceded the point and war was declared, the opposition gained very little, as the government in effect put into practice exactly what they had been demanding. By 1740 the faction led by William Pulteney had decisively split with other Whigs such as those who belonged to Cobham's connection, while the death of Wyndham ended an effort to make common cause with the rump of Tories at Westminster. Somehow Walpole had escaped again, and the Patriots were reduced to a marginalized presence in parliament, unable to make enough alliances to damage the ministry.

Pope kept up social contacts with Cobham, Lyttelton, Marchmont and others in the opposition. However, he would never again be regarded as a spokesman for the Patriot cause. Instead, he went back to his roots, and devoted himself to private life, as well as managing the publication of his earlier works, carrying out endless improvements to the house and garden at Twickenham – above all, to the grotto which had become a kind of monomania. In November 1739 he lost another old friend in Charles Jervas, who left him £1,000, should he survive the painter's widow. This bequest seems to have embarrassed Pope, and if he could have known that he would be the first of the pair to die it would have caused him no regret. His mood was generally good, with happy days spent in the company of Bathurst, Burlington, Bethel and Allen. Only the state of his health cast a shadow over his life: by now the effects of his spinal curvature had steadily reduced the lung cavity, giving rise to difficulties with breathing diagnosed at the time as asthma. So matters stood when the turbulent 1730s drew to a close.

EPILOGUE: AFTER WALPOLE

> A few good deeds done me, a few valuable friendships allowed me ... are what I pray for and am content with; and I do not exaggerate the matter at all, when I say I prefer some ten or twelve months of my whole life spent at Cirencester, Dawley, and so forth, to a long and glorious reign of an hundred years upon Parnassus after my death.
>
> Pope to Bathurst, 8 October 1737[1]

Early in 1742, events finally caught up with Robert Walpole. A year before he had survived an attempt to unseat him, led by a doughty Whig and henchman of Pulteney named Samuel Sandys. But this time he could hold on no longer. The vice in which he had gripped the House of Commons for more than two decades slipped from his hands. Gradually his majority had shrunk to nothing, and when it fell on 2 February to a minority of sixteen, he promptly tendered his resignation to the reluctant King. The Tories played a part in his downfall, almost the first time they had affected the course of major events since they suffered eclipse in 1715.

For an instant, the political world stood still. A generation was growing up who could barely remember a world with anyone else at the head of the government. The Prime Minister had enormous staying power, built around some remarkable qualities – shrewdness, self-confidence, patience, a mixture of compliance in some areas with brutal determination in others. People found him a loyal friend but an implacable enemy. While he did not exactly possess a sophisticated grasp of what we would call economic theory, he had an unrivalled knowledge of public finances. He had a thick skin, and never courted popularity, as long as he was able to rustle up enough votes in parliament. Walpole is no longer a household name, even among those with an interest in politics. The fact that he held office longer than any subsequent British premier comes up occasionally among trivia questions in a pub quiz, but few people realize the scale of his achievement in putting the nation back on an even keel after it had floundered in the waves of the South Sea Bubble. He helped to promote not just the growth of political stability, but also the maintenance of a civil society in which religious toleration expanded, economic activity burgeoned, and the world of commerce and manufacturing began to play a larger part in national affairs. Many of the dreams that the revolutionaries of 1688 harboured, under the inspiration of John Locke, had to wait for the reign of Walpole before they could be implemented.

Meanwhile Pulteney and Carteret joined a reformed administration, which kept in place some old loyalists such as the Pelham brothers and Lord Hardwicke. Even Samuel Sandys gained a reward with a place as Chancellor of the Exchequer. If it was not exactly what most of the opposition had been seeking, at least they could bask in the knowledge that their oldest enemy had gone. With him went a large part of their *raison d'être*, and efforts to mount an impeachment did not come to much – people maybe recalled the failure of the Whig vendetta against the Earl of Oxford, a quarter of a century ago. In fact George II awarded the fallen minister a peerage, with the confusingly similar title of Earl of Orford. He was also offered a pension of £4,000 a year, but did not immediately claim this in case it stirred up further resentments. Possibly the strangest appointment concerned Lord Wilmington, formerly Spencer Compton, now an avowed member of the opposition. Despite the comprehensive proofs he gave of inadequacy for the role in 1727, he was made First Lord of the Treasury, a genuine triumph of hope over experience. Just over a year later, the King ditched him for the last time. Henry Pelham took over the leadership, and before long Carteret too was ousted. In 1746 Pulteney attempted to form a ministry, but it lasted barely forty-eight hours. Walpole himself had died one year earlier, but his 'Old Corps' of followers clung on to power for another decade. The total upheaval that had been so long expected would somehow never quite occur.

What of Pope? At the time of Walpole's resignation he had rather more than two years to live. Within a few weeks he produced a supplementary fourth book to his great mock-epic, known as *The New Dunciad*. Eighteenth months later came a fully revised version of *The Dunciad in Four Books*, the poet's last major contribution to literature. He wrote nothing else of substance after 1740.

The fourth book differs from its predecessors in several ways. It largely eschews the sustained narrative which had supported Books I–III. Its setting no longer uses the specifics of London, as what action there is seems to take place mainly in a sort of throne-room where a mixed collection of aspirants to fame have assembled at the call of Queen Dulness. The targets are much broader than earlier in the poem, with less emphasis on strictly literary matters; now opera singers, antiquarians, virtuosi, collectors, scientists, grammarians, theologians and other groups figure as prominently as the denizens of Grub Street. The cast list has shifted upmarket, and the participants belong in the salons of Westminster and the combination-rooms of Oxford rather than in the environs of the Fleet Ditch. There are also some tributes to the great and good, whereas only Swift had been given his own direct commendation in the work as previously published. This time Pope included a section that singles out Wyndham, Murray and Pulteney; elsewhere he mentions Lord Chesterfield with approbation.

The author undertook extensive revisions to the first three books. He augmented the pedantic annotations of Martin Scriblerus with the contributions of another foolish commentator, easily identifiable as Dr Richard Bentley. The great classical scholar had put his reputation in jeopardy when he produced an improved version of *Paradise Lost* (1732), inserting a little matter of 800 conjectural emendations. Thus Milton's immortal phrase from the opening book, 'No light but rather darkness visible' was found to be illogical, requiring the editor to propose his favoured version of the line: 'No Light, but rather a TRANSPICUOUS GLOOM'. On top of this, Pope made changes to the fourth book, as it appeared in *The New Dunciad* of 1741, including the addition of a climactic passage describing the eclipse of light on earth by 'Universal Darkness'. (This was adapted from the former conclusion to Book III.) Fresh elements include a new 'Advertisement', signed 'W.W.' (Warburton) but doubtless written by Pope; a mock declaration 'By *Authority*'; another parody of Bentley's editorial manner, written by Warburton and titled 'Ricardus Aristarchus of the Hero of the Poem'; a reprint of the prefatory note from 1742; and an appendix on the office of the poet laureate, taken from a piece that appeared in the *Grub-Street Journal* in 1730. Other supplementary items are retained from *The Dunciad Variorum*.

However the most important change operates throughout *The Dunciad in Four Books*, and this involves the replacement of Theobald as King of the Dunces by Colley Cibber. Pope had personal reasons for bringing on Cibber as a substitute at this late stage of the game. The two men had engaged in skirmishes for twenty-five years, back to the time of *Three Hours after Marriage* and *The Non-Juror*. Here the contemptuous allusions to the poet laureate start early in the first book and appear right up to the end. Pope was able to enlist a large amount of detail drawn from Cibber's life as an actor, a playwright, a manager and a composer of inept laureate odes. One aim is to strike at the court through its appointed public bard. But the poem also brings in the statuary work of his enemy's father, the sculptor Caius Gabriel Cibber, who had created stone figures of mania and depression over the gates of Bedlam, near the spot where the dunces gather early in the poem. These allusions finally goaded Cibber into a serious act of retaliation, and he struck back with vigorous pamphlets, *A Letter from Mr. Cibber. To Mr. Pope* (1742), *A Second Letter from Mr. Cibber* (1743) and *Another Occasional Letter* from *Mr. Cibber to Mr. Pope* (1744), all making effective points against Pope.[2] Cibber may also have helped Lord Hervey in writing a further attack on Pope, *The Difference between Verbal and Practical Virtue* in 1742.

Unquestionably the installation of Cibber in this key role sharpened the political point of *The Dunciad*. He held a royal patent as manager of Drury Lane; he was a loyal Whig who gave strong support to the Hanoverian regime, and got his reward. His vicious caricature of a Jesuit plotter in *The Non-Juror* helped to whip up popular feeling against the Catholic community after the Jacobite rising. A colourful figure in Augustan society, at the meeting-point of culture and commerce, he has only limited fame today; it was not just *The Dunciad* that helped to bring him down, but also Fielding's *Shamela*, which ruthlessly exposed the egocentric ramblings of the self-revelatory *Apology for the Life of Colley Cibber Comedian* (1740). Above all, the injudicious elevation of the actor-manager to the post of the nation's official poet – a decision for which Walpole's henchman the Duke of Newcastle was probably responsible – gave Pope an easy chance to relate bad writing to the taste of the court.

Not that either the King himself or Walpole got away unscathed. The assembly portrayed in Book IV recalls a levee held by a monarch or a minister. It suggests in places a gathering of loyal knights, such as the installation ceremony for the Order of the Bath or the Garter, to which Walpole (against custom, as a commoner and not a peer) had been admitted in 1726.

> Walpole, as usual, made the most of the occasion. His installation ceremony featured such expensive and elaborate pageantry that it was compared to a new coronation. The following year his feast at Windsor outmatched in extravagance that of any nobleman who had recently received the Order of the Garter.[3]

When writing Book IV, Pope may have had a preview of a poem by a Cobhamite, Gilbert West, *The Institution of the Order of the Garter*, which Dodsley published in February 1742, just over one month before *The New Dunciad*. This 'dramatic poem', set in Windsor Great Park in the age of Edward III, includes enough bards and druids to satisfy the most ardent Patriot antiquarian. Implicitly it casts the Prince of Wales as the patriot king who would revive both chivalry and virtue. When Pope echoed this ceremonial in *the Dunciad*, readers would have noted the contrast between St George, patron of the order, and George II, the man who should be preserving the nation's honour. It is worth adding that West contributed 'fine petrifactions' to the grotto at Twickenham, and Pope remembered him in his will.

The Institution of the Order of the Garter may have left some mark on a projected epic on the legendary figure of Brutus, since in his outline scheme Pope allots a major role to druid priests who welcome the hero on his arrival in ancient Britain. This of course refers not to Marcus Brutus, but to a mythical descendant of Aeneas who had voyaged from Troy to establish 'the first foundations of the British monarchy'. Pope had also been reading the works of William Stukeley (1687–1765), clergyman, physician, antiquarian and archaeologist. Some firsthand contact may have arisen, not documented, since both men belonged to the Gentleman's Society at Spalding, a club of antiquarians, and both were freemasons, though Stukeley in a more active capacity. He had done pioneering work at sites such as Stonehenge and constructed an imaginative version of early British history in the light of his findings. Pope may well have incorporated certain aspects of Stukeley's vision. Unfortunately the sketch of the planned epic is too brief to show everything that the poet had in mind. Beyond doubt the work would have aimed to show how Brutus prevails, 'having reduced the fortresses of superstition, anarchy and tyranny', so that 'the whole island submits to good government'.[4] How far this constituted a restatement of Bolingbroke's ideas on virtue and kingship remains a matter of doubt.

One final encounter with Curll lay in store. On 30 May 1741 the bookseller issued the last volume of his series of Pope's literary correspondence. It actually comprised *Dean Swift's Literary Correspondence for Twenty-Four Years*, and claimed to have been reprinted from the Dublin edition of Swift, a device for avoiding copyright restrictions through the unstable state of Anglo-Irish law on the point. In truth, Curll had simply reprinted a London edition. On 14 July, Pope wrote to Ralph Allen and gave him a summary account of what followed: 'That Rascal Curl has pyrated the Letters, which would have ruin'd half my Edition, but we have got an Injunction from my Lord Chancellor to prohibit his selling them for the future, tho doubtless he'l do it clandestinly' (*Corr.*, vol. 4, p. 350). Pope had indeed obtained an injunction forbidding Curll to sell the book; the case went before the court of Chancery, and on 17 June the Lord Chancellor issued a lastingly significant verdict. This laid it down that the physical letter sent by A to B remains B's property, but the copyright still belongs to the writer A. Essentially the ruling has prevailed in Anglo-American copyright law until the present day. Curll may have gone on marketing the volume. He had included in the volume one of the fillers that so often made up for the absence of relevant materials in his books. This was an item by John Arbuthnot, and when it appeared separately the doctor's son promptly sued Curll for infringing his rights as his father's heir. In both of these cases it was William Murray who acted on behalf of the plaintiff.

By this date Pope confined his literary activity almost entirely to preparing a collected version of the *Works*. His fragile health worsened still further: in 1740 he had been forced to undergo a painful operation, performed by his friend William Cheselden, to deal with a strangulation of the urethra. Realizing his days were now short, he set about consolidating his legacy. Together with the industrious Warburton, who had edged out the poet's other friends to become *de facto* literary executor, he began to assemble what is generally called the 'deathbed edition'.[5] Only a few poems had been made ready when, a few weeks before his death, he saw the earliest segment in proof. Drily he remarked to Joseph Spence, 'Here am I, like Socrates, distributing my morality among my friends, just as I am dying' (*Anecdotes*, vol. 1, p. 261). After he died, survivors in his circle felt alarmed about some of the new material in the *Moral Essays*, especially those lines on the fearsome Atossa which could be applied either to the Duchess of Buckingham, recently deceased but with influential friends, or the Duchess of Marlborough, who lived on to the following October. The volume was accordingly suppressed. In taking this step Bolingbroke seems to have been actuated by a growing distrust of Warburton, who had in some measure supplanted his own relationship with Pope.[6]

During 1743 and 1744 Bolingbroke returned to England for long periods, and in the poet's last days he spent a good deal of time with Pope. If he felt dismayed by the role into which Warburton had wormed himself, he was totally astonished by something that came out only after Pope died. This was the discovery that his friend had deceived him over *The Idea of a Patriot King*. In 1739 Bolingbroke had allowed Pope to print a few copies of the manuscript for private circulation. Unknown to its author, Pope had arranged for no less than 1,500 copies of the text to be printed, though not circulated, with a few revisions of his own. Enraged by this act of bad faith, Bolingbroke asked Lord Marchmont to retrieve any copies that could be located and burn them. In 1749 he produced an authorized edition of his own, and in his remaining years he engaged in bitter recriminations against the poet, to which Warburton replied with equal vehemence. It makes for an unedifying story, reflecting no great credit on any of the participants.

We do not know exactly what prompted Pope to prepare this secret version and then to leave it unpublished. Most scholars who have explored the issue believe that he intended to bring it out with great fanfare after the death of Bolingbroke, his senior by a decade – but by 1744 that was obviously not going to be the way things happened. Apart from this, the *Idea* seemed less germane to events in the new decade: after the Prince of Wales and Bolingbroke both died in 1751 it became a museum piece, only briefly brought back to attention when Frederick's son, later George III, came to adulthood. What had once seemed a powerful strike by the opposition against Walpole's way of doing things soon lost immediacy and point. At the end of the day Pope need not have striven quite so officiously to keep this harmless polemic from the eyes of the nation.

In his final months Pope suffered from a variety of ailments of growing severity, almost all complications of his underlying condition. The immediate cause of his death lay in a breakdown of the functions of his heart and lungs, proceeding from the kyphoscoliosis he had contracted long before. As the spinal curvature proceeds over time, it causes failure in both cardiovascular and respiratory systems.[7] His friends rallied round to give what comfort they could. Those he saw regularly included Ralph Allen, Bathurst, Hugh Bethel, Burlington, Marchmont and Orrery. Near the end he received visits from Anne Arbuthnot (the doctor's daughter), Bolingbroke, Martha Blount and Lyttelton. The last rites were administered on 29 May 1744 by a Benedictine monk, the son of Pope's valued legal advisor Nathaniel Pigott, and in the evening of the next day he died. He had survived a week after his fifty-sixth birthday. When the will was read, it emerged that he had left money to the Rackett family, as well as books and pictures to most of his friends, with gifts to his gardener John Serle and a bequest to impoverished residents of the parish. Much to the affront of Magdalen Rackett, the residuary legatee was Martha Blount.

The burial took place at Twickenham parish church on 5 June. It must have been a simple service, as the churchwardens' accounts record a charge of just one pound. Pope had asked for his body to be carried to the grave by six poor parishioners. Alexander's name, and nothing more, went on to the memorial that he had already set up for his parents in the north gallery. This was too plain by half for Warburton, and in 1761 he had a large monument in the shape of a pyramid erected there. With typical insensitivity, he added some lines that Pope had written years earlier, 'Epitaph, for one who would not be buried in Westminster Abbey'. Perhaps the bishop, as he now was, considered it unworthy of a major poet to lie anywhere else but in the great national mausoleum. If so, he badly misunderstood the nature of the poet. Although he gained an unrivalled position of literary eminence and great social standing, Pope had always been an outsider. His religion, his origins and his invalid condition had all ensured that much. His highest art offers a challenge to the powerful, the fashionable, the idly rich and the manipulators of taste, and derides all pretentious dullness. It makes perfect sense that he was laid to rest alongside his revered mother, in a humble church standing close to the villa that had become an emblem of his proud resistance.

NOTES

Introduction

1. *The Prose Works of Alexander Pope*, vol. 1, *The Earlier Works, 1711–1720*, ed. N. Ault (Oxford: Blackwell, 1936), p. 24.
2. The most complete assessment of this issue will be found scattered throughout M. Mack, *Alexander Pope: A Life* (New Haven, CT: Yale University Press, 1985). A good short outline is A. R. Humphreys, 'Pope, God, and Man', in P. Dixon (ed.), *Writers and their Background: Alexander Pope* (London: Bell, 1972), pp. 60–100.

1 Nature and Nurture

1. Mack, *Pope: A Life*, p. 20.
2. G. Sherburn, 'New Anecdotes of Alexander Pope', *Notes and Queries*, 5 (1958), pp. 343–9, on pp. 348–9.
3. For the best account of Edith and Pope's sister Magdalen, see V. Rumbold, *Women's Place in Pope's World* (Cambridge: Cambridge University Press, 1989), pp. 24–47.
4. D. Defoe, *A Tour thro' the Whole Island of Great Britain*, ed. J. McVeagh, in *Writings on Travel, Discovery and History by Daniel Defoe*, gen. ed. W. R. Owens and P. N. Furbank, 8 vols (London: Pickering & Chatto, 2001–2), vols 1–3, in vol. 3, p. 56.
5. Mack, *Pope: A Life*, p. 19.
6. G. Sherburn, *The Early Career of Alexander Pope* (Oxford: Clarendon Press, 1934), p. 29.
7. Mack, *Pope: A Life*, pp. 813–14.
8. Ibid., p. 3.
9. Ibid., p. 21.
10. Unless otherwise stated, details of Pope's early life are taken from Mack's account in ibid.
11. J. Stow, *A Survey of the Cities of London and Westminster*, 2 vols (London: A. Churchill et al., 1720), vol. 1, book II, p. 163.
12. For details of the burial, see Mack, *Pope: A Life*, p. 820.
13. For the high values of property in this area, see C. Spence, *London in the 1690s: A Social Atlas* (London: Centre for Metropolitan History, Institute of Historical Research, 2000), p. 51. For the cluster of shops in Lombard Street, see p. 125.

14. A. J. Henderson, *London and the National Government, 1721–1742: A Study of City Politics and the Walpole Administration* (Durham, NC: Duke University Press, 1945), pp. 80–2.
15. Defoe, *A Tour thro' the Whole Island of Great Britain*, vol. 2, p. 80.
16. Ibid., vol. 2, p. 80.
17. N. Rogers, *Crowds, Culture and Politics in Georgian England* (Oxford: Clarendon Press, 1998), p. 23.
18. Mack, *Pope: A Life*, pp. 36–7.
19. T. Boreman, *The Gigantick History of the Famous Giants in the Guildhall, London* (London: Tho. Boreman, 1741), quoted by C. Hole, *English Sports and Pastimes* (London: B. T. Batsford, 1949), pp. 129–30. See further P. Rogers, *Literature and Popular Culture in Eighteenth-Century England* (Brighton: Harvester, 1985), pp. 31–2.
20. O. Ruffhead, *The Life of Alexander Pope* (London: C. Bathurst et al., 1769), p. 419.
21. G. S. De Krey, *A Fractured Society: The Politics of London in the First Age of Party, 1688–1715* (Oxford: Clarendon Press, 1985), pp. 58–9.
22. The following material is drawn in part from a paragraph that I contributed to the essay by Brian Young, 'Pope and Ideology', in *The Cambridge Companion to Alexander Pope*, ed. P. Rogers (Cambridge: Cambridge University Press, 2007), pp. 118–33, on pp. 118–19.
23. T. E. May, *The Constitutional History of England*, 2nd edn, 2 vols (London: Longmans, 1863–5), vol. 2, p. 321.
24. Statutes are quoted from W. C. Costin and J. S. Watson (eds), *The Law and Working of the Constitution: Documents, 1660–1914*, 2nd edn, 2 vols (London: Black, 1961), vol. 1, pp. 61–2.
25. Sherburn, *The Early Career of Pope*, p. 36.
26. W. E. H. Lecky, *A History of England in the Eighteenth Century*, 8 vols (London: Longmans Green and Co., 1892), vol. 1, pp. 352–3. Lecky's account of the 'perpetual insecurity' of Catholics in this period remains of value.
27. For the few facts, see Mack, *Pope: A Life*, pp. 815–16.
28. Defoe, *A Tour thro' the Whole Island of Great Britain*, vol. 2, p. 136.
29. W. Thornbury and E. Walford, *Old and New London: A Narrative of its History, its People, and its Places*, new edn, 6 vols (London: Cassell Petter & Galpin, 1893), vol. 6, p. 530.
30. T. Faulkner, *The History and Antiquities of the Parish of Hammersmith* (London: Nichols & Son, 1839), p. 242.
31. Thornbury and Walford, *Old and New London*, vol. 6, p. 531.
32. On Dame Mary, see D. B. Wyndham Lewis, *A History of the Benedictine Nuns of Dunkirk* (London: Catholic Book Club, 1957), pp. 17–55.
33. Faulkner, *The History of Hammersmith*, p. 252.
34. Ibid., pp. 244–5.
35. He may later have joined the recusant family of William and Mary Holman, who lived near Banbury, and were connected to the Eyres.
36. Sherburn, *The Early Career of Pope*, p. 39.

2 The Flowers of the Forest

1. Rumbold, *Women's Place*, p. 27.
2. M. H. Nicolson and G. S. Rousseau, *'This Long Disease, My Life': Alexander Pope and the Sciences* (Princeton, NJ: Princeton University Press, 1968), pp. 8, 82.
3. Ibid., p. 20.
4. Mack, *Pope: A Life*, p. 67.
5. Rumbold, *Women's Place*, p. 5.
6. Ibid., p. 24.
7. O. Rackham, *The Last Forest: The Story of Hatfield Forest* (London: Dent, 1989), p. 38.
8. S. Schama, *Landscape and Memory* (London: HarperCollins, 1995), p. 147.
9. Ibid., p. 155.
10. For a convenient chart, see E. P. Thompson, *Whigs and Hunters: The Origins of the Black Act*, rev. edn (Harmondsworth: Penguin, 1977), p. 35.
11. Schama, *Landscape and Memory*, pp. 158–9.
12. Thompson, *Whigs and Hunters*, pp. 40–7.
13. *The Victoria History of the County of Berkshire*, ed. W. Page and P. H. Ditchfield, 5 vols (London: St Catherine Press, 1906–27), vol. 3, p. 118.
14. Thompson, *Whigs and Hunters*, p. 32.
15. *The Works of Alexander Pope*, ed. W. Elwin and W. J. Courthope, 10 vols (London: John Murray, 1871–89), vol. 1, p. ix.
16. G. Sherburn, 'Letters of Alexander Pope, Chiefly to Sir William Trumbull', *Review of English Studies*, 9 (1958), pp. 388–406, on p. 393; *Corr*, vol. 1, p. 32.
17. W. Blackstone, *Commentaries on the Laws of England*, 4 vols (Oxford: Clarendon Press, 1765–69), vol. 2, p. 201.
18. J. Bossy, *The English Catholic Community, 1570–1850* (New York: Oxford University Press, 1976), p. 102. To be precise, the Blounts lived on the north bank of the Thames.
19. See Rumbold, *Women's Place*, pp. 48–82.
20. Mack, *Pope: A Life*, p. 257.
21. E. Harlan, *Elijah Fenton, 1683–1730* (Philadelphia, PA, 1937), p. 177.
22. *The Works of Pope*, ed. Elwin and Courthope, vol. 1, p. ix.
23. Ibid., vol. 1, p. ix.
24. Ibid., vol. 1, p. x.
25. Ibid., vol. 1, p. ix.
26. *The Correspondence of Jonathan Swift*, ed. D. Woolley, 4 vols (Frankfurt: Peter Lang, 1999–2005), vol. 3, p. 593.
27. Sherburn, *The Early Career of Pope*, p. 46.
28. Sherburn, 'New Anecdotes of Pope', p. 347.
29. Congreve survived until 1729 and Granville until 1735, but both were peripheral figures before the time of their death.
30. *The Last and Greatest Art: Some Unpublished Poetical Manuscripts of Alexander Pope*, ed. M. Mack (Newark, DE: University of Delaware Press, 1984), pp. 19–23.

3 The Piping Time of Peace

1. J. Dennis, *Reflections Critical and Satyrical, upon a late Rhapsody, call'd, An Essay on Criticism* (London: Bernard Lintott, 1711), p. 29.
2. Ibid., p. 27.

3. J. Swift, *Journal to Stella*, ed. H. Williams, 2 vols (Oxford: Clarendon Press, 1948), vol. 2, p. 516.
4. J. Lees-Milne, *Earls of Creation: Five Great Patrons of Eighteenth-Century Art* (London: Hamish Hamilton, 1962), p. 31.
5. P. Ackroyd, *Thames: The Biography* (London: Chatto & Windus, 2007), p. 11.
6. Swift, *Journal to Stella*, vol. 2, pp. 507, 633–4
7. The founding document here is J. R. Moore, '*Windsor-Forest* and William III', *Modern Language Notes*, 66 (1951), pp. 451–4. For the suggestion about Louis XIV, see H. Weinbrot, *Britannia's Issue: The Rise of British Literature from Dryden to Ossian* (Cambridge: Cambridge University Press, 1993), pp. 283–96.
8. Thompson, *Whigs and Hunters*, p. 41.
9. *The Works of Michael Drayton*, ed. J. W. Hebel et al., 5 vols (Oxford: Basil Blackwell, 1961), vol. 5, p. 234.
10. Sherburn, *The Early Career of Pope*, p. 52.
11. M. Mack, *Collected in Himself: Essays Critical, Biographical, and Bibliographical on Pope and Some of His Contemporaries* (Newark, DE: University of Delaware Press, 1982), p. 464.
12. *Pope's Windsor Forest 1712*, ed. R. M. Schmitz (St Louis, MO: Washington University, 1952), p. 40.
13. Mack, *Collected in Himself*, p. 21.
14. Swift, *Journal to Stella*, vol. 2, p. 635.
15. J. V. Guerinot, *Pamphlet Attacks on Alexander Pope, 1711–1744: A Descriptive Bibliography* (London: Methuen, 1969), p. 247.
16. For Pope's attitude to the 'little Senate' at Button's, see M. Ellis, *The Coffee House: A Cultural History* (London: Weidenfeld & Nicolson, 2004), pp. 155–6.
17. Swift, *Journal to Stella*, vol. 1, p. 97.
18. *The Prose Works of Pope*, vol. 1, p. 62.
19. *The Prose Works of Jonathan Swift*, ed. H. Davis et al., 14 vols (Oxford: Basil Blackwell, 1939–74), vol. 8, p. 5.
20. *The History of Parliament: The House of Commons, 1690–1715*, ed. E. Cruickshanks, S. Handley and D. W. Hayton, 5 vols (Cambridge: Cambridge University Press, 2002), vol. 3, p. 1084.
21. Mack, *Collected in Himself*, p. 461.
22. Bossy, *The English Catholic Community*, p. 101.
23. *The Correspondence of Swift*, vol. 2, p. 70.

4 Civil and Religious Rage

1. *The Correspondence of Swift*, vol. 2, p. 47.
2. For these developments, see D. Foxon, *Pope and the Early Eighteenth-Century Book Trade*, ed. J. McLaverty (Oxford: Clarendon Press, 1991), especially pp. 51–101 on the 'business' of the Homer translations.
3. Sherburn, 'Letters of Pope', p. 398.
4. *The Prose Works of Pope*, vol. 1, p. 254.
5. Ibid., vol. 1, p. 197.
6. D. Szechi, 'The Jacobite Theatre of Death', in E. Cruickshanks and J. Black (eds), *The Jacobite Challenge* (Edinburgh: John Donald, 1988), pp. 57–74, on p. 57.

7. *Weekly Packet*, 18 August, 29 September 1716. News of James's escape came in Read's *Weekly Journal* on 15 December.
8. J. O. Payne, *Records of the English Catholics of 1715* (London: Burns & Oates, 1889), pp. 143–4. In 1722 young Sir John married Mary, the only daughter of Pope's good friend Edward Bedingfield.
9. L. Gooch, *The Desperate Faction?: The Jacobites of North-East England, 1688–1745* (Birtley, Durham: Casdec Ltd, 2001), p. 55. Other members of the extended family were captured and put on trial: John Thornton, a first cousin of Sir William and schoolfellow of Lord Derwentwater in Paris, was convicted of high treason in July 1716, but was reprieved and later released. His estate was forfeited, but he managed to buy it back secretly after a series of bogus transactions (ibid., pp. 103–4). The ancient line could point to long experience as rebels: around 1400 Sir William Swinburne fought in the Earl of Northumberland's retinue for Owain Glyndŵr.
10. *Weekly Remarks and Political Reflections*, 14 April 1716. In 1722 Mary Swinburne left a will, apparently not granted probate. It leaves only small bequests to family members including her brother John Englefield and her sisters, all nuns at Cambrai or Paris. She requests her son and heir Sir John Swinburne to be kind to his brothers as 'you are the only friend they have to depend on'. Edward Swinburne had made a will in August 1715, making William Gilpatrick his sole executor, but had added a codicil stating 'it's only meant by me for Security's Sake, and that I intend my Brother James Swinburne to be understood' (Northumberland Collections Service, ZSW/513/1, 514). Thanks to Joanne Paterson for help in obtaining a digital copy. These documents illustrate some of the plight of beleaguered families such as the Swinburnes.
11. Payne, *Records of the English Catholics*, p. 104.
12. W. S. Gibson, *Dilston Hall: or, Memoirs of the Right Hon. James Radcliffe, Earl of Derwentwater, a Martyr in the Rebellion of 1715* (London: Longman, Brown, Green & Longmans, 1850), p. 43.
13. R. Arnold, *Northern Lights: The Story of Lord Derwentwater* (London: Constable, 1959), pp. 176, 187. Much of my information on the Radcliffe family's financial situation is drawn from this book, a popular biography of outstanding quality.
14. Sir Henry's father had been imprisoned during the Popish Plot. The family was suffering economically and he left his son (father of Mary Agnes) a document which indicates that they now possessed only a quarter of their former revenue: quoted by Valerie Rumbold in *Women's Place*, p. 66. Sir Henry acted as a trustee for Caryll family settlements: see Parliamentary Archives, HL/PO/JO/10/1/470/877.
15. Rumbold, *Women's Place*, p. 73.
16. University of Reading, Museum of English Rural Life, MS 145/EN 1/3/44.
17. Sir John's second wife was Helen, daughter of Sir Richard Moore of Fawley – a family related to the Blounts of Mapledurham. Some of the Moores were well known to Teresa and Martha, and almost certainly Pope, in their youth (Rumbold, *Women's Place*, p. 55). The sister of Pope's friend in Binfield, John Dancastle, had also married into the family. When Sir John died in Aix-la-Chapelle in 1745, his wife set up a monument with an inscription praising him as a model for English Catholics and a comforter of the afflicted. He was apparently on the run as a royal warrant had been issued for his arrest (National Archives, SP 36/70/40).
18. In fact the Blount girls had a separate relationship with the Earl, less important at this juncture. As we have seen, their aunt Mary had married William Swinburne, whose

mother was a step-daughter of the first Earl of Derwentwater, James Radcliffe's grandfather.
19. Mack, *Collected in Himself*, pp. 467–9.
20. C. J. Rawson, 'Some Unpublished Letters of Pope and Gay', *Review of English Studies*, 10 (1959), pp. 371–87, on p. 377.
21. Thomas Burnet, quoted by P. Smithers, *The Life of Joseph Addison*, 2nd edn (Oxford: Clarendon Press, 1968), p. 361.

5 Toil, Trouble, South Sea Bubble

1. R. Hatton, *George I: Elector and King* (London: Thames and Hudson, 1978), pp. 170–210. Especially important for Pope is the section on the quarrel in the royal family, pp. 201–10.
2. See N. Ault, *New Light on Pope* (London: Methuen, 1949), p. 179.
3. *TE*, vol. 6, p. 184; Ault, *New Light on Pope*, pp. 176–81.
4. Mack, *Pope: A Life*, p. 340; *Corr.*, vol. 2, pp. 25–6.
5. Mack, *Pope: A Life*, p. 25.
6. C. Cibber, *A Letter from Mr. Cibber, to Mr. Pope* (London: W. Lewis, 1742), p. 13.
7. T. J. Goddard-Fenwick, *Stanton Harcourt: A Short History* (privately printed, 1967), p. 6.
8. On Pope's dealings with Rowe, Ault's chapter in *New Light on Pope*, pp. 128–55, remains a good starting-point.
9. On the physical surroundings, see A. Beckles Willson, *Mr Pope and Others at Cross Deep Twickenham in the 18th Century* (Twickenham, privately printed, 1996). On the political and cultural implications of Pope's settling at Twickenham, see the classic account of Maynard Mack in *The Garden and the City: Retirement and Politics in the Later Poetry of Pope, 1731–1743* (Toronto: University of Toronto Press, 1969), pp. 3–115.
10. See M. R. Brownell, *Alexander Pope's Villa* (London: Greater London Council, 1980), pp. 14, 40–1.
11. For the history of the Company and the lead-up to the crisis, see J. Carswell, *The South Sea Bubble*, 2nd edn (Stroud: Sutton, 2001).
12. *The Poetical Works of John Gay*, ed. G. C. Faber (London: Oxford University Press, 1926), p. 166.
13. *The Works of Pope*, ed. Elwin and Courthope, vol. 1, p. ix.
14. H. Erskine-Hill, *The Social Milieu of Alexander Pope: Lives, Example and the Poetic Response* (New Haven, CT: Yale University Press, 1975), pp. 83–4.

6 A Dull Duty and a Public Cause

1. *The Complete Letters of Lady Mary Wortley Montagu*, ed. R. Halsband, 3 vols (Oxford: Clarendon Press, 1965–7), vol. 2, p. 37.
2. For the original lines, see below. In 1735, after mending fences with William Broome, Pope substituted the more general form of words, retained in the long standard edition of Warburton in 1751.
3. Mack, *Pope: A Life*, p. 388.
4. *The Letters of John Gay*, ed. C. F. Burgess (Oxford: Clarendon Press, 1966), p. 43.
5. *The Prose Works of Alexander Pope, vol. 2, The Major Works, 1725–1744*, ed. R. Cowler (Hamden, CT: Archon, 1986), p. 197.

Notes to pages 127–64 239

6. S. Johnson, *Lives of the English Poets*, ed. G. B. Hill, 3 vols (Oxford: Clarendon Press, 1905), vol. 2, p. 262.
7. *The Works of Pope*, ed. Elwin and Courthope, vol. 1, p. x.
8. Mr Gerard, *An Epistle to the Egregious Mr. Pope* (London: for the author, 1734), p. 7, typography normalized. A note adds, 'In his Proposals he made Use of the Expression *Undertaken by A. Pope*, and by this poor Fallacy deceived his Subscribers' – again the phrasing suggests a Bubble-type fraud.
9. R. Trickett, *The Honest Muse* (Oxford: Clarendon Press, 1967), p. 195.
10. S. Johnson, *The Vanity of Human Wishes* (London: R. Dodsley, 1749), p. 25.
11. Erskine-Hill, *The Social Milieu of Pope*, p. 74.
12. Quoted by P. S. Fritz, *The English Ministers and Jacobitism between the Rebellions of 1715 and 1745* (Toronto: University of Toronto Press, 1975), pp. 147–55.
13. W. Wynne, *The Defence of Francis, late Lord Bishop of Rochester* (London: Jonah Bowyer, 1723), p. 41.
14. *Tory and Whig: The Parliamentary Papers of Edward Harley, third Earl of Oxford, and William Hay, M.P.*, ed. S. Taylor and C. Jones (Woodbridge: Boydell Press, 1998), p. 241.
15. Mack, *Collected in Himself*, p. 398.
16. *Journal of the House of Lords*, 22 (1722–6), pp. 218–20.
17. Sherburn, *The Early Career of Pope*, pp. 226–7.
18. *The Correspondence of Swift*, vol. 2, p. 621.
19. Thompson, *Whigs and Hunters*, p. 287.
20. Ibid., p. 280.
21. Ibid., p. 293.
22. Ibid., p. 293.
23. Voltaire, *Letters concerning the English Nation* (London: C. Davis and A. Lyon, 1733), p. 215.
24. *The Correspondence of Swift*, vol. 3, p. 44.
25. See ibid., vol. 2, pp. 399–408, vol. 4, p. 289; as well as G. Sherburn, 'An Accident in 1726', *Harvard Library Bulletin*, 2 (1949), pp. 121–3.
26. *The Works of Pope*, ed. Elwin and Courthope, vol. 1, p. x.

7 Dunce the Second Reigns

1. John, Lord Hervey, *Some Materials towards Memoirs of the Reign of King George II*, ed. R. Sedgwick, 3 vols (London: Eyre & Spottiswoode, 1931), vol. 1, p. 22.
2. *The History of Parliament*, vol. 3, p. 669.
3. Hervey, *Some Materials towards Memoirs*, vol. 1, pp. 23–4.
4. Ibid., vol. 1, pp. 25–6.
5. *The Correspondence of Swift*, vol. 3, p. 140.
6. *The Poems of Jonathan Swift*, ed. H. Williams, 3 vols (Oxford: Clarendon Press, 1958), vol. 2, p. 536.
7. *The Works of Jonathan Swift* (Dublin: George Faulkner, 1746), vol. 8, p. 159.
8. *The Prose Works of Pope*, vol. 2, p. 89.
9. This expressive phrase is borrowed from Jeremy Black's excellent political biography, *George II: Puppet of the Politicians?* (Exeter: University of Exeter Press, 2007), p. 77.
10. Guerinot, *Pamphlet Attacks*, p. 174.

11. Pope exchanged a number of letters with Slingsby, whom he probably got to know through the merchant's brother Hugh, one of the poet's most intimate friends. He also stayed at Bethel's house on Tower Hill. Slingsby was named after the Whig republican and sheriff of London whom Dryden portrayed as Shimei in *Absalom and Achitophel*. He procured Pope claret and madeira. A representative excerpt from their correspondence occurs in Pope's letter of 31 October 1739: 'I have not been in London but one day these 3 months, & not one day in the City (I think) since I saw you. This day I intended to have made you a Visit at Towerhill, being to pass most of the day in the City upon business' (*Corr.*, vol. 4, p. 197). Bethel also acted as a kind of investment banker for Pope (*Corr.*, vol. 4, pp. 299, 365, 401, 447, 496–7, 513).
12. *The History of Parliament*, vol. 3, pp. 151–2.
13. W. Thornbury, *Old and New London: A Narrative of its History, its People and its Places*, 2 vols (London Cassell Petter & Galpin, 1872), vol. 1, p. 322.
14. *The Correspondence of Swift*, vol. 3, p. 529. Swift replied on 11 September 1732, 'I think I saw, in my youth, a lord mayor's show with all that pomp, when Sir Thomas Pilkington ... made his procession' (vol. 3, p. 541). Significantly, this was the famous show of 1689, described in the text. The best short account of Pope's use of the Lord Mayor's procession remains A. Williams, *Pope's Dunciad: A Study of its Meaning* (London: Methuen, 1955), pp. 29–41. On Barber, see C. A. Rivington, *'Tyrant': The Story of John Barber, Jacobite Lord Mayor of London, and Printer and Friend to Dr. Swift* (York: William Sessions, 1989).
15. *Daily Journal*, 26 October 1732.
16. *The Historical Register ... for the Year 1727*, vol. 12 (London: S. Nevill, [1727]), pp. 278–81.
17. W. Maitland, *The History of London from its Foundation to the Present Time*, 2 vols (London: T. Osborne et al., 1756), vol. 1, p. 542.
18. *The Correspondence of Swift*, vol. 3, p. 297.
19. *The Life and Character of John Barber, Esq; late Lord-Mayor of London* (London: T. Cooper, 1741), pp. 3–5; Rivington, *'Tyrant'*, pp. 5–6. The 1741 biography, published by Thomas Cooper, is not wholly reliable in detail, but the overall account is scarcely in doubt.
20. *The Correspondence of Swift*, vol. 3, pp. 655, 686.
21. *The Prose Works of Pope*, vol. 2, p. 450.
22. *Spectator*, 69 (19 May 1711); 3 (3 March 1711); 2 (2 March 1711).
23. For the first, see I. Kramnick, *Bolingbroke and his Circle: The Politics of Nostalgia in the Age of Walpole* (Ithaca, NY: Cornell University Press, 1992), esp. chs 2, 3, 8. For the second, see C. Nicholson, *Writing and the Rise of Finance: Capital Satires of the Early Eighteenth Century* (Cambridge: Cambridge University Press, 1994). Nicholson, pp. 177–201, has many interesting things to say on *The Dunciad*; but unlike the discussion here his account concentrates on Book IV, and isolates Colley Cibber as the key figure representing the new commercialism.

8 Libels and Satires

1. Guerinot, *Pamphlet Attacks*, p. 241.
2. *Grub-Street Journal*, 6 December 1733.
3. *The Correspondence of Swift*, vol. 3, p. 269.
4. Rumbold, *Women's Place*, p. 256.

5. Sherburn, 'New Anecdotes', p. 348.
6. For the fullest account of this puzzling affair, see H. Erskine-Hill, 'Pope and the Poetry of Opposition', in *The Cambridge Companion to Alexander Pope*, ed. Rogers, pp. 134–49.
7. G. V. Bennett, *The Tory Crisis in Church and State, 1688–1730: The Career of Francis Atterbury Bishop of Rochester* (Oxford: Clarendon Press, 1975), p. 250.
8. *The Letters of John Gay*, p. 130.
9. D. Nokes, *John Gay: A Profession of Friendship* (Oxford: Oxford University Press, 1995), p. 537.
10. Will of Margaret Scudamore, National Archives, PROB 11/491.
11. For a good discussion of the origins of the quarrel between the two, stressing their opposing views on Walpole's government, see I. Grundy, *Lady Mary Wortley Montagu* (Oxford: Oxford University Press, 1999), pp. 268–74.
12. Guerinot, *Pamphlet Attacks*, p. 224
13. Ibid., p. 222.
14. Mack, *The Garden and the City*, p. 135.
15. G. H. Jones, *The Main Stream of Jacobitism* (Cambridge, MA: Harvard University Press, 1954), p. 184, quoting the Stuart papers at Windsor. When the scheme was defeated, the Common Council of the City voted to return thanks to Barber for his efforts to resist the excise: it is cited by Henderson, *London and the National Government*, p. 157. The standard authority is P. Langford, *The Excise Crisis: Society and Politics in the Age of Walpole* (Oxford: Clarendon Press, 1975).
16. *The Works of J.S, D.D.*, 4 vols (Dublin: George Faulkner, 1735), vol. 2, p. 372.
17. The best short account of the property and its owner is J. Bryant, *Marble Hill House, Twickenham* (London: English Heritage, 1988). Pope had a portrait of Henrietta Howard, perhaps by Charles Jervas, hung in 'the best room fronting the Thames' at his villa (Mack, *The Garden and the City*, p. 248).
18. Hervey, *Some Materials towards Memoirs*, vol. 2, p. 382.
19. *The Correspondence of Swift*, vol. 3, p. 745.

9 Friendship and Opposition

1. W. Blake, *The Marriage of Heaven and Hell* ([London], [1790]), Plate 20.
2. P. Martin, *Pursuing Innocent Pleasures: The Gardening World of Alexander Pope* (Hamden, CT: Archon, 1984), p. xx.
3. Ibid., p. xxii.
4. Ibid., p. 14.
5. Lees-Milne, *Earls of Creation*, pp. 44, 46.
6. Mack, *Pope: A Life*, p. 641.
7. For a fuller account of Peterborough's death, see P. Rogers, 'The Last Days of Lord Peterborough: The Earl, the Opera Singer, and a New Letter by Pope', *Philological Quarterly*, 83 (2004), pp. 237–57.
8. Mack, *The Garden and the City*, p. 307.
9. Erskine-Hill, *The Social Milieu of Pope*, p. 99.
10. C. Gerrard, *The Patriot Opposition to Walpole: Poetry, Politics, and National Myth, 1725–1742* (Oxford: Clarendon Press, 1994), p. 42.
11. Lees-Milne, *Earls of Creation*, p. 44.
12. R. Macfarlane, *The Wild Places* (London: Granta, 2007), pp. 316–17.

13. Horace, *Epistles Book II and the Epistle to the Pisones*, ed. N. Rudd (Cambridge: Cambridge University Press, 1989), pp. 1–3.
14. Mack, *Pope: A Life*, p. 683.
15. Mack, *The Garden and the City*, pp. 131–2.
16. Gerrard, *The Patriot Opposition to Walpole*, p. 88.
17. See N. O. Brown, *Life against Death: The Psychoanalytical Meaning of History*, 2nd edn (Middletown, CT: Wesleyan University Press, 1985), pp. 179–201.
18. *The Parliamentary History of England from the Earliest Period to the Year 1803*, 36 vols (London: Hansard, 1806–20), vol. 8, pp. 1026–7.
19. Mack, *The Garden and the City*, p. 251.
20. Ibid., p. 121.
21. Gerrard, *The Patriot Opposition to Walpole*, p. 68.

Epilogue: After Walpole

1. A. Pope, *Selected Letters*, ed. H. Erskine-Hill (Oxford: Oxford University Press, 2000), p. 279.
2. Guerinot, *Pamphlet Attacks*, pp. 310–11, 316–19.
3. Gerrard, *The Patriot Opposition to Walpole*, p. 224.
4. Ruffhead, *The Life of Pope*, pp. 410–21.
5. On the deathbed editions, see Foxon, *Pope and the Early Eighteenth-Century Book Trade*, pp. 144–52.
6. See the judicious comments in B. S. Hammond, *Pope and Bolingbroke: A Study of Friendship and Influence* (Columbia, MO: University of Missouri Press, 1984), pp. 105–9.
7. Nicolson and Rousseau, *'This Long Disease, My Life'*, pp. 73–81.

WORKS CITED

Manuscript Material

National Archives
    PROB 11/491.
    SP 36/70/40.
Northumberland Collections Service, ZSW/513/1.
Parliamentary Archives, HL/PO/JO/10/1/470/877.
University of Reading, Museum of English Rural Life, MS 145/EN 1/3/44.

Published Sources

Ackroyd, P., *Thames: The Biography* (London: Chatto & Windus, 2007).

Anon., *The Life and Character of John Barber, Esq; late Lord-Mayor of London* (London: T. Cooper, 1741).

Arnold, R., *Northern Lights: The Story of Lord Derwentwater* (London: Constable, 1959).

Ault, N., *New Light on Pope* (London: Methuen, 1949).

Beckles Willson, A., *Mr Pope and Others at Cross Deep Twickenham in the 18th Century* (Twickenham, privately printed, 1996).

Bennett, G. V., *The Tory Crisis in Church and State, 1688–1730: The Career of Francis Atterbury Bishop of Rochester* (Oxford: Clarendon Press, 1975).

Black, J., *George II: Puppet of the Politicians?* (Exeter: University of Exeter Press, 2007).

Blackstone, W., *Commentaries on the Laws of England*, 4 vols (Oxford: Clarendon Press, 1765–69).

Blake, W., *The Marriage of Heaven and Hell* ([London], [1790]).

Boreman, T., *The Gigantick History of the Famous Giants in the Guildhall, London* (London: Tho. Boreman, 1741).

Bossy, J., *The English Catholic Community, 1570–1850* (New York: Oxford University Press, 1976).

Boyce, B., *The Benevolent Man: A Life of Ralph Allen of Bath* (Cambridge, MA: Harvard University Press, 1967).

Brown, N. O., *Life against Death: The Psychoanalytical Meaning of History*, 2nd edn (Middletown, CT: Wesleyan University Press, 1985).

Brownell, M. R., *Alexander Pope's Villa* (London: Greater London Council, 1980).

Bryant, J., *Marble Hill House, Twickenham* (London: English Heritage, 1988).

Carswell, J., *The South Sea Bubble*, 2nd edn (Stroud: Sutton, 2001).

Cibber, C., *A Letter from Mr. Cibber, to Mr. Pope* (London: W. Lewis, 1742).

Costin, W. C., and J. S. Watson (eds), *The Law and Working of the Constitution: Documents, 1660–1914*, 2nd edn, 2 vols (London: Black, 1961).

Defoe, D., *A Tour thro' the Whole Island of Great Britain*, ed. J. McVeagh, in *Writings on Travel, Discovery and History by Daniel Defoe*, gen. ed. W. R. Owens and P. N. Furbank, 8 vols (London: Pickering & Chatto, 2001–2), vols 1–3.

De Krey, G. S., *A Fractured Society: The Politics of London in the First Age of Party, 1688–1715* (Oxford: Clarendon Press, 1985).

Dennis, J., *Reflections Critical and Satyrical, upon a late Rhapsody, call'd, An Essay on Criticism* (London: Bernard Lintott, 1711).

Dickinson, H. T., *Bolingbroke* (London: Constable, 1970).

Drayton, M., *The Works of Michael Drayton*, ed. J. W. Hebel et al., 5 vols (Oxford: Basil Blackwell, 1961).

Ehrenpreis, I., *Swift: The Man, his Works and the Age*, 3 vols (London: Methuen, 1962–83).

Ellis, M., *The Coffee House: A Cultural History* (London: Weidenfeld & Nicolson, 2004).

Erskine-Hill, H., *The Social Milieu of Alexander Pope: Lives, Example and the Poetic Response* (New Haven, CT: Yale University Press, 1975).

—, 'Pope and the Poetry of Opposition', in *The Cambridge Companion to Alexander Pope*, ed. P. Rogers (Cambridge: Cambridge University Press, 2007), pp. 134–49.

Faulkner, T., *The History and Antiquities of the Parish of Hammersmith* (London: Nichols & Son, 1839).

Foxon, D., *Pope and the Early Eighteenth-Century Book Trade*, ed. J. McLaverty (Oxford: Clarendon Press, 1991).

Fritz, P. S., *The English Ministers and Jacobitism between the Rebellions of 1715 and 1745* (Toronto: University of Toronto Press, 1975).

Gay, J., *The Poetical Works of John Gay*, ed. G. C. Faber (London: Oxford University Press, 1926)

—, *The Letters of John Gay*, ed. C. F. Burgess (Oxford: Clarendon Press, 1966).

Gerard, Mr, *An Epistle to the Egregious Mr. Pope* (London: for the author, 1734).

Gerrard, C., *The Patriot Opposition to Walpole: Poetry, Politics, and National Myth, 1725–1742* (Oxford: Clarendon Press, 1994).

Gibson, W .S., *Dilston Hall: or, Memoirs of the Right Hon. James Radcliffe, Earl of Derwentwater, a Martyr in the Rebellion of 1715* (London: Longman, Brown, Green & Longmans, 1850).

Goddard-Fenwick, T. J., *Stanton Harcourt: A Short History* (privately printed, 1967).

Gooch, L., *The Desperate Faction?: The Jacobites of North-East England, 1688–1745* (Birtley, Durham: Casdec Ltd, 2001).

Gregg, E., *Queen Anne*, rev. edn (New Haven, CT: Yale University Press, 2001).

Grundy, I., *Lady Mary Wortley Montagu* (Oxford: Oxford University Press, 1999).

Guerinot, J. V., *Pamphlet Attacks on Alexander Pope, 1711–1744: A Descriptive Bibliography* (London: Methuen, 1969).

Hamilton, E., *The Backstairs Dragon: A Life of Robert Harley, Earl of Oxford* (London: Hamilton, 1969).

Hammond, B. S., *Pope and Bolingbroke: A Study of Friendship and Influence* (Columbia, MO: University of Missouri Press, 1984).

Harlan, E., *Elijah Fenton, 1683–1730* (Philadelphia, PA, 1937).

Harley, E., *Tory and Whig: The Parliamentary Papers of Edward Harley, third Earl of Oxford, and William Hay, M.P.*, ed. S. Taylor and C. Jones (Woodbridge: Boydell Press, 1998).

Harris, F., *A Passion for Government: The Life of Sarah Duchess of Marlborough* (Oxford: Clarendon Press, 1991).

Hatton, R., *George I: Elector and King* (London: Thames and Hudson, 1978).

Henderson, A. J., *London and the National Government, 1721–1742: A Study of City Politics and the Walpole Administration* (Durham, NC: Duke University Press, 1945).

Hervey, J., *Some Materials towards Memoirs of the Reign of King George II*, ed. R. Sedgwick, 3 vols (London: Eyre & Spottiswoode, 1931).

The Historical Register ... for the Year 1727, vol. 12 (London: S. Nevill, [1727]).

The History of Parliament: The House of Commons, 1715–1754, ed. R. Sedgwick, 2 vols (London: HMSO, 1970).

The History of Parliament: The House of Commons, 1690–1715, ed. E. Cruickshanks, S. Handley and D. W. Hayton, 5 vols (Cambridge: Cambridge University Press, 2002).

Hole, C., *English Sports and Pastimes* (London: B. T. Batsford, 1949).

Holmes, G., *British Politics in the Age of Anne*, rev. edn (London: Hambledon, 1985).

Horace, *Epistles Book II and the Epistle to the Pisones*, ed. N. Rudd (Cambridge: Cambridge University Press, 1989).

Humphreys, A. R., 'Pope, God, and Man', in P. Dixon (ed.), *Writers and their Background: Alexander Pope* (London: Bell, 1972), pp. 60–100.

Johnson, S., *The Vanity of Human Wishes* (London: R. Dodsley, 1749).

—, *Lives of the English Poets*, ed. G. B. Hill, 3 vols (Oxford: Clarendon Press, 1905).

Jones, G. H., *The Main Stream of Jacobitism* (Cambridge, MA: Harvard University Press, 1954).

Kramnick, I., *Bolingbroke and his Circle: The Politics of Nostalgia in the Age of Walpole* (Ithaca, NY: Cornell University Press, 1992).

Langford, P., *The Excise Crisis: Society and Politics in the Age of Walpole* (Oxford: Clarendon Press, 1975).

Lecky, W. E. H., *A History of England in the Eighteenth Century*, 8 vols (London: Longmans Green and Co., 1892).

Lees-Milne, J., *Earls of Creation: Five Great Patrons of Eighteenth-Century Art* (London: Hamish Hamilton, 1962).

Macfarlane, R., *The Wild Places* (London: Granta, 2007).

Mack, M., *The Garden and the City: Retirement and Politics in the Later Poetry of Pope, 1731–1743* (Toronto: University of Toronto Press, 1969).

—, *Collected in Himself: Essays Critical, Biographical, and Bibliographical on Pope and Some of His Contemporaries* (Newark, DE: University of Delaware Press, 1982).

—, *Alexander Pope: A Life* (New Haven, CT: Yale University Press, 1985).

Maitland, W., *The History of London from its Foundation to the Present Time*, 2 vols (London: T. Osborne et al., 1756).

Martin, P., *Pursuing Innocent Pleasures: The Gardening World of Alexander Pope* (Hamden, CT: Archon, 1984).

May, T. E., *The Constitutional History of England*, 2nd edn, 2 vols (London: Longmans, 1863–5).

Montagu, M. W., *The Complete Letters of Lady Mary Wortley Montagu*, ed. R. Halsband, 3 vols (Oxford: Clarendon Press, 1965–7).

Moore, J. R., 'Windsor-Forest and William III', *Modern Language Notes*, 66 (1951), pp. 451–4.

Nicholson, C., *Writing and the Rise of Finance: Capital Satires of the Early Eighteenth Century* (Cambridge: Cambridge University Press, 1994).

Nicolson, M. H., and G. S. Rousseau, *'This Long Disease, My Life': Alexander Pope and the Sciences* (Princeton, NJ: Princeton University Press, 1968).

Nokes, D., *John Gay: A Profession of Friendship* (Oxford: Oxford University Press, 1995).

The Parliamentary History of England from the Earliest Period to the Year 1803, 36 vols (London: Hansard, 1806–20).

Payne, J. O., *Records of the English Catholics of 1715* (London: Burns & Oates, 1889).

Pearce, E., *The Great Man: Sir Robert Walpole, Scoundrel, Genius and Britain's First Prime Minister* (London: Jonathan Cape, 2007).

Plumb, J. H., *Sir Robert Walpole*, 2 vols (London: Cresset Press, 1956–60).

Pope, A., *The Works of Alexander Pope*, ed. W. Elwin and W. J. Courthope, 10 vols (London: John Murray, 1871–89).

—, *The Prose Works of Alexander Pope, vol. 1, The Earlier Works, 1711–1720*, ed. N. Ault (Oxford: Blackwell, 1936).

—, *The Twickenham Edition of the Works of Alexander Pope*, ed. J. Butt et al., 11 vols (London: Methuen, 1938–68).

—, *Pope's Windsor Forest 1712*, ed. R. M. Schmitz (St Louis, MO: Washington University, 1952).

—, *The Correspondence of Alexander Pope*, ed. G. Sherburn, 5 vols (Oxford: Clarendon Press, 1956).

—, *The Last and Greatest Art: Some Unpublished Poetical Manuscripts of Alexander Pope*, ed. M. Mack (Newark, DE: University of Delaware Press, 1984).

—, *The Prose Works of Alexander Pope, vol. 2, The Major Works, 1725–1744*, ed. R. Cowler (Hamden, CT: Archon, 1986).

—, *Selected Letters*, ed. H. Erskine-Hill (Oxford: Oxford University Press, 2000).

Rackham, O., *The Last Forest: The Story of Hatfield Forest* (London: Dent, 1989).

Rawson, C. J., 'Some Unpublished Letters of Pope and Gay', *Review of English Studies*, 10 (1959), pp. 371–87.

Rivington, C. A., '*Tyrant*': *The Story of John Barber, Jacobite Lord Mayor of London, and Printer and Friend to Dr. Swift* (York: William Sessions, 1989).

Rogers, N., *Crowds, Culture and Politics in Georgian England* (Oxford: Clarendon Press, 1998).

Rogers, P., *Literature and Popular Culture in Eighteenth-Century England* (Brighton: Harvester, 1985).

—, 'The Last Days of Lord Peterborough: The Earl, the Opera Singer, and a New Letter by Pope', *Philological Quarterly*, 83 (2004), pp. 237–57.

Ruffhead, O., *The Life of Alexander Pope* (London: C. Bathurst et al., 1769).

Rumbold, V., *Women's Place in Pope's World* (Cambridge: Cambridge University Press, 1989).

Schama, S., *Landscape and Memory* (London: HarperCollins, 1995).

Sherburn, G., *The Early Career of Alexander Pope* (Oxford: Clarendon Press, 1934).

—, 'An Accident in 1726', *Harvard Library Bulletin*, 2 (1949), pp. 121–3.

—, 'Letters of Alexander Pope, Chiefly to Sir William Trumbull', *Review of English Studies*, 9 (1958), pp. 388–406.

—, 'New Anecdotes of Alexander Pope', *Notes and Queries*, 5 (1958), pp. 343–9.

Smithers, P., *The Life of Joseph Addison*, 2nd edn (Oxford: Clarendon Press, 1968).

Spence, C., *London in the 1690s: A Social Atlas* (London: Centre for Metropolitan History, Institute of Historical Research, 2000).

Spence, J., *Observations, Anecdotes, and Characters of Books and Men*, ed. J. M. Osborn, 2 vols (Oxford: Clarendon Press, 1966).

Stow, J., *A Survey of the Cities of London and Westminster*, 2 vols (London: A. Churchill et al., 1720).

Swift, J., *The Works of J.S, D.D.*, 4 vols (Dublin: George Faulkner, 1735).

—, *The Works of Jonathan Swift* (Dublin: George Faulkner, 1746).

—, *The Prose Works of Jonathan Swift*, ed. H. Davis et al., 14 vols (Oxford: Basil Blackwell, 1939–74).

—, *Journal to Stella*, ed. H. Williams, 2 vols (Oxford: Clarendon: Press, 1948).

—, *The Poems of Jonathan Swift*, ed. H. Williams, 3 vols (Oxford: Clarendon Press, 1958).

—, *The Correspondence of Jonathan Swift*, ed. D. Woolley, 4 vols (Frankfurt: Peter Lang, 1999–2005).

Szechi, D., 'The Jacobite Theatre of Death', in E. Cruickshanks and J. Black (eds), *The Jacobite Challenge* (Edinburgh: John Donald, 1988), pp. 57–74.

Thompson, E. P., *Whigs and Hunters: The Origins of the Black Act*, rev. edn (Harmondsworth: Penguin, 1977).

Thornbury, W., *Old and New London: A Narrative of its History, its People and its Places*, 2 vols (London Cassell Petter & Galpin, 1872).

Thornbury, W., and E. Walford, *Old and New London: A Narrative of its History, its People, and its Places*, new edn, 6 vols (London: Cassell Petter & Galpin, 1893).

Trickett, R., *The Honest Muse* (Oxford: Clarendon Press, 1967).

The Victoria History of the County of Berkshire, ed. W. Page and P. H. Ditchfield, 5 vols (London: St Catherine Press, 1906–27).

Voltaire, *Letters concerning the English Nation* (London: C. Davis and A. Lyon, 1733).

Weinbrot, H., *Britannia's Issue: The Rise of British Literature from Dryden to Ossian* (Cambridge: Cambridge University Press, 1993).

Williams, A., *Pope's Dunciad: A Study of its Meaning* (London: Methuen, 1955).

Wyndham Lewis, D. B., *A History of the Benedictine Nuns of Dunkirk* (London: Catholic Book Club, 1957).

Wynne, W., *The Defence of Francis, late Lord Bishop of Rochester* (London: Jonah Bowyer, 1723).

Young, B., 'Pope and Ideology', in *The Cambridge Companion to Alexander Pope*, ed. P. Rogers (Cambridge: Cambridge University Press, 2007), pp. 118–33.

INDEX

Works by Alexander Pope (AP) appear directly under title; works by others under author's name.

Act of Settlement (1701), 22–3
Addison, Joseph, 1, 65–7, 72–3, 76–7, 79, 84–5, 88, 101, 105, 114, 119
   Cato, 66
   Freeholder, 101
   see also *Spectator*; *Tatler*
Aislabie, John, 121, 133
Allen, Ralph, 209–10, 215, 220, 223, 229–30
Anne, Queen, 2, 22, 39, 53, 56–8, 62, 68, 76–8, 80, 87, 107, 113, 132, 142, 168
anti-Catholic legislation, 4, 213, 79, 89, 96–7, 100, 138
Arbuthnot, George, 125, 205
Arbuthnot, John, 1, 61, 67, 69, 70–1, 76, 78, 80, 88–9, 96, 104, 11, 114, 124, 129, 135, 145, 156, 159, 182–3, 197, 204–5, 229
Arbuthnot, Robert, 84, 135
   see also *Imitations of Horace* (AP), *Epistle to Arbuthnot*
Argyll, John Campbell, 2nd Duke of, 90, 105–6, 108, 124, 222
asiento, 55
Atterbury, Francis, 2, 4, 53, 77, 111, 114, 119–20, 123, 126, 129–31, 133–8, 143, 146, 181, 187–8, 221
Atterbury plot (1722–3), 2, 123, 133–7, 139, 215

Bagshot, Surrey, 24, 36
   Bagshot Heath, 8, 108

Banister, John, alias Taverner, 24, 26
Bank of England, 20, 22, 186
Barber, John, 124, 131, 139–40, 168–73, 195
Barnard, Sir John, 217, 22
Bath, 1st Earl of see Pulteney, William
Bath, Somerset, 80–1, 209
Bathurst, Allen, 1st Earl, 4, 43, 45, 56, 61, 84, 108, 111–12, 113–14, 119, 124, 133–5, 138, 145, 147–8, 163, 167, 175–6, 179, 181–2, 184, 188–9, 200–2, 207, 210, 213, 215, 220–1, 223, 225, 230
   see also *Moral Essays* (AP), *Epistle to Bathurst*
Beach, Mary, 10, 24, 29, 32, 145, 177–8
Bedingfield, Frances, 25–6, 40
Bedingfield family, 25–6, 44, 91, 108
Bellenden, Mary, 103, 105
Bentley, Richard, 84, 227
Berkshire, 4, 10–11, 24, 31, 40, 42, 76–7, 81, 118, 167
Bethel, Hugh, 124, 199, 220, 223, 230
Bethel, Slingsby, 167, 173, 199
Betterton, Thomas, 2, 46–8, 51
Bevis Mount, Hampshire, 125, 202, 206, 215
Binfield, Berkshire, 4, 11, 24, 32, 35–6, 39–40, 46, 78, 108
   see also Pope, homes
Blackmore, Sir Richard, 160, 217
Blount, Edward, 79, 90, 108, 111, 124

Blount, Lister, 40, 43, 109
Blount, Martha (mother of next), 109–10, 177
Blount, Martha (friend of AP), 9, 30, 40–4, 73, 78, 81–2, 88, 91–4, 98, 103, 107–11, 114, 116, 119, 151, 161, 177, 197, 206, 209, 220, 230–1
  see also *Moral Essays* (AP), *Epistle to a Lady*
Blount, Michael, 40, 43, 93–5, 108–9
Blount, Teresa, 40, 43, 73, 78, 81–2, 88, 91–5, 98, 100, 103, 107–11, 114, 116, 119, 176–7
Blount family, 4, 10, 37, 42
Blunt, Sir John, 121, 186, 188
Bolingbroke, Henry St John, 1st Viscount, 1, 4, 49, 53–4, 60, 62, 69, 72, 76–7, 80–1, 83–4, 87, 113, 129, 143, 146, 151, 155, 175, 181, 188, 190–1, 193–4, 197, 199, 201–2, 220–1, 229, 230
  AP addresses Horatian imitation to, 216–17
  AP and *Essay on Man*, 194
  Craftsman, 201
  Idea of a Patriot King, 230
  joins the Pretender, 87
  restored, 138
  returns to England, 230
  returns to France, 201
Bond, Denis, 218–20
Bononcini, Giovanni, 124–5
Bounce to Fop (AP and Swift), 210
Bowyer, William, 106–7
Boyle, John *see* Orrery, 5th Earl of
Boyle, Richard *see* Burlington, 3rd Earl of
Bracknell, Berkshire, 35, 46
Broome, William, 126–7, 131, 148
Browne, Sir George, 73, 75
Brutus (AP; projected), 221, 228–9
Brydges, James *see* Chandos, 1st Duke of
Buckingham, John Sheffield, 1st Duke of, 49–50, 83, 107, 125, 131, 163, 166
  see also *Works of Buckingham* (ed. AP)
Buckingham, Katherine Sheffield, Duchess of, 107, 124, 139, 145, 207, 230
Burlington, Richard Boyle, 3rd Earl of, 45, 88, 98, 100, 110–11, 119, 124, 163, 179–81, 202, 210, 223, 230

  see also *Moral Essays* (AP), *Epistle to Burlington*
Butler, James *see* Ormonde, 2nd Duke of
Butler, Samuel, 170–1

Caesar, Mary, 127–8
Cambridge, Cambridgeshire, 84
Campbell, John *see* Argyll, 2nd Duke of
Caroline, Queen, 3, 83, 103, 105–6, 108, 116, 124, 128, 145, 151–3, 156, 163, 165, 169–70, 186, 197, 205, 211, 214
Carteret, John, Baron, 140, 155, 222, 226
Caryll, John, 25–7, 40–2, 44, 72–4, 78, 82–3, 91–2, 95, 97–9, 108–10, 120–1, 133, 138, 143, 176–7, 182–3, 199, 210, 221
Caryll, Philip, 133, 143
Caryll family, 4, 33
Catholic community, 21–2, 40, 43–4, 84, 86
Cervantes, Miguel Saavedra de, 66, 163
Chandos, James Brydges, 1st Duke of, 55, 70, 83, 124, 128, 180, 183, 189
Charles I, King, 38–9, 62
Charles II, King, 17, 25, 39, 46, 52, 84, 107
Charteris, Francis, 184–5
Chaucer, Geoffrey, 31, 86, 167
Chaucer, imitations of (AP), 51
Cheselden, William, 94, 130, 229
Chesterfield, Philip Stanhope, 4th Earl of, 202, 227
Chiswick (Middlesex), 111, 200, 202
  see also Pope, homes
Churchill, John *see* Marlborough, 1st Duke of
Churchill, Sarah *see* Marlborough, Duchess of
Cibber, Caius Gabriel, 15, 27
Cibber, Colley, 2, 15, 104, 112, 157, 166, 175, 227
  The Non-Juror, 112, 227–8
Cirencester, Gloucestershire, 112–13, 124, 176, 202–4, 213, 215, 225
Civil War, English, 9, 40
Cobham, Richard Temple, 1st Viscount, 124, 142, 175, 197–8, 200, 202–3, 210, 221, 223
  Cobham's Cubs, 195, 202, 216
  see also *Moral Essays* (AP), *Epistle to Cobham*

Commons, House of, 55, 66, 70, 91, 222, 225
Compton, Spencer, 152–3, 226
Congreve, William, 1, 49, 78, 85, 124, 135, 203
Coningsby, Thomas, 1st Earl, 87–8, 100, 121, 147, 176, 187–90
Cook, Japhet, 185, 218
Cooper, Thomas, 172, 217
Cooper family, 8–9
copyright, 208–9, 229
Court Ballad (AP), 103–6
Craggs, James, Jr, 109, 114–15, 120, 122–3, 127, 135, 186
Cromwell, Henry, 48, 51, 148
Cromwell, Oliver, 18, 60, 144
Curll, Edmund, 48, 76, 99, 101, 104–5, 107, 112, 119, 127, 139–40, 145, 148–9, 155–6, 160–3, 176, 192–3, 207–9, 212, 216, 229

Dancastle, John, 4, 35, 40, 45, 108
Dancastle, Thomas, 40, 108, 118
Dancastle family, 35–6
Dawley, Middlesex, 138, 145–6, 203, 220, 225
Deane, Thomas, 26–7
Defoe, Daniel, 8, 12, 14–16, 25, 63, 198
  Tour thro' the Whole Island of Great Britain, 8, 14
Dennis, John, 52, 78, 80, 104, 160, 163
Derwentwater, Anna Maria, Countess of, 91, 93–5
Derwentwater, James Radcliffe, 3rd Earl of, 3, 25, 84, 91–5, 116, 197, 219
Digby, Mary, 147–8, 176, 190
Digby, Robert, 112, 114, 134, 147, 176, 189–90, 196, 213
Digby, William, 5th Baron, 133–4, 147, 196
Dodd, Anne, 161, 190
Dodsley, Robert, 212, 217
Dormer, James, 202, 213
Douglas, Charles and Catherine *see* Queensberry, 3rd Duke and Duchess of
Drayton, Michael, 59–60
Dryden, John, 31, 44, 46–7, 107, 220
  MacFlecknoe, 166

Dublin, 80, 114, 145, 151, 154, 160–1, 208, 215
Dunciad, The (AP), 3, 17–19, 47, 68, 99, 112, 114, 125–6, 139, 149, 156, 158, 160, 161–73, 175–6, 179, 184, 191–3, 204, 208, 216, 218, 226–8
Dunciad in Four Books, The (AP), 226–8
Dunciad Variorum, The (AP), 162
  civic pageantry, 168–70
  origins, 163
  politics, 165–7
  presented to the King, 163
  publication, 161
  responses, 161–2, 164
  role of the City, 168–73
Duncombe, Sir Charles, 20, 168, 173

Easthampstead, Berkshire, 44–6, 127
East India Company, 20, 63, 185
Eckersall, James, 120–1
elections, 3, 87, 153
Elegy to the Memory of an Unfortunate Lady (AP), 106
Elizabeth I, Queen, 222
Eloisa to Abelard (AP), 101, 106
Empire, British, 63
Englefield, Anthony, 40–1, 91
Englefield, Henry, 95
Englefield family, 25, 37, 40, 42–3, 74, 109
'Epigram upon Two or Three' (AP), 76
Epilogue to the Satires (AP) *see Imitations of Horace*
Epistle to Arbuthnot (AP) *see Imitations of Horace*
Epistle to a Lady (AP) *see Moral Essays*
Epistle to Bathurst (AP) *see Moral Essays*
Epistle to Burlington (AP) *see Moral Essays*
Epistle to Cobham (AP) *see Moral Essays*
'Epistle to Miss Blount on her leaving the Town' (AP), 34, 81, 106
Epistle to Oxford (AP), 128–30, 208
Epistles (AP) *see Imitations of Horace*
epitaph on Atterbury (AP), 137
Erasmus, Desiderius, 30, 68, 86
Erskine, John *see* Mar, 6th Earl of
Essay on Criticism (AP), 3, 51–3, 106, 178

Essay on Man (AP), 132, 147, 183, 193–4, 196, 198–9, 208, 217
Eusden, Laurence, 160, 166
Excise scheme (1733), 2, 170, 186, 195
Exclusion crisis (1679–81), 15, 17

Farewell to London (AP), 88
Fenton, Elijah, 46, 126–7, 130, 132, 148
Fermor, Arabella, 43, 73–4, 84, 94, 128
Fielding, Henry, 158, 191, 106, 210, 219, 228
Financial Revolution, 13, 185–6
Ford, Charles, 81, 18, 130
Fortescue, William, 71, 120, 177–8, 181, 190–2, 207
Frederick, Prince of Wales, 195, 201–2, 210–12, 218, 220–2, 230
Full and True Account (AP), 99
Further Account (AP), 99

Garter, Order of, 61, 179, 228
Garth, Sir Samuel, 46–7, 49–50, 73, 107, 114, 128
Gay, John, 1–2, 67–9, 71–2, 76, 80–1, 83, 85, 88, 104–5, 107, 110, 114, 120, 126, 128, 130, 135, 145–6, 151, 154, 156–60, 176, 181–3, 187, 221
  The Beggar's Opera, 139, 157–60, 176
  early poems, 72
  Fables, 149, 158
  Polly, 176
  The What d'ye Call It, 72, 86
George I, King, 2, 13, 22, 39, 54, 61, 66, 76, 81, 104–6, 108, 112, 119, 128, 144–5, 151, 153, 158, 165, 186
George II, King, 2, 103–6, 108, 116, 124, 128, 151–3, 156, 163, 165–6, 168, 170, 186, 191, 199, 202, 211, 214, 225–6, 228
Gibbs, James, 14, 124, 175
Gildon, Charles, 47–8, 140
Gilliver, Lawton, 190, 199
Gloucestershire, 113, 148
Godolphin, Sidney, 1st Earl, 50, 53–5, 69
Granville, George, 1st Baron Lansdowne, 49, 56–7, 60–1, 83–4, 89–90, 133–4
Great Fire of London (1666), 12, 14, 62
Great Plague (1665), 62

Grub Street, 50, 76, 127, 158, 164, 204, 226
Grub-Street Journal, 175–6, 227
Guardian papers (AP), 113

Halifax, Charles Montagu, 1st Earl of, 49, 66, 83–6, 88, 119
Hall Grove, Surrey, 24, 177
Hamilton, Elizabeth, Duchess of, 108, 207
Hammersmith, Middlesex, 24–26, 32
  see also Pope, homes
Hampton Court, Middlesex, 97, 103, 115
Handel, George Friderick, 2, 70, 107, 125, 156
Harcourt, Simon (friend of AP), 61, 108
Harcourt, Simon, 1st Viscount, 83, 112, 135, 138, 140, 143, 207
Harley, Edward (Auditor of the Imprest), 70, 134, 188
Harley, Edward *see* Oxford, 2nd Earl of
Harley, Robert *see* Oxford, 1st Earl of
Harley, Thomas, 134, 188
Heathcote, Sir Gilbert, 20, 168, 172–3
Herefordshire, 87, 113–14, 129, 147–8, 180, 188–9
Hervey, John, Baron, 2, 103, 153–3, 176, 191–2, 197, 200, 204–5, 218, 222, 227
Hervey, Mary, Baroness, 103, 124
Hill, Aaron, 218, 222
Holme Lacy, Herefordshire, 147, 189
Homer, translation (AP), 72, 101, 103
Horace (Quintus Horatius Flaccus), 124, 176, 190, 193, 199, 212, 214, 216
  see also Imitations of Horace (AP)
Howard, Henrietta, Countess of Suffolk, 43, 103, 124, 151, 153, 197, 203, 210

Iliad, translation (AP), 66, 78, 85–6, 88, 106–7, 111, 118, 122, 126
Imitations of Donne (AP), 179, 197–8, 208
Imitations of Horace (AP), 33, 139, 179, 190, 197, 217, 221
  Epilogue to the Satires, 86, 217–18
  Epistle to Arbuthnot, 7, 9, 66, 71, 77, 86, 110, 178–9, 204–5, 208
  Epistle I.i, 216
  Epistle I.vi, 216
  Epistle II.i, 158, 214–15
  Epistle II.ii, 212–14

Satire II.i, 86, 175, 190–3
Satire II.ii, 199
Sober Advice from Horace, 199–200, 209

Jacobites
  invasion (1719), 119
  rising (1715–16), 2–3, 23, 40, 63, 88, 90–1, 93, 96, 101, 104, 112–13, 119, 178, 187, 228
  rising (1745–6), 221
Jacobitism, 4, 77, 87, 133–4
  see also Pope, politics
James II, King, 2, 15, 17, 19, 21, 23, 27, 39, 62
James Edward Stuart, the Pretender, 2, 23, 54–5, 60–1, 63, 77, 86–8, 90–1, 96, 104, 107, 113, 133, 138–9, 178, 221
Jervas, Charles, 78–9, 81, 89, 100, 106, 115, 124, 128, 145, 148, 223
Johnson, Esther ('Stella'), 64–5, 154
Johnson, Samuel, 127, 131, 158, 212
  Lives of the Poets, 47, 85
Jonson, Ben, 31, 176, 190

Kent, William, 116, 175, 212
Key to the Lock (AP), 75, 86–7
Kneller, Sir Godfrey, 78, 108, 118, 145
Knight, Robert, 121, 186
Kyrle, John, 148, 181, 183–4, 189–90

Lansdowne, 1st Baron *see* Granville, George
Lechmere, Nicholas, 138, 188
Letter to a Noble Lord (AP), 192
Lintot, Bernard, 51, 72–3, 82, 87, 100, 103, 106–7, 127–8, 210
Locke, John, 16, 194, 222, 226
London, 12–20, 57, 109, 139
  Bank of England, 13–14
  Button's coffee-house, 65, 72, 140
  Charing Cross, 77, 99
  Cheapside, 18–19
  City of London, 16, 20, 165–73, 195
  Cornhill, 13, 15
  Covent Garden, 31, 65
  Drury Lane theatre, 66, 104, 112, 157, 227
  East India House, 13–14
  Exchange Alley, 13, 16–17
  Fleet Ditch, 167, 226
  General Post Office, 13–14, 16
  Gracechurch Street, 12, 15
  Guildhall, 13, 18, 169–70
  guilds, 15–16, 169, 172
  Haymarket theatre, 107, 124
  Leicester Fields, 151, 153, 211
  Lincoln's Inn Fields theatre, 127, 157
  Lloyd's coffee-house, 13, 186
  Lombard Street, 11–12, 14, 24, 29, 173
  Monument, 15
  Newgate, 157–8
  Plough Court, 11–13, 15, 173
    see also Pope, homes
  Royal Exchange, 10, 12, 14, 16–17, 169, 173
  St Edmund the King, 11, 13
  St James's Palace, 67, 211
  St Paul's Cathedral, 14, 53
  South Sea House, 13–14
  The Strand, 36, 99
  Threadneedle Street, 10, 13
  Tower of London, 61, 63, 72, 90–1, 93, 129, 133, 136
  Westminster Abbey, 81, 131, 170, 181–2, 211, 231
  Westminster Hall, 52, 135
  Whitehall, 14, 151, 176
  Will's coffee-house, 31, 47–8
Lord Mayor's Show, 17–19, 166, 168–9
Lords, House of, 53, 55, 93, 136, 139, 207, 222
Louis XIV, King of France, 55, 58–9, 100
Lyttelton, George, 1st Baron, 203–3, 220, 223, 230

Mack, Maynard, 4, 8, 11, 17–18, 32, 64, 110, 126, 194, 204
Mansfield, 1st Earl of *see* Murray, William
Mapledurham, Oxfordshire, 37, 42–3, 79, 81, 89, 110
Mar, John Erskine, 6th Earl of, 84, 90, 134
Marble Hill, Middlesex, 151, 197, 203
Marchmont, Hugh Hume, 3rd Earl of, 202, 220–1, 223, 230
Marlborough, John Churchill, 1st Duke of, 1, 50, 53–6, 60, 69, 84–5, 87, 125, 131–3

Marlborough, Sarah Churchill, Duchess of, 50, 56, 86, 132, 199, 220, 230
Mary II, Queen, 19
see also William and Mary
Masham, Abigail, 56, 86
Mawhood family, 9, 34–5
Memoirs of Scriblerus (AP and Scriblerus Club), 67–8, 71, 114
Merlin's Cave, Richmond, 116, 211
Messiah (AP), 65, 106
Milton, John, 97, 127, 205, 220, 222
Paradise Lost, 72, 97, 227
Miscellanies (AP and Scriblerus Club), 68, 71, 151, 155–6, 158, 181, 208, 210
Mississippi Bubble (1719–20), 111, 121
Montagu, Charles *see* Halifax, 1st Earl of
Montagu, Lady Mary Wortley, 2, 4, 8, 49, 81, 100, 105–8, 114–15, 118, 124–5, 191–2, 200, 205, 207
Moral Essays (AP), 3, 179, 198, 206, 208, 229
Epistle to a Lady, 43, 206
Epistle to Bathurst, 3, 45, 56, 121, 148, 168, 180–1, 183–90, 193, 206, 219–20
Epistle to Burlington, 45, 179–80, 183
Epistle to Cobham, 198
Moore's Worms (AP), 101, 159
Mordaunt, Charles *see* Peterborough, 3rd Earl of
Motte, Benjamin, 145, 155, 158, 160, 208
Murray, William, 1st Earl of Mansfield, 197, 216, 227, 229

Newcastle, Thomas Pelham-Holles, 1st Duke of, 155, 226, 228
Newton, Sir Isaac, 1, 85

Odyssey, translation (AP), 46, 125–8, 144
Ogilby, John, 30, 126
'On a Lady who Pisst at the Tragedy of Cato' (AP), 76, 159
opposition to Walpole, 2, 4, 138, 175, 195, 197, 201–4, 211–12, 217
Opus Magnum (AP; planned), 179
Orford, 1st Earl of *see* Walpole, Robert
Ormonde, James Butler, 2nd Duke of, 61, 84, 89–90, 116, 134

Orrery, John Boyle, 5th Earl of, 215–16, 221, 230
Ovid (Publius Ovidius Naso), 30, 59–60
Oxford, 84, 100, 108, 112, 124, 128, 131, 212, 226
Oxford, Edward Harley, 2nd Earl of, 32, 129, 145, 148, 151, 163, 175, 181, 184, 188, 197, 205, 210, 221
Oxford, Robert Harley, 1st Earl of, 1, 4, 50, 54, 56, 59, 61–2, 67–70, 72–3, 76–7, 81, 86–8, 100–1, 112–14, 119, 121, 128–30, 134–5, 138, 156, 186–8, 221

Pangbourne, Berkshire, 10–11
Parnell, Thomas, 67–9, 72, 80, 96–7, 107, 114, 128, 183
Pastorals (AP), 44, 48–50, 56, 106
patriot king, 201, 221
Patriots, 220–3
see also opposition to Walpole
Pelham, Henry, 155, 226
Pelham-Holles, Thomas *see* Newcastle, 1st Duke of
penal laws *see* anti-Catholic legislation
Peri Bathous (AP and Scriblerus Club), 3, 68, 114, 126, 158–60
Peterborough, Charles Mordaunt, 3rd Earl of, 19, 71, 124, 143, 181, 191, 197, 200, 203, 205–6, 221
Petre, Robert, 7th Baron, 41, 72–4, 91
Petre family, 44, 73–5
Pigott, Nathaniel, 91, 116, 146, 231
Poems of Parnell (ed. AP), 130
Poems on Several Occasions (ed. AP), 107
Pope, Alexander, Sr, 4, 7, 9–12, 15–17, 19, 23–4, 30, 34, 40, 48, 110–11, 168, 173, 186
Pope, Alexander
biographic and personal references
attacks on, 52, 162, 164, 192–3
battles with Curll, 76, 99, 112, 155–6, 162, 207–9, 229
birth, 2, 12
care of parents, 110–11, 145, 151, 177, 196, 204
childhood, 7–27
death, 2, 231
early reading, 30–1

early mentors, 44–8
education, 26–7
youth, 29–50
characters in AP's poetry
  Atossa, 207
  Atticus, 119
  Sir Balaam, 168, 187–8, 190
  the Baron, 75
  Belinda, 43, 74–5, 86–7, 99
  Bufo, 204
  Lord Fanny, 176
  Man of Ross, 181, 183, 189
  Sir Plume, 73
  Sapho, 205–6
  Sporus, 204–5
  Timon, 180, 183–4, 189, 191
correspondence, 207, 212
health
  accident with cow, 32
  deformity, 31–2
  dwarfism, 31
  final illness, 230–1
  headaches, 31, 51
  Pott's disease, 31–2, 223
  urinary condition, 229
homes
  Binfield, 4, 11, 12–14, 27, 29–30, 33–9, 45, 64, 81, 88–9, 96–8, 100, 118, 167–8
  Chiswick, 11, 40, 88, 96–8, 100, 168
  departure from the Forest, 97–100, 108
  grotto, 117–18
  Hammersmith, 7, 11, 12, 27, 98, 168
  Plough Court, 1–17, 26, 118, 223
  Whitehill House, 29, 31, 34–5
  Twickenham, 4, 29, 83, 97, 103, 115–18, 120, 122–4, 155, 167, 202, 209, 220
  villa and garden at Twickenham, 117–18, 203, 223
interests
  country pursuits, 33–4
  dogs, 202, 210
  landscape gardening, 115, 118, 147–8, 175, 180, 203–4, 221
  painting, 78
  rambles, 100, 110, 124, 200, 215

money
  finances, 14, 126, 128
  gives pension to Savage, 158
  investments, 109, 120–1
  pension offered, 85, 128
  subscriptions, 79, 82–5, 103, 127–8, 130, 140, 178
  taxation, 96–7, 100, 138–9
politics
  arrest, possible (1723), 140
  arrest, threatened (1737), 215
  break with Whigs, 65–7, 78–9, 88, 101, 114
  City of London politics, 4, 166–73, 217
  connections with Waltham Blacks affair, 140–4
  effect of Jacobite rising, 86, 89–90, 92–7
  relations with Frederick, Prince of Wales, 201–2,
  relations with George II, 103–6, 124, 165–6, 191, 197, 214, 228
  relations with Patriot group, 195, 201–4, 216, 218, 220–3
  relations with Queen Caroline, 103–4, 106, 124, 165–6, 186–7, 211, 214
  relations with Walpole, 142–4, 178, 194, 200, 205, 214, 217, 228
  subscription lists, 83–5, 127–8, 130
  supposed Jacobitism, 52–3, 57, 60–3, 75, 85–7, 112, 134
religion
  Catholicism, 4, 23–4, 79, 81–2, 111
  Catholic friends, 40–4, 84–5, 91–5, 125
works *see individual titles*
Pope, Edith, 7–8, 11, 19, 25, 30, 34, 40, 43, 110, 145, 151–2, 177, 182, 196
Preston, battle of (1715), 90–1
Pretender *see* James Edward Stuart
Prior, Matthew, 1, 61, 76, 78, 83–5, 88, 100, 107, 118–19, 188
Prior Park, Somerset, 209, 215
Pulteney, William, 1st Earl of Bath, 1, 124, 153, 155, 195, 197, 201, 223, 225–7

Queensberry, Charles Douglas, 3rd Duke of, and Catherine Douglas, Duchess of, 124, 154, 176, 181, 187, 204

Rabelais, François, 68, 163
Rackett, Charles, 24, 37, 140–1, 143, 177
Rackett, Magdalen, 9, 11, 24, 26, 32, 110, 119, 140–1, 177, 231
Rackett, Michael, 141, 143
Rackett family, 123, 140–1, 143, 177
Radcliffe, James *see* Derwentwater, 3rd Earl of
Rape of the Lock (AP), 3, 41–3, 51, 64–5, 72–5, 81, 86–7, 91, 99, 103, 106, 178, 190
Ratcliffe, Charles, 91, 219
Reading, Berkshire, 35–7, 40, 42, 46
Revolution of 1688, 19, 22
Richmond, Surrey, 115, 124, 151–2
　Richmond Lodge, 116, 151
　Richmond Park, 116, 211
Riot Act, 88–9
Riskins, Buckinghamshire, 202
Robinson, Anastasia, 124–5, 181, 205, 215
Rousham, Oxfordshire, 202, 212
Rowe, Nicholas, 1, 76, 84, 97, 114, 128, 130–1, 166
Rumbold, Valerie, 33–4, 177

Sacheverell, Henry, 53, 77, 87, 112, 152
　Sacheverell affair (1709), 53–4, 99
St Germain-en-Laye, château of, Paris, 55, 91
St John, Henry *see* Bolingbroke, 1st Viscount
Sandys, Samuel, 1st Baron, 225–6
'Sandys's Ghost' (AP), 159
Satires (AP) *see Imitations of Horace*
Savage, Richard, 158, 162, 191
Schama, Simon, 37–8
Scriblerus Club, 65, 67–72, 72, 76, 80–1, 84, 114, 149, 159, 163, 183, 205
Scudamore, Frances, Viscountess, 114, 134, 147–8, 176, 188–90
Scudamore, James, 3rd Viscount, 147, 188
Settle, Elkanah, 139, 165, 168, 170–2
Severn, River, 148, 189, 213
Shakespeare, William, 42, 130, 178, 220
Shakespeare edition (AP), 127, 130–2, 144
Sheffield, John *see* Buckingham, 1st Duke of

Sheffield, Katherine *see* Buckingham, Duchess of
Sherborne, Dorset, 147
Sherburn, George, 23, 96
Shrewsbury, Charles Talbot, 1st Duke of, 49, 76, 108
Sober Advice from Horace (AP) *see Imitations of Horace*
Society, the, 61, 69
Somers, John, Baron, 49, 84
Sophia, Electress of Hanover, 22, 76
Southcott, Thomas, 75, 84, 178
South Sea Bubble (1720), 2, 13, 17, 109, 119–22, 123, 126–8, 133, 141, 143, 146, 148, 184, 188, 225
South Sea Company, 55, 59, 61, 63, 87, 109, 11, 119–21, 186
Spectator, The, 65, 67, 72
Spence, Joseph, 19, 26, 29–30, 66–7, 85, 101, 116, 183, 190, 229
Spencer, Charles *see* Sunderland, 3rd Earl of
Spenser, Edmund, 31, 220
　Faerie Queene, 72
Stanhope, James, 1st Earl, 84, 100, 104–5, 123
Stanhope, Philip *see* Chesterfield, 4th Earl of
Stanton Harcourt, Oxfordshire, 112–13
Staveley family, 10–11, 37
Steele, Sir Richard, 1, 65–7, 69–70, 76, 84, 88
　Guardian, 65–6
　see also Tatler
Stonor, Oxfordshire, 108
Stonor family, 44, 108
Stowe, Buckinghamshire, 175, 180, 198, 203, 222
Strafford, Thomas Wentworth, 3rd Earl of, 84, 88, 115, 133–4, 138, 210
Stukeley, William, 228–9
Suffolk, Countess of *see* Howard, Henrietta
Sunderland, Charles Spencer, 3rd Earl of, 84, 96, 100, 104–5, 121, 123
Swift, Jonathan, 1–2, 35, 41, 48, 53, 55–6, 61, 64–5, 67–8, 69–70, 71–2, 76–80, 83, 87, 100, 107, 114, 118–20, 125–6, 128, 130, 132, 139, 142–3, 149, 154–61, 163, 168, 172,

175–6, 181–3, 192, 196–7, 199, 205, 210–11, 215–16, 218–19, 226, 229
and *The Dunciad*, 156, 160, 163
visits England (1726–7), 145–6, 151, 154
works
'Cadenus and Vanessa', 159, 181
Conduct of the Allies, 69
'Contests and Dissentions', 156
Examiner, 69
'Famous Prediction of Merlin', 156
Gulliver's Travels, 69, 114, 145–6, 151, 159–60
The Importance of the Guardian, 70
'A Libel on Dr Delany', 158
'A Modest Proposal', 181
'On Poetry: A Rhapsody', 158
Pastoral Dialogue, 197
'Satirical Elegy', 132
Tale of a Tub, 68, 172
'To Mr. Gay', 154–5
Verses on the Death of Dr Swift, 161
Virtues of Sid Hamet's Rod, 69
Swinburne, Mary, 25, 40, 90, 92–3
Swinburne, Sir William, 92–3
Swinburne family, 40, 92

Talbot, Charles *see* Shrewsbury, 1st Duke of
Tatler, The, 65
Teddington, Middlesex, 115–16
Temple, Richard *see* Cobham, 1st Viscount
Temple of Fame (AP), 86, 167
Ten Mile Act (1689), 11, 23, 89
Thames, River, 10, 24, 29, 36, 40–2, 57–8, 60, 64, 86, 89, 98–9, 115–17, 137, 213
Theobald, Lewis, 131, 139, 149, 163, 165, 175, 227
Thomas, Elizabeth, 48, 148–9, 162
Thompson, E. P., 38–9, 142–4
Thomson, James, 183, 222
Thorold, Sir George, 165–6, 168
Three Hours after Marriage (AP and Scriblerus Club), 68, 71, 104, 107, 114, 227
Tichborne family, 93–5, 109
Tickell, Thomas, 66, 140
Tonson, Jacob, Sr, 48, 118, 130, 180
Tonson, Jacob, Jr, 127, 130–2

Townshend, Charles, 2nd Viscount, 84, 104–5, 123
Trumbull, Sir William, 4, 39, 44–6, 49–50, 61–2, 82–3, 95, 98, 100, 127, 142
Turner, Elizabeth, 9, 51
Turner family, 8–9, 34
Twickenham, Middlesex, 9, 115–16, 125, 127, 145, 151, 203, 231
see also Pope, homes
Twyford, Hampshire, 26–7

Utrecht, Treaty of (1713), 2, 55–7

Voltaire (François-Marie Arouet), 14, 210

Walpole, Robert, 1st Earl of Orford, 1, 4–5, 39, 84, 87, 91, 99–100, 104–5, 116, 122–3, 125, 132–4, 138, 141–2, 144, 151–5, 157–8, 163, 165, 169–70, 173, 176–7, 180, 183, 186, 191, 194–5, 197, 199–202, 211–12, 214–15, 217–18, 221, 223, 225–6, 228, 230
Atterbury plot, 133–4
Dunciad, 163, 166
Houghton Hall, 180
Southcott affair, 178
see also opposition to Walpole; Pope, politics, relations with Walpole
Walsh, William, 46–9
Walter, Peter, 184, 218–19
Waltham Blacks, 37–9, 140–4, 177, 191
War of Jenkins's Ear (1739–42), 212
War of the Austrian Succession (1740–8), 212
War of the Spanish Succession (1701–14), 19, 54, 75
Warburton, William, 171, 193, 210, 229–31
Ward, John, 218
Webb, Sir John, 25, 93–5
Welsted, Leonard, 160, 193
Wentworth, Thomas *see* Strafford, 3rd Earl of
West, Gilbert, 202, 228
Wharton, Philip, 1st Duke of, 115, 137, 185, 198
Whig split (1716–17), 100, 104–6
Whigs and Tories, 54–5, 61, 79

Whitehill House, Binfield, 29, 31, 34–5, 44, 97
   see also Pope, homes
Whiteknights, Berkshire, 37, 40–2, 74, 109
Wild, Jonathan, 157–8, 169
William I, King, 58–9, 144
William II, King, 58–9
William III, King, 2, 12, 15, 17–18, 21, 39, 41, 44, 52, 58–9, 70, 80, 85, 144, 188, 222
William and Mary, 2, 11, 17, 19, 39, 168
Windsor, Berkshire, 35–7, 57, 167
Windsor Castle, 36, 38, 57, 61, 228
Windsor Forest, 7, 23–4, 29–50, 58, 98, 100, 108, 113, 141–2
Windsor-Forest (AP), 2–3, 39, 45, 49, 57–65, 79, 89, 106, 129, 131–2, 144, 167, 184

Wokingham, Berkshire, 35–7, 40, 52
Woolley, David, 169, 172
Works of Buckingham (ed. AP), 107, 131, 133, 139–40, 170, 207
Works (AP)
   1717 edition, 106–7, 118, 208
   1735 edition, 193, 208
   planned 'deathbed' edition, 229–31
Wren, Sir Christopher, 13, 85
Wycherley, William, 32, 40, 46, 48, 50–1, 107, 163
Wye, River, 148, 189
Wyndham, Sir William, 61, 77, 84, 89–90, 113, 133, 195, 202, 221, 223, 227

York, 8–9, 25